SCREENS OF TERROR:

representations of war and terrorism in film and television since 9/11

EDITED BY PHILIP HAMMOND

Published 2011 by arima publishing

www.arimapublishing.com

ISBN 978 1 84549 501 5

Printed and bound in the United Kingdom

Typeset in Garamond 11/14

Abramis is an imprint of arima publishing.

arima publishing
ASK House, Northgate Avenue
Bury St Edmunds, Suffolk IP32 6BB
t: (+44) 01284 700321

www.arimapublishing.com

Contents

Acknowledgements

The essays in this collection first came together at a conference, held at London South Bank University's Centre for Media and Culture Research in September 2010, on representations of the 'war on terror' in film and television. I would like to thank all those colleagues who helped with the planning, funding and organisation of the conference, especially Jenny Allan, Ricardo Domizio, Safron Drew, Chris Elliott, Colin Harvey, Alison Jones, Donatella Maraschin, Paul McDonald, Mike Molan, Jenny Owen, Anna Reading and Patrick Tarrant. Special thanks to Ceri Dingle and her team of volunteers from WorldWrite.

As editor, I would like to dedicate this volume to the memory of the screenwriter, critic and *cinéaste* Branko Vukojević (1956-2003) who would, I hope, have enjoyed it.

Introduction: Screening the War on Terror

Philip Hammond

Right from the first moment, the 11 September 2001 attacks and the ensuing 'war on terror' were closely associated with film and media. There was the widespread sentiment at the time that the act itself was 'like a movie'. There was the US military's bizarre decision to recruit a 'group from the entertainment industry' in the immediate aftermath of 9/11, to help them 'think outside the box' – essentially asking for advice on how to handle terrorist threats, as if life really was like an action movie.[1] And there were various meetings bringing together Hollywood film and television executives and creatives with government officials (notably senior presidential advisor Karl Rove), which appeared to raise the possibility that an official propaganda line would guide future production of films and TV dramas.

From some in Hollywood there was an enthusiastic response to these overtures. Screenwriter and producer Bryce Zabel, for instance, then chair of the Academy of Television Arts and Sciences, proclaimed that: 'We are willing to volunteer to become advocates for the American message' (quoted in Cooper 2001). Although there were many who responded very differently, in a sense the prominence of celebrities such as Sean Penn or George Clooney as anti-war voices sustained the impression that the film industry is central to the contemporary politics of war. Certainly the military seemed convinced of its importance, commissioning Hollywood art director George Allison to design the 'set' for press announcements at Centcom, the Central Command base in Doha during the 2003 Iraq invasion. By far the biggest production number to come out of Centcom was the story of the rescue of a wounded soldier, Private Jessica Lynch, from a hospital in al-Nasiriyah in Iraq. Filmed by the soldiers who undertook the mission, the episode was almost invariably reported by journalists under headlines alluding to Steven Spielberg's *Saving Private Ryan* (1998). It soon transpired that the 'rescue' had not been 'the heroic Hollywood story told by the US military, but a staged operation that terrified patients and victimised the doctors who had struggled to save her life' (Lloyd-Parry 2003). According to one of those doctors, Anmar Uday, interviewed by the BBC in May 2003:

> It was like a Hollywood film. They cried 'go, go, go', with guns and blanks without bullets, blanks and the sound of explosions. They made a show for the American attack on the hospital – action movies like Sylvester Stallone or Jackie Chan.
>
> (Quoted in Kampfner 2003)

To complete the circle, Lynch's story – or rather, a mythologised version of it – was almost immediately turned into a TV-movie for NBC titled, inevitably, *Saving Jessica Lynch* (2003).[2]

War Movies

Of course, Hollywood myth-making is nothing new. Yet when ideas were first floated in the weeks following 9/11 about a major, long-term propaganda offensive, harking back to the films of the early Cold War era or even those of World War Two, there were good reasons to doubt that we would see any such thing. Not least was the fact that, as Guy Westwell notes in the opening chapter of this volume, the war film genre short-circuited in the late 1960s and 1970s, unable to reconcile its staple heroic myths with the reality of defeat in Vietnam. George Bush Sr.'s declaration, after the 1991 Gulf War, that the US had 'kicked the Vietnam Syndrome' (Chesterman 1998) – overcoming years of corrosive self-doubt about American power and values – soon proved premature, and similar sentiments from the government of George Bush Jr. sounded no more convincing. Yet in the realm of popular culture, although the Vietnam defeat produced a slew of critical, more or less anti-war movies, these gradually gave way to revisionist films which tended to rehabilitate the war. Westwell locates today's Iraq war combat movies within this context of the genre's development, examining the claim that the 'greatest generation' cycle of Second World War films produced in the late 1990s and 2000s signalled the rise of a 'New American Militarism' (Bacevich 2005) and a return to something like the myth-making of the 1940s. He argues that although the Iraq war has prompted many critical responses from film-makers, these have largely proved unpopular with audiences; while the few films that have been relatively successful have also tended to be much less critical.

Westwell's main example in the latter respect is Kathryn Bigelow's Oscar-winning film *The Hurt Locker* (2008), which studiously avoids engaging with the politics of the war by focusing narrowly on the individual soldier. The film seems to recover an idea of heroism, but its protagonist (a bomb-disposal expert) is heroic insofar as he is humanitarian, obeying a moral imperative to save lives. This is a crucial point, not only because of how the Iraq war was presented at the time (as a mission to save and liberate Iraqis), but also because of how military intervention has developed since, with the 2011 'humanitarian bombing' of Libya. The necessity to challenge 'humanitarian' justifications for contemporary military action, as argued in a number of chapters in this volume, is a blind-spot for some critics: Douglas Kellner (2010: 18), for example, contrasts the 'militarist interventionism' of George W. Bush's administration with the 'Clinton-Gore era of relative peace and prosperity'. Yet under President Bill Clinton the US sent troops to Haiti in 1994, sent NATO into action in Bosnia in 1994 and 1995, launched cruise missiles against Sudan and Afghanistan in 1998, led the 78-day bombing of Yugoslavia in 1999, and kept up a near-constant bombardment of Iraq (along with devastating economic sanctions) throughout the decade. It was precisely in this era of 'peace' that the sort of 'humanitarian' military interventionism seen in Afghanistan and Iraq after 2001 became standard operating procedure for Western governments.

The Hurt Locker – and the 'terrains of debate' that surround it – is also one of the key examples discussed by Martin Barker in his chapter on Iraq war films. The film has been widely understood in terms of post-traumatic stress disorder (PTSD) even though, as Barker shows, it does not really fit in the way that critics have assumed. Tracing the history of the category of PTSD, Barker identifies it as a Foucauldian 'system of knowledge'; not simply a clinical diagnosis but an ideological proposition. He critically examines how this widely accepted discourse has developed in relation to the war on terror, and the Iraq conflict in particular, as a point of consensus between Left and Right in emphasising sympathy for the troops, and as a way to re-cast the US military as victim rather than perpetrator. A second example discussed in his chapter, *In the Valley of Elah* (2007), illustrates this very clearly: the film altered the real story on which it is based in such a way as to remove blame from the troops and to explain their murder of a fellow soldier in terms of PTSD.

The motif of the victim-soldier is also at the centre of Mark Straw's discussion of ostensibly critical war on terror films. *In the Valley of Elah* is again a key example here, alongside Robert Redford's film about the war in Afghanistan, *Lions for Lambs* (2007). Homing in on the question of 'ethical spectatorship', Straw's chapter examines in detail how these movies portray soldiers as victims, not only of US foreign policy, but also of contemporary visual culture. Both films thereby individualise responsibility for war, hectoring us as passive spectators much as Redford's Vietnam-era professor lectures his apathetic student about the latter's lack of political awareness. Straw argues that, although they attempt a reflexive critique of war and media, ultimately these films offer only a narcissistic sense of altruism, encouraging spectators to revel in the feeling of 'worthy' engagement.

The limitations of seemingly critical war on terror films discussed in these opening chapters lend some support to Matthew Alford's argument that Edward Herman and Noam Chomsky's (2002) 'propaganda model' of news media can be applied to Hollywood. Alford discusses a number of possible objections and limitations to doing so, but overall he finds that Herman and Chomsky's five 'filters' – concentrated ownership, the influence of advertisers, the use of 'official sources', vulnerability to flak, and the internalisation of an 'anti-Other' ideology – fit this very different context surprisingly well. His chapter draws attention to the structural constraints within which mainstream commercial fare is produced, and in doing so helps to explain the political limits of 'liberal' Hollywood.

Despite such limitations, however, the fact remains that many responses to 9/11 and the war on terror in film and TV have at least attempted a critique. Sounding a more optimistic note, Liane Tanguay's chapter looks at one of the

most critical cinematic responses to date, Brian de Palma's *Redacted* (2007).
Bringing a literary perspective to bear, Tanguay develops a comparison between
the way that Joseph Conrad's 1898 novella *Heart of Darkness* subverts the
conventional detective story, and with it the Victorian imperial aesthetic, and the
way that *Apocalypse Now* (1979), Francis Ford Coppola's transposition of
Conrad's story to the context of the Vietnam war, achieves something very
similar in relation to the hegemonic aesthetic of American 'victory culture'
(Engelhardt 2007). Addressing the contemporary context, Tanguay shows how
Redacted accomplishes the same manoeuvre in comparison with *Black Hawk
Down* (2001), Ridley Scott's dramatisation of the 1992 US-led 'humanitarian
mission' to Somalia, employing similar aesthetic techniques – a gritty, hyperreal
style and handheld-camerawork producing an 'apparently unassailable *truth-
narrative*' – but turning them to very different effect.

Popular Pleasures

Of course, cinematic reactions to the war on terror have not been limited to the
war film genre, however broadly defined. As Jean-Michel Valantin's (2005)
useful category of 'national security cinema' suggests, some of the most
interesting filmic treatments of contemporary foreign-policy concerns are often
those which take a more allusive and allegorical, or at least a less direct and
literal tack. Though the head-on approach of war films has seemed, for the most
part, to leave audiences cold, more popular genres have found other ways to
address the post-9/11 world.

Kathryn Bigelow may have beaten her ex-husband James Cameron at the
2010 Oscars, winning the Best Picture award for *The Hurt Locker*, but it was
Cameron's *Avatar* (2009) that was the winner in commercial terms, rated, at the
time of writing, the highest-grossing picture of all time. *Avatar* is among the
examples discussed by Fran Pheasant-Kelly in her chapter on fantasy films,
along with *The Dark Knight* (2008) and the *Harry Potter* and *Lord of the Rings* series.
Both visually and thematically, these different films mediate the experience of
terrorism and war, offering spectators a 'safe' way of experiencing death and
destruction, she argues. The indirect messages conveyed about the war on terror
in these films vary markedly: Pheasant-Kelly identifies an undertone of
militarism in *Lord of the Rings*, a liberal critique of such values in *Avatar*, but more

11

indirect and ambiguous mediations in *Harry Potter* and *The Dark Knight*. What these films have in common, though, is that in reflecting contemporary concerns they represent a kind of 'working through' of shared cultural memory.

The so-called 'torture porn' genre analysed by Graham Barnfield has also been held to offer audiences a 'safe scare' – and for that reason to be particularly popular with US combat troops. Barnfield's chapter offers a careful reappraisal of the genre – questioning, in fact, how far it really exists as a distinct and identifiable genre in the way many critics have assumed – and sets contemporary debates in the context of earlier trends in (and moral panics about) films depicting graphic violence and horror. He rejects as simplistic the notion that the on-screen representations of torture in films such as the *Hostel* series are responsible for encouraging or excusing real-life torture (such as in Abu Ghraib),[3] in part precisely because the screen violence is gratuitous, as opposed to the plot-driven violence of shows such as *24*, where torture is presented as a rational choice. Rather, Barnfield argues, critics and audiences have latched on to 'torture porn' because the irrational threat dramatised in such films provides a kind of focal point for a wider social unease.

Some popular genres, though, have taken a more direct approach to engaging with the war on terror. As Michael Frank observes in his chapter on the figure of the 'enemy alien' in both science fiction films and official discourse, Spielberg's 2005 remake of *War of the Worlds* was explicitly intended to evoke 9/11 and to revisit the recent experience of Americans being attacked by an unknown enemy. Though it stops short of simply equating aliens and terrorists, Frank argues, the film does echo official constructions of the enemy as radically 'Other'. Frank returns to the observation that 9/11 was 'like a movie', interrogating the different assumptions that often underpinned this long-running analogy. The narratives already familiar from countless sci-fi movies in some senses provided a script for the response to 9/11; a 'political imaginary' through which political leaders and officials sought to explain the necessity for a war against 'alien' terrorists.

Such official perceptions are the target of dark humour in *Four Lions* (2010), one of the comic films about the war on terror discussed in my own chapter for this collection. I argue that such comic treatments – other examples discussed here are *In the Loop* (2009), *The Men Who Stare at Goats* (2009), and *Team America: World Police* (2004) – in some respects offer greater insight into the politics of contemporary war and terrorism than 'straight' films, including those that attempt a critique. While more conventional (critical) portrayals tend to stay within the boundaries of a traditional conception of Left/Right politics, comic treatments acknowledge that, after the end of the Cold War, we are in a wholly different political universe. Though arguably limited in various ways, comedies are nevertheless able to get at some essential truths – about the emptiness of Western political life and the correspondingly incoherent character of Al-Qaeda-style terrorism.

Us and Them

The satire of official misconceptions about Muslims in *Four Lions*, and the film's representation of suicide bombers as part of mainstream British culture, are effective because they resonate with real uncertainties. In recent years UK Muslims have found themselves both demonised as the 'enemy within' and simultaneously flattered by politicians worried about offending their sensitivities. Indeed, the first point that Karl Rove reportedly emphasised in briefing film and television industry executives after 9/11 was that 'the war is against terrorism, not Islam' (Cooper 2001) – a point also highlighted in the internal editorial guidelines issued by the BBC in September 2001.[4] Saying who the enemy was not, however, did not settle the question of exactly who the enemy was – especially when worries about offending or inflaming Muslim opinion coexisted with fears of 'home-grown' terrorists.

How enemies are depicted is of course a perennial issue in war propaganda, and also in fictional and dramatic representations of war, in which it is generally felt necessary to have some 'baddies'. But while it may be a long-standing issue, that is not to say it is an unchanging one. Two major events have shaped the context in which we now think about the question of enemies: 9/11 itself, of course, but prior to that the end of the Cold War in 1989.

In the early 1990s, foreign-policy analysts started to discuss the problem of what they called 'enemy deprivation syndrome'.[5] One might think that not having enemies would be an unequivocally good thing, but from a certain point of view it also has major downsides. Most obviously, in the international arena the lack of a clear enemy raised all sorts of awkward issues. If the Soviets had quit the battlefield, what exactly were Western militaries and defence establishments for? Who were they trying to deter? What threats were they protecting against? What was the point of strategic organisations such as NATO? What, indeed, was the strategy; what was the national interest? All these formerly straightforward questions were suddenly much more difficult to answer. Over the course of the 1990s there were various attempts to suggest that new enemies had appeared. Former allies, such as Saddam Hussein, found themselves abruptly re-cast in the role of the 'new Hitler'. Places that most of us had barely heard of before, like Bosnia-Herzegovina or Kosovo, suddenly became the front line in an epic battle between Good and Evil. The new enemies were seldom very convincing, and rarely did they last for very long. Saddam Hussein, Slobodan Milošević, Haitian generals, Somali 'warlords' – they came and went with baffling speed as the media spotlight briefly picked them out then moved on someplace else.

But the second major event seemed to change that. After 9/11, it appeared that the problem of 'enemy deprivation syndrome' might be about to be resolved for the foreseeable future. Radical Islamists and Arabs, it was suggested, might be able to fill the enemy-shaped hole left by the Russians, perhaps in the form of a 'clash of civilisations'. In the event, such was the diffuse and elusive character of Al-Qaeda – and of the phantom menace posed by Iraqi 'weapons of mass destruction' – that the construction of these new enemies has not always been as straightforward as some had feared and others had hoped. This makes it all the more important an issue for us to consider. How have Muslims and Arabs been depicted as enemies? Have they been unfairly demonised? What sorts of political and cultural resources do contemporary representations of enemy Others draw upon?

As Bernd Zywietz observes in his chapter examining the portrayal of 'evil Arabs', post-9/11 accusations of Western 'Islamophobia' can be understood as the latest version of long-standing concerns about the portrayal of Arabs and Muslims in US film and television (Shaheen 2001). Zywietz does not take these concerns at face value, however: discussing the debates that surrounded two pre-9/11 films, *True Lies* (1994) and *The Siege* (1998), he carefully uncovers the shifting criteria by which stereotypical images have been found wanting, suggesting that critics have made inconsistent and unrealistic demands. Through a detailed comparison with a quite different cinematic tradition – India's 'Bollywood' film industry – he emphasises the importance of genre conventions in the way that stock characters and situations are formed. Bollywood's generically eclectic 'masala movies' include overtly nationalistic messages about an idealised Hindustan and stereotypical 'evil-terrorist' Muslims – but they also encompass stock storylines that reject official views of conflict with India's Muslim populations and that acknowledge the 'outrage and grief' these communities have suffered at the hands of official policy. There are lessons here for Hollywood, Zywietz suggests, and some signs that these have already started to be learned in the last decade.

The attempt to imagine a different way of doing things also runs through the chapter by Joe Parker and Rebekah Sinclair on representations of the 'subaltern' – understood here as 'illiterate rural women from the global South' – a usually marginal figure who seemed suddenly to have become the centre of elite attention as Western states engaged in 'nation-building' in Afghanistan and Iraq. Focussed on documentary film but reading across to fictional drama, Parker and Sinclair draw on post-structuralist theory to point up the limitations and possibilities of filmic encounters with the Other. Challenging the 'totalising narrative of liberal humanitarianism' they discuss how 'films-yet-to-come' might devise more ethical and politically effective strategies of representation.

While Parker and Sinclair make a forceful case against the 'universalist subject' of Western liberal discourse, in the war on terror it has often seemed that political elites have had as much trouble articulating a sense of the Western Self as they have identifying the enemy Other. A further downside of 'enemy deprivation syndrome' – perhaps, in fact, the main one – was summed up very perceptively by the neoconservative writer Irving Kristol, who said in 1989: 'We may have won the Cold War, which is nice…But this means that now the enemy is us, not them.'[6] Kristol recognised that having the negative example of the USSR had been a valuable political asset. With the sudden demise of the Soviet Union, Western societies now had to stand entirely on their own terms, and it was suddenly much more difficult to say exactly what it was that they stood for. Perhaps this is why, over the years that have followed, political leaders have engaged in an almost incessant discussion of values – Western values, American values, British values, European values, 'shared' values – although, amid all the values talk, one is hard pressed to find any very coherent or convincing account of what those values might be.

The problem of conceptualising the Western Self is addressed in Hugh Ortega Breton's chapter on what he calls a 'paranoid style' in contemporary politics and popular culture. Ortega Breton successfully takes on the challenge of connecting a fine-grained analysis of textual characteristics with the larger political and cultural context within which these are used to convey recurring themes. Like Parker and Sinclair he reads across both documentary and fictional programming, and through close audio-visual analysis uncovers how the representation of subjectivity in terrorism narratives is shaped by the West's post-Cold War 'crisis of meaning and identity'. One key narrative theme, for instance, is conspiracy theories: Ortega Breton shows how TV programmes dramatising or discussing conspiracy give expression to the contemporary alienation from political agency, depicting the active political subject as malevolent while portraying people positively only when they are vulnerable, fearful and passive.

Somewhat similar concerns frame Jack Holland's analysis of *The West Wing*, a television series beloved of American liberals in the desolate Bush years as a kind of alternative 'good' White House. Holland examines a particularly heightened experience of the crisis of political meaning identified by Ortega Breton, when, in the immediate aftermath of 9/11, an elite 'failure to narrate' the attacks exacerbated the sense of shock and disorientation. With official voices silent or inarticulate, popular culture filled the 'void of meaning'. In a departure from its normal storylines, *The West Wing* offered a special episode explicitly teaching the audience how to understand and respond to terrorism – in part by equating 'Islamic extremists' with the Ku Klux Klan and comparing the Taliban with the Nazis. Notwithstanding the show's liberal reputation, Holland demonstrates how it closely followed official US foreign policy stances both before and after 9/11, sometimes espousing even more hawkish views than the Bush Administration.

The final chapter of this collection, Brigitte Nacos's essay on another popular topical TV drama, *24*, also scrutinises the relationship between screen images and real-world experience, challenging the sharp division that researchers usually draw between news and entertainment media. In a bid to win back dwindling audiences, news organisations have created hybrid 'infotainment' forms, she observes, and in any case researchers have questioned whether audiences maintain such a strict fact/fiction separation when they incorporate media messages into understandings of the world (Entman and Rojecki 2000). Fictional characters and situations matter in real-world contexts, argues Nacos, noting how *24*'s protagonist – counterterrorism agent Jack Bauer – has figured in classroom discussions, think-tank deliberations and even election debates. The key question that the series dramatised so effectively, of course, was whether it was legitimate to torture terrorist suspects: *24* provided endless iterations of the 'ticking time bomb' scenario much discussed by lawyers, journalists and politicians. Such was the impact of the show, indeed, that personnel at the Joint Task Force Guantánamo detention facilities not only watched it but reported that it influenced their treatment of 'enemy combatants'.

After a decade of turmoil and instability in world affairs, after two wars that have left hundreds of thousands dead and injured, it may seem frivolous to focus on fictional film and television drama. The impulse to do so, however, is in part given by the nature of the war on terror itself, designed by its architects to be a media-friendly event. Staging the spectacle of 'war on terror', complete with sound-bites and photo-opportunities inspired by Hollywood, was an attempt to offset the Western elite's loss of purpose and vision, to fill the 'void of meaning' in Holland's phrase. It could never accomplish that. But what it did do – not so much through the meetings with entertainment industry executives as through its very failure and incoherence – was to prompt others to try to make sense of the contemporary experience of war and terror in ways that aimed to connect with popular audiences. Ten years on, this volume brings together European and North American scholars working in politics and international relations as well as in literature, film, media and cultural studies to take stock and assess the shape and significance of the post-9/11 cultural moment.

Notes

[1] 'Hollywood on terror', Australian Broadcasting Corporation, 21 October 2001, www.abc.net.au/correspondents/s397008.htm. Military cooperation with the entertainment industries was facilitated by the Institute for Creative Technologies at the University of Southern California: see further Burston (2003), Der Derian (2001), and Michael Frank's chapter in this volume.

[2] Lynch herself has rejected the 'elaborate tales' constructed by the US authorities around her experiences (MacAskill 2007), and said of the film: 'Not all of it was accurate, so I couldn't keep watching it' (in Cole 2005).

[3] Kellner (2010: 9), for example, worries that audiences for popular torture films such as the *Saw* franchise are 'potential recruits' as 'torturers and killers'.

[4] The guidance, written by Stephen Whittle, Controller Editorial Policy, states: 'We must avoid giving any impression that this is a war against Islam', noting that 'we must be careful not to fuel the flames of prejudice and intolerance' (BBC 2001a).

[5] As one commentator puts it: 'as soon as the initial euphoria over the Soviet Union's collapse had passed, most of the American foreign-policy cognoscenti...began to search for a substitute enemy' (Harries 1997).

[6] 'Responses to Fukuyama', *The National Interest*, Summer 1989, available at www.wesjones.com/eoh_response.htm.

Chapter 1

In Country: Mapping the Iraq War in Recent Hollywood Combat Movies

Guy Westwell

This chapter aims to begin the process of establishing how the recent cycle of US war movies showing wars in Iraq and Afghanistan might be located in relation to the development of the US war movie genre more generally, and especially in relation to the genre's most recent cycles, including the Vietnam war cycle, and the pre-9/11 'greatest generation' cycle. A brief description of the core myths of the war movie genre will provide a context for a series of more specific observations about *The Hurt Locker* (2008), the most successful of the recent Iraq war movies. I am particularly interested in the question of whether the contemporary war film conforms to the war movie genre's general tendency, ideologically speaking, to make an argument for war (Westwell 2006: 109-16).

Core myths and earlier cycles

During World War Two, the war movie functioned as propaganda and became one of Hollywood's staple genres. In support of a strident, jingoistic nationalism, the war movies of the 1940s celebrated individual and group heroism, the self-sacrifice of individual desires to higher ideals/goals, and the effectiveness of military command and technology. War films advocated the need for strong leadership (with potentially fascistic overtones), celebrated war as both an exciting and spectacular experience, and as a rite of passage, with boys becoming men and in doing so confirming and defining conventional masculine identity. The cultural imagination of war via the war movie was also governed by a severely restricted point of view (usually via the experience of a small military unit or squad) and the prejudicial construction of cultural otherness. A grim, bloody realism was also an essential part of the formula, reminding the viewer that the nation (and the ideals it embodies) is built on the honourable sacrifice of young, citizen soldiers (Boggs and Pollard 2007: 13-15). After the war, these propagandist elements (what Thomas Schatz calls 'Hollywood's military Ur-narrative') remained central to the genre, with even the bloodiest war movies tending to show war as a 'progressive' activity, entered into reluctantly but ultimately necessary and productive (Schatz 2002: 75).

Most scholars tend to agree that the war movie genre leaves these core myths relatively intact and unquestioned until the late 1960s and 1970s, when the experience of losing a war in Vietnam causes something of a short circuit (Young 2003). As a result, it is claimed that films such as *The Deer Hunter* (1978) and *Apocalypse Now* (1979) challenge and question many of the genre's core myths, though they never manage to escape them completely (Boggs and Pollard 2007: 90-1). However, after this brief cycle of what might be considered critical (if not resolutely antiwar) movies, the genre (and the positive view of war enshrined in it) rallied. Vietnam was increasingly constructed as an ahistorical nightmare registered primarily through the experience of the ordinary combat soldier, or grunt, and this paved the way for a series of revisionist war films – from *Coming Home* (1978) to the *Rambo* trilogy (1982-1988) – that sought to alleviate the traumatic experience of the veteran and in doing so restore credibility for war (Sturken 1997: 85-122).

As a result of this (and wider processes of cultural forgetting), a cycle of films in the late 1990s and early 2000s – including *Saving Private Ryan* (1998), *Pearl Harbor* (2001), and *We Were Soldiers* (2002), and sometimes referred to as the 'greatest generation' cycle – were again able to present war in ways proximate to the propagandist genre staples of the 1940s (Boggs and Pollard 2007; McCrisken

20

and Pepper 2005; Stahl 2009; Westwell 2006). This reclamation of war as noble, positive, and necessary, prompted Andrew Bacevich to argue that:

> …Americans in our own time have fallen prey to militarism, manifesting itself in a romanticized view of soldiers, a tendency to see military power as the truest measure of national greatness, and outsized expectations regarding the efficacy of force. To a degree without precedent in US history, Americans have come to define the nation's strength and well-being in terms of military preparedness, military action, and the fostering of (or nostalgia for) military ideals.
>
> (Bacevich 2005: 2)

This New American Militarism is the latest iteration of what Michael Sherry describes as a wholesale militarisation of US popular culture that can be traced back to the early 1950s, and the beginnings of the Cold War. Sherry argues that from this point of origin '…war and national security became consuming anxieties and provided the memories, models, and metaphors that shaped broad areas of national life' (Sherry 1995: xi). It is claimed that this 'militarised' public sphere, with the war movie genre just one part of a wider culture that fostered a revisionist, mythologised, and nostalgic view of war in the 1980s and 1990s, primed Americans to respond enthusiastically to the belligerent rallying cries of their political leaders in the aftermath of the 9/11 terrorist attacks.

Significantly though, Bacevich's book was published before the release of the cycle of war movies that I am attempting to contextualise in this chapter. The question is, then, do his claims still hold true? In order to answer this question I will provide a brief overview of contemporary war cinema and then examine three points of comparison between the contemporary war movie cycle (with a particular focus on *The Hurt Locker*) and the wider war movie genre: first, the construction of a certain model of heroic masculinity; second, the description of war via a narrow, limiting point of view; and, third, the foregrounding of the suffering of the ordinary soldier as a redemptive move, marking America as victim and justifying further military action.

Contemporary War Cinema

It is possible to identify a significant cycle of feature films relating to America's current wars, including (in order of theatrical release): *GI Jesus* (2007), *The Situation* (2007), *Home of the Brave* (2007), *In the Valley of Elah* (2007), *Lions For Lambs* (2007), *Redacted* (2007), *Badland* (2007), *Grace is Gone* (2008), *Conspiracy* (2008), *Stop-Loss* (2008), *The Lucky Ones* (2008), *The Hurt Locker* (2008), *The Objective* (2009), *Brothers* (2009), *The Messenger* (2010), and *Green Zone* (2010). Two television series, *Over There* (2005) and *Generation Kill* (2008), also provide useful points of comparison.[1] The films' release dates coalesce around winter 2007-08, and most are set in the period of adjustment following the Iraq invasion, when jingoistic 'mission accomplished' rhetoric confronted the reality of a strengthening insurgency. Even later releases such as *The Hurt Locker* (on wide release in the US from mid-2009) and *Green Zone* belong to this point in the timeline (as both were held back after the poor performance of their predecessors).[2] Box office figures clearly show that on the whole these films failed to find an audience in the US. In fact, the only films to make a profit on theatrical release in the US are *The Hurt Locker* and *Brothers*, and the success of these will be crucial to my argument as it develops. These contemporary war movies can be organised into two distinct groups: a home front cycle (although films in this cycle do contain scenes of combat these scenes are usually short and contextualised as a flashback of some sort) and an Iraq war cycle. Iraq is the more significant of the two post-9/11 shooting wars, while the largest group of films overall is the home front cycle. So, we might observe that recent wars are being considered largely via the experience of the Iraq-based combat soldier and his/her journey from the front-line to home front and back again.[3]

Heroism

From Alfred Hitchcock's *Sabotage* (1936) to Anthony Minghella's *The English Patient* (1996), the intrinsic drama of a ticking bomb has long attracted filmmakers. Yet, in *The Hurt Locker*, Kathryn Bigelow eschews the convention that the unexploded bomb be placed at the zenith of the film's narrative arc and instead chooses to document the day-to-day experiences of bomb disposal technician, Staff Sergeant William James (Jeremy Renner), utilising a denotative, almost documentary-style approach. Amy Taubin suggests that the film could be titled 'Seven Instances of Dismantling an Improvised Explosive Device' (Taubin 2009: 32).

Joshua Clover argues that *The Hurt Locker*'s loose, repetitive narrative structure emulates the aimlessness of the invasion and occupation, and the circular, endless, and ultimately impossible task of imposing order. He compares the film to the HBO television series, *Generation Kill*, which he argues has an 'episodic aimlessness' that '...summons up the unnarratability of the Iraq adventure, its unreason, and inevitably the idea that there was no reason to start with' (Clover 2009: 9). Counter to this, I wish to argue that the film's structure calls on the viewer's sense of the war (gleaned from television news reportage) but then works towards a more positive formulation, a formulation focused on the counter-entropic quest to locate and defuse IEDs before they detonate. Against a backdrop of news reporting in which the war had become, according to Susan Carruthers, '...just one damn IED after another', Bigelow's instinct is to repeat the bomb disposal scenario, each time using the resources of a fictional narrative to find a more redemptive line. As such, each act of bomb disposal is replete with the potential to redeem the experience of roadside bombs, military stalemate, and steadily growing casualties (Carruthers 2008: 73).

The bombs James defuses, for example, prevent a United Nations building and its civilian workers from being destroyed (we might recall that the UN headquarters in Baghdad was bombed in August 2003) and he attempts to save an innocent Iraqi, press-ganged into being a suicide bomber. Most dramatically, he risks his own life to prevent the desecration of a dead child's body. The underlying humanitarian impulse behind each of these acts leads Taubin to describes James as an conventionally heroic 'equal opportunity saviour' and it is clear that not one of these sequences shows an IED in its most commonly used scenario, as a roadside bomb targeting US convoys (Taubin 2009: 35).

Through his instinctive commitment to effective action James offers a corrective to the inertia that had come, by 2004, to typify the standoff between heavily protected US forces (only vulnerable when moving by road) and the guerrilla tactics of the insurgents. James's work of bomb disposal retains and reclaims a sense of the heroic, effective, US soldier who puts his life at risk in pursuit of a mission informed by a moral imperative. As Robert Alpert notes, when James arrives to begin his rotation '…he removes the plywood boards from his living quarters, since he both wants the sunlight and refuses to separate himself from the risk of incoming mortars' (Alpert 2010). Similarly, James refuses to use the bomb disposal 'bot', or to be encumbered by the bomb suit, indicating how, through sheer force of will and courage, he can break through the mediated, prophylactic, stalemate of the war. In addition to this, in the film's one conventional combat sequence, James behaves effectively, commanding his men, and prevailing over the enemy.

Ultimately, the type of heroism on offer here is a powerful antidote to the news coverage of the war, and is congruent with that shown in the World War Two propaganda film *Bataan* (1943), a film that, like *The Hurt Locker*, was made during a time when a war was not going well, and which Jeanine Basinger considers paradigmatic of the combat movie more generally (Basinger 1986: 40-52). We have here also an extension of the logic described by Susan Faludi in *The Terror Dream*, in which the narrative trope of *rescue* became a key mechanism for dealing with the experience and aftermath of 9/11, with the emergency services lauded as heroes, and with their commitment, obedience, and bravery dovetailing with a wider culture of jingoism that consolidated the move to war (Faludi 2007). Like those other heroes of 9/11, James is not mired in atrocity, nor even actual combat, but is instead actively attempting to save lives and establish order. The tagline for the film reads: 'You don't have to be a hero to do this job. But it helps.' The implication is clear enough – *The Hurt Locker* seeks to reclaim (in the face of considerable challenges from films such as *Redacted, In the Valley of Elah*, and *Badland*) a certain conventional model of male, soldierly behaviour. This dynamic is echoed in the HBO documentary, *Baghdad ER* (2006), which Pat Aufderheide describes as '…one life-or-death medical drama after the next. The gurneys roll in and the problem is presented. We hope they live, and some of them do. It's a race, a performance, a drama. There are heroic moments every time' (Aufderheide 2007: 60).

The film is driven here by a desire to convert the intractable political, ethnic and religious conflicts that had come to define the war in Iraq into tangible, reducible and solvable problems. The bomb disposal technician's carefully demarcated role, peripheral relationship to the military, and potentially neutral position in relation to the wider aims and objectives of the war, serves as an accessible and redemptive cipher for the experience of the war more generally. Or, as Slavoj Žižek puts it:

> This choice is deeply symptomatic: although soldiers, they do not kill, but risk their lives dismantling terrorist bombs destined to kill civilians – can there be anything more sympathetic to our liberal eyes? Are our armies in the ongoing War on Terror, even when they bomb and destroy, ultimately not just such EOD [explosive ordnance disposal] squads, patiently dismantling terrorist networks in order to make the lives of civilians everywhere safer?
>
> (Žižek 2010)

This positive spin on the war is indicative of a clear act of act of differentiation taking place across the cycle of contemporary war movies between a group of so-called 'atrocity films' (claimed as critical and left-aligned responses to the war on terror) and more conventional (at least in genre terms) combat movies. Stephen Hunter, for example, describes *In the Valley of Elah*, as *agit prop*, objecting to the depiction of a US soldier pretending to be a doctor in order to torture prisoners of war, arguing that this is 'pretty much the case of all the Iraq-war movies; they seem entirely atrocity-driven, based on the conceit that combat turns men axiomatically evil and that evil is to be taken as a surrogate for the evil policies that spawned them' (Hunter 2009: 78). By contrast, *The Hurt Locker* is taken to be a combat movie (it is described as such by its director), and combat is markedly distinct from torture, atrocity, war crimes, and so on (Macaulay 2009). The work of war here is shown to be justifiable and progressive, carefully demarcated, and in pursuit of desirable goals. Separating what might be called 'valid' combat experiences from atrocities in this way is indicative of the attempt to retain a territory within which war can still be described according to positive formulae. Atrocity films that are willing to confront extremely difficult facets of the war – torture, rape, murder – offer a considerable challenge to Bacevich's claims but their deselection, their identification as somehow not war films because of the very subject matter and behaviour they describe, seems a clear indication of the genre's intrinsic limitations. That is, if a film shows war to be barbaric, atrocity-fuelled and damaging to all involved, it *by definition* cannot be considered a war movie. In contrast, *The Hurt Locker* fits within the tradition of 'noble grunt' films which acknowledge that the work of war is difficult and bloody (the 'war is hell' paradigm) but also show the work is shouldered in good faith and with positive results.

Point of View

The positive characterisation of James as hero, and the symbolic meaning of his actions as redemptive, is augmented through the careful emulation of a documentary style and an extremely narrow and limiting point of view system. In the bomb disposal sequences, for example, clever direction and careful technical choices (the latter the work of Barry Ackroyd, Ken Loach's long-time cinematographer), cultivate a 'documentary feel' that immerses the viewer in the action alongside the bomb disposal squad, in fear for their lives while trying to do a good job. This 'documentary feel' was cultivated via the choice to shoot on location in Syria (a country that borders Iraq), and through the casting of Iraqi refugees as extras. The decision to use Aaton XTR-prod cameras and Super 16mm (the documentary filmmaking standard before the shift to digital video), as well as to shoot handheld 90% of the time, further ensured a documentary 'look' (Thomson 2009). Similarly, the film's large sets (often in excess of 300m) were orchestrated as '360 degree active', with four camera teams given license to roam and shoot footage as they saw fit, in emulation of war reportage. In addition to this, physical effects were preferred to CGI in order to create what Bigelow describes as realistic-looking, '...very dense, black, thick, almost completely opaque explosions filled with lots of particulate matter and shrapnel' (Thomson 2009: 47). These carefully staged elements combine to produce a powerful 'reality effect' that underpins the fictional narrative lending the film credibility and a claim to authenticity (Barthes 1986).

In interview, Bigelow has described how she set out to try to depict the experience of fighting in Iraq (in her words, 'a war of invisible, potentially catastrophic threats') by focusing tightly on the experience of the combat soldier and showing the war from his point of view (Macaulay 2009: 33). As such James is the key focaliser, with Sanborn (Anthony Mackie) and Eldridge (Brian Geraghty) also given a significant amount of screen time. As Alpert notes, other points of view are utilised:

> Throughout the film Bigelow shows us all perspectives – a shot from behind Iraqi snipers or a videographer taking pictures of Eldridge, a close-up of the eye of the cab driver focusing on James holding a pistol on him, a long shot of James' squad from behind the bars of a window, a foreshortened close-up of a white building seen through the scope of a rifle, or a helicopter seen high above through the visor to Thompson's helmet. 'There's lots of eyes on us,' Sanborn says at one point with fear in his voice.
>
> (Alpert 2010)

But these frantic cutaways, appearing in the heat of the film's action sequences, are commonly point of view shots looking on at James and his men from diegetically unanchored positions (using techniques that harness the unsettling potential of off-screen space). Occasionally these point of view shots are embodied but they remain at all times thoroughly decontextualised, with no attempt at characterisation. For example,

> ...during the defusing of the car bomb next to the UN compound, Sanborn and Eldridge are clearly unnerved by the videographer, both a voyeur to and a likely participant in the violence. In the factory where the squad finds the young boy's body wired with a bomb, we see the bombers' tools left in the open, the unexploded ordinances, the cigarette still smoking, the camera on the tripod, all left behind only moments ago, as though caught mid-shoot.
>
> (Alpert 2010)

The effect of these cutaways is to make the threat more apparent: when the film switches back to seeing through the bomb squad's gun sights, the viewer, like James and his team, feels surveilled from all quarters. By such means a reversal of power relations is effected, with the Americans portrayed as imperilled, powerless and victimised, in contrast to the realities of the balance of power between an insurgency and the world's most powerful army. This sense of limited perspective is reinforced by the way in which the film isolates the squad from wider military command structures. Hunter notes, for example, that their support and intelligence systems are rendered '...almost as shadowy nuances' (Hunter 2009: 78). Reviewing the film in the *New Yorker*, David Denby writes that it '...narrows the war to the existential confrontation of man and deadly threat' allowing it to be enjoyed '...without ambivalence or guilt' (Denby 2009: 84). Denby's comments indicate how the film's realist/documentary aesthetic and narrow point of view license a detachment from the wider discourses pertaining to the war, a detachment that limits understanding and allays critique.

Marilyn B. Young argues that Vietnam war movies of the late 1980s kept a similarly tight focus on the individual fighting man, erasing history and politics in favour of 'an emotional drama of embattled individual survival' (Young 2003: 255). However, Young claims that films such as *Platoon* (1986), *84 Charlie Mopic* (1989), *Full Metal Jacket* (1987), and *Casualties of War* (1989), through their depiction of the effects of the war on the Vietnamese, conflict within the military, and US culpability in war crimes, still managed to show war through a critical lens. In contrast, *The Hurt Locker* offers a similar narrowed perspective to that offered by the 'greatest generation' cycle, which is itself thoroughly beholden to the conventions of the war movie genre as a whole. Young argues that '...by screening out everything save the immediate context in which [the US combat soldier] fights, recent war movies, wherever they are set, serve as all-purpose propaganda instruments' (Young 2003: 255).

Robert Sklar argues that *The Hurt Locker*'s limited point of view is compounded by the fact that the Iraqis in the film are represented in prejudicial terms (Sklar 2009). As noted already, most Iraqis are seen at a distance (often through the sights of a rifle) and in the small number of sequences where characters come into focus – James's standoff with a taxi driver, his surreal conversation with an academic who claims to work for the CIA – the film refuses to convey any clear information. Presumably this is intended to reflect the difficulty James faces trying to make sense of the war, but it also has the effect of casting all Iraqis as inscrutable, masked, and potentially dangerous. In perhaps the most powerful dramatic line through the film, James befriends an Iraqi child, nicknamed 'Beckham'. As a result of his friendship with James,

Beckham is kidnapped and killed and his body is discovered stuffed with explosives surrounded by the paraphernalia of Islamic fundamentalists. In the absence of any reporting of similar cases or of any imaginable strategic purpose to the preparation of a body bomb of this sort, this scene must be read as a mechanism designed to symbolise the absolute barbarity and inscrutability of the enemy, as well as positing Iraq as a civil struggle (with Iraqi killing Iraqi) in which America has no role.[4]

A number of films in the recent cycle follow this template for the orchestration of focalisation and point of view, namely *Home of the Brave*, *The Lucky Ones* and *Brothers*. However, there are signs of a desire to seek alternatives. The restricted point of view that governs the investigation at the heart of *In the Valley of Elah*, for example, ensures that the question of what can be known and how remains open and difficult. *Redacted* offers multiple perspectives as a defining principle of its construction; while *Green Zone* and *The Situation* strive towards a form of limited social realism, with narratives that attempt to triangulate between the different perspectives of Americans, Iraqis, soldiers, civilians, men, women, and so on. In a reversal of the comrades-in-arms tendency of the 'greatest generation' cycle, where war is reduced to the duty to die in defence of one's fellow soldiers, the tag-line for *Stop-Loss*, reads 'The bravest place to stand is by each other's side', referring instead to the soldiers' families, friends, and lawyers, all striving to find ways to refuse to fight.

PTSD and Resolution

Sklar (2009) claims *The Hurt Locker*'s title comes from a saying among bomb squad members that an explosion puts you in 'the hurt locker', i.e. the title is synonymous with a period of immense, inescapable physical and emotional pain that it will be difficult to overcome. Although at one level, and as already noted, James is presented in fairly conventional heroic terms, he is also shown to be suffering post-traumatic stress disorder (PTSD) – he is addicted to war, disobeys orders, and is prone to lapses of judgement. Crucially though, James's combat stress is not triggered as a result of being a perpetrator of, or a witness to, atrocity (as is the case in a number of films in the cycle), but is instead a result of the incremental day-to-day strain of saving lives and helping people. The war in

Iraq has put the US – figured here as an irrepressible, skilful, decent, young man harmed as a result of his desire to do good – 'in the hurt locker'. Žižek argues that this resolute focus on the suffering of the soldiers, is '…ideology at its purest: the focus on the perpetrator's traumatic experience enables us to obliterate the entire ethico-political background of the conflict' (Žižek 2010).[5]

This suffering allows *The Hurt Locker* to negotiate a number of contradictions, or ambiguities, around James's heroism, and the attendant qualities of bravery, selflessness and the desire to do good. For example, one aspect of the film that has been lauded by reviewers (the source of many of the claims that it somehow indexes reality/the truth) is its willingness to acknowledge that for some men war, even an unpopular war like the one in Iraq, carries an intrinsic dramatic charge. The film prefigures its action, for example, with a quotation from journalist Chris Hedges, stating: 'The rush of battle is often a potent and lethal addiction, for war is a drug' (Hedges 2002). Admittedly this is a truth not often acknowledged in Hollywood war movies – where killing is usually presented as grim work in the pursuit and/or defence of noble ideals. However, unlike the soldiers who appear in Joanne Bourke's book, *An Intimate History of Killing*, and who testify to the pleasure of killing in battle, James engages in very little killing *per se* (Bourke 1999). The war he loves is replete with humanitarian acts of bravery designed to save lives. And it is made relatively clear that he is embarked on a trajectory that will lead either to his own death or to nervous breakdown. James's addiction to the adrenaline rush that comes with bomb disposal is extenuated by the harm his desire to do his job well will ultimately do to him. Put simply, James's emerging combat stress extenuates his love of war.

In an article for *The New York Times*, A.O. Scott tracks the widespread denial of politics/ideology in Iraq war movies and argues that a resolute focus on PTSD is the defining feature of many films and that this is leading to the Iraq war (like Vietnam before it) being reduced to a resolutely American experience (Scott 2010). Yet, such a generalisation misses important nuances in the way PTSD is portrayed. In contrast to a number of Vietnam war movies, such as *First Blood* (1982) and *Born on the Fourth of July* (1989), and unlike other films in the contemporary war cycle, such as *In the Valley of Elah* and *Stop-Loss*, which explore the idea that PTSD is precipitated if the soldier's actions run counter to a wider cultural sense of moral propriety, *The Hurt Locker* shows PTSD simply as an inevitable consequence of soldiering. As with Captain Miller (Tom Hanks) in *Saving Private Ryan*, whose shaking hand testifies to the toll the work of war has taken on a humble and decent soldier, *The Hurt Locker* presents PTSD as an inevitable response to combat, something to be toughed out and dealt with later after the war has been won.

Contemporary war cinema's resolute focus on traumatised young men also enables a redemptive narrative of therapeutic healing to be brought to bear, a narrative that we have seen before in relation to Vietnam. At first glance, a move towards resolution does not seem to be a key feature of the cycle. In *The Hurt Locker* James returns from Iraq and is confronted with the glossy surfaces of US consumerism and the grinding chores of family life. He confesses to his infant son that he only loves one thing, and in the next shot we see him striding towards an unexploded bomb. A similar desire to return to the war gives shape to other films in the cycle, including *Home of the Brave* and *The Lucky Ones*. Even a seemingly critical, antiwar, film such as *Stop-Loss*, in which desertion is considered and seems merited, ends with a soldier deciding to drive back to his unit.

As such, the combat and home front cycles are clearly entangled, with combat giving way to stories of a return to America, usually followed by a decision to return to war. At the time these films were made the war was still being fought, so perhaps this lack of resolution is unsurprising. However, the eschewal of the therapeutic move and the return to war feels provisional, more like a temporary deferral, and this circular movement contrasts markedly with the neurotic journeying that typifies the 1970s Vietnam war movie (Willard's return to the jungle in *Apocalypse Now*, for example), a journeying that marked the continued irreconcilability of the experience of Vietnam in the decade following the end of the war. In contrast, the contemporary war movie cycle has troops willingly returning to action, duty-bound to finish what has been started. Once the task is completed, the ideological model for dealing with the returning soldier, a model tried and tested in more pliant and recuperative war movies – from *Coming Home* (1978) to *Courage Under Fire* (1996) – shows that trauma can be worked through, masculine capability can be re-established (often via the love of a good woman), and the honourable hard work of soldiering can be reclaimed and remythologised.

It is significant then that James is divorced but living as if married, almost as if the structures are remaining in place, ready for him to be reintegrated (if his wife would only listen and understand him, for example). In *Brothers*, the only other commercially successful film in the cycle, Captain Sam Cahill (Tobey Maguire) finds the courage to tell his wife (named Grace) of the atrocity he has committed (the murder of a fellow soldier, a fratricide that recalls *Platoon*'s 'We did not fight the enemy, we fought ourselves') and the film shows Grace and Cahill's family pulling together to help heal the wounds the war has inflicted. Douglas Kellner writes that the logic here is clearly '...to redeem the terrible losses of the destructive invasion and occupation through the heroic struggle for recovery and redemption of the returning US soldiers' (Kellner 2010: 222). Read alongside one another, *The Hurt Locker*'s moral heroism, limited and prejudicial point of view, and decontextualised PTSD present us with a positive formulation of the war on the ground, while *Brothers* enfolds the returning traumatised combat veteran in discourses of healing and redemption, discourses that will likely shape the stories of return that will follow in the future.

Conclusion

So what of Bacevich's and others' claims of an all-pervasive New American Militarism shaping US popular culture and underwriting the waging of war in the early twenty first century? This chapter has demonstrated that the late 2000s have witnessed the release of a considerable number of films operating at the absolute limits of the war movie genre, and in a way not seen since the 1970s (in part, explaining their lack of an audience and the admonitions of some right-wing critics that these are not war movies at all). Within the set of bounded possibilities available to filmmakers working in Hollywood, and at a time when US troops are still being killed on the battlefield, a cycle of war movies has been made that could be said to be largely critical of war. Filmmakers have been willing to face up to difficult, irreconcilable facts: that US troops have committed atrocities, that the wars have not been a success and may even have been counter-productive, that political leaders and jingoistic constructions of national identity can be harmful, and so on. As Kellner puts it, '…the cycle testifie[s] to disillusionment with Iraq policy and help[s] compensate for mainstream corporate media neglect of the consequences of war' (Kellner 2010: 222). Taken together with the myriad documentaries focusing on the war, this critical coverage of a conflict as it has taken place is almost without precedent.[6]

So, has what Roger Stahl (2009: 140) describes as the 'militainment bubble' that shaped the first half of the decade been pricked by the grim, real experience of a quagmire in Iraq and Afghanistan, and a raft of cultural production that attempts to seek out and show this reality? Stahl suggests the latter part of the decade has suffered an 'Iraq syndrome' that may well prove as difficult to shift as the Vietnam syndrome before it. He writes:

> It could be argued that the arrival of this 'syndrome' signaled a collective critical awakening, one that increasingly questioned the underlying narratives that made the consumption of war possible. In other words, certain realities could no longer be held at bay, the field of deliberation and debate widened, and an increased skepticism towards wartime public relations took root. One may conclude that the consumption of war became an endeavor fraught with new complexity.
>
> (Stahl 2009: 141)

Maybe Stahl is right. *But*, and it is a big but, many of the films that might be said to be fraught with this new complexity remain largely unseen in the US and, as I have demonstrated, by far and away the most successful film in the cycle, *The Hurt Locker*, displays a strong tendency to make an argument for war, or at least to begin to clear the way for that argument to become possible once more.

Different accounts have been offered to explain the 'absent audience' for recent war movies but surely the most straightforward answer is that people support the war, and have been conditioned to do so, as shown by their preference for war movies such as *The Hurt Locker* that show war according to more conventional formulae (Barker 2011; Murray 2010). And, in a move that already mirrors something of the way in which the experience of the Vietnam war was eventually contained and screened, the dominant trope emerging (even in seemingly antiwar films such as *In the Valley of Elah* and *Redacted*) is one of the war being *brought home*, i.e. figured as the traumatic, psychologised experience of individual soldiers, and available to discourses of forgiveness and healing. I hope that this chapter has shown that while contemporary war cinema is varied, and has some critical bite, the fact that audiences have not rushed to see a cycle of bleak and critical films, and instead have gravitated towards those that are more conventional, might well speak to the success of the New American Militarism, in which a constant state of war, and trickle of US casualties, is now considered an acceptable and necessary part of the status quo.

Notes

[1] A number of Iraq war films by non-US directors have also received a limited distribution, including *The Short Life of José Antonio Gutierrez* (2006), *Invierno en Bagdad/Winter in Baghdad* (2005), *Return to the Land of Wonders* (2004), *Kurtlar Vadisi: Irak/Valley of the Wolves: Iraq* (2006), and the British productions *Battle for Haditha* (2007) and *The Mark of Cain* (2007).

[2] The release of *The Hurt Locker* was phased, with a long, award-winning tour round the festival circuits in 2008/early 2009, where it picked up garlands and critical acclaim, as well as a distributor: Summit Entertainment. The film was then given a wider release in the US from 26 June 2009, eventually showing in 535 theaters. According to Box Office Mojo (www.boxofficemojo.com), the production budget was $15m, with domestic gross of $16.4 and a foreign gross of $32.2m. As of August 2010, the film had taken $48.6m at the box office. As these figures indicate, roughly two thirds of the film's profits came from non-US markets. Also, as of August 2010, US sales of the DVD numbered $30.3m. The film was nominated for nine Academy Awards in 2010 and won six including Best Picture and Best Director for Kathryn Bigelow, the first woman to win this award. *The Hurt Locker* also won six BAFTA Awards. The figures clearly indicate the film was commercially successful in a difficult climate for movies showing the war.

[3] There are, of course, other possible ways of grouping the films, and these alternative groupings have their corollaries in previous periods. For example, it might be possible to talk of a eulogy cycle (by definition this tends to be conservative), a road movie cycle, and possibly also a salvation/rescue cycle.

[4] This is pushed to laughable extremes in *Home of the Brave*, where a scene of US soldiers petting a dog is contrasted with a scene of insurgents preparing to use a dog as a bomb (surely not a predictable or safe enough delivery method). See also *Four Lions* (2010) where a bomb attached to a crow has tragic consequences in a satire of these kinds of rhetorical moves.

[5] Žižek compares *The Hurt Locker* to two Israeli films about the 1982 Lebanon war, *Waltz With Bashir* (2008) and *Lebanon* (2010), arguing that they share a similar ideological function to *The Hurt Locker*, that is, casting a powerful, oppressive military force as victim.

⁶ A large number of documentaries have depicted recent wars and an initial viewing of these documentaries suggests that they certainly cannot be accused *en masse* of perpetuating Bacevich's New American Militarism. See for example: *Fahrenheit 9/11* (2004), *Occupation: Dreamland* (2005), *The Blood of My Brother* (2005), *The War Tapes* (2006), *Iraq in Fragments* (2006), *Iraq for Sale: The War Profiteers* (2006), *My Country, My Country* (2006), *The Ground Truth* (2006), *No End in Sight* (2007), *Ghosts of Abu Ghraib* (2007), *Taxi to the Dark Side* (2007), *Jerabek* (2007), *Body of War* (2007), *Standard Operating Procedure* (2008), and *Restrepo* (2010), all of which offer a considerably broader and more critical view than the cycle of feature films discussed in this chapter.

Chapter 2

'America Hurting': Making Movies About Iraq

Martin Barker

On the night of 7 March, at the 2010 Academy Awards ceremony, the film *The Hurt Locker* triumphed, winning six Oscars including Best Picture, Best Director and Best Original Screenplay. Introduced at the Awards by its writer, Mark Boal, as 'exemplifying the spirit of the independent film-maker', and celebrated as the first such award to a female director, this was the culmination of a longer process. As the BBC's Will Gompertz (2010) had commented just days before, this was the final showdown, after skirmishes at the Golden Globe and BAFTA Awards. On the one side was *Avatar* (James Cameron, 2009), hugely successful at the box office and effective champion of emergent 3D technologies, while variously critiqued as a bad example of bloated Hollywood film-making, showy special effects, and predictable story; or as anti-war, anti-military, and anti-American. On the other side, 'brave' Kathryn Bigelow, ex-wife of James Cameron (just to add personal spice and venom to the encounter), making a small but special film for just $11m. What did this victory mean? For Bigelow, without hesitation, it was about the soldiers. In her acceptance speech she dedicated the film to 'the women and men in the military who risk their lives on a daily basis in Iraq and Afghanistan and around the world. May they come home safe.' For Boal, accepting his Oscar for Best Original Screenplay, it was for 'these men in the front line of an unpopular war'.[1] Both insisted that this was not a political position or a political film. And all those Awards appeared to vindicate this position.

That was, though, a position that others wanted to dispute. For example, from the left, Jonathan Rosenbaum (2009) came close to denouncing it. This was a film in denial, refusing to say anything about why America is in Iraq. Its central character was 'myopic to the point of insanity'. Bigelow herself carries some blame, he said, for making claims such as that 'there is no politics in the trenches'. From the right, Nile Gardiner (2010) crowed over its success over 'one of the most left-wing films' to come from Hollywood in years. *The Hurt Locker* was not an overtly political film, he asserted, but was 'a tremendously patriotic film which pays tribute to the courage of American troops serving in Iraq.' In one respect even its most ardent critics agreed. As *The Hollywood Reporter* put it, 'To earn its gold, "Hurt Locker" had to break what producer Greg Shapiro called "The Iraq War Curse", referring to all the movies touching on that conflict that had failed to find an audience' (Block 2010). Well, yes, in a way – but one of the striking things about the film is that, at the time of its Awards, it had actually made a loss at the box office. Only the 'bump' to DVD rentals and sales which traditionally follows Oscar success took the film clearly into profit.

These kinds of debates are important, not least because they reveal the terrains of debate over what will count as being pro- or anti-war and pro- or anti-American. I take this notion of 'terrains of debate' (although not the precise phrase) from the work of Janet Staiger (1992) who has argued that the meaning of a film is not to be derived by scholars from textual features alone. Rather, meaning is an outcome of interactions between formal and narrative features, and the frames of interpretation which different actors and groups bring to bear on a film. This reception approach to films has proved successful and insightful in very many ways. And importantly, by an extension of this analytic process, it becomes possible to see, through the range of reactions and judgements enacted upon a film, what assumptions, expectations and sensitivities are in play around its topics.

Unfortunately, on Staiger's approach it becomes much harder to identify and address those things which reviewers and commentators take as common ground: the things which pass effectively unnoticed, because they are so taken for granted. I want to argue in this chapter that one such 'commonsense' assumption is critical to understanding *The Hurt Locker*. It not only helps to explain some otherwise puzzling responses to the film, but will suggest the inadequacy of those responses to the film which got caught up in it *despite* disliking what they saw as its overt politics. This is well exemplified by Bernard Weiner who, writing in the critical *Countercurrents*, declared: 'I despise the implicit pro-Iraq war politics of *The Hurt Locker*....But I cannot deny the movie's aesthetic power' (Weiner 2010). Making the film's aesthetics into a separate zone, a neutral achievement, eliminates the possibility of exploring what *kind* of persuasive fascination is created by *The Hurt Locker*. To get at this, I believe, one needs to come at the film in a slightly different way than Staiger, exploring a fundamental paradox in what is one of the most common features of its reception, which ought literally to make no sense.

Let me illustrate this paradox through one post-Oscars response, one which was generated for and communicated within a small special interest group:

> Last night's top honors for *The Hurt Locker*, a film that successfully embeds the audience with an explosive ordnance disposal (EOD) unit in Iraq, can only help build awareness and support for the real people who have suffered the physical and mental traumas of war. There has been some flak about the movie's authenticity....But there's no questioning the larger role hyperbaric oxygen therapy might play in soldiers' recovery. In the past couple months we've been following progress in new clinical studies of HBOT for traumatic brain injury (TBI) and new funding for veterans experiencing posttraumatic stress disorder (PTSD). We will continue our coverage of this vital topic, with a new condition page for PTSD and the occasional push for a TBI indication.
>
> (Anon 2010)

There is something intriguing in itself about this kind of crossover between a fiction film and real-life medico-political processes. The blog is confident of the film's 'successful embedding of the audience', but at the same time acknowledges that *The Hurt Locker* was not perfect for their purposes. That, of course, only goes to show how closely this particular audience was inspecting the film for its possibilities of use.[2] This incorporates a direct challenge to those who might say that fiction entirely inhabits its own world and operates by its own rules. But it is beyond that in its specificity – here, a film circulates into a distinct discursive world and is called upon as a potential resource, persuasive to others, therefore of benefit to these folk. Companies, doctors and researchers promoting this specialist and expensive treatment, hyperbaric oxygen therapy, look on hopefully at an opportunity for expanding their reach.

But there is something inherently paradoxical about the use of *The Hurt Locker* as a means to promote a treatment for post-traumatic stress disorder (PTSD) – at least, if we take the film simply in and of itself. Bigelow's film, based on a screenplay written by Mark Boal who worked as an embedded journalist with American troops in Iraq, tracks specialist Sergeant William James, whose skill is in defusing roadside bombs. James arrives in Iraq to replace a previous specialist whom we have seen killed by a bomb at the start of the film. The film follows his time in Iraq, showing us episodically his defusings. He is cool, committed, unfazed by the dangers. He loves the adrenalin buzz his work gives him. After action, James releases pressures in barracks by getting drunk, and doing serious play-fighting with his platoon-mates. But he also cares mightily – including searching for a small Iraqi boy who sells dodgy DVDs in their camp then disappears. Finding the boy's body packed with explosives, James cares enough to risk his own life to free the corpse so it can be properly buried. He also drags two soldier buddies into a hugely risky sortie to locate bombers in some back-alleys, nearly leading to disaster. This is one good but dangerous guy. But the one thing he cannot do is return to 'normality'. At the end of the film, he has tried to return home to his partner and young child, and cannot bear the dull routines. The film's closing shot is of him back in Iraq, suited up, and walking jauntily towards yet another bomb.

Whatever you say about Sergeant William James, he does *not* suffer from PTSD. This has always been a very loosely defined syndrome, at best, but the standard lists of defining symptoms include: feeling fearful or numb, and helpless; bad dreams or nightmares; intrusive memories and flashbacks (paradoxically also presenting as suppressions or forgettings); intense physical reminders of the stress; avoidance of situations which might remind; loss of concentration, inability to sleep, hyper-vigilance, and being easily startled.[3] It would be hard to make a case for James suffering from any of these, at all. Even the attempt, which the blog quoted above hints at, to expand the range of admitted symptoms to include Traumatic Brain Injury, would not fit him. At no point does the film suggest that James has suffered such blast (or equivalent) injuries. As a film in itself, it would simply not sustain such uses. But looking at James and *The Hurt Locker* in other ways can make this much more understandable.

William James is not just a soldier. He is offered as a new role model of 'The American Soldier'. He is what soldiers need to be, ought to try to be. He is a millennial version of Alvin York (the World War I soldier whose life was recovered and heroised in the late 1930s). He is John Wayne (the star who 'forgot to fight' in World War II, but who could in a dozen or more movies weld together willing but unschooled recruits into a fighting force). America, perhaps more than any other country in the world, has long invested heavily in heroising its soldiers. From the late 1930s onwards, in highly concerted ways, government, military authorities, and film-makers have worked closely (if not always entirely without tensions) to create and distribute images of ideal soldiering. In World War II, this became systematised as government and military directly recruited sociologists (led by Samuel Stouffer), communications researchers (led by Paul Lazarsfeld), and film-makers such as Frank Capra, to propagandise their own troops, about whose loyalty and conviction they were quite seriously worried. Capra made the 'Why We Fight' series of films, as part of this persuasion offensive. Post-war, relations became more codified, run through established offices in Washington. Some of the ways in which this has been confidentially managed have recently come to light in David Robb's (2004) excoriating exposures of Pentagon manipulation of Hollywood. The tactics for ensuring this working association change, of course – but there is no doubt that in the case of the 2003 invasion and occupation of Iraq the embedding of journalists was a key way of ensuring that they stayed on-side. Scriptwriter Mark Boal was one such embedded journalist. And the story he enacts through Sergeant James is a Pentagon wet dream.

But in the case of *The Hurt Locker*, this is about more than James's behaviour. It becomes, I would argue, part of the film's aesthetic strategies. In a long central scene in the film, James's role in shaping and driving the film is strikingly revealed. Returning from a patrol, his unit encounters a group of stranded soldiers. At first distrustful, the Americans relax when they learn that these are British mercenaries bringing in captives. But as they try to help them, they come under fire. In the film, this is evoked through wild camera movements and jumpy editing. Their world has gone crazy. But as James exerts his influence, lining up one of his mates as a counter-sniper, his presence, his words, his calm breathing soothe and smooth the camerawork and editing. To him, it is a game of exciting chance. As the last of their attackers is taken out, his quiet words close the scene: 'Goodnight and thank you for playing.' James is a man who has swallowed 'PTSD', and made it his. He is a perfect new role model because he has taken this 'illness' and made it into his motivational source. He *lives and breathes* PTSD, and thus he is the new hero because under his influence others might too make it into a positive feature – at the price of dissociation from all questioning, all critical engagement, all politics.

What is PTSD?

So, what is 'PTSD'? The concept of post-traumatic stress disorder only in fact emerged in 1980, as a name for a range of 'conditions' identified as needing labelling in the third edition of the *Diagnostic and Statistical Manual of Mental Disorders* (DSM-III). The property of the American Psychiatric Association (APA), but used widely by legal, insurance and political bodies, DSM is not some neutral record of medical knowledge. It contains within itself the signs of the epistemologies and systems of medicine currently predominant in the USA. DSM's first version emerged in 1952, at the height of the popularity of psychoanalysis, and that first version shows all the signs of this. The second version, in 1968, was transitional in many ways – but among the points of transition was the disappearance of one condition identified in 1952: 'gross stress reaction'. In its 1950s incarnation, there was nothing special about this – stress was a part of life, and it was presumed that people would naturally recover

over time. By 1968 there seemed little reason to keep the label and it was quietly dropped, almost without debate. The 'condition' no longer existed.

But with veterans returning from the Vietnam war in the 1970s, disturbed in many ways, a campaign was mounted by veterans' associations, and some doctors and therapists, for its reinsertion as 'combat stress'. The problem was that by this point the dominant medical epistemologies had shifted. By now, under the influence of the pharmaceutical companies and medical equipment industries, a predominant individualism put chemical and brain sciences at the heart of the APA. As the third revised edition was being prepared, those leading the revisions were working hard to remove all traces of psychoanalytic concepts, languages and explanations. Now, mental disorders only gained entry if they could be defined by a consistent symptomatology; no reference to putative causes was admitted. PTSD simply would not fit that model. It could only be defined and understood by reference to putative causes. The problem, of course, was that not every case or situation of stress led to trauma. To suggest so would have made DSM-III look foolish. Therefore considerable work had to go into clarifying that just being very upset did not make you medically, and thus legally, traumatised.

The story of DSM is the story of America's troubled love affair with psychiatry, in its many incarnations. Its namings have always had a normative, politicised strand. The biggest argument in the run up to 1980, which revealed the extent to which such namings were not merely medical but ideologically loaded, was over the demand by gay groups for the removal of 'homosexuality' from the list of disorders requiring treatment. (The story of this struggle has been brilliantly recovered by several researchers – see for instance Kirk and Kutchins 1992; Mayes and Horwitz 2005). This normative/political distortion spilt over into the arguments that would lead to the characterisation of PTSD. The initial impetus for this struggle to gain recognition for combat stress reveals a terrible irony. Wilbur Scott (1990), who has told this part of the history most acutely, points to its beginning with a young New York therapist angry at being laughed at by colleagues when she tried to recount to them the story of her patient, a Vietnam veteran. He was convinced that he was being hunted down by former colleagues, because he could tell a story of atrocities committed by them. She wanted him admitted for special treatment, for symptoms of 'paranoia'. Her colleagues dismissed the story, which involved a place called…My Lai. The depoliticisation of Vietnam which can be seen within the suggestion that he was paranoid tells a great deal, as we will see. After a considerable struggle, a compromise was reached, under which a variety of conditions – from suffering personal traumas ranging from rape, kidnapping to car crashes, to being disturbed by watching horrible events on television – coalesced into PTSD. It was always a sore thumb, now being effectively the only 'condition' defined by its putative cause. But its suitability for use for the military made it popular. Funding programmes supported major studies of its causes, incidence and the effectiveness of different treatments. Journals were established to carry the research results. Lobbying groups – from veterans' associations, to military-friendly media, to research groups and universities – sought its wider recognition, and resources for its treatment. When in 1994 DSM was updated to a fourth edition, a re-description of PTSD's symptoms tidily increased supposed incidence levels by up to 50% (Breslau and Kessler 2001).

My argument is that the emergence of PTSD was not some simple process of discovery and naming. Rather, it was a highly politicised process under which some *real* problems – people sorely distressed for a whole range of reasons – came under the gaze of a Foucauldian system of 'knowledge'. Ways of looking and asking became established. Catalogues of events took on meaning. Treatments emerged which suited powerful interest groups. There are in here distinct and self-contained 'regimes of truth' protecting doctors, therapists and researchers from outside evaluation. And the *appeal* of PTSD was that it made those who could be said to suffer it, innocent. Here, then, is a distinctly Foucauldian system of knowledge, with some special features. First, there is unlikely to be resistance by its 'objects'. It could be worthwhile in so many ways to get that diagnosis. No stigma appeared to attach to the condition. It carried the probability of public sympathy. It promised regimes of care and treatment, and financial benefits. And it excused things you might have done. Second, this classification runs right the way to the centre of American politics. Contrary to Foucault's attempts to see systems of power/knowledge as distributed, uneven, and in conflict with each other, this one is supervenient. It is assuredly an ideology, in the full original sense of the term. But it is an ideology badly in need of narrative embodiment. It is pretty imperative that people should *feel* 'what it must be like'. Hence the importance of film versions.

Once in place, PTSD could be retroactively applied (irrespective of the lack of its distinctive symptoms). There is something almost delightful about finding, on the Internet Movie Database, a description of the film *Heroes*, as follows: 'A Vietnam veteran suffering from post traumatic stress disorder breaks out of a VA hospital and goes on a road trip with a sympathetic traveler to find out what became of the other men in his unit'.[4] *Heroes* was released in 1977.

The 'Cycle of Failures'

I return to that phrase cited in *The Hollywood Reporter*, that Bigelow had to escape 'the Iraq war curse'. This notion was very widespread across the period 2004-10. Any film made about the Iraq conflict was doomed to failure, at least at the box office, if not in its very soul. *Variety*, Hollywood's house magazine, greeted news that Bigelow was going to make *The Hurt Locker* by wondering if she knew what she was doing in working within such a 'toxic genre' (Thompson 2008). The American media were indeed full of predictions, explanations, regrets and gloatings over the repeated perceived 'failure' of all the films which sought to address the conflict. One very typical example – screenwriter John Nolte:

> In March of 2008, *Stop-Loss* was about to open, but the *Washington Post* had already its obituary written: 'After five years of conflict in Iraq, Hollywood seems to have learned a sobering lesson: The only things less popular than the war itself are dramatic films and television shows about the conflict. A spate of Iraq-themed movies and TV shows haven't just failed at the box office. They've usually failed spectacularly, despite big stars, big budgets and serious intentions. The underwhelming reception from the public raises a question: Are audiences turned off by the war, or are they simply voting against the way filmmakers have depicted it?' The *Post*, as you can see, followed the studio narrative in lamenting the box office failure of 'Iraq-themed' films, as opposed to what they really are:

pro-defeat films that in some cases are outright anti-American and too often defame the troops.

(Nolte 2008)

Even in a relatively neutral context – Nolte was contributing to a dedicated film site – the general expectations of failure have to be noted, and sides have to be taken. Hollywood's films were doomed to fail. And yet – this is the surprising part – there were overall so many of them. Even discounting those addressing it indirectly, through metaphor and allegory (as has been said of the so-called 'torture porn' films), at least the following have to be acknowledged alongside Bigelow's: *American Soldiers: A Day in Iraq* (Sidney J Furie, 2005); *Badland* (Francesco Lucente, 2007); *Battle for Haditha* (Nick Broomfield, 2007); *Body of Lies* (Ridley Scott, 2008); *Conspiracy* (Adam Marcus, 2008); *Day Zero* (Bryan Gunnar Cole, 2007); *GI Jesus* (Carl Colpaert, 2006); *Grace Is Gone* (James C. Strouse, 2007); *Home of the Brave* (Irwin Winkler, 2006); *In the Valley of Elah* (Paul Haggis, 2007); *The Kingdom* (Peter Berg, 2007); *Lions for Lambs* (Robert Redford, 2007); *The Lucky Ones* (Neil Burger, 2008); *The Marine* (John Bonito, 2006); *The Mark of Cain* (Marc Munden, 2007); *The Messenger* (Oren Moverman, 2010); *The Objective* (Daniel Myrick, 2008); *Redacted* (Brian de Palma, 2007); *Rendition* (Gavin Hood, 2007); *The Situation* (Philip Haas, 2006); *Stop-Loss* (Kimberley Pierce, 2008); and *War. Inc.* (Joshua Seftel, 2008). A few of these – notably *The Marine*, and *The Objective* – were frankly opportunistic cuckoos trying to feed off what they hoped the cycle might generate. *Green Zone* (Paul Greengrass, 2010) comes after *The Hurt Locker* and essentially tries to become 'Jason Bourne does Iraq'. This leaves a lot of films trying, in serious fashion, to address various aspects of the conflicts in Iraq (and by extension, in Afghanistan). Of these, an overwhelming proportion put at their heart the issues of 'courage', 'morale' and 'stress' among American troops. And the same proportion – and very often the same films – make two simultaneous modal moves: they ensure that their stories are understood to be *fictional* (so that characters' responses are not to be read directly onto the world);[5] but simultaneously they insist that they are based upon real events, situations, people, requirements. Whatever the reasons for this (explored in Barker 2011), the effect on the films, I would argue, is to make their pivotal characters look like *proposed models* of soldiering. They are not individuals, so much as *kinds*.

In the space of this chapter I can only touch on what this *kind* is made out to be, and how this unstitches those attempts I illustrated to separate the *ideas* of the films from their *aesthetic achievement*. I use one film to illustrate my argument, for a very particular reason: *In the Valley of Elah*. *Elah* stars Tommy Lee Jones as Hank Deerfield (with Susan Sarandon as his wife), father to Mike who has been serving in Iraq. One morning, Hank receives a phone call to say his son, home from Iraq (without his knowledge) has gone AWOL. As an ex-military policeman and wholly devoted to military ideals, Hank cannot believe this, and travels to the environs of his son's camp to search for him. The military authorities either can't or won't help him, but he manages to secrete Mike's phone from which gradually across the film he receives recovered bits of filming. Eventually, Mike turns up, dead – his body cut to pieces and burnt. Suspicions first fall on a Latino soldier, with implications of drug trading. But that is disproved (though not before Hank has badly beaten him). Finally, after much wrangling and covering up, but with the aid of a local policewoman (played by Charlize Theron), the truth emerges. Mike was killed by his platoon-mates after a trivial row. The soldier who eventually confesses this presents many symptoms of PTSD. Hypertense, withdrawn, Cpl Steve Penning (Wes Chatman) appears to have lost 'affect' (although that is not an official symptom, it kind of fits). From the confession Hank also learns that his son was involved in the torture of prisoners in Iraq – for fun. But by the time we learn this, we are expected to have become convinced by these representations of stressed-out soldiers who have been 'sacrificed' to the war. Their behaviour is not so much excused, as externalised.

The first thing to say about this film is that it is *very well done*. The film is, it is true, topped and tailed with deliberately provocative symbolic scenes about how the American flag should be displayed, rather baldly declaring a 'message' of crisis in the nation. But this aside, all the acting is controlled, measured, underplayed. Jones and Sarandon are simply impressive as the desperate, despairing parents. The film shifts ground from being a 'thriller' (its marketing tag) to being a quiet exposé of military inaction and uncaring over American soldiers' suffering. The confession scene is stark and brutal in its combination of still faces showing almost no emotion, and a sense of just-suppressed exhaustion and helplessness in Cpl Penning's face. There is a near-final shot, of Mike Deerfield stepping out of his military vehicle, defying orders to get the fuck back in, to take a photograph of the body of a boy he has been ordered to run over ('we never stop when we're out on patrol…'). His face is tight, empty, without hope. This is the revelation of what is supposed to have driven him over the edge – though, rationally, it is not clear why guilt at killing a boy should free a torturer's tendency in him. That is not asked, but emotionally, aesthetically and narratively the film has asked us to go there with him.

But there is another story behind *Elah*. As with so many of the films, this one is based on 'real events': in this case, the story of the real death at the hands of his platoon-mates of Specialist Richard Davis. The writer of *Elah*, who adapted the story from his own journalism, was the same Mark Boal who went on to write the Oscar-awarded screenplay for *The Hurt Locker*. Boal's original investigation of Davis's murder was published in *Playboy*. There, another possible explanation for the murder is discussed – that Davis was silenced by his fellow soldiers because he was threatening to report their rape of an Iraqi woman. The explanation, says Boal (2004), was a persistent rumour around the case. Any sense of this is excised from *Elah*, which invites us unreservedly to go with the 'PTSD' explanation.

The American Right, of course, and those with military connections, largely condemned the film. It presented the military authorities pretty much as sacrificing its front-line soldiers, and then hiding their crimes. And of course it is unacceptable to talk of American soldiers' crimes – until they become impossible to deny (think Abu Ghraib – although it is remarkable to me that among all those 24 films I cannot think of one which explicitly refers to those revelations – the nearest any comes is the very first, *American Soldiers*, which hints at our knowledge of this). Then, they are the results of individuals, errors, bad apples.

The Discursive Functions of PTSD

Post-traumatic stress disorder has been playing a quite central ideological role in recent American debates around Iraq. It has provided one point where Right and Left could appear to unite. It has allowed the Left to duck and dive on the (undeniably difficult) issue of their attitude to the American troops. It is the core of an enormously well-funded raft of institutes, hospitals, treatment regimes, research programmes and the like whose virtual failure to 'cure' anyone is one of the better-kept secrets of the whole sorry and horrible affair. The winners are, surprise, surprise, the medical drug and hardware companies, the private medical institutes, and the wider network of companies thoroughly invested in ripping the financial heart and soul out of Iraq, for the sake of profit. The name of that common interest, publicly presented, is 'ideology'. The sad thing is to see the American liberal left so caught in promoting its end of this, without realisation.

Boal himself offered an explanation of the changes from the actual events. In the course of a long discussion of the film in the *Independent on Sunday* reviewing the relationship between film and real events, Rob Sharp revealingly quotes him:

> When *In the Valley of Elah* was released in the US late last year, it was lauded by the critics but it did not prove popular with cinema-goers. Those close to the real events it depicts have weighed in with criticism, too. Matt Thompson says: 'It's hard to enjoy the movie because I knew what really happened. People say the real story would have been the better movie. They changed it too much.' Lanny [Richard's father] takes issue with a scene in the film that shows the soldier based on Richard getting kicked out of a strip club, something he believes never happened. He is frustrated by the film-makers' suggestion that his son had a hash pipe (a claim he denies), and infuriated by the depiction of his son's killers as fine, upstanding American citizens who were turned into psychopaths by the madness of war; their documented histories contradict this. The film's screenwriter was Mark Boal. Speaking from set on the final day's shooting of *The Hurt Locker*...Boal says that crucial decisions needed to be made when Lanny's story was adapted for the screen. 'It's a fictional

piece, and so at various junctures Paul [Haggis] and I thought we should change Lanny's story to make it feel more universal.'

(Sharp 2008)

The decision to 'go universal' was one which stripped out a bit of the real politics of the Iraq conflict, offering instead the ideological story of PTSD. If *Elah* takes us inside the mind of a soldier 'corrupted into torture' by the stress of the Iraq war, and his murderous colleagues made sympathetic because they have been through the same, then *The Hurt Locker* goes one better. It shows us one soldier rising above the 'disorder', containing and using his stress to survive and become horribly noble. The undeniable power of *The Hurt Locker* lies then in its subordination of the film to Sergeant William James. The disease becomes the beauty and the beauty becomes the disease.

Notes

[1] For both speeches, see 'Oscar Acceptance Speeches', NDTVMovies.com, 8 March 2010, http://movies.ndtv.com/movie_Story.aspx?id=ENTEN20100134095&keyword=&subcatg=.

[2] Too few audience studies have focused on the way special interest groups go about watching films for these kinds of purposes. One notable example of such an examination is Tom Poe's (1998) study of the historical reception of Stanley Kramer's *On The Beach*, a film which frightened the authorities in America because of its depiction of nuclear nightmare. Poe explores some very particular 'audiences': the FBI, the American government, and the Catholic Legion of Decency, and the ways they watched the film as through the eyes of others they were worried about.

[3] For such standardised lists, see either: http://helpguide.org/mental/post_traumatic_stress_disorder_symptoms_treatment.htm or http://ptsd.about.com/od/symptomsanddiagnosis/a/PTSDsymptoms.htm.

[4] See: www.imdb.com/title/tt0076138/.

[5] A classic cover-note on this comes in the Extras to the DVD of *Badland*. The film's central character has harangued a man whom he is about to kill with a raging attack on god as a myth that America uses to justify its action, and who simply doesn't exist. The Extras cover themselves by insisting that this is just the character in despair, not the view of the film-makers.

Chapter 3

Ethical Encounters and Passive Spectators: Looking on at Hollywood's War on Terror

Mark Straw

There seems to be a compelling theme emerging in the recent war on terror cycle of combat films, namely a focus on spectatorial inactivity and passivity. This passivity is either embodied in characters in the film, or takes the form of an explicit or implicit accusation levelled at the audience. This is not quite the same passivity spoken of in 1970s film theory, whereby the spectator is figured as being located within a matrix of 'voyeuristic active/passive mechanisms' (Mulvey 1975: 18), but is rather an *ethical* charge that contemporary Western audiences are culpable collaborators in a certain political/cultural apathy and disengagement leading to the invasion and occupation of Iraq and Afghanistan.[1] In this chapter, I will analyse how certain war on terror films set up these accusations and present a specifically ethical charge to the spectator. As a consequence of this charge, I will ask: what are the spectatorial implications of watching fictionalised accounts of catastrophe and trauma, specifically when this involves films that address the war on terror?

To get a handle on these questions, I wish to examine the impact on the spectator of these films' stylistics, and how one is drawn into what I shall refer to as 'ethical encounters' with the films. By this I mean moments when one becomes acutely aware of the filmic nature of one's audio-visual immersion; moments of unsettling self-awareness that cause one to question the appropriateness of one's spectatorial position. In other words, one is incorporated into a regime of self-questioning focussed on whether one *ought* to be watching what is occurring on screen.

For the purposes of this analysis I will focus on two films, *Lions for Lambs*, and *In the Valley of Elah*. These were both mainstream Hollywood productions, released in the same year (2007), which share similarities in their narrative trajectories and aesthetic preoccupations. In the first instance, they both possess incredibly tonally downbeat endings, and we are offered corporeally, morally, and emotionally damaged men by way of emotional routes into the film. Secondly, the films make use of the contemporaneous visual style of modern warfare, in particular what Garrett Stewart has referred to as the 'instantaneous videography' of war (2009: 48). This means the films are linked by their visual style in that they, in part, use digital video to ape the style of the vernacular practices of recording video using mass market hand-held digital cameras, camera-phones and the like. The effect of this is to place these films within the context of the 'digitally mediated narratives' (Stewart 2009: 45) that form the popular consciousness of contemporary wars, and in particular the occupations of Iraq and Afghanistan.

Ethics and Spectatorship

It is important first to delineate what is meant by an *ethical* encounter, as opposed to a *moral* one. Ethics is not the same as morality, and emotional and sensory engagement with a film is not necessarily ethical. As Michele Aaron states, 'being moved…marks [an] experience as moral but not ethical: involuntary emotion is the opposite of reflection and implication' (2007: 116). Ethical spectatorship therefore is not defined by emotive pleas to a spectator's morality, but is founded in generating a sense of self-awareness, and a degree of responsibility for our active role in looking on, as is the case in so many films (and in visual culture in general), at the suffering of others. It is a form of spectatorship that can be delineated as 'interrogation, and as resistance to affective capitulation to acculturated norms' (Downing and Saxton 2010: 3).

This of course means that a film can sometimes be immoral and ethical, or unethical and moral.

Lisa Downing and Libby Saxton have pointed out that 'ethics designates a way of responding to the encounter between self and others, while suspending the meaning of the subject-object relation, with its implicit dynamic of dominance and subordination' (2010: 3). So there is the crucial question in ethical spectatorship of encounter with the other, and ensuring that the other does not become objectified and aestheticised. Emotional engagement or feelings of empathy are not enough: critical attention must be paid to the position of the spectator in the dynamics of constructing our relationship to images and narratives. In this respect, many critics studying film and ethics find the work of the philosopher Emmanuel Levinas useful. It is Levinas's concept of the 'face-to-face', or *visage*, discussed at length in his volume *Totality and Infinity* (1979) that provides the structural framework for conceiving of an ethics of cinematic spectatorship. This is rooted in Levinas's idea that encounter with the other can produce transformations and processes of subversion in the self, in which one's experience of the world is troubled and shaken up. He specifically states that 'we name this calling into question of my spontaneity by the presence of the other ethics' (Levinas 1979: 43). Sarah Cooper, in discussing this idea of ethics, states that it is 'a primordial relation, obligation and responsibility to others on the part of the self' (2006: 5). Accordingly, we see here the crucial role of responsibility: ethical spectatorship is not just about formulating a moral sense of the goodness of how others are treated and represented on the screen, but rather stresses how we might be culpable for the dominating systems of representation that cast others in their objectified, de-subjectivised states. Cooper goes on to delineate that 'the way in which the encounter with alterity is figured in his thinking is primarily through his notion of the *visage* (face)'[2] and so therefore it is in 'the face-to-face encounter between self and other' that Levinas's ethics 'challenge the sovereignty of the self, which is constituted by being thrown into question by alterity' (2006: 5). For Levinas, the absolutism of the self is replaced by recognition of the other, a manoeuvre that in itself exposes the interplays of subordination, submission, dominance and control that inform social relations. Accordingly, the ethics of spectatorship in the context of war on terror films has the ability to expose our spectatorial subordination to dominant narratives and representational regimes. This is therefore a useful tool for interrogating the neo-imperial domination by the US of Iraq and Afghanistan through confronting the spectator with the subordination of ethnic and racial alterity upon which US cultural authority might be argued to depend.[3]

So why is Hollywood seemingly preoccupied with *attempting* to produce ethically implicated and culpable spectators? Since ethical filmic notions of alterity are so bound up with dominance and subordination, it seems strange that Hollywood should be concerned with following a route that entails the casting out of one of its central representative regimes. This regime is one that emphasises difference (rather than promoting ethical encounter with the other) and manufacturing narrative and aesthetic intrigue from the re-entrenchment and re-articulation of boundaries, whether these be defined by race, class, gender, or sexuality. As Sharon Willis (1997: 1) states, our 'contemporary investments' in highly visible indicators of difference, such as race and gender, 'have tended to eroticize and aesthetize'. Accordingly, cinema seems to deploy a 'volatile affective range' in order to enhance spectatorial desire for these sensational and highly legible markers of difference. The motives behind Hollywood's turn to the ethics of spectatorship will be one of the central questions explored here.

For the purposes of this analysis, and since I am focussing on ethical spectatorial encounters, I am keen to explore moments in war on terror films which may be categorised as ruptures in our safe, interpellated subject positions. By this I mean moments which cause us to reflect on what Louis Althusser identified as 'the imaginary relationship of individuals to their real conditions of existence' (1971: 153). Hence, they are moments when, either through the use of textual or narrative techniques or through meta-textuality, we come to a heightened self-awareness regarding our relationship to the image. In a way, these moments may be categorised as when we no longer ask, 'why is this image being presented to me?' and instead start to ponder, 'why is this image so uncomfortable, so unsettling, and yet I continue to watch?'. As Cooper (2006: 5) puts it, 'the catalyst for this process is a primordial encounter with alterity which disturbs our solitary enjoyment of the world, our illusory position of omnipotence and sovereignty.'[4]

Catherine Wheatley, in her discussion of the cinema of Michael Haneke, observes that his films extra-diegetically raise questions of 'complicity, responsibility, and guilt' which are viewed as analogous to the 'acts of film-going and film-viewing' (2009: 4). In other words, the films, narratively speaking, engage with the morality of guilt and complicity and use this moral engagement as not only a metaphorical consideration of these self-same issues when it comes to a spectator viewing a film, but also as a direct mode of implication to the spectator, a form of cinematic ethical call to arms. The source of this is that his films are 'formally reflexive – they reflect on their own construction' (Wheatley 2009: 5). It is precisely this fascination with the apparatus of constructing a cinematic piece of work and drawing attention to the artifice and deceits upon which cinematic modes of representation are predicated (for example, continuity editing, the limitations and movement of the frame, post-production sound editing, and so on) that induce this reflexive mode. In turn, this 'aesthetic reflexivity is conducive to the spectator's moral reflexivity' (Wheatley 2009: 5). Here, seemingly, Wheatley conflates morality and ethics, yet I do not believe that the aesthetic reflexivity of a film will ever cause a self-interrogation of one's codes and values. What it can provoke, however, through highlighting the constructed nature of the film text, is a self-consciousness of the act of looking on. This is a purely ethical engagement, since it depends on a spectatorial self-regard and scrutiny, one that exposes the sovereignty of the viewing subject to critical attention. Through interrogating and drawing attention to the formal techniques of cinema, the spectator cannot help but notice the constructed nature of the filmic text, hence ruining any reality effect/suspension of disbelief. This brings the spectator directly into confrontation with questions such as 'how are we complicit with the apparatus? What are the moral consequences of this?' (Wheatley 2009: 5).

As Wheatley accurately states, the self-awareness that results from the unpleasurable emotions provoked by these sudden 'ruptures' or moments of aesthetic reflexivity, leads to a sense of shame or guilt. If war on terror films levy accusations of inactivity and passivity at Western vernacular visual culture, and as a consequence inculcate feelings of guilt and shame, and induce a profound sense of disquiet to do with the spectatorial position of viewing atrocity, then this is in need of close investigation as to the reasons why and the political and cultural motivations behind it. As such, not only will I look at Hollywood's turn to ethics, I will examine how war on terror films depict violence and atrocity and will critique their attempts to implicate the spectator in a consistent regime of passivity and inaction.

Crucial in this depiction, and in attempts to draw the spectator into an ethical encounter, are the textual and narrative pleasures offered up by these films. As Jayne Stadler asserts, 'physicality of narrative film is central to its impact' and this in turn leads us, through empathic emotional engagement, 'to better understand other people's circumstances in a felt, experiential, embodied sense' (2008: 165). So the tactile, sensual world of cinema is a central component in permitting emotional connections and regulating ethical encounters. This doesn't just become about the realm of empathy, but the lived, corporeal sensations of film: ethical engagement is a matter for the *cinematic body*, one that is intimately bound to the narrative processes and apparatus of film, mediating our emotional liaisons and then stepping aside to allow us to literally *feel* the force of collision when reflexively-derived rupturing ethical encounters arrive. This *cinematic body* owes something to Steven Shaviro's (1993) proposition of a visceral and embodied conception of film spectatorship, one that is also self-consciously bound up in the economics and politics of the contemporary Western liberal subject. Shaviro's conception of spectatorship flies in the face of the commonly held idea, especially in Marxist and early psychoanalytical film theory, that the spectator searches for self-identity and wholeness in the 'better than real' scenarios presented on the cinema screen. Shaviro instead asserts that 'cinema seduces its viewers by mimetically exacerbating erotic tension'; in other words, we can only stand by, looking on, in a state of tension, in 'visual fascination' (1993: 56). Cinematic spectatorship is therefore at its heart a seeking of, even an infatuation with, loss of control. The surface pleasures of the text manufactured through production design, close-up shots, and immersive sound design, all contribute to this seduction. Accordingly, analysis of the tactile, intimate and sensuous realm of the cinematic text reveals the mechanisms by which this seduction of the spectator works, and reveals how the cinema may attempt to draw us into ethical encounters.

However, it is crucial to maintain, as stated earlier, that emotional engagement is not the same as ethical encounter, it is merely one of the interceding forces in this encounter. Ethical encounter can only occur when a matrix of emotional engagement, aesthetic and spectatorial reflexivity develops, and the nature of these ethical encounters depends on the relationships between each of the aspects of this matrix.

Lions for Lambs and Spectatorial Passivity

First I shall examine a film that was described by Peter Bradshaw in *The Guardian* as 'pure fence-sitting liberal agony' (Bradshaw 2007), namely, *Lions for Lambs* (Robert Redford, 2007). The film features three interwoven narratives, depicting: an interview between a veteran journalist (Janine Roth, played by Meryl Streep) and a US Senator, Jasper Irving (Tom Cruise), with foreign policy responsibilities; a discussion between an idealistic university professor (Stephen Malley, played by Redford) and one of his students (Todd Hayes, played by Andrew Garfield); and the harrowing experiences of two US marines (Rodriguez and Finch, played by Michael Peña and Derek Luke, respectively) stranded in the hostile environment of the Afghan mountains with Al-Qaeda troops closing in on them. Garrett Stewart describes this particular form of grandiose cross-cutting editing as 'a geopolitics of montage' (2009: 47), which certainly rings true: the editing relies on creating a juxtaposition between the various scenarios on display, and serves to underline the political and geographical tensions between these spaces. Unfortunately, *Lions for Lambs* does little to let the spectator attach meanings to these juxtapositions, it being such a verbose film. As Nathan Rabin (2007) has pointed out, the film commits one of the cardinal sins of film-making in disobeying the rule of 'show, don't tell': characters embark on lengthy polemical and ideological discussions and monologues almost compulsively, and the film patronises and preaches at every turn, with its ideas being writ large through dialogue and melodramatic acting.

Stewart places contemporary war films within a trend of 'digitally mediated narratives' (2009: 45). The problem of conveying the war on terror audio-visually is symptomatically demonstrated in the reliance on layered narration and obscure/obscuring aesthetic and editing practice. As Stewart argues, 'battle fatigue has grown stylistic, afflicting the picturing as well as its scene' (2009: 45). Films addressing the war on terror can be seen to be struggling to negotiate the space between the traditional/classical war film and the 'new plots of surveillance paranoia', and therefore necessarily are seemingly concerned with issues of the ethics of watching and the accounts of inactivity/passivity which accompany this. Stewart also suggests that it is possibly the fact that the film was made while the violence in Afghanistan and Iraq was still ongoing that contributes to the lack of narrative clarity, of a 'clear ethical and political perspective' (2009: 48). If this is true, then it is crucial to examine what precise ethical perspectives are conjured by contemporary American engagements with the war on terror in this film.

In the Finch and Rodriguez strand of the film, we see them spend a good two thirds of the screen-time in a hopelessly desperate situation, stranded in the Afghan mountains in full winter conditions with Al-Qaeda troops unrelentingly closing in on them. Through their inevitably victimised and vulnerable status, they become empathic points of emotional connection for spectators, and objects of a certain contemporary, mediated 'imperial' gaze (after Kaplan 1997). This is courtesy of the fact that their position on the mountainside is monitored, via satellite and drone video footage, by the military commanders back at their base. The commanders look on, bark instructions about a swift emergency rescue, and ultimately watch helplessly as Finch and Rodriguez are gunned down by Al-Qaeda forces. In the meantime, smart bombs target the enemy troops, but as Stewart points out, once the ammunition has run out and the bombs stop falling, 'the doomed soldiers must at last face the enemy gunmen across real rather than mediated space' (2009: 50).

The manner in which they 'face the enemy gunmen' is also interesting. They take their deaths standing up, with Rodriguez declaring 'not like this, not lying down...help me up!' So leaning on each other, half frozen, with no ammo, they deliberately invite their deaths, pointing their unloaded guns at the enemy to provoke shooting. As David Savran (1998: 38) might say, they 'take it like a man', and hence this scene is revealing in the way in which it conflates Americanness, masculinity, masochism and self-negation. When the Al-Qaeda troops open fire, the sound of the bullets is muted and replaced with a mournful string soundtrack. In a conceit of editing, the strobing effect of the gunfire is used to intersperse the scene with flashbacks of Finch and Rodriguez at college, and the satellite and drone video footage flares into a brilliant white. Their victimhood is stretched out over narrative time and incorporated into the aesthetic regime of the new technologies of war. Accordingly, they are at once eulogised as victims of US foreign policy, but also as victims of the culture of watching, mediation and digital fatigue that typifies contemporary visual culture.

The implication here is that we as spectators are being included in this condemnation of contemporary visual culture. This is one of the more clunky points the film makes in its over-long passages of dialogue. Professor Stephen Malley (Redford) declares in an unintentionally hilarious melodramatic moment that: 'Rome is burning!…The problem's with us. All of us who do nothing. We just fiddle.' In his excruciating office hour with his underachieving student, he challenges the younger man to ιe-engage with the world and do something to make a difference. A similar problem confronts Janine Roth: Senator Irving disparages modern journalists as 'windsocks', passive and pliant, and yet this provokes moral doubt regarding whether Roth should swallow whole Irving's talk of winning the war through a new military strategy. In the end it appears her morals have taken a pummelling since we see Todd Hayes (the underachieving student) watching television with his housemates, the story regarding the new military strategy appearing verbatim on the rolling ticker tape at the bottom of the screen.

There are severe problems with this condemnation of passive spectatorship. Firstly, the film lectures its audience on the importance of action and making a difference, making appeals to leftist political idealism, and yet it locates the spectator in a position of pleasurable enjoyment of its aesthetic regime and its narrative format. The second problem arises in the manner in which the film constructs its aesthetic regime, especially in the narrative concerning Finch and Rodriguez. Janine Roth comments at one point, when Senator Irving promises her news network exclusive access to 'the infra-red and gun camera images', that 'Great, those are our most popular downloads', obviously intended as a critical comment on the sedentary, passive nature of contemporary television spectatorship, on the technology of war and its transference into screened multimedia entertainment. However, in the Finch and Rodriguez strand, this is exactly the kind of aesthetic we are treated to, since we experience the grainy satellite and drone video night-vision imagery. We also experience the frenzied experiences of the two soldiers on the ground, courtesy of rapid cutting, shaky hand-held camera work, and a focal position that aligns the spectator with the soldiers' experiences – the enemy are always in the distant shadows of the icy rocks and obscured by snow storms. These scenes construct for us the sort of imagery Streep's character describes as 'our most popular downloads', and so the film castigates a passive spectatorial interest in US forces' video images of war, and yet all too readily supplies scenes which visually replicate major sources of this spectatorial interest.

The audio and visual strategies cajole the spectator into an encounter with the stated moral concern of the film, that of looking on, but make the act of looking on a pleasure that is rooted in the (fictional and stylised) suffering of others. In other words, inactive and passive spectatorship is indicted as ruinous for contemporary democracy and for fostering unchecked neo-imperial US foreign policy, but the film uses narrative and stylistic techniques in order to encourage the spectator to remain glued to the screen, thus sustaining this inactive and passive state. Through its dialogue and use of digital mediation and the instantaneous videography that surrounds the war on terror, it then condemns this self-same state of political and moral inertia.

The effect is also to equate the spectator position with one of victimhood, as we are manipulated into a position of empathy with the US soldiers. The vague, open-ended nature of the film's close serves to feed this too. The final scene is of Todd Hayes and other college students sitting on a sofa watching vacuous entertainment news on an enormous flat-screen television. They make the occasional amused remark to each other about the celebrity gossip being presented on screen. Most of this is filmed using shots at a skewed angle to the people sitting on the sofa and is inter-cut with straight on close-up shots of the television. This visual regime is then slightly disturbed when Todd notices the scrolling sound-bites relayed to Janine Roth sliding past at the bottom of the screen. The camera pushes in on this scrolling ticker-tape and then switches back and forth to shots which show Todd front on, each successively pushed in a little closer, him wearing a concerned, unsettled expression. The aesthetic strategies here clearly link Todd's sudden realisation of his inactive and vacuous spectatorial position with his subjectivity. However, since this arrives at the very conclusion of the film, there is no definite culmination or closure to the narrative: we are left hanging on. There is no suggestion as to how to break out of this spectatorial passivity, just a lingering set of shots conveying the inactivity and vacuity of white US domestic vernacular visual culture. Despite the spectator being bound to an emotive engagement/empathy with the characters by the very representational processes and strategies of the film itself, we can deny our own subjection and subjugation in this scenario by pointing at traumatised characters and internally whispering 'no, it is *their* pain, confusion, trauma, not mine'. Accordingly, we can gloss over the ethical encounter attempted by the film through deriving satisfaction from the solipsism of the position of the 'concerned' and 'thoughtful' spectator, one who can indulgently acknowledge the ruinous regimes of passivity bound up in contemporary mass media visual culture, and then disavow its effects through feeling the pain and victimhood of this scenario.

In the Valley of Elah, Male Trauma, the War on Terror and the Liberal Spectator

In the Valley of Elah takes digital mediation, US male victimhood, and spectatorship to another level. The film's title is a reference to the story of David and Goliath, the eponymous valley being the land that separates the massed armies of the Philistines and the Israelites. The US is therefore figured as David fighting a 'monster', and accordingly it is implied that the US is the courageous underdog.[5] The film concerns Hank Deerfield (Tommy Lee Jones) attempting to piece together the mysterious circumstances of the murder of his son (Mike, nicknamed Doc) and the subsequent burning of his body. Mike had recently returned from a tour of duty in Iraq and had been out drinking with his army buddies. Deerfield clandestinely steals Mike's mobile phone and hands it to a friend with the technology to recover the corrupted media files saved on it. The unravelling of the mystery of what these audio-visual documents depict runs hand in hand with the unravelling of the exact circumstances of Mike's murder, and although the two strands are not intrinsically linked, they are presented as corroborating, or complementary narratives.

Digital imagery seems to be the chief concern of a film that, in its *mise-en-scène* and editing, conforms to the basic precepts of classical Hollywood cinema. The majority of the *film* shots (as opposed to the *digital* audio-visual files on Mike's phone) are static, or slow and ponderous pan and track, with little handheld work. Despite this considered, formal filmic style, from the very first few frames we can see the interest in, even obsession with, digital imagery. The familiar CGI Warner Brothers logo slithers into the darkened space of the frame, but reflected in the metallic border to the logo, we see bursts of visual white noise (akin to a detuned TV), and crackles of static, giving the impression that the studio logo is infected with the distorted and corrupted digital imagery that plagues the film. It is an interesting image with which to commence the film, and seems to imply a certain linkage between the global business of multinational entertainment industries such as Warner Brothers, and the vernacular, handheld forms of populace-derived media.

The first images of the film are a brief scene from a corrupted video file that depicts some random panning over some Iraqi children on a dusty street. The credits and this scene are accompanied with snatches of disconnected and seemingly random speech that have an almost incantatory or hallucinatory effect. These include crackling and desperately harrowing sounding voices declaring 'Let's go, Mike, now!', 'What are you doin'?!', and 'Get back in the vehicle!'. There is also a lone weak and croaky voice pleading, groping in the dark almost, repeating 'Dad..? Dad..?' The former snatches of speech are obviously in the context of military operations in Iraq, given the visual information, but the latter portion of speech is much more ambiguous and forms its own miniature mystery within the film. The poignant and disembodied pleas for the father continue throughout the film and always accompany Deerfield's scenes. It turns out that these bits of speech are Deerfield's memories of the last telephone conversation he had with his son, Mike, and hence they haunt the film. We are gathered into the private world of Deerfield's grief and traumatic memory, one which is essentially auditory. It is implied through this technique of disembodied voices accompanying his scenes when he is depicted on the cusp of sleep or waking, that not only is he haunted by the memories of this last telephone conversation, but that we should experience this too. Hence, we as spectators are invited into sharing a position of traumatised subjectivity (in the sense of our experience of this auditory technique) with Deerfield.

Towards the conclusion of the film, all the corrupted imagery and 'dirty' media fades away for us to be given a narrative account of what the files were attempting to convey. It becomes clear that Mike and his fellow squad members had captured an enemy soldier and were transporting him with them in the back of their armoured vehicle. The enemy soldier has serious open wounds, to which Mike's response is to stick his fingers into one of these wounds declaring 'Where does it hurt? Right there?' The soldier's response is understandably a series of blood-curdling screams conveying the physical pain and distress this is causing him.

However, are there any disavowed or unannounced pleasures in looking on at these mutilated and damaged bodies? The film is certainly populated with numerous images of burned bodies, usually courtesy of the corrupted videos on Mike's mobile phone. These images arguably do not invoke a turning away, but rather underline a certain fascination with the broken human body. It is curious the manner in which the camera lingers over these images, inviting the spectator to observe, recoil in disgust, then keep watching, transfixed. The images crackle and jump, decay and return to wholeness; they also are characterised by the 'blocky' pixilation of low definition digital images, light sources rendered a brilliant white and areas of darkness just a fuzz of black and grey. Through this squall of corruption and distortion one can faintly pick out the movements of Mike when he tortures the Iraqi soldier, and hear the desperate screams from the victim, the blank inquiring voice of the perpetrator, and the collusive, dead-eyed laughter of the onlookers.

There is potential here to take pleasure from feeling ethically troubled and entangled with the film. The spectator is positioned in relationship to what Cynthia Weber (2006: 5) has identified as the competing trajectories of 'morality' and 'vengeance' in post-9/11 cultural discourse. In a sense, we adopt a punished, victimised, even assaulted subject position through bearing witness to traumatic scenes of violence and carnage, but we remain safely distanced and can disavow our implication in the cinematic happenings the more extreme they are, since they bear no relation to the perceivable reality we encounter on a daily basis.

However, the distancing and disavowal depends on aping the style and format of the relentless videography characteristic of the war on terror. Accordingly, the visual pleasures of regarding the textures and tactile sensations of the corrupted digital images and the narrative investment associated with the revelation of Mike's complicity in torture, plus the numerous scorched corpses that litter the film all point towards a fascination with the terrifying effects of the traumatic experiences of the US soldiers in Iraq.

In engaging with serious, downbeat, and 'worthy' films about the war on terror such as *Lions for Lambs* and *In the Valley Of Elah*, we as Western, (sometimes) liberal, democratic spectators are wholly culpable in our collusion with the textual and narrative pleasures of the suffering of others. Yet we can disavow this collusion by culturally investing in 'worthy' cultural productions, since they provide the emotional and ethical catharsis to make ourselves feel better. These actions contribute to a self-delusional status of political engagement, where we *believe* we are resistant and anti-authoritarian, when in reality we are tools, agents of the dominant fiction of globalised media and entertainment. A sense of narcissistic altruism is fostered in lieu of ethical action and self-reflexivity. Our capacity to be reflective and interrogate our relationship to images of suffering and crisis is buried by the sense of worthiness that goes hand-in-hand with the spectatorship of ostensibly critical films. The emotional engagement and tactile intimacy of the film text that is supposed to draw us into ethical encounter with the other become merely the means by which one can emotionally invest in the film and then cast aside any culpability for constructing and maintaining the spectacles of suffering contained within.

It is seemingly the case that our ethical culpability and sense of guilt is a product of our narratological manipulation, and that this sense of guilt and responsibility, as Wheatley states, is a product of 'not having *done* wrong, but from mere *desiring*' (2009: 184). So crucially, since, in the context of cinema, our capacity for action is limited we are powerless to act and hence ethically compromised. The ethics of our position as feeling, emotionally engaged spectators is typified by 'not a process of acting, but a process of overcoming: an overcoming of the desire for oblivion, an overcoming of nature, and an overcoming of cinematic systems of interpellation' (Wheatley 2009: 184). At this point Wheatley once again conflates morality with ethics, but her general point is still valid. Our spectatorial position is defined by our internal resistance to the illicit pleasures and excitations we have comfortably subscribed to, but the true nature of which we have then been critically jolted into self-awareness of by the aesthetic reflexivity and narrative techniques of the films under discussion. Ethical calls to arms such as the accusations of spectatorial passivity embodied in *Lions for Lambs* and *In the Valley of Elah* invoke guilt and shame at having consented to the abject pleasures of witnessing suffering, and revelling in the aesthetic values and narrative content of such spectacles. Therefore, the strategies by which these ethical calls to arms are issued have the effect of closing off any radical spectatorial interaction with images and narratives. Ethical reflexivity encourages a departure from the excitations and embodied critical pleasures of watching films, and in a sense, sublimates the transgressive in favour of fixity and coherence. This is achieved on a basic level by calling into play our interpretative and sense-making faculties when attempting to deduce the significance of the ruptures and collisions depicted in these films, but also through invoking a rationalising vision with which to acknowledge the emotional engagement and empathic alignment of ethical reflexivity, and then compartmentalise this affective realm of sensation as part of the pleasure-producing machinery that entrenches unquestioned, unchallenged desires pleasurably to consume spectacles of suffering and pain.

Conclusions: War on Terror Films and Neo-Liberal Spectatorship

One of my foundational questions was why do these films go to such lengths to point the finger at us, the audience? This can be answered through reference to the rise of neo-liberalism, and how it interacts with the notions of ethical spectatorship explored so far.

Neo-liberalism is a normative political theory that commits to the primacy of the state, the capitalist market, and the status quo (Lamy 2001: 182). It asserts the supremacy of market freedom and private enterprise over state intervention and control, espouses an inherent ideological linkage between capitalism and democracy, and consistently stresses the sovereignty of the individual in determining his/her economic and physical health (Grugal 2002: 87-90).

With Hollywood pointing an accusatory finger at war on terror film audiences, we see a manifestation of this neo-liberal ideology. There is no *cultural* or *social* exploration or interrogation of culpability for US foreign policy actions, but rather an assignment of guilt and responsibility to the individuated contemporary Western spectator. Ethical culpability and reflexive interrogation of one's relationship to images of suffering and catastrophe are reconfigured as expressions of the neo-liberal subject's de-socialised and de-cultured agency. Critical reflection, ethical encounter and irreducible alterity are all bypassed in favour of stressing the individual's liability. This is no longer about interaction with the other calling into question the self's sovereignty, or critiquing difference through the lens of reflexivity. Instead, this is about crucially *bolstering* an illusion of sovereignty, or omnipotent agency, swelling the apparent self-importance of individual responsibility to the exclusion of the state, the social, and the cultural.

It is an illusion of sovereignty since individual liability for colluding in images of military and neo-imperial violence is asserted in order assign the subject responsibility, but crucially not the power or the ability to do anything about this responsibility. Neo-liberalism furnishes the subject with an imaginary mastery in which social and political power is suggested as solely in the dominion of the individual. However, as is the case with the ethical charge presented to the contemporary viewer of war on terror films, the subject has been divested of any genuine empowerment, and so is sited in an almost paralytic position in relation to this ethical charge.

This dynamic of empowerment and disempowerment of individuated subjectivity that eradicates the social and the cultural is also the precept by which US exceptionalism operates. Its economic, military (and cultural) might is the pretext by which its interventionist international relations strategies flourish; a self-styled pre-eminence and uniqueness (McCrisken 2003). This pre-emptive mode also results from a styling of the US as a victim in the sphere of contemporary geo-political conflict and power, as seen in neo-conservative think-tank publications such *America the Vulnerable* (Lehman and Sicherman 2000). So furnishing contemporary Western spectators with initially a self-image of victim (through the assaultive sensory environments of contemporary war films and through emphasising the mental and corporeal dismantlement of the

US soldier), and then with a sense of guilt for the responsibility of their passivity and inaction, acts to reinforce the precepts of neo-liberalism.

Recalling Cooper's argument that our 'encounter with alterity…disturbs our solitary enjoyment of the world, our illusory position of omnipotence and sovereignty' (2006: 3), it might be argued that, in this sense, ethical encounter can be utilised as a means by which to stress the loss of this sovereignty and to jolt the subject back into awareness of his/her lost grip on the outlines of his/her omnipotence. Ethical reflexivity can shatter our illusory sovereignty, but it can also draw attention to its sudden lack or absence, and has the potential to hurl the subject back into a recuperative zone, one that resists alterity and the dissolution of boundaries of difference. The aforementioned techniques by which war on terror films invoke emotional empathic protagonists that offer up a crucial sense of victimhood assist in turning round moments of ethical encounter into ones of intense self-regard. This secures the primacy of the spectator's emotions, through empathising with an assaulted or traumatised subjectivity, and fixes the spectator's position in relation to state power by securing him or her as an agent of the status quo.

The superficial impression of ethical encounter that some war on terror films invoke stops short of interrogation and critical reflexivity. Accordingly, the exceptionalism and neo-liberalism on which US foreign policy has been based become both the political effect of blaming the individuated responsibility of contemporary Western spectators, and also its motivating factor. This means that US foreign policy (and specifically its Bush doctrine incarnation) is bolstered by reinforcing the neo-liberal precept of individual responsibility. Our recruitment to this politics is disguised by draping it in the veils of liberal moral hand-wringing over standing by whilst war was consented to, and then leaving the films with ambiguous doleful endings. Since we have been furnished with the political agency by which to assert our neo-liberal sense of sovereignty, in the light of these doleful endings (once one is acculturated to the neo-liberal concepts seeded in these films), the only logical conclusion can be that a robust and belligerent foreign policy is the only way out of this ethical and political mire. In accepting our guilt as passive spectators to catastrophe and suffering, we accept that we are individually responsible, and hence are already a long way towards accepting a neo-liberal account of subjectivity and personal and social agency. The implied trajectory – especially in *Lions for Lambs*, in which enlisting is presented as a supreme moral (but not ethical) interrogation of one's political stance on US international relations; and in *In the Valley of Elah*, in which the closing image is of the US flag hung upside down as a 'distress signal' – is that rescue and recuperation can be achieved through military strength and engagement with US exceptionalism uncritically, on its own terms.

This is why it is now more important than ever that our relationship to images of suffering and catastrophe, whether they be real or fictional, ethical or unethical, authentic or inauthentic, is critiqued. The precepts of economic liberalisation, privatisation and deregulation that define neo-liberalism are perilous to democracy. Ethical spectatorship can go some way to resisting the privatisation and colonisation of individuated liberal subjectivity by these precepts and can contribute to a rejection of self-regarding 'responsibility', and assert the primacy of our responsibility to the other. In the altericidal practice of refusing ethical spectatorial encounter by acculturation to neo-liberal concepts of self-regard, we can disavow any accountability for what we witness, and revel in a narcissistic position of victimhood and existential contemplation. In stressing an inward turn to self-regard and soul-searching contemplation of one's disabused spectatorial passivity, then, these films above all assert the ascendancy of Western liberal subjectivity.

Notes

[1] This is an outrageous manoeuvre, considering the extent of public and media protest and dissent, especially in the lead up to the invasion of Iraq in 2003. The reasons for this are explored later in this chapter.

[2] It is important to note that the *visage* is not simply the 'face' as we know it, and rather speaks of the presentation of the other to the self. It is not literally the human face, more of a philosophical concept for explaining the call and response initiated through encounter with the other, and our responsibility to these others.

[3] John Carlos Rowe (2004: 576-80) has noted that the US, in cultural terms, has a propensity to 'import' alterity in order to render differences, be they political, cultural, ethnic etc., aspects of US national identity. This form of 'internal colonization' transforms US neo-imperialist ventures into reflections or iterations of US-specific national anxieties. Hence, racial and ethnic alterity becomes subordinated to US monocultural power.

[4] Cooper's specific textual remit is avant-garde film and specifically French documentary cinema. This is somewhat removed from mainstream Hollywood war film, however her

theorisation of ethical culpability is more universal than the textual specificity of genre, in that it can cope with the hybridisations and trans-nationalisations that typify the visual style and cultural circumstances of mainstream US cinema post-9/11.

5 The film sets up the meaning of the title by having Deerfield read a bedtime story to a child. Deerfield tempers his narration of the David and Goliath story by explaining 'that's how we fight monsters…lure them in.' It is relevant also that this position is narrated into place in the context of an old man telling a child a bedtime story. Both characters fill in for each other's absences, the child having no father figure, and Deerfield having lost a son. Paternity and masculinity coalesce around the subject of US military victimhood.

Chapter 4

Why Not a Propaganda Model for Hollywood?

Matthew Alford

In the two decades following Edward Herman and Noam Chomsky's original proposal of a Propaganda Model (PM) to account for the politics of news media, several theorists have argued that it can be applied more broadly to understand political discourse, particularly intellectual culture (Herring and Robinson 2003; Phelan 2006; Jensen 2007). Both Herman (2003) and Chomsky[1] have stated that the PM can be applied across the spectrum. I have proposed a 'Hollywood Propaganda Model' (Alford 2008) based very closely on the original PM, as an explanation for why films do not challenge what Chomsky (1989: 45) calls the 'bounds of the expressible' about the US role in the international system. The model consists of five filters – concentrated ownership, the economic importance of advertising, the centrality of the government as a source of information, the ability of the powerful to issue flak, and a dominant ideology of a superior 'us' in the West versus a backward 'them' overseas – which in Herman and Chomsky's words 'cleanse' information from the real world leaving only the 'residue' which is acceptable to established power systems (Herman and Chomsky 2002: lx).

To test this theory, I examined mainstream American films released between 1991 and 2002 that represented the application of US power overseas. I predicted that mainstream Hollywood products would assume, almost without exemption, that the US is a uniquely 'worthy' and benevolent entity in world affairs. I found that this was the case and, in addition, that there was a significant body of films that actively endorsed the application of US force against official enemies (with the resultant 'unworthy' victims), in stark contrast to the oft-cited characterisation of Hollywood as 'anti-American' and 'anti-military' (Medved 1993; Alford 2008, 2010).

Is the Hollywood Propaganda Model (HPM) an adequate explanation for the conformist nature of Hollywood cinema? If so, then it would indeed be a useful tool in understanding the parameters of the debate about the war on terror declared by President Ronald Reagan in 1985 and given a reboot by the Bush administration in 2001. However, the scholarly community has raised its objections, as we shall see. Let us first consider how the model can be applied by examining the pertinence of each filter before moving on to the criticisms of the original model and, especially, its derivative.

The Five Filters

1) Concentrated Corporate Ownership

Just six theatrical film studios, known collectively as 'the majors', control the vast majority of the world's movie business. These are: Disney (owned by The Walt Disney company), Sony Pictures Entertainment (Sony), Paramount (Viacom Inc.), Twentieth Century Fox (NewsCorp), Warner Brothers (TimeWarner Inc.) and Universal (Comcast/General Electric). These companies produce, finance and distribute their own films and also pick up projects initiated by independent filmmakers. The studios' parent corporations also have substantial holdings in other industries beyond entertainment and are well integrated into the prevailing order, which tames their output within standard ideological parameters (Bagdikian 2004; McChesney 2007). Indeed, those parents have even occasionally interfered deliberately in the output of their subsidiaries, guided by their broader interests (see Alford, forthcoming).

As Herman and Chomsky (2002: 14) observe with regard to news media, the majors are subject to the 'sharp constraints' of the market and a collective interest in keeping production costs high to exclude weaker, less resource-rich rivals from taking their market share – hence the emphasis on expensive stars and special effects in the world of mainstream motion pictures. In 2007, the last year for which data were released, the average cost of producing and marketing a studio movie had reached $106.6 million (Motion Picture Association of America, Inc. 2007: 7). Smaller production companies have significant distribution capabilities in specialised markets, but not the considerable access to capital necessary to handle such broad theatrical product lines (Vogel 2004: 49-50). There are overseas owners – NewsCorp (Australian), Vivendi (French), Sony (Japanese) – but Washington limits foreign ownership to 25%, provides various state subsidies, and control of studio output remains in California and New York (Miller 2005: 187-9). This has squeezed out competition from foreign films, which accounted for nearly 10% of the North American market in the 1960s, 7% by the mid 1980s, and just 0.5% by the late 1990s (McChesney 2000: 33; Miller et al. 2001: 4). Of the 1,000 foreign language films which entered the US market since 1980, 70% scored less than $1 million and only 22 more than $10 million. For each successful foreign release there are dozens if not hundreds of failures; most never make it to the country (apart from screenings at some film festivals) nor ever enter distribution (Mueller 2010).

What impact does this concentration of ownership among a very small group of US-based multinationals have on film content? First of all, whilst of course Hollywood is aware of its international markets, it is liable to make films about and for America and Americans, marginalising the importance of foreigners. This is not necessarily 'unfair' or unusual but it does mean that the notion of America as a culturally internationalised, globalised melting pot should not be overstated. Secondly, films will tend to avoid political narratives that are unfamiliar to audiences. '[Filmmakers] don't do the unexpected, they're too scared – the prices are too high', says producer Robert Evans (Rich 2005). Former President of Paramount David Kirkpatrick agrees that the result is that: 'You need a homogenized piece of entertainment...something that is not particularly edgy, particularly sophisticated' (Kirkpatrick 2001).

2) Advertising

Although movies are not dependent on advertising revenue (unlike most TV stations and newspapers), product placement and merchandising deals are widespread and attractive to movie-makers because even if the movie fails the manufacturer incurs the loss. Product placement in motion pictures is valued at $1.2 billion annually (Kivijarv 2005), and the majority of Fortune 500 companies are involved in the practice (Segrave 2004: 180). Therefore, for financial security the major producers sell markets (film goers) to buyers (advertisers). As such, the film producers compete for their patronage and – as Herman and Chomsky (2002: 16) describe it with regards to news media – 'develop specialized staff to solicit advertisers and explain how their programs serve advertisers' needs.' Consequently, many films are under pressure to avoid raising 'serious complexities and disturbing controversies' because this would interfere with the 'buying mood' in the media outlet. Instead, they will more likely 'lightly entertain' and thus 'fit in with the spirit of the primary purpose of program purchases – the dissemination of a selling message' (Herman and Chomsky 2002: 17-18). Egregious examples include the science fiction blockbuster *Fantastic Four* (2005), which was produced with an intimate relationship with Chrysler.[2]

3) Sourcing

As Herman and Chomsky (2002: 19-20) observe, government and corporate bureaucracies such as the Pentagon have vast and well-funded public relations divisions which offer special access to the media. Unlike journalists, Hollywood creatives and producers do not rely on the Pentagon for daily news or the military itself for protection in a war zone. However, for over half a century filmmakers have made use of Pentagon advice and material to save costs and create authentic-looking films, in exchange for carefully constructed script re-workings that ensure good coverage of the military for recruitment and public relations. At least a quarter of major 1991-2002 films depicting the application of US force received full cooperation from the Pentagon, including *True Lies* (1994), *Executive Decision* (1996), *Air Force One* (1997), *Rules of Engagement* (2000) and *Black Hawk Down* (2001). The CIA also appears to have exerted significant influence over films such as *The Recruit* (2003) and *Charlie Wilson's War* (2007) (Alford 2010; Roddy 2007), and there were even some unusually direct requests from Washington to Hollywood about how to represent the War on Terror and the War on Drugs (Alford and Graham 2008; Forbes, 2000).

4) Flak and the Enforcers

Punishment, or 'flak' refers to the 'negative responses to a media statement or program', which 'may take the form of letters, telegrams, phone calls, petitions, law suits, speeches, bills before Congress, and other modes of complaint, threat, and punitive action' (Herman and Chomsky 2002: 26). Whilst flak may be organised locally or consist of 'entirely indepeandent actions of individuals', the ability to produce effective flak is related to power (2002: 26-8). The government is a major producer of flak, 'regularly assailing, threatening, and "correcting" the media, trying to contain any deviations from the established line' and the business community has also sponsored the creation of organisations, such as the right-wing Accuracy in Media, whose sole purpose is to produce flak (2002: 27).

On the occasions when radical movies do emerge that challenge US power, reactions from enforcers can be intense. This happened most dramatically with the 'Hollywood Blacklist', which began in 1947 and continued until the end of the 1950s, whereby film-making professionals were denied employment in the field because of their political beliefs or associations with Communism, whether verified or not. More recently, in 2008, Hillary Clinton ended her financial relationship with the Turkish producers of *Valley of the Wolves Iraq* (2006), a film which portrayed the US military as brutal invaders (Cooper 2008). Numerous filmmakers who have raised their voices about injustice have been on the wrong end of industry isolation, vigilante violence (notably Michael Moore – see Democracy Now 2010), multi-million dollar legal action by government members (notably Costa-Gavras – see Lewis 1987), and even false imprisonment (notably Jane Fonda – see Hershberger 2004). 'All publicity' is not necessarily 'good publicity' when filmmakers knock up against the limits of tolerance in the US political system, just as journalists face risks when they embark on a dissident career path.

5) Anti-'Other' as Control Mechanism

Hollywood narratives are frequently based on polarised representations of good and evil, with the audience encouraged to root for the 'good guys'. Throughout the Cold War, Communists provided convenient enemies in countless moving pictures from *The Red Menace* (1949) to *Rambo III* (1988) and beyond. Herman and Chomsky (2002: 29) argue that Communism has always been seen by the powerful as the 'ultimate evil' because it 'threatens the very root of their class position and superior status'. Since the concept of Communism is 'fuzzy', they suggest, it can be used against anyone 'advocating policies that threaten property interests or support accommodations with Communist states and radicalism.' With Communism presented as the worst imaginable result, the support of repressive regimes abroad is 'justifiable' as a 'lesser evil' (2002: 29).

Herman concedes that the filter perhaps should have been termed 'the dominant ideology' so as to include the merits of private enterprise and one's own government. In the end though, 'anti-Communism' was selected primarily to emphasise the ideological elements that have been most important in terms of disciplining and controlling mechanisms (Wintonick and Achbar 1994: 108). Chomsky stresses 'Otherness' as part of the 'dominant ideology', explaining that:

> [I]t's the idea that grave enemies are about to attack us and we need to huddle together under the protection of domestic power. You need something to frighten people with, to prevent them from paying attention to what's really happening to them. You have to engender fear and hatred, to channel the kind of fear and rage – or even just discontent – that's being aroused by social and economic conditions.
>
> (Chomsky 2003: 41)

Since the end of the Cold War, it has been fashionable to associate the Other with the East, particularly Islam and specifically its 'radical' form. As early as 1992, former National Security Council member Peter Rodman, writing in the *National Review*, explained that 'now the West finds itself challenged from the outside by a militant, atavistic force driven by hatred of all Western political thought, harking back to age-old grievances against Christendom' (Rodman 1992: 28). Harvard professor and founder of the Middle East Forum Daniel Pipes (1995) explains that in radical Islam there are 'no moderates' and that it is 'closer in spirit to other such movements (communism, fascism) than to traditional religion'. Another Harvard professor, Samuel Huntington, popularised the phrase 'Clash of Civilisations', claiming that the West had to face up to this new paradigm for international relations, and that Islam had 'bloody borders' (Huntington 1993). President George W. Bush took on similar rhetoric, initially dubbing the 'war on terror' operation in Afghanistan 'Infinite Justice' and a 'crusade' (BBC 2001b).

Edward Said (1979) explained that this kind of 'Orientalist' thought associated history, narrative, speech, complexity, and development with the West, and image, stasis, and myth with the East. For example, where the likes of Rodman (1992) talk about 'the politics of rage' and Islam being driven by 'resentments' and 'material inferiority', Said (1997: xviii) asks: 'Does every one of the billion Muslims in the world feel rage and inferiority?' He concludes that such assertions can be made because the Islamic stereotype 'stands charged and convicted without the need for supporting arguments or modulating qualifications' (1997: xviii).

This does not mean that the Other will necessarily be presented as wholly aggressive. Stuart Hall broadly concurs with Said's assessment but explains that:

> [F]or every threatening image of the black subject as marauding native, menacing savage or rebellious slave, there is the comforting image of the black as domestic servant, amusing clown and happy entertainer – an expression of both a nostalgia for an innocence lost forever to the civilized, and the threat of civilization being over-run or undermined by the recurrence of savagery, which is always lurking beneath the surface; or by an untutored sexuality threatening to 'break out'.
>
> (Hall 1993: 287)

Ella Shohat and Robert Stam (1994) wrote about these binary representations of the Other in the Western movie genre, where different tribes of Indians become classified as 'good' (to be patronised and rescued) or 'bad' (to be destroyed). Shohat and Stam further argue that such a binarism 'persists...even in revisionist, "pro-Indian" (or "pro-Arab") films' with the result that stories are told from the perspective of the powerful (1994: 109).

As the foregoing discussion suggests, the five filters of the Propaganda Model map quite neatly onto the Hollywood film industry. Still, do these help or obfuscate our understanding of the politics of motion pictures?

Limitations and Debates

There are limitations to the utility of the PM and debates around this have been well rehearsed (Herring and Robinson 2003). Much discussion revolves around the question of which is the more significant part of the process: the active 'manufacture of consent' (agency), or the more passive 'filtering out' (structure) of critical discourse. Herman and Chomsky's work emphasises that structure is more important than agency: they accordingly stress that the model is not a conspiracy theory. However, critics seem to have been misled by the one-off but prominent use of the word 'propaganda', which John Corner calls Herman and Chomsky's 'calculated shock effect',[3] but which prompts unfortunate and inflated charges of functionalism (Edwards 2001a; Edwards 2001b).

Ultimately, perhaps one cannot expect too much of the PM. Corner emphasises that it should engage with other radical thinkers like Jürgen Habermas, Ralph Miliband and Michel Foucault,[4] but can any model sufficiently digest, process and incorporate such dense and extensive material? Why should Herman and Chomsky – or anyone – be obliged to use specified academic texts, or texts that are European or even old or obscure? In the words of Herman (2003), the PM deals with 'extraordinarily complex sets of events, and only claims to offer a broad framework of analysis, a first approximation, that requires modification depending on local and special factors, and that may be entirely inapplicable in some cases'. Similarly, Chomsky acknowledges that 'there's no algorithm for judging relative importance [of each filter] abstractly. It varies from case to case'.[5]

Such caveats and limitations – and the responses to them – hold true for the Hollywood Propaganda Model too. More important to explore in this chapter is what additional criticisms have been levelled specifically at the HPM. The main objections are as follows: that it is harder to measure; that narrative conventions in entertainment are more salient considerations in the de-radicalisation of products; that Hollywood is only responding to audience demands for standard political orientations; that the model underplays the diversity of screen entertainment; that it is less appropriate to critique entertainment products in political terms; and that there is a powerful liberal community in Hollywood. In what follows I examine each of these in turn.

Entertainment products are harder to analyse politically

Robert Kolker (2000: 11) explains that the formal conventions of Hollywood film tend to 'downplay or deny the ways in which it supports, reinforces and even sometimes subverts the major cultural, political and social attitudes that surround and penetrate it.' In contrast, news media convey their messages in more straightforward terms. They are less liable to obfuscate the political points they are making, even whilst they might hide behind claims to 'objectivity', since their remit is to provide clear, digestible information about the real world.

Nevertheless, the comparatively opaque nature of Hollywood fiction that Kolker highlights has little impact on the attempt to apply the PM to the motion picture industry. Herman and Chomsky essentially identify a benevolent meta-narrative of US power which assumes without question that the US deploys military force to further common principles and values based on human rights and consciously or unconsciously classifies victims of political violence as 'worthy' and 'unworthy' depending on their utility. The extent to which media products adhere to these 'exceptionalist' assumptions corresponds to how closely they conform to the predictions of the PM. Such representations are usually not hard to identify in fictionalised entertainment, since we are typically able to agree on what is happening in the story, whether the military or government is presented in a favourable light, and which characters, with which national and institutional affiliations, are heroes, villains and victims. We can identify whether the film presents in any form (through dialogue, imagery, etc.) any ideas that are challenging to real-world power structures. We can also ensure that we focus on those films that are most widely lauded as offering challenges to powerful interests, such as *Three Kings* (1999), *Buffalo Soldiers* (2001) or *Hotel Rwanda* (2004), just as the PM pays closest attention to cases such as the Vietnam war where the news media appeared to adopt an adversarial role.

There are some additional complications in a PM reading of cinema but they can be negotiated. Where individuals in the government or military are rendered villainous, it does not follow that the system itself is necessarily being significantly criticised. In fact, the existence of internal enemies is often the catalyst that is needed to demonstrate the essential decency of US power. As Robert Ray (1985) argues, such 'problem pictures' critique large social issues but ultimately have happy endings that belie those problems. Even an unusually challenging film such as *Rendition* (2007) provides a happy ending, whereby the Muslim-American wrongly kidnapped by the CIA is returned to his wife and newborn child, providing a certain level of comfort for the viewer. Even in this extreme case, in a blunt way the system eventually provides some relief.

It is important to be careful in HPM readings of fictional films, as even the most reactionary pieces are liable to make nods towards more dissenting views, which can obscure their more central political message. So just because the *Rambo* franchise has its hero sometimes dress like a hippy does not mean that the spirit of the film is all 'flower power'. Films may hold internal ideological contradictions and this is not in opposition to the predictions of the HPM. British film scholar Brian Neve comments that the PM presumes that 'stridently ideological, conservative texts' will result – an assumption which derives, perhaps, from Herman and Chomsky's use of the word 'propaganda' in the title of their model (though they are much more careful in its usage elsewhere). The model actually predicts only that texts will be 'cleansed' of any seriously critical content and could be either conservative or liberal in flavour (Herman and Chomsky 2002: 2). Neve concedes that the influence of the Pentagon on certain productions 'may be problematic, especially at times when a real or imagined threat from outside is central to official thinking', but, he asks 'is it really useful to use the term propaganda in this context? Are we then comparing *Top Gun* [1986] with [the Nazi propaganda film] *Triumph of the Will* [1935]?'[6] Well, in terms of the film text itself – yes. The HPM itself tells us nothing about the character or intent of the government backers, only the nature of the media message.

Entertainment products are less well suited than news media to providing information that interrogates established power structures

With genre as the paramount consideration when making a film, it might be that little room remains for dissent. Generic conventions oblige certain kinds of stories, offering certain kinds of audience pleasures: action adventures must prioritise spectacle, comedies must be funny, and so on. However, genres are not fixed. Given the will and demand Hollywood could in principle exclusively produce socially-responsible documentaries.

Indeed, even if Hollywood was obliged to produce only a certain range of genres, this would not in itself preclude the generation of more challenging, 'dissident' material, since all major genres have produced critical pictures at some stage in the history of screen entertainment: *Dr Strangelove* (comedy), *Syriana* (political drama), *Apocalypse Now* (war film) and *Starship Troopers* (science fiction). Nor is there any inherent need for Hollywood to emphasise American exceptionalism in even the most violent or dumbed-down genre narrative, as has been demonstrated in countless films from *Reservoir Dogs* (1992) to *Kick Ass* (2010).

Audiences routinely demand mainstream products with standard political orientations
'If you want to send a message,' says the old Hollywood adage, 'send a telegram'. It is widely believed, quite reasonably, that audiences do not want to feel that they are being encouraged to buy a particular political argument. However, there is also another popular saying in the business: 'Nobody knows anything' (Goldman 1996: 39) and this also has some validity – witness huge surprise hits like *The Shawshank Redemption* (1994) or *Titanic* (1997) and some political surprise successes such as *Silkwood* (1983).

Additionally, Hollywood's business leaders make crucial decisions that affect the success of these products. It is not possible to know how much better more dissenting films might do at the box office were studios to invest in them as heavily as they do more conventional fare. *The New York Times* reported that test audience reaction to *The Quiet American* was 'OK' when Miramax acquired the film on 10 September 2001 (Thompson 2002: 1). According Miramax co-chairman Harvey Weinstein:

> What freaked me out after the 10th was the 11th. I showed the film to some people and staff, and they said: 'Are you out of your mind? You can't release this now, it's unpatriotic. America has to be cohesive, and band together'. We were concerned that nobody had the stomach for a movie about bad Americans anymore.
>
> (Quoted in Thompson 2002: 1)

Miramax released the film in two cities for two weeks, reportedly because its star, Michael Caine, pressed the studio to recognise that the film could make a lot of money if he won the Oscar for Best Actor (this requires a minimum one-week commercial run in Los Angeles to qualify) (Wiener 2002).

Similarly, although *Variety* claimed that the military farce *Buffalo Soldiers* (2001) was 'the wrong film at the wrong time' because of 'public opinion' (McCarthy 2001: 25), in fact its dreadful box office showing was unavoidable after Miramax released it in just two cities. Meanwhile, despite lamentable reviews, Disney unexpectedly decided in August 2001 to extend *Pearl Harbor*'s nationwide release window from the standard two-to-four months to seven months, meaning that this 'summer' blockbuster continued screening until December. Sometimes, films seem to be shaped at a fundamental level by conscious political decisions – for instance when Twentieth Century Fox released *Australia* (2008) the film was intimately tied into the country's major new tourism campaign (Ferguson 2008). Herman and Chomsky's 'filters' seem to be very much at play, to some degree in opposition to audience desires: demand does not always create supply – supply also promotes demand.

Hollywood's output is more critical and contradictory than the model assumes
It is certainly true that a range of political ideas are presented by Hollywood but, just as the PM examines the most mainstream news and pays less attention to smaller and independent media outlets, so the HPM examines the most mainstream Hollywood products. Even the most visible radical productions are poorly distributed as cinematic releases. *War, Inc* (2008) was released in only 33 cinemas nationwide, for example; *Redacted* (2007) in just 15. *In the Valley of Elah* (2007) opened in nine screens in the US but 216 in the UK – an indication that the superpower is less willing to interrogate itself than those who live outside its borders may be.

Furthermore, even amongst the lower budget range, screen entertainment products are surprisingly constricted ideologically. Reactionary fodder like *In the Army Now* (1994), *Stealth Fighter* (1999), *Air Marshal* (2003) and the *Left Behind* (1999-) series is plentiful. Perhaps most disturbingly, more high-brow films may raise issues about US power and take new and challenging political angles, but on closer inspection these frequently turn out to be more conformist. *Hotel Rwanda* (2004), for example, condemns America's unwillingness to stop the 1994 Rwandan genocide but it stays within the established political narrative of the genocide, ignoring evidence of more active Western support for the Rwandan Patriotic Front, which contributed to the disaster (Herman and Peterson 2010). *The Kingdom* (2007) gives a leading role to an Arab actor but also lionises gun-toting US authorities as they clean up Saudi Arabia (Shaheen 2008). *Three Kings* (1999) suggests that the problems of Iraq can only be solved by the application of US force, though of the 'right', humanitarian sort. Although *Munich* (2005) was condemned by various Israeli groups as being opposed to Israeli policy, in fact director Steven Spielberg said explicitly that 'Israel had to respond (to the Munich massacre), or it would have been perceived as weak: I agree with Golda Meir's response' (Ebert 2006: 14-15). The most celebrated 'anti-war' scene (Reich 2006) in the film is a two-and-a-half minute exchange between an Arab and an Israeli, which at most points out that Palestinians are motivated by a desire for 'home' but, more saliently, suggests that their struggle is futile and immoral.

Films given 'full cooperation' by the Pentagon are predictably less subtle. *Black Hawk Down* (2001) removes those elements of the book on which it is based that point to soldiers' brutality and unseemly US actions/motivations in Somalia (see further Alford 2010). *Iron Man* (2008) was a 'pacifist' film, according to several reviewers (see, for example, *Chicago Sun Times* 2008), but really only in the sense that the weapons-dealer hero decides that he is no longer comfortable selling arms that kill Americans, instead designing new attack armour allowing him to venture out and kill Afghan villains. *Rules of Engagement* (2000) suggests that US massacres are understandable, even noble, when dealing with foreign populations that are infested with – in fact, in total sympathy with – Al-Qaeda terrorists.

It can be argued that in times of heightened public cynicism – such as during the latter years of the Bush and Blair governments, when the popularity of political leaders plummeted – there may also be a 'darkening' of mainstream movies, as manifest in films such as *War of the Worlds* (2005), *There Will Be Blood* (2007) and *The Dark Knight* (2008). However, these examples – cited specifically to me by a film scholar – have little to do directly with American power (indeed, very few films of any kind even mention American power directly, so in this sense the HPM is vindicated). The darkening of tone is a double-edged sword politically too: *War of the Worlds* actually envisions a heroic American military response to invasion, complete with 'special thanks' to the Pentagon on the credits to the film; *The Dark Knight* can readily be understood as a parable that is highly favourable to neoconservative ideology – K.D. Killian (2007) makes a convincing case for this in relation to the previous movie in the franchise, *Batman Begins* (2005).

Films which offer some challenge to elite power are important, but as Herman (2003) puts it, why thrust these into the foreground 'except as a means of minimizing the power of the dominant interests, inflating the elements of contestation, and pretending that the marginalized have more strength than they really possess?'

It is less appropriate to criticise entertainment products
'It is the responsibility of intellectuals to speak the truth and to expose lies,' Chomsky (1967) famously stated. People working in the fields of media, academia and politics are obliged to be honest about the world. Entertainers, however, have a responsibility to entertain. Do they really have the responsibility to speak the truth and expose lies? If a product is entertaining but has conventional politics, is it so worthy of criticism? Should we take the politics of entertainment as seriously as we do that of news providers?

We may say we want films for 'just entertainment', but in reality few people want or expect our entertainers to be telling lies, supporting falsehoods or mythologising for the government. There is actually a good case to be made that filmmakers should have comparable responsibility for their output. No one knows the actual effects of film products on audiences, but even if they were minimal that still does not change the fact that cinema warrants a critical approach. Still, let us assume that there is less moral imperative for fictional artists to expose lies or to prioritise telling the truth. Let's assume that they should have no responsibility at all. Does this change our analysis? Surely not – regardless of the moral question, we can still try to determine the extent to which Hollywood is part of a de facto propaganda apparatus which is significantly generated by its involvement in larger commercial and political power systems. Likewise, just because audiences may be able to differentiate between reality and fiction does not change the fact that this is a model about media performance, not effects.

Liberal networks are a powerful force in Hollywood

Hollywood is indeed characterised by liberal ideas. 'Far from being conservative or reactionary forces in the society as many academics insist is the case', argue Stephen Powers et al. (1996: 3), 'elite directors, writers and producers now usually espouse liberal or leftist perspectives.' However, there are crucial qualifiers left unsaid here. Liberal views have frequently been consistent with endorsing the use of US military force, as indicated by the old adage that 'Politics stops at the water's edge', and actualised by President Barack Obama's intervention in Libya. The notion of liberal influence also overplays what liberals are actually prepared to do. Ben Dickenson (2006: xiv-xvi) argues that 'the fruit of the last twenty five years of activist and ideological battle in the arena of American cinema is the emergence in the twenty first century of a new radical Hollywood left' which has embarked upon a 'tumultuous path' to 'social justice' and whose influence he declares is dependent on 'how far they can understand the recent social, political and economic history'. Yet Marc Cooper (1999) points out that the 'authentic Hollywood left that functions beyond the parameters of narrow electoral politics' was 'virtually unchanged through the eighties and nineties...because it is so small'.

Actually, liberal Hollywood has been remarkably unconcerned by America's actions beyond its borders in the modern era. In the build-up to the 1991 Gulf War, for example, the *Washington Post* reported that Hollywood's 'most visible liberals' were 'maintaining low profiles when it comes to the war' (Hall 1991: D2). The fear, reportedly, was that any protest against US policy could be misunderstood as a criticism of American troops, as had occurred over Vietnam. So, on the eve of the conflict, 100 Hollywood celebrities – including Tommy Lee Jones, James Woods, Jean-Claude Van Damme, Meryl Streep, William Shatner, Michelle Pfeiffer, Kurt Russell and Kevin Costner – recorded a charity record, 'Voices That Care', which praised American troops without explicitly commenting on the legitimacy or otherwise of their presence. When American troops returned home in April 1991, Hollywood held a 'Welcome Home Desert Storm' parade, which deliberately excluded peace messages collated by a body of social activists (United Press International 1991). Similarly, at the height of NATO's 1999 bombing campaign against Serbia, an extensive interview with leading 'dissenting' Hollywood stars appeared on the pages of *The Nation*, yet none of them even mentioned foreign policy, aside from a brief (though pertinent) comment from actor Tim Robbins, who alluded to the ongoing calamity in Iraq:

> You talk about the Hollywood Left, where the hell are they? The same people who will be absolutely crazy about animals being sacrificed in the name of medical research will not raise a voice about human beings who are killed in the name of oil.

(Biskind 1999: 14)

Even with regard to the exceptionally controversial 2003 Iraq war, Hollywood was split. Lara Bergthold, former executive director of the Hollywood Women's Political Committee, which had been the town's most active opponent of the Reagan administration's intervention in South America during the 1980s, said that there was a behind-the-scenes 'conversation' about the 'antiwar response' but that the debate 'should begin and take place in Washington' (Broder 2002: 22), echoing the organisation's lack of a public stance over Iraq in 1991 (Hall 1991: D2).

Mostly, though, there has been apathy about US power in a political environment dominated by money and narrow self-interest. Even right-wing activist David Horowitz, who despises what he sees as Hollywood's liberal agenda, concurs, saying that '98% of people in Hollywood have no politics to speak of, or their politics are an inch deep. People do what they have to do to get ahead in this town' (Corn 1999: 52). As a consequence, movie texts are produced according to the internal logic of the industry, which naturally strives for profit and is therefore subject to the filters of the Propaganda Model.

Additionally, although the political beliefs of celebrities are frequently discussed, in truth this is something of a side issue rather than providing any decisive insight into the communications industry. Justin Lewis observes in the documentary *The Myth of the Liberal Media* (Media Education Foundation 1997) that studies examining the political beliefs of writers 'assume that it is the journalists rather the owners, the advertisers, the news-shapers or news-makers that control the manufacture of news. That's a bit like saying...the workers on the factory floor decide what the car industry produces.' Powerful media owners, such as Rupert Murdoch, have considerably different agendas from those further down the ladder. Chomsky explains further that:

> You could find that 99% of journalists are members of the Socialist Workers Party or some Maoist group and that in itself would prove nothing about the media output. The issue is whether the media are free. Are the media by their institutional structure free to allow expression of opinion from whatever source and look at whatever topic and so on and so forth?
>
> (Media Education Foundation 1997)

This is different from claiming that there is censorship of any kind in the media, even self-censorship. When British journalist Andrew Marr asked Chomsky, 'How can you know that I'm self-censoring?' Chomsky replied: 'I don't say you're self-censoring....If you believed something different you wouldn't be sitting where you're sitting.'[7]

Overall, Hollywood's opposition to US foreign policy in the contemporary era is all too easily exaggerated. Celebrity apathy towards, and complicity with, the stances of state and private power sets the context for understanding how entertainment conglomerates produce movies that invariably support the idea that the US is a benevolent power in world affairs and frequently endorse the application of US force.

Conclusions

Does the Hollywood Propaganda Model help us to understand better the ways in which the war on terror has been represented? As with any theoretical perspective in the social sciences, the HPM cannot account well for nuance and there have always been limitations to what any configuration of the PM can do. Indeed, it may be more appropriate to call it primarily a 'de-radicalisation model' rather than associating it so much with the more active implications of 'propaganda'. Still, the PM does offer a useful paradigm, namely that it coherently challenges the crucial and well-worn idea that the media typically adopt an adversarial stance towards elites. As demonstrated, the model is equally applicable to mainstream US cinema. Hollywood is a liberal town but, as former Motion Picture Association head Jack Valenti (1998) commented, it sprang 'from the same DNA' as Washington, especially when it comes to foreign policy – and so a cultural framework was laid for the war against terrorism that fitted neatly with the broader objectives and narratives of the US government.

Notes

[1] Email to the author, 26 March 2006.

[2] See www.youtube.com/watch?v=My2-42lzYdU.

[3] Email to the author, 7 September 2010.

[4] Email to the author, 9 September 2010.

[5] Email to the author, 10 December 2006.

[6] Email to the author, 8 July 2010.

[7] *The Big Idea*, BBC2, 14 February 1996, available at http://video.google.co.uk/videoplay?docid=-4827358238697503#.

Chapter 5

Redacted: The *Heart of Darkness* Trope in Representations of Empire

Liane Tanguay

The question of 'screens' raises the question of what the popular cultural productions of the past decade or so contribute to our understanding of the Bush administration and the war it waged on 'terror'. Our 'screens', as we know, were the Bush administration's most pervasive means of dominating public discourse with its militaristic objectives, particularly following what might be (so far) the greatest mass screening of all – the images, seared into popular consciousness, of the Twin Towers collapsing, floor upon floor, in the wake of a terrorist attack unprecedented in its global reach and consequences. Screens have been, insofar as popular culture is concerned, the principal vehicle for this 'war' and its manifold representations, both from within the establishment and without – and by 'without' I imply not only the rise of Al Jazeera and other Arab networks but also the ostensibly anomalous appearance of scenes of torture, inhumanity, and cruelty inflicted upon 'illegal combatants' by the putative footsoldiers of Progress itself. Screens have both promoted and contested the Progress narrative, having increasingly become a terrain of contention in a present-day war of images.

Yet this same Progress narrative, for all that the neoconservative 'end of history' or 'posthistorical' paradigm has set against it – insofar as 'History' (the struggle towards universal, liberal-democratic capitalism) had for neoconservatives reached its pinnacle on a global scale with the end of the Cold War – has long been, and remains, still very much in play. And save for its progressive incarnations from within the printed medium through to the evolution of cinematic and broadcasting techniques, it remains very much the same, in structure and principle, as ever: it is still the narrative of capitalist modernity, of the West overtaking the 'rest' as liberal capitalism has progressively overcome, over centuries, the natural boundaries imposed by space (or distance) and time. And its full and final realisation as such a conquest is an illusion – commodities, in reality, must still undergo the arduous and time-consuming process of extraction, development and transportation – to which the screen is ideally suited; the fact of instant transmission overrides in an aesthetic sleight of hand the truth that what powers the world as we know it remains subject to material and, yes, historical conditions. But what is the nature and origin of this sleight of hand, and why and how does it work? And perhaps more importantly, for the purposes of this chapter, where, and how, does it fail?

The following pages seek to explore this question and suggest some possible answers, with reference not only to contemporary popular culture but also to the Victorian era in Britain. For if the Progress narrative can be said to have had its heyday, insofar as the discourse of imperialism and its reality as experienced at home can be said to have squared up, then this was almost certainly in late nineteenth-century England, which held sway over about a quarter of the Earth's land mass, dwarfing the achievements of prior and concurrent Western empires and in the process vastly enriching its cultural and economic standing. And its position in the world, like America's today, demanded a sustaining ideological framework and an accompanying aesthetic with which to 'suture' the individual to the 'imagined community' of the nation and hence to its global dominance and presumed cultural superiority. In terms of popular culture, the fictional narratives of Victorian Britain, such as Rudyard Kipling's and Robert Louis Stevenson's, which – in their content as well as in their adherence to generic conventions and, more importantly, their faith in linear narrative itself as a means of ordering reality – became, with the development of leisure time among the burgeoning middle class, a key ideological underpinning of the new imperial reality. The 'suturing', or what Louis Althusser (1984) calls 'interpellation' – the ideological construction of a subject *as subject* – required also an aesthetic counterpart to such narratives, one which could embody in spatial form the temporal notion of Progress and bring the modern self into alignment with the Victorian world order. This aesthetic, I will argue – an 'aesthetics of hegemony' – is instantiated in the phenomenon of the 'world fair', of which a most notable example was Britain's Great Exhibition of 1851.

The advent of modernism, however, cast a shadow across this blind faith in narrative, this identification with aesthetic totality as a means of constituting a European 'self' against its 'others'. Linear, logical narrative was dealt a blow by the continual upheavals and ceaseless transformations of capital, the melting of 'all that is solid' into 'air'; and in the realm of the aesthetic as embodied in popular literature, so was, notably, the most epistemologically satisfactory sort: the detective story, which for Russian formalist Tzvetan Todorov (2000: 122—3), combined two distinct layers of narrative, the one (the story) '[telling] "what really happened"' and the other explaining 'how the reader (or the narrator) has come to know about it.' To this extent the detective story is what Peter Brooks (1984: 25) calls the 'narrative of narratives, its classical structure a laying-bare of the structure of all narrative in that it dramatises the role of *szujet* and *fabula* and the nature of their relation.' The crime (the equivalent of the 'story') is anterior to the narrative, and the plot has the detective follow – retrace – the criminal's footsteps in order to reach the solution. The detective's actions, in other words, 'retell' the story of the crime. It is the Storyteller's narrative in the Benjaminian sense, affording a closure which sheds light on the beginning and the middle (Benjamin 1968: 83). And the incursion of modernism upon this insular, totalising form, I argue alongside Brooks (1984: 25), is best illustrated by Joseph Conrad's *Heart of Darkness*, a deliberate and troubling distortion of the genre that makes of it a 'detective story gone modernist.'

Beginning with this idea of the Victorian imperial aesthetic 'gone modernist' and thus undermined, I will move forward through what Tom

Engelhardt (2007) sees as the narrative paradigm of American 'victory culture' –
the Western – and its own undoing in Francis Ford Coppola's reconfiguration of
Conrad's message in *Apocalypse Now* (1979). I will pay particular attention to the
effect on this message of the cinematic medium, and thenceforth on cinematic
techniques as these have developed since the late 1970s to enable a still more
direct identification between the viewer and the screen. Such techniques, I will
argue, allow films like *Black Hawk Down* (2001) to reinforce the aesthetics of
hegemony. I will conclude, however, by demonstrating how films like Brian de
Palma's *Redacted* (2007) can turn the very same techniques against the hegemon
itself. In other words, the screen, while a powerful aesthetic means of 'suturing'
the viewer to a national narrative – as were the world's fairs of the nineteenth
century – can also serve to disrupt that identification, generating unease by the
same means as it can also enjoin fear, credulity and mindless nationalism.

The Crystal Palace and the Heart of Darkness

The Great Exhibition of 1851, housed in the spectacular Crystal Palace, is but
one instance of the phenomenon of the 'world fair' in the era of nineteenth
century European imperialism; as such, however, it is emblematic of the
aesthetic and the narrative that sustained, domestically, Britain's overseas
adventures, fostering among the citizenry an appreciation, or at least a general
acceptance, of the nation's imperial conquests. Before we come to the
dissolution of the Victorian narrative structure and its accompanying aesthetic –
the ways, I will argue, in which its own logic can be turned against it – it is
essential to discuss the ways in which the Great Exhibition and subsequent
world fairs (though not as spectacular) projected the impression of a
harmonious totality of well-nigh global empire. Displaying 'the Works of
Industry of All Nations', the Crystal Palace showcased not only British
technological innovations, the machinery that made it the 'workshop of the
world', but also the spoils of victory – presented, of course, less as 'spoils' than
as the raw materials of an organic, smoothly functioning global economy in
which all nations worked together ostensibly to their mutual benefit. The
collection of all of these exotic, diverse and seemingly disparate objects and their
harmonious integration within the transparent walls of the Crystal Palace

furnished the iconic imperialist aesthetic that Britain needed to celebrate, in tangible, visual form, its achievements.

Collecting, like narrative, is a means of appropriating, ordering, classifying, and thereby representing; and by transposing objects from their original environments into a centralised venue such as the Crystal Palace, it is also a means of embedding them into a specifically Western narrative, that of the 'Industry of All Nations' and the promises this afforded (as well as, less distinctly, its imperialist underpinnings). As Carol Breckenridge (1989: 196) points out, collected objects 'undergo a metamorphosis' and come to be 'valued in modes that [are] radically different' from those of their original context. In the process, they help to act upon the 'social formations' of the metropole, constituting the body politic at once against its colonial 'others' and, somewhat paradoxically, as continuous with them. For Breckenridge, world fairs such as the Great Exhibition 'situated metropole and colony within a single analytic field', creating a global discourse that harmoniously encompassed particular cultures – cultures no longer constrained geographically but now integral, functional components of the landscape of Empire. As for the Great Exhibition itself, it is in particular the glass walls of the Palace that translated imperial discourse into the realm of the visual, enclosing as they did a number of actual trees (thus 'naturalising' the business of empire) and enacting, by means of transparency, the continuity between imperial self and imperialised other. Nothing opaque separated viewer from object, and the former was afforded the privilege of a 'gaze' that could take in the whole world at once. Combined with the increasing appeal of overseas adventure, and the development of photography as an additional means of appropriation of the 'other', this aesthetic of imperialism was ultimately one of knowledge and therefore of control. What the Great Exhibition did, perhaps better than any subsequent world fairs, was to add spectacular visual effect to the narrative that bolstered the machinations of Empire; and in so doing it helped 'suture' the citizen to the nation and its widespread imperial reach.

This convincing aesthetic organicism, as noted above, had its literary counterpart in popular narrative, in particular genres such as the detective narrative, with its epistemological satisfaction, uniting disparate elements into a cohesive whole, revealing the mechanisms of narrative, or of making narrative, as it were, 'transparent'; and also the adventure tale, the narrative in which a protagonist comes to be defined against a backdrop of exotic, if menacing, surroundings. In both cases, indeed, and irrespective of literary point-of-view, it is the protagonist's gaze – effectively the Western gaze – that dominates, assimilates, makes sense of otherness and, in the process, of the self; disparate elements of reality are ordered in a temporal, logical whole that satisfies the desire for closure and reinforces the binary of self and other.

Joseph Conrad's *Heart of Darkness* presents itself initially as precisely this sort of narrative – both a detective narrative and an adventure tale featuring a Western protagonist's drama as it unfolds against an exotic, in this case African, background. I will focus, however, on one reading in particular of the novella as a model that undermines that very aesthetic by exposing its internal contradictions. Over and above its content it is its narrative form that bears the most scrutiny here, as Marlow, protagonist and narrator at one remove, undercuts the sensationalist appeal of the adventure tale by miring his listeners (and the reader) in a series of contradictions and uncertainties that portend not the formation but the dissolution of the imperial self as constructed by the master narratives of empire.

I turn to *Heart of Darkness* in part because it reminds us that we have been in our contemporary situation before – in a geopolitical dis/order threatened by imperial overreach, marred by atrocities, fraught with *fin de siècle* anxiety. Further, by directing the techniques of the imperial narrative to its anti-imperialist ends in ways that will soon become apparent, the novella serves as a paradigm for the study of narrative, of representation, of modernity and modernism, and for what it says about imperial civilisation in decline. No other 'great book' in my opinion has so astutely grasped and confronted the relationship between narrative form and both the events and the spirit of its time – events and spirit that have found a new incarnation in our own. Finally, the relationship Conrad identifies between narrative form and geopolitical realities in the novella remains dispiritingly pertinent today – the setting has undoubtedly changed, as has the imperial powerhouse and the technologies of domination, but one has only to look beyond these surface details to see how what I call the 'Heart of Darkness trope' continues to apply.

Heart of Darkness, as noted, brings together the generic conventions of the adventure tale and the detective story. It is, after all, based on Conrad's own 'adventures' in the Belgian Congo, only now it incorporates into its structure a 'crime' of murky implications, which Marlow, partway into his adventure, is called upon to resolve. Marlow, his story framed by the narrating consciousness of one of his listeners (our primary narrator, unnamed), is sent to recover the rogue Kurtz, a man of 'great potential' who has vanished upriver and is now beyond reach of the Company that employs him. He narrates his retracing of Kurtz's path into central Africa, a retracing which draws him ever closer to the mystery of the man's 'unsound methods' and his related disappearance, progressively distancing him from the markers of 'civilisation' until he arrives at what he finally declares his 'answer': Kurtz's wholesale repudiation of 'civilisation' itself – his having, in the terminology of the time, 'gone native', turned his back on the signifiers of European society and looked directly into the abyss, the unrepresentable, or to state it in quite obvious terms, the heart of darkness itself. Marlow is at pains to demonstrate how this is the 'answer' he had sought, an answer encompassed in Kurtz's famous final words, 'the horror, the horror':

> He had something to say. He said it. Since I had peeped over the edge myself, I understand better the meaning of his stare that could not see the flame of the candle but was wide enough to embrace the whole universe, piercing enough to penetrate all the hearts that beat in darkness. He had summed up – he had judged. 'The horror!' ... After all, this was the expression of some sort of belief; it had candour, it had conviction, it had a vibrating note of revolt in its whisper, it had the appalling face of a glimpsed truth – the strange commingling of desire and hate ... I like to think my summing-up would not have been a word of careless contempt. Better his cry – much better. It was an affirmation, a moral victory paid for by innumerable defeats, by abominable terrors, by abominable satisfactions. But it was a victory.
>
> (Conrad 2006: 70)

But, as Brooks (1984) asks in his reading of the novella, *is* this a 'summing up'? Marlow seems desperate, that is, to impose his *own* 'summing up', to provide a definitive 'answer' to the riddle he set out to solve; yet what he brings forth as an 'answer' lies stubbornly beyond the bounds of the representable. 'The horror,' that is, escapes the grasp of what can be signified within the discourse of 'civilisation' as we understand it; it is therefore excluded, absent, 'invisible', and it makes of Marlow's conclusion an impenetrable mystery. Whatever justifications Marlow fabricates to shed light on the beginning and the middle of his tale, we as readers sense the emptiness at its very core, indeed at the 'heart of darkness' that gives the novella its name. 'Exterminate all the brutes' – Kurtz's scrawled 'exposition of a method' on an otherwise 'magnificent' paper written for the 'International Society for the Suppression of Savage Customs' (Conrad 2006: 50), reveals to Marlow 'the unbounded power of eloquence – of words – of burning noble words' while revealing to the reader a hint of the irresolvable contradiction to come: a contradiction inherent to the imperial enterprise in itself, to the unfettered imposition of liberalism upon other cultures, we might say, 'at the barrel of a gun'.

Conrad, it seems, had his finger on the pulse of the era – on the actual horrors of imperial capitalism as these are *not* revealed to the metropole and on the imminent breakdown of an overstretched regime – and he gave us Brooks's 'detective story gone modernist', displaying 'an acute self-consciousness about the organizing features of traditional narrative, working with them still, but suspiciously, with constant reference to the inadequacy of the inherited orders of meaning' (Brooks 1984: 238). Even a cursory re-reading of the text with Brooks's thesis in mind brings to the fore this 'inadequacy' – the narrative is thoroughly aware of itself, and in this awareness it points to the falsehood of narrative discourse (imperial discourse in particular) and ultimately frustrates our expectations as readers, our *desire* for the ending to shed 'light', so to speak, on the beginning and the middle. Our identification with Marlow, our complicity, is revealed in a way we can only find unsettling, identified, as we are, with the all-encompassing 'gaze' of the West.

The hegemonic aesthetic embodied in the Great Exhibition as one of the more prominent world fairs of the late nineteenth century – this aesthetic, that is, and the narrative it implies – is thus turned in upon itself in *Heart of Darkness*, 'twisted' to reveal the hollowness at the heart of colonial discourse and the impossibility of conveying such emptiness in language. The organicist aesthetic embracing the harmonious integration of 'the industry of all nations' is inherently contradictory: by laying claim to universality, by denying its own limitations – which imperialism, or imperialist discourse, does – it denies, in effect, its own being. For a system without limitations – represented in the blending of metropole with colony as embodied in the Crystal Palace, the liberal dream of transcendence of time and space, the imperial subject as one with the universe – is really no system at all; it is, to the contrary, revealed as empty, as devoid of meaning, and as therefore resistant to codification within the symbolic order. Conrad's aesthetic is ultimately not that of the world fair or the Great Exhibition, though he enjoins our complicity in invoking it by promising the satisfactory totality of the adventure narrative, the detective story, the constitution of self against a backdrop of otherness. But in *Heart of Darkness* the self, instead, dissolves against the impossibility of an imperial totality, along with the promise of narrative fulfilment, as totality itself is revealed as a logical nonentity. Kurtz, with 'nothing either above nor below' him (Conrad 2006: 66), embodies this impossibility by enacting the unrestrained ego, the self without limits that, for this very lack of limits, is reduced to hollowness incarnate.

From Crystal Palace to Silver Screen: The American Western and *Apocalypse Now*

If there is a modern-day counterpart to exhibitions like the Crystal Palace and the world order it displayed, then it is surely manifested in the realm of the screen, both televisual and cinematic. Indeed the screen has often served as a window onto conquered lands, first the American frontier – as represented in the Western – and subsequently foreign territory, assimilating this 'otherness' as did the world fair into a narrative paradigm constituting both the American viewer and his narrative-image of the world at large. Like the pre-cinematic and pre-photographic exhibitions that assembled, ordered, and linked to the metropole the spoils of nineteenth-century European imperialism, the present-day screen affords its own 'aesthetics of hegemony', a powerful ideological paradigm premised still on the mythical logic of unbounded totality – the totality of capitalist empire, now enhanced by the technologies of instant transmission and the truly global reach of a superpower unparalleled in its military and economic might.

I will therefore take as an example of a distinctly American structural equivalent to Victorian narrative the generic conventions of the Western, which, like the classic adventure tale, sends the protagonist – a rugged individualist like Marlow, only more so – beyond the 'frontier' or the limits of what is known. Evoking the battles against nature and natives that paved the way for the settlement of the West and as such have a permanent place in American foundational mythology, the genre creates a paradigm not dissimilar to that of European imperialism. The subordination of otherness is once again justified in the name of civilisation and cloaked in the particularly American mythology of honour and justice, as Tom Engelhardt aptly demonstrates in *Victory Culture* (2007). Already popular in literature prior to the advent of cinema, the Western constituted its (white) protagonists against a barren landscape (populated only, if at all, by hostile native Americans); such a landscape, like the 'blank' maps of Africa that attracted Conrad's protagonist, afforded a *tabula rasa* ripe for colonisation, for the triumph of honour over anarchy. Granted, the antagonists are not invariably native Americans but can be 'outlaws' having crossed the border into an uncharted, uncivilised wilderness; in either case, however, violence is the only logical means of imposing order on chaos, and is thoroughly justified by the underhanded (read dishonourable) tactics of the outlaws or Indians themselves. Transposed to the cinematic screen, the Western implicates the viewer in its narrative of conquest, enjoining a continuity between viewer and spectacle and thus, like the Crystal Palace before it, constituting the American subject, along with the hero, as an agent of civilisation.

The problem with the American frontier, of course, is that beyond the Pacific coast it ceases to exist. The conquest of outlaw territory can from that point of reference on be only global in nature, and American foreign policy with its undercurrent of 'manifest destiny' takes the form of conquest and annexation beyond its natural borders, transcending these as did the empires that preceded it. Following the 'victory culture' engendered by World War Two, however, the mutually assured destruction promised by the Cold War restricted its foreign policy endeavours to protecting its national interests in 'lawless' places such as Vietnam, and it is therefore to Coppola's *Apocalypse Now*, a reconfiguration for the screen of *Heart of Darkness*, that this chapter now turns.

Coppola's representation of 1970s Vietnam constitutes a faithful cinematic re-enactment of the dissolution of self portrayed by Conrad. Some 80 years after the publication of *Heart of Darkness*, we are confronted once again with the same narrative structure, the same enticing mystery, and finally the unsettling revelation that within the context of a discourse that lays claim to universality, to illimitability, representation ends up devoid of any value. In other words, as with European imperialism, the eradication of limits is implied in this particularly American form of expansion, and with it the eradication of meaning. Now, of course, the exposure of this contradiction in the aesthetics of hegemony is presented cinematically, positioning the viewer in specific relations to the action depicted on screen – a development the consequences of which will become more evident later.

Those who criticised the final third of *Apocalypse Now* for being overly 'metaphysical' and 'pompous' (Cook 2000: 62) surely missed the director's fidelity to his original source. Coppola's Kurtz is faithful to Conrad's, even if the cinematic medium demands that he articulate his 'philosophy' slightly more intelligibly; *Apocalypse Now* is in its relationship to a burgeoning American imperialism very much like *Heart of Darkness* in relation to the Belgian incursion into the Congo. But the medium, in this case – the screen – necessarily changes the consumer's relation to the text. The complicity now – the 'suturing' of subject to nation – consists in the very act of *viewing*: in the subject position and perspective of the viewer in relation to, perhaps most notably, the 'Ride of the Valkyries' scene, which depicts an indiscriminate slaughter from the vantage point of a Huey helicopter and, ingeniously, from a mainly first-person perspective. The scene, distasteful as it is, approaches the Kantian sublime in its magnitude and the Burkean in the terror it invokes (terror being for Burke a necessary condition of the sublime), and in doing so it brings the viewer into the protagonist's position, one from which, in Kurtz's words, 'we can not judge'. How can we judge, after all, having 'taken part' in that brutal, unforgiving spectacle, experiencing in the process that degree of *jouissance* that only the cinematic sublime can afford? Again, the text unsettles, and not only by virtue of its vivid, catastrophic imagery; it is the inadequacy of representation in the face of such a totalising vision that destabilises the sense of self.

Further, the identification factor afforded by the cinematic medium inverts the 'gaze' such that it is no longer the 'other' but the imperial 'self' (sutured, implicitly, to the viewer) that is threatened as Willard travels against the immensity of the jungle upriver into Cambodia. Willard's voiceover indeed frames the narrative but cannot in the end reconstitute this 'self' that dissolves over the course of the film and finally in the encounter with Kurtz; the boundaries of this self are thereby blurred, the psyche contaminated by a wilderness it cannot, by force of will, encompass. Once again it is this narrative self-awareness, like that of Conrad's tale, that exposes the contradictions of the hegemonic aesthetic, by means of its ambiguous conclusion, the twists and turns of Kurtz's 'philosophy', and the final revelation that representation, in the context of imperial atrocity, is stripped of its referent. The taken for granted duality of referent and representation is further undone by the blurring between audience and spectacle, the cameo appearance of Coppola himself directing the soldiers as he films them, the slippage between cinematic direction, newsreel direction, and the brute reality the film attempts to convey. The medium itself is used to lead us to question the frameworks bolstered for so long by the classical narrative of imperialism, frameworks in which we once had confidence – objectivity, mediation, rational selection and combination, linear narratives, questions raised and answered, resolution as a whole.

Coppola's film, like Conrad's text, flies in the face of narrative and structural tradition, only in this case it is also the tradition of the American Western – the incursion into uncharted lands, the 'justified' slaughter of natives or outlaws as an integral element of American foundational mythology – that comes under attack. In Coppola's film as in Conrad's novella one can see how taken-for-granted discourse can so readily be undermined, not simply in the sense that a 'revisionist' text would do, but at a deeper structural level, namely that of narrative itself, narrative that presumes – like imperialist discourse – to encompass at once the whole world. By such means do these texts reveal, like

Kurtz's last words, the senselessness of a system without limitations. The aesthetic of hegemony constructed in the traditional Western gives way, with Coppola, to a final revelation of the inadequacy of representation – a revelation fully consistent with that of his Victorian predecessor.

The 'War on Terror' and the Revival of Victory Culture

In his foreword to *The End of Victory Culture*, Engelhardt (2007: x) looks back upon the years when America 'stood alone, enemy-less and seemingly confused in a world of midget bad guys (quickly dubbed "rogue states")'. But following the attacks of 9/11 – in which, arguably, the screen struck back against the viewer – George W. Bush's neoconservatives quickly

> invoked an old tradition of American triumphalism…which had by the end of the Vietnam War essentially collapsed. They brought back much of its language and many of its images, while promising 'victory' in a new, generations-long, Manichean struggle against 'evil' enemies.
>
> (Engelhardt 2007: xi)

That in itself is easy enough to discern. The imperialist proclamations that followed the attacks, the flagrant disregard for international conventions and international law, the assault on civil rights at home and abroad, spoke to the emergence of a new, almighty America whose dominance would never again be challenged, even at the cost of the very 'freedoms' the country was ostensibly fighting to defend.

The Bush administration, armed with a mixed bag of neoconservative thought in which Francis Fukuyama's (1989) 'End of History' thesis paradoxically coexisted with Samuel Huntington's 'clash of civilisations', embarked on a quest to bring liberal-democratic capitalism to a civilisation defined by 'bloody borders' (Huntington 1996: 254), a civilisation that threatened otherwise to destroy all that was prized in the West. They pursued a path that even Francis Fukuyama, the RAND corporation's champion of global liberal-democratic capitalism, was himself to denounce some years into the foundering war in Iraq. This path, to be sure, was only one of several that Bush could have taken: cultural critic Stuart Croft (2006) speaks of a 'decisive intervention' that took place between September 2001 and January 2002, a period during which one of any number of possible narratives was selected, imposed, and promoted; and this intervention, as we know too well, was that of the 'War on Terror'. The window of intervention, to be sure, was short: an attack of unprecedented scale and scope, made instantly 'traumatic' on a national scale by the broadcast media with their power to create of the event a real-time spectacle, *demanded* that a decision be taken without hesitation, and the decision taken would have to restore the victorious narrative of the New American Century. By the start of 2002, then, we had a full-fledged 'War on Terror' underway, with a 'State of the Union' that had 'never been stronger' (Bush 2002) and a reasonably solid international coalition having toppled the Taliban regime in Afghanistan. In later years, of course, the rhetoric took on a less robust tone, suggesting ominously that this new 'War on Terror', ostensibly begun at 'Ground Zero', the site of the former World Trade Center, was not going to unfold into the triumphant narrative that Bush's neoconservatives thought it would; the question of whether a larger attack on American soil would ever take place yielded to that of whether a 'war' on 'terror' could ever achieve its objectives, leaving a tale so neatly be told to 'our children and our children's children'. And it is for this reason that there is now some question as to whether 'Vietnam Syndrome', or at any rate something like it, has returned at a different time and in a different guise, amplified at least in part by the very technologies that (according to the architects of that earlier war) assisted its emergence some thirty years previously.

The revival of 'victory culture' took place less in the halls of power or in the sands of Afghanistan and Iraq than in the living rooms and cinemas of the United States, in the mass cultural production that engendered the dominant 'cultural imaginary' of the time. Plenty has been written about the content of such products, and indeed this content has spoken powerfully to precisely the resurrection of 'victory culture' that Engelhardt identifies. As such, a close reading of cultural production, including network news coverage as well as TV and film, is essential to some understanding of how, for so long, the American public was coerced into buying the dominant line as well as how they might be motivated to reject it. But precious little analysis has delved into the *formal* aspects of these products, in particular the aesthetic that dominates and holds them together, that enjoins either identification with America's mission or, more uncommonly until recent years, a rejection of it. In other words it is the aesthetic paradigm that 'frames' historical events – that selects, filters, and presents them to the viewing public – that demands to be more closely investigated. For it is more than a matter of choices made at the administrative level – more than the 'pool' or 'embedded' system of war coverage, even though the latter indeed forms an integral part of that aesthetic. It involves a way of transmitting and perceiving that once again enjoins the complicity of the viewing public and that has proven, until recently, to be more in line with the 'aesthetics of hegemony' than with an 'aesthetics of resistance'. In further suturing the individual to the nation by means of enhanced cinematic techniques it becomes what Walter Benjamin (1968: 242) would have called the 'aestheticisation of politics' to the overall stultification of the 'masses' and the emancipatory potential inherent in genuine class consciousness.

However, as I have argued, an aesthetics of hegemony is always contradictory and hence always a double-edged sword: what makes it so effective in favour of the imperial endeavour – its claim to encompass a global totality to which the American aspires – can also undercut this latter at a stroke. And we are finally beginning to see evidence of this in films like *Redacted* and *Battle for Haditha* (2007), never mind *The Hurt Locker* (2008), which swept the award for Best Picture from its more populist (and wildly popular) rival at the 2010 Academy Awards. Enjoining complicity by means of the 'aesthetics of hegemony' is a dangerous game, particularly if you happen to be doing it to win the sympathies of a mainstream audience in a time of global upheaval; there's no guarantee, that is, that the same techniques that are effective in some settings will work again, when intelligently deployed, in others.

To illustrate how this can be the case, I will first provide a reading of Ridley Scott's *Black Hawk Down* that reveals it as a prime instantiation of the aesthetics of hegemony, ideally suited to the immediate post-9/11 cultural climate into which it was released, before moving on to more recent Iraq war cinema – namely, Brian de Palma's *Redacted* – as an instance of how the same (or very similar) aesthetic techniques can be deployed to the opposite effect, raising the spectre of a renewed 'Vietnam Syndrome' for our times.

The Contemporary Aesthetics of Hegemony: *Black Hawk Down*

Black Hawk Down – bumped forward in its release following the attacks of September 11 – juxtaposes, like the Western, honour with dishonour, order with chaos, altruism with barbarity. As such I invoke it prior to demonstrating how more recent films invert this dominant aesthetic in the tradition of Coppola and Conrad. *Black Hawk Down* unapologetically enjoins viewer complicity in suturing self to nation, only with no trace of the self-awareness of the former, more subversive texts; it purports to achieve that identity between representation and reality that *Apocalypse Now* and *Heart of Darkness* reveal to be impossible.

Cinematic techniques have evolved since the time of Coppola's masterpiece to incorporate computer simulation and to overcome some of the limitations imposed by older cinematic technology. The hand-held camera – or the ability to create the illusion of one – allows for an aesthetic not dissimilar to the first-person video game, which interpellates its subject to an unprecedented degree; indeed, instead of the 'mass spectacles' that for Benjamin constituted a sort of Lacanian mirror-stage, enjoining viewer identification with a fabricated collectivity, it is an aesthetic 'beyond the looking glass' with which we are forced to grapple now, placed as we are in the position of the soldier himself. And by means of the film's particular content – an American mission gone dreadfully wrong, resulting in the deaths of 18 soldiers – it reinforces the victim-complex required to shore up support for a retaliatory strike on a barbaric enemy with no clear reason to hate 'us', the American saviours. The classic Western paradigm that 'justifies' slaughter is here deployed anew and in the context of 1990s Somalia – outlaw territory beyond the frontier – and the aesthetic cuts deeply into the viewer's sensory experience of the film to enjoin an unthinking, unreflective and thoroughly credulous identification that 'justifies' the only remaining rationale for militarism in an age of unrivalled American superiority: the legitimate defense of one's own life (see Link 1991: 42-3). Huntington's 'clash of civilisations', in which rational debate is impossible – and in which, as Walter Benn Michaels (2000: 653-4) pervasively argues, only one's *subject position* can dictate his stance – is made manifest here by the hordes of frenzied Somalis, armed and ready to kill without discernible purpose, and viewed, moreover, from the first-person perspective of the American soldier under threat. Scott's earnest attempt to present the incident 'as it really was' instead puts us in the position of the victim – the former 'liberal idealist' faced down by a terrifying, incomprehensible enemy – and this is a 'position' which is inherently ideological in its strike against ideology (in this case liberal ideology) itself. If, as Fredric Jameson (1979: 145) suggests, a 'fidelity' to reality does not imply an absence of ideology but to the contrary a surfeit of it, then *Black Hawk Down* constitutes perhaps the aesthetics of hegemony at its cinematic best, implicating the viewer in a position that can only lend support to the militarism being promoted by the powers that be. To place the viewer in a subject position from which self-defense is the only legitimate option allows the aesthetics of hegemony to crystallise around a number of distinct but related phenomena: the removal of the mediating narrative that might otherwise afford a critical perspective and the 'suturing' of the viewer to a fully reconstituted imperial self, under threat but maintaining its integrity against a backdrop of barbarity and inscrutable 'otherness'. The illusion of totality promised by earlier films is further realised as the barrier between viewer and viewed is almost entirely effaced, creating a sense of continuity between imperial self and imperialised other that, in this case, serves the revival of 'victory culture' quite well.

Undoing the Aesthetics of Hegemony: The Iraq War Film

Certainly a compelling case can be made – as often it is – for the dominance of a mainstream film industry that churns out, with the help of the Pentagon, the CIA and other imperial bodies, film after film that reinforces the goals, implicit or explicit, of the American global enterprise. This is to neglect, however, the critical potential of Hollywood audiences as well as the persistence of Jameson's 'political unconscious', a cultural undercurrent attuned to injustice and amenable to a more genuine sense of a progressive collectivity. In other words, it is neither the case that Hollywood commands a mass audience of muppets nor that it is the 'liberal' establishment its neoconservative enemies so stridently believe it to be. As a producer of commodities, to be sure, it will respond to what the audience purportedly 'wants', and, granted, in many cases these *are* the simplified, regressive (and therefore inherently conservative) narratives, combined with novel technology and special effects, that films such as James

Cameron's *Avatar* (2009) provide. Also, when it comes to films dealing expressly with political subject matter – such as *Rendition* (2007) or *Redacted*, the latter of which was screened at only 15 theatres nationwide (Alford 2010: 17) – the system of production and distribution is usually manipulated such that their box-office returns are kept to a minimum. There is no doubt, in other words, that the industry caters to the production and distribution of films that are at best not progressive in their approach to American foreign policy, either falling back upon the de-historicised 'few bad apples' scenario or a context in which America goes in to a situation with good intentions but insufficient information to pull off a successful campaign and restore order to the 'failed' states in question.

That said, this is surely not the only possible interpretation. To the contrary, the lack of an overarching political narrative in mainstream American cinema does not *have* to imply that America's intentions are inherently good. The recurrent critique of such films on the basis of their reluctance to summon a broader historical narrative and, in the case of anti-Iraq war films, their limited release, does not condemn them to eternal impotence. *Redacted*, for instance, is not Conrad's or Coppola's tale of imperial leadership gone mad; however, it is similar in that it is a tale of leadership gone altogether, leaving young, inexperienced troops with no direction or security but, quite importantly, with an excess of firepower. And it is this very absence of leadership that throws into question America's right to invade, hinting at a lack of direction that permeates the establishment right through to its upper echelons. The force and more importantly the legitimacy of narrative depends on a narrator as an 'authority', so to speak; in the absence of such authority, legitimacy comes into question, and with it – in this case – the legitimacy of the American enterprise as a whole. Granted, without a leader, and given also the grittingly realistic first-person perspective mobilised by Scott in the service of American imperialism, we have only Michaels's (2000) 'subject position' to go on, only the ethos of 'kill or be killed' that structures the experience of video games and blockbuster films that share their visual premise; however, in sharp contrast to *Black Hawk Down*, a number of recent Iraq war films employ the logic of the hegemonic aesthetic to strike *against* the ideologues of the American 'victory narrative' rather than to justify the slaughter of the other and, in so doing, to constitute the self at the centre of an imperial totality.

A political unconscious responsive to and productive of fissures within the given social order is always already a threat to the micromanagement of imagery both real and fictitious that the ruling orders conspire to sustain. Were it not, Hollywood's ideological efforts would be unnecessary. The fissure between representation and referent – no matter how ostensibly faithful to reality that representation strives to be – resurfaces again to reveal the impossibility of the self-identity that Ridley Scott strives to enjoin. What we encounter in recent war films is yet a further aesthetic development of the anti-narratives in *Apocalypse Now* and *Heart of Darkness*; the handheld, gritty, hyperreal, apparently unassailable *truth*-narrative encoded in the aesthetics of hegemony is just as effectively mobilised *against* the dominant narrative.

This is achieved in one of a number of films that carry on the tradition of their countercultural predecessors, even if it is more heavy-handed in its narrative self-awareness: namely, Brian de Palma's *Redacted*. Were there ever to be an award for the film most acutely aware of the problems of narrative representation, *Redacted* would surely be a contender. What is important in this film is how the drive towards authenticity that defines militaristic films like *Black Hawk Down*, as well as the ideology embedded in 'embedded' reporting, reveals all the more acutely the flaws inherent in the assumption that reality can be adequately represented in writing or on screen, particularly against a backdrop of imperialistic warfare that lacks the legitimating premise it so desperately needs. In the case of *Redacted*, the removal of the mediating 'context' so central to the distance between narrator and narratee brings the viewer into complicity with the rape and murder of a 15-year-old girl and her family – into a nightmarish visualisation of 'the horror' that takes place beyond the frontier.

De Palma is keenly aware of what needs to be 'redacted' in order for the imperial narrative to function, and this is not only the atrocity itself but realist visuals from numerous other narrative sources, which he therefore makes a point of including – the jihadists' website, the Arabic networks, the American networks, the French documentary, the surveillance cameras on base and in the psychological evaluation and interrogation rooms, the webcams of families and random Americans, and most importantly the handheld camera of a young recruit trying to document the 'truth' of the war (unsuccessfully, as he quickly becomes the victim of a retaliatory beheading). In each case, de Palma implies, there is something left out, something abandoned; in other words, he foregrounds the imperative of redaction *as a structural necessity of narrative itself*, as the absent evidence of what is untold. And by giving us the uncompromising realism that the new generation of moviegoers demands – all the while acknowledging, implicitly, that true realism is finally impossible – he may be giving us more than we bargained for: complicity not only in warfare but in a vicious crime, as well as in the cover-up that follows. There is no need in this case for a detective story to 'go modernist', as did the tale told by Marlow; instead, if there is any remnant of the detective framework at all, it is inverted such that the crime takes place before our very eyes, with the aspiring filmmaker's night-vision camera inverting, crucially, the taken-for-granted order of darkness and light. This is why de Palma's message, delivered with a sledgehammer though it may be, is so important. While it seizes upon the video-game aesthetic that in films like *Black Hawk Down* lays claim to uncompromising realism, it turns it around by 180 degrees to make 'us' not the victims but the victimisers – very much as we are in the 'Valkyries' scene, but now even closer to the horror. The narrative of the Wild West remains, but only in spectral form, and only to reveal how utterly degraded even that paradigm has become.

Conclusion: Vietnam Syndrome Revisited

The profound unease with which the viewer of *Redacted* is left is reminiscent of that which underlies 'Vietnam Syndrome' – the American cultural pathology deemed 'cured' by George Bush Sr. following the 1991 Persian Gulf War. We cling to the illusion that we can see it all firsthand – all 'our' conquests, in their gritty and triumphant realism – but the great frustration is that we cannot: that what can be shown is never equivalent to what is. A shadow is cast over the hegemonic aesthetic of *Black Hawk Down* by the aesthetic of films like *Redacted* – and this is why the latter film, while undeniably heavy-handed and transparent in many respects, is such an important one for the time of its production. It is at the aesthetic level – not at the level of plot, or story, or official rhetoric – that we are afforded a truly critical opportunity. For at this level, the level of the body, the fissure in the dominant aesthetic –between representation and referent – becomes most glaringly apparent, and the space is opened up for a heightened awareness. The 'subject position' has changed; to change the 'subject position' in what once may have seemed a desperate fight for one's own life is to change, in an important sense, the subject; and to change the subject, in turn, is to open up the possibility for the resurgence of politics proper.

This latter may well be a while in coming; that is, what Benjamin would refer to as the politicisation of art is but one aspect of what is required at a much broader level in order to bring about genuine change. At the very least, however, the aesthetic twist I have attempted to emphasise throughout – the *Heart of Darkness* trope – brings back to America the spectre of the Vietnam war, a war which to be sure was not 'lost' by the presence of the camera but which the camera helped to undermine, contributing to a cultural malaise that would not be 'defeated' until the first Gulf War; and in so doing it may yet contribute to a self-examination that brings the current imperialism, with all its atrocities, to an end. Indeed the Bush administration's master narrative itself remained troublingly inconclusive: the 'mastermind' of 9/11 was not found under his watch; the weapons of mass destruction purportedly stashed away in Iraq were never unearthed; fundamental American values (as well as domestic and international laws) have been flagrantly violated; and now thousands of troops in their twenties are returning from the wars to an extended sentence of unemployment in a battered economy, never mind the roughly 5,000 dead, the countless maimed for life, and the unnumbered Afghans and Iraqis sacrificed to the administration's goals. The disconnect between the rhetoric and what was increasingly apparent on our screens brought one opportunity for the undercurrent of dissent to emerge into the broader public consciousness: that 'the United States does not torture' clashed with the practice of 'extraordinary rendition', and the justification of the wars on humanitarian grounds was dealt a devastating blow with the release of images of abuse and degradation sent from Guantánamo Bay and Abu Ghraib. The administration's increasingly panicked responses to such revelations expose the twisted logic of the line 'this mission does not exist, nor will it ever exist' that kickstarts the narrative of *Apocalypse*

Now, as well as the implicit critique built into nearly all of the Iraq war films – namely, that the sheer absurdity of a war in which, as Bush once put it, '[there are] no rules' means that representation and reality need no longer coincide. In 'real life' as in cultural production, sometimes this critique takes place at the recognisable level of plot; sometimes it is ingrained in the narrative form and/or in the very aesthetics of film itself; but in all cases it points to a re-emergent strain of 'Vietnam Syndrome', returned to destabilise the putative moral certitude that legitimated the 'just war' waged after 2001.

Thus have recent war films shown not the heroism of combat against the 'enemies of freedom', nor even the brotherhood that forms among soldiers on the front, but a sprawling sort of despair, a 'horror', not unlike that invoked by Coppola and Conrad. The genealogy from *Heart of Darkness* through to recent war films constitutes a cyclical recurrence or 'return of the repressed' whereby what seems at first to be a solid narrative promising a satisfactory conclusion becomes, through sheer excess, what Peter Brooks deems 'unreadable': the disconnect between representation and reality that these texts reveal widens to the point that the consumption-satisfaction of the conventional narrative and its accompanying aesthetic is entirely disabled. In the end there can be no 'solution', much less a sense of moral justification of the sort that this conventional narrative – detective, Western, or other – provides. 'The horror' cuts across the narrative itself, reminding us that behind the safe world of fictional representation is a chasm that eludes the reach of the symbolic – yet, a chasm that can afford us a necessary moment of critical detachment – and it is in this fleeting moment that, as Benjamin once hoped, the aesthetic might be politicised, rather than the other way around.

Chapter 6

Ghosts of Ground Zero: Fantasy Film Post-9/11

Fran Pheasant-Kelly

A growing number of films retell, document or reflect on events relating to the terrorist attacks of 11 September 2001. Some focus on the unfolding of that particular day, and others on the subsequent 'war on terror', with science fiction and fantasy proving particularly fertile ground for oblique mediations of 9/11. Generally, the reception of these various genres has been uneven. Although two films released in 2006 that relived specific aspects of 9/11, *United 93* (Paul Greengrass) and *World Trade Center* (Oliver Stone), fared well at box office, subsequent films that centred on the war on terror have been less successful commercially. In contrast, worldwide all-time box office data (see table) reveals that fantasy films, especially those referring to 9/11 and the subsequent war on terror, constitute the most lucrative genre since 2001, with many of the all-time highest grossing movies released in the decade following 9/11.

In his analysis of 'The Easternisation of the West', Colin Campbell (2010) attributes the increasing prominence of fantasy to a more generalised cultural change e within the West that has emerged over the past 50 years. He argues that this preoccupation with fantasy is congruent with a more pervasive acceptance of Eastern values. Noting a 'turn from realistic to fantasy fiction that has been such a marked feature of popular culture over the last 40 years', Campbell concludes that 'it has occurred because historical narratives are no

All-Time Worldwide Box Office Figures

Rank	Title	US$
1	*Avatar* (2009)	2,781,505,847
2	*Titanic* (1997)	1,835,300,000
3	*The Lord of the Rings: The Return of the King* (2003)	1,129,219,252
4	*Pirates of the Caribbean: Dead Man's Chest* (2006)	1,065,896,541
5	*Toy Story 3* (2010)	1,062,984,497
6	*Alice in Wonderland* (2010)	1,023,285,206
7	*The Dark Knight* (2008)	1,001,921,825
8	*Harry Potter and the Philosopher's Stone* (2001)	968,657,891
9	*Pirates of the Caribbean: At World's End* (2007)	958,404,152
10	*Harry Potter and the Deathly Hallows: Part 1* (2010)	946,080,434
11	*Harry Potter and the Order of the Phoenix* (2007)	937,000,866
12	*Harry Potter and the Half-Blood Prince* (2009)	933,956,980
13	*Star Wars: Episode I - The Phantom Menace* (1999)	922,379,000
14	*The Lord of the Rings: The Two Towers* (2002)	921,600,000
15	*Jurassic Park* (1993)	919,700,000
16	*Harry Potter and the Goblet of Fire* (2005)	892,194,397
17	*Ice Age: Dawn of the Dinosaurs* (2009)	887,773,705
18	*Spider-Man 3* (2007)	885,430,303
19	*Shrek 2* (2004)	880,871,036
20	*Harry Potter and the Chamber of Secrets* (2002)	866,300,000
21	*Finding Nemo* (2003)	865,000,000
22	*The Lord of the Rings: The Fellowship of the Ring* (2001)	860,700,000
23	*Star Wars: Episode III - Revenge of the Sith* (2005)	848,462,555
24	*Transformers: Revenge of the Fallen* (2009)	835,276,689
25	*Inception* (2010)	817,068,851
26	*Independence Day* (1996)	811,200,000
27	*Spider-Man* (2002)	806,700,000
28	*Star Wars: Episode IV - A New Hope* (1977)	797,900,000
29	*Harry Potter and the Prisoner of Azkaban* (2004)	795,458,727
30	*Shrek the Third* (2007)	791,106,665

Source: Internet Movie Database, Worldwide All-time Box Office, May 2011, available at www.imdb.com/boxoffice/alltimegross?region=world-wide (accessed 16 May 2011).

longer seen to be credible' (2010: 748). Conversely, Ted Friedman suggests that the turn to fantasy is a much more recent phenomenon, its current ubiquity deriving from 'two intertwined preoccupations of our era: technology and nature' (2008). Clearly, the popularity of fantasy films that depend on developing technologies, such as computer-generated imagery (CGI), motion capture, and animation, lends support to Friedman's claim. The market potential of fantasy franchises, as well as high profile directors and stars, also have a significant part to play.

While these aspects are important to the development and status of the genre, I suggest that fantasy's post-9/11 dominance also reflects its potential to re-articulate traumatic histories. For example, both *Harry Potter and the Philosopher's Stone* (Chris Columbus, 2001) and *The Lord of the Rings: Fellowship of the Ring* (Peter Jackson, 2001), released immediately after 9/11, performed exceptionally well at the box office. Kathy Smith suggests that this success arose because, 'in the wake of the realisation of events previously confined to disaster movies, the global audience looked for a different kind of fantasy into which to escape, a "guaranteed" fantasy, the reality of which was securely beyond imagination' (2005: 69-70). For fantasy, as Katherine Fowkes (2010) tells us, constitutes a genre that audiences perceive substantially deviates from reality.

Smith's comment indicates that there is some kind of relief inherent in the fantasy genre. However, this seems incongruous with the fact that, similar to many top-grossing fantasy films, the *Harry Potter* series and *The Lord of the Rings* (*LOTR*) trilogy are dark and nihilistic. Indeed, their entire underpinning themes are persistently those of death. Moreover, post-9/11 fantasy films, including the *Potter* series and the *LOTR* trilogy, almost inevitably provide direct or oblique mediations of 9/11 and the war on terror. For example, death and violence dominate *The Dark Knight* (Christopher Nolan, 2008), the seventh highest grossing film of all time, and one which also contains clear allusions to 9/11. Similarly, *Avatar* (James Cameron, 2009), currently the highest grossing film of all time, contains obvious analogies with the war on terror in relation to pre-emptive attack, the Iraq wars, and 'oil' as a motivating factor for these. While films such as *Harry Potter*, the *LOTR* trilogy and *Avatar* particularly illustrate Campbell's point about an increasing Easternisation of values in their qualities of magic and spiritualism, whilst also depending, and indeed, reflecting on 'technology and nature', their engagement with themes and imagery connected to 9/11 raises other possibilities. One might suggest that such fantasies offer 'safe' ways subconsciously to re-enact, or work through traumatic memories of 9/11 for viewers reluctant to witness realistic depictions of death and destruction. They may also allow acknowledgement of issues arising from the subsequent war on terror, for example, revelations about the abuse of prisoners at Guantánamo Bay, and the failure to find weapons of mass destruction in Iraq. *Avatar*'s director, James Cameron, certainly made this explicit when he said, 'We went down a path that cost several hundreds of thousands of Iraqi lives. I don't think the American people even know why it was done. So it's all about opening your eyes' (in Hoyle, 2009). Fantasy films such as *Pan's Labyrinth* (Guillermo del Toro, 2006) and *The Chronicles of Narnia: The Lion, The Witch and The Wardrobe* (Andrew Adamson, 2005) that are set against a backdrop of war may function in similar ways, enabling audiences experiencing the current war on terror to find a connection with a fictionalised wartime setting.

In articulating 9/11, fantasy film does not always utilise the conventional visual vocabulary of traumatic cinema, such as the flashback. Nor does it necessarily deploy the conventionally traumatic narrative. More usually, deriving from its quality of being 'substantially beyond reality', the post-9/11 fantasy film translates terror and anxiety into various forms of spectacle. The nature of spectacle offers a way of dealing with terror through the concept of the 'arresting image', which, according to Barbara Klinger (2006), has the capacity to mobilise spectator emotion. The arresting image may also serve to fetishise terror, in the way that it simultaneously draws attention to loss whilst disguising it (Elsaesser, 2001: 200). Cinematography and framing are often vital to the 9/11 connotations of such images. For Klinger, the 'arresting image' (2006: 24) mobilises spectator emotion through its associations and is thus an important concept in considering how fantasy 9/11 narratives operate. Klinger continues that 'arresting images are often generated by juxtaposing incongruous elements' (2006: 30) which confers a surreal quality on them, whilst the narrative's temporality tends to distort or slow down. The very nature of fantasy is consistent with such surreal elements, while spatial and temporal distortion is a distinctive feature of the films considered here. Arguably, the single spectacular image or sequence may encapsulate an entire narrative, evoking the emotion of the grand narrative through the associations that Klinger describes. Thus, while we may specifically remember the falling bodies from the Twin Towers, these do not exist as an isolated memory, but as part of the bigger catastrophe.

Moreover, spectacle may take many forms, manifesting as a kinetic 'impact aesthetic' (King, 2000), as the terrifying sublime, as abject horror or as action or technological spectacle. Fantasy films thus not only depend on technological innovation but also highlight technology as spectacle. Visually, fantasy may further provide arresting imagery in its characterisation and settings. Characterisation has the capacity to articulate concerns about terrorism through the 'other', fantasies reconfiguring the terrorist as technological, genetic, cybernetic or action spectacle (the Joker, Voldemort, and Sauron being obvious examples). Settings too may be visually striking or memorable, serving to mobilise terror, fascination, or disgust through inter-textual references that further reflect on 9/11. This chapter therefore aims to examine several fantasy films made since 2001, and consider the ways in which they mediate the events of 9/11.

Avatar

Avatar predominantly questions America's role in Iraq and Afghanistan, channelling these concerns through the unstable identity of its protagonist, Jake Sully (Sam Worthington). The fantasy world of Pandora that Cameron constructs represents the oil rich nations of the East, which the US military attack with wanton disregard for life. Indeed, the film continually points to the 'gung ho' hyper-masculinity of the US army, whilst representing Pandora as a maternal, nurturing place and its inhabitants, the Na'vi, as 'Other'.

The film tells the story of a paraplegic ex-marine, Jake Sully, who undertakes his twin brother's mission on the fictional planet of Pandora, a site of a valuable mineral called unobtainium. His mission is to assume the identity of an avatar and infiltrate the Na'vi, a humanoid species inhabiting Pandora. Increasingly, however, Sully opposes the American military's intention to attack the Na'vi. His equivocation and eventual transition to a constructed avatar identity thus reflects critically on the shortcomings of the war on terror, and condemns the decision to invade Iraq. The film encourages the spectators' consistent identification with Sully and thus enlists their support for his rejection of American military strategy. It achieves this identification through Sully's voiceover, and by utilising camera shots from his point of view. The film also highlights the 'natural' beauty of Pandora and further persuades us by its unethical destruction.

The opening scenes present Pandora as a mystical, fantastic world in an overhead tracking shot. Sully's voiceover firstly informs the viewer of his injuries, and secondly, about his dreams of flying. Stating that, 'Sooner or later you always have to wake up', the camera then cuts from his fantasy of flying to a forensically filmed close-up of his open eye, signifying the harsh reality of being unable to walk. Initially, the film therefore emphasises the fact that Sully is a paraplegic, and is highly suggestive of the symbolic castration of America during the 9/11 attacks, since US national identity derives significantly from its military strength. Relating to losses in Iraq and Afghanistan, the film implies that one soldier is expendable and easily replaceable with another. For example, one official tells Sully, whose dead twin brother was initially intended for the avatar programme, 'you can step into his shoes'. Subsequently, we see his brother cremated, with Sully's voiceover commenting, 'one life ends, another begins'. There is therefore an implicatin of the death, loss, and replacement associated with war, and the suggestion that individual identities are unimportant. In some ways, this compares to the life cycle of renewal on Pandora, although departing from it in the lack of compassion for life.

We then see Sully transfer to Pandora where the other marines run out from the aircraft while he lags behind as he swings his legs over into a wheelchair. The other soldiers continually humiliate him because of his disability, one describing him as 'meals on wheels'. Despite these negative connotations, his voiceover encourages the spectator to identify with him. We mostly see events unfolding from Sully's perspective (he sits in a wheelchair and is thus low down), with low-angle shots of military equipment, as well as close-ups of weaponry, emphasising the signifiers of US power and dominance. When Grace (Sigourney Weaver), who is leading the Avatar team, finds out that Sully is joining them, she further suggests a condemnation of US military action, commenting, 'The last thing I need is another trigger happy moron out there'.

On Sully's first outing into Pandora, slow sweeping pans reveal it as a lush green place with exotic flora and fauna. The *mise-en-scène* persistently signifies Pandora as a magical and mystical fantasy world where plants are illuminated and have their own energy, while extreme low-angle shots of floating mountains emphasise their spectacular nature. The focus on 'feeling', and bonding with fauna is completely antithetical to the approach of the military, who are merely preoccupied with money and killing. The military's usual technology does not work on Pandora because of a 'flux vortex' – it is thus anti technological.

We see Sully documenting his observations of Pandora to a video log, directly addressing the spectator and thereby further encouraging us to identify with him. However, he appears increasingly disorientated in his daily reports to the log, commenting 'the days are starting to blur together'. Eventually, he loses his sense of identity and slowly withdraws from reality, remarking 'everything is backwards now – out there is the real world...here is the dream', and 'I don't know who I am anymore'. Ultimately, he rebels against the US army and supports the Na'vi, his desire to remain as an avatar indicating the moral dilemmas of the Iraq/US conflict, and uncertainties about US national identity.

Though the military personnel persistently label the Na'vi as savages, the unfolding of the film from Sully's perspective reveals them as a caring, highly sensitive group who have spiritual and mystical beliefs. In line with Campbell's claims for an increasing 'Easternisation of the West', *Avatar* seems to place value on such qualities, the 'Eastern' qualities of Pandora being especially apparent in discussions about the 'flow of energy', and the essential bonding with animals. For example, Neytiri (Zoe Saldana) tells Sully when mounting one creature to 'feel her heartbeat, feel her breath' in order to form a psychic bond with it.

While the Na'vi hunt, they aim for a 'clean kill', showing they are humane and have respect for animals, unlike the US military who do not seem to have respect for life. Referring to their imminent attack on the Na'vi, the Army Colonel says 'we'll drop them out with gas first – it'll be more humane...*more or less*'. He also talks of 'pre-emptive attack' saying 'we will fight terror with terror', clearly alluding to Iraq's alleged weapons of mass destruction.

The US army also appear bigoted, and construct the Na'vi as 'Other' in relation to Western values. For example, one commands, 'Find out what the blue monkeys want – we try to give them medicine, education, roads but no, that's not what they want...killing the indigenous looks bad – but there's one thing shareholders hate more than a bad press, and that's a bad quarterly statement'. The construction of the Na'vi in this way has undertones of slavery and racism, harking back to the past as well as reflecting the more recent events of 9/11, and perhaps symbolises America's efforts to shore up its own sense of crippled masculinity since 2001. Moreover, the army devastate the home of the Na'vi in order to procure the unobtainium, extreme low-angle shots showing their bulldozers devastating the planet. The film thus makes clear its opinion about the motivations of the US in the Gulf Wars.

While allusions to the war on terror persist in the references to unobtainium, analogies to the destruction of the Twin Towers are apparent in the attack on the Hometree. Our first view of the tree occurs in an extreme low-angle shot from Sully's perspective. We also see it in long shot, its huge size emphasising its parallels to the Twin Towers. In later scenes, long shots of its height repeatedly intercut with quickly edited close-ups and medium close-ups at ground level where we see the suffering its destruction causes. In further allusions to the Twin Towers, Sully reports to the Colonel on the interior detail of the Hometree, stating, 'your scan doesn't show its interior structure', as if it is a building, and further describes its outer row of columns as: 'real heavy duty. There's a secondary ring here and an inner ring and a core structure like a spiral. The secondary ring is also load-bearing.' This description recalls the discussions of building structure in relation to the unanticipated collapse of the Twin Towers on 9/11. Indeed, when the US army destroy the tree, the ends of its broken trunk distinctly resemble the remains of the steel structures of the Twin Towers. Thus, *Avatar* addresses visually a range of issues that resonate with contemporary audiences, namely, 9/11, the war on terror, and anxieties about environmental catastrophe, as well as narratively questioning the invasion of Iraq.

The Dark Knight

Like *Avatar*, *The Dark Knight* clearly allegorises 9/11, entailing scenes of suicide bombers and coercive 'interrogation' that allude to Guantánamo Bay and Abu Ghraib. As well as presenting imagery reminiscent of the Twin Towers, *The Dark Knight* also offers perspectives that in themselves invoke fresh horrors. These include the viewpoint of the aircraft that crashed into the Towers, and that of those who jumped to their deaths from within them. While exploring fears of terrorism through generalised associations, the film also reflects on the nature of terrorism and raises questions concerning counterterrorist measures. Its 9/11 inferences are mediated chiefly through the characterisation of the Joker, while the theme of ambiguous identity that pervades the film is symptomatic of anxieties about terrorism. Although *The Dark Knight* is primarily a Batman narrative, the character of Batman serving as a metaphor for the Bush Administration, the film paradoxically retains a focus on the Joker, who represents the anonymous face of terrorism.

The film's plot centres on the activities of Batman (Christian Bale) working in conjunction with Lieutenant Gordon (Gary Oldman) and new district attorney Harvey Dent (Aaron Eckhart). Their aim is to thwart the Joker's intention to throw Gotham City into chaos. In their attempts to stop him, the Joker seriously injures Harvey Dent and kills his girlfriend, Rachel Dawes (Maggie Gyllenhaal), as well as inflicting chaos in general. the Joker is a central figure of *The Dark Knight*, his transgressive behaviour driving the film's plot forward. According to one character, mob moss Maroni (Eric Roberts), the Joker 'has no rules', while the Joker himself states: 'I'm not a schemer. I try to show the schemers how pathetic their attempts to control things really are.' He also comments: 'Nobody panics if things go according to plan, that...if tomorrow I tell the press a truckload of soldiers will be blown up, nobody panics because it's all part of the plan...but upset the established order and everything becomes chaos, I'm an agent of chaos.' This latter comment, pointing to losses in the Iraq and Afghan Wars, also establishes him as a disruptive force. At many points in the film, the Joker causes places of order to become chaotic. One example of his ability to instigate chaos is apparent visually in his attempt to kill the Mayor at Commissioner Loeb's memorial. A number of overhead, high-angle camera shots emphasise the uniformity of the police officers' positions. Suddenly, the emergence of the Joker causes the scene to escalate into chaos, a subsequent high-angle shot showing the police officers dispersing randomly.

The Joker is also disorderly in appearance and behaviour: his hair is wild and unkempt, his loose clothing tends to flap open and fly back, and his face is prone to distortion. His tongue darts in and out of his mouth, while his often maniacal laughter reveals yellowing teeth. Even his voice has an erratic, wide-ranging tonality in comparison to Batman who talks in a deep monotone. Overall, his appearance is antithetical to the chiselled features of Batman. In their analysis of *The Dark Knight*, Alan Lovell and Gianluca Sergi (2009: 32-3) identify a 'sensual pleasure' that pervades the film in general. The authors attribute this sensuality to various aspects of the Joker, generally describing a chaotic style, with unexpected movement and a voice that is alternately high and low. I suggest that the instability implied in his ill-defined appearance and the havoc that he wreaks have qualities more consistent with terrorism and his capacity for causing chaos. Indeed, his visual representation as 'alien other' corresponds to the politics of fear embedded in US foreign policy as a means of 'constructing and sustaining collective identity' (Jackson, 2007: 187). For example, in the hospital scene with Harvey Dent, he boasts 'look what I did to this city with a few drums of gas and a couple of bullets', referring to the explosions that killed Rachel and destroyed Dent's face.

The Joker thus lacks any sense of a normal moral perspective, providing a distinct contrast with the scientific, technological, and rational nature of Batman. In addition to his sadistic impulses, the Joker appears masochistic, and apparently thrives on the thought of his own demise as well as that of others. In several scenes the Joker invites Batman to 'hit me, hit me – I want you to do it', his suicidal drive partly intended to corrupt Batman's moral stand, but also a reference to the terrorists who executed 9/11. In fact, the Joker is not at all motivated by money but by causing suffering. In one of the film's clearest allusions to 9/11, Alfred (Michael Caine) comments, 'Some men aren't looking for anything logical like money...they can't be bought, bullied, reasoned or negotiated with...some men just want to watch the world burn' (*verbatim*). This obsession with suffering further materialises in the Joker's execution videos, which simulate those of Al-Qaeda displayed on the Internet or television news bulletins after 9/11.

However, the Joker is a compelling character. This partly stems from the filmic aspects of his bizarre appearance and disturbing persona, as well as uncertainty about his origins. His character also generates excitement in the extreme measures he takes to create complex strategies and spectacular modes of death for his victims, which inevitably depend on exact timing. One example of this is the attempted murder of Rachel and Dent, whom he attaches to devices that are set to explode simultaneously. This attention to timing is important to the narrative because Batman only has enough time to save one of them. Another example of spectacular modes of death dependent on concurrent timings occurs in the ferry scene. Here, the Joker instructs the passengers of two ferries, one carrying convicted felons, the other carrying civilians, to detonate explosive devices aboard the other ferry at a specific time in order to save their own lives. While the Joker succeeds in killing Rachel, he fails to convince the ferry passengers to kill each other, implying the morality of convicted felons relative to terrorists. Clearly, this attention to spectacle and timing alludes to the nature of the plane hijackings of 9/11 and the intended co-ordinated destruction of their final destinations.

The film as a whole tends towards scenes of spectacular destruction, deploying the impact aesthetics typical of the action film (see further, King 2000: 91-116). For example, in the opening scene, fireballs billow out towards the spectator, followed by an explosion in which glass shatters outwards towards the screen. A similar spectacular effect was also apparent in documentary images of 9/11. Jean Baudrillard describes how the realness of these images added a further dimension of fascination:

> in this case [9/11], then, the real is superadded to the image like a bonus of terror, like an additional *frisson*; not only is it terrifying, but, what is more, it is real. Rather than the violence of the real being there first, and the *frisson* of the image being added to it, the image is there first, and the *frisson* of the real is added.

(Baudrillard 2003: 29)

Similarly, in *The Dark Knight*, aspects of reality emerge in the Gotham Hospital explosion scene through evoking traumatic memory – and become more potent because of this. Here, the Joker, dressed as a nurse, leaves Dent's hospital bed and approaches the camera. Behind him, explosions occur sequentially, fragments of debris flying towards the spectator. Subsequently, we see him centre-framed against the backdrop of the hospital, which begins to collapse. The windows blow outwards, with a low-level camera angle revealing the scene from a different perspective. Fragments of paper shower from the falling building, resembling one of the most memorable images of the Twin Towers' destruction. An overhead shot then recaptures the explosions, while the ensuing overhead shot of the site shows the whole area burnt to the ground, another direct allusion to Ground Zero. We are then able to re-watch this spectacle again on a news bulletin, much in the way that 9/11 was repeatedly replayed.

Fascination with the Joker also undoubtedly arises because of the 2008 death of Heath Ledger. Ledger's death not only heightens the Joker's spectral qualities but also reinforces his sense of obscurity. For when the Joker is imprisoned, the police officers are unable to determine any single aspect of his identity. As Commissioner Gordon notes, '[the Joker has] no matches on prints, DNA, dental...no name...no other alias.' Indeed, the entire narrative structure of *The Dark Knight* revolves around ambiguous identity. Questions relating to the respective real identities of both the Joker and Batman underpin the film, signifying anxieties about the pervasive but intangible nature of terrorism, specifically the anonymous nature of the individual terrorist. As Baudrillard (2003: 20) asks, 'might not any inoffensive person be a potential terrorist?'

Further to the characterisation of the Joker, other aspects of the *mise-en-scène* mediate traumatic memories of 9/11. One indication is the light beam directed skyward that the Commissioner uses to summon Batman's help. While the beam is iconic of the *Batman* movies, here it has special significance. Although the huge lamp that radiates the light lies at an angle, the first light beam seen to project skyward is actually vertical, similar to the twin beams of *The Tribute in Light* that radiated into the sky to mark the site of the Twin Towers after their collapse.

Also noticeable are the various explosions that punctuate the film, as the Joker blows up first the police headquarters and then Gotham City Hospital. Following the explosion at the police headquarters, the film's sound temporarily disappears and there is an immediate cut to a surreal shot of the Joker leaning out of a stolen police car, swaying maniacally. The acuteness of the silence implies his madness and isolation, while its persistence into the ensuing apocalyptic scene of fire fighters silhouetted against the burning buildings conveys the sight as traumatic memory. The silence dissects it from the film's narrative, the imagery again reminiscent of Ground Zero.

The film's most distinctive reminder of 9/11 occurs in scenes where Batman dives off high buildings, and although typical of the genre, these also closely resemble 9/11 footage. For example, in several sequences Batman dives from a skyscraper with the camera revealing his point of view of the drop below before cutting to frame him in long shot, much in the same way that we saw bodies falling from the World Trade Center. In another example, Batman seizes one of his adversaries, Lau (Chin Han), from the upper floors of a skyscraper in Hong Kong, before attaching himself onto a low flying aircraft. The low-angle shot of the aeroplane highlights its close proximity, profoundly echoing 9/11, while the subsequent reaction shot of one of Lau's colleagues shows his disbelief, mirroring similar reactions of onlookers when the Towers were attacked.

In addition to its 9/11 imagery, the film's cinematography offers perspectives that invoke fresh horrors. After the opening sequence of full-frame fireballs, the camera tracks directly towards a skyscraper, its motion simulating the flight path of the planes that flew into the Twin Towers. When almost at point of impact, a window explodes outwards. The ensuing sequence continues to reflect 9/11 as two masked men emerge from the broken window to rig a wire across to an adjacent building at similar elevation, and then abseil across. As they set up the wire, the camera, positioned within the building, rapidly tracks towards the open window and then tilts down to reveal a high-angle shot of the street below, creating a lurching effect for the spectator, which gives the sensation of falling or jumping from the window.

9/11 allusions and the implications of the war on terror further materialise in the thematic aspects of the film. As in many fantasy films, the narrative's central theme is one of good versus evil, *The Dark Knight* persistently exploring the relationship between these. The blurring of the boundary between them is apparent in certain similarities between the Joker and Batman, and is made more potent by Harvey Dent's degeneration into vigilantism. His turning from good to evil follows Rachel's murder in the explosion triggered by the Joker that partly destroys Dent's face, his identity thus compromised both physically and morally. Dent's earlier nickname of Harvey Two Face calls attention to this duality, and perhaps points to the way that terrorism may arise in previously upstanding citizens. Batman's coercive 'interrogation' of the Joker whilst the latter is in custody also alludes to scenes of Guantánamo and Abu Ghraib, perhaps condemning the methods used there, though in many ways, the film seems to justify illegal or subversive responses to extreme provocation. This is not only evident in Commissioner Gordon's tacit approval of Batman's torture of the Joker, but is further apparent in Batman's unethical surveillance of Gotham City. Despite Lucius Fox's (Morgan Freeman) disapproval of Batman's methods, he complies with them in order to capture the Joker.

The relationship between the Joker and Batman is thematically relevant to a film about terrorism. They are opposites in almost every sense, Batman symbolising Western values as a wealthy capitalist in scenes that see him arrive by private helicopter, or sail aboard a private yacht. In contrast, the Joker signifies the abject Other who cares little for money. Indeed, he sets fire to his stolen stash of money, and says to Dent, 'It's not about money, it's about sending a message.' However, Batman and the Joker have similarities in that both have dual identities and operate on the fringes of society in subversive ways. Like Baudrillard's claim that, 'perhaps that is the terrorist's dream: the immortal enemy. For, if the enemy no longer exists, it becomes difficult to destroy it' (2003: 55-56), the Joker's words to Batman – 'What would I do without you. You complete me. To them, you're just a freak, just like me' – imply that Batman is his *raison d'être*. The implication in *The Dark Knight* is that terrorism exists merely because of the war waged against it, with the film making much of the consequences of a war against terrorism, namely the deaths of innocent civilians. Though Batman's flight into the shadows at the film's finale again suggests a need to act subversively, thus justifying his actions (and those of the Bush Administration), the film seems inconclusive. Narratively, it does not offer closure, and resists the temptation of a 'happy ending', recognising that 9/11 is still an open wound.

The *Harry Potter* Films

While *The Dark Knight* sustains a focus on terrorist action, the *Harry Potter* films repeatedly replicate the destruction of the Twin Towers. Although Harry Potter (Daniel Radcliffe) initially lives with his step-parents, The Dursleys, at their Surrey home, the principal setting for the *Potter* series is Hogwarts School of Witchcraft and Wizardry. Within this magical realm, the films chart the progress of its protagonist towards a coherent subjectivity and his quest to uncover his secret past. Potter, together with his friends Hermione Granger (Emma Watson) and Ron Weasley (Rupert Grint), also has a mission to defeat the evil Lord Voldemort (Ralph Fiennes), requiring him to overcome various challenges involving tests of morality, and physical and psychological endurance. Like Batman in *The Dark Knight*, Harry at times appears morally ambivalent, once succumbing to 'bad' magic when he almost kills his adversary and fellow student, Draco Malfoy (Tom Felton). Other characters, too, are ambiguous, notably Severus Snape (Alan Rickman), and even Albus Dumbledore's (Richard Harris/Michael Gambon) reputation comes into question. Therefore, as in *Avatar* and *The Dark Knight*, there is a common narrative paradigm of good overcoming evil, although often some ambiguity between these, perhaps questioning America's actions in the war on terror. Here, however, such ambiguity tends to be peripheral to Harry's central quest of defeating Voldemort. Instead, magic and myth are foregrounded in the films, with bewitched spaces constituting a world parallel to the real places of London and Surrey, existing invisibly alongside these. Campbell suggests that the success of *Harry Potter* derives from earlier literary works of fantasy, such as *LOTR*:

> It is impossible to imagine the current popularity of the Harry Potter books...had there been no *Lord of the Rings* or *The Chronicles of Narnia*. In

this respect J.R.R. Tolkien and C.S. Lewis...played a critical part in pioneering the turn from realistic to fantasy fiction.

(Campbell 2010: 748)

As well as harking back to its literary forebears, the complex visual rendering of the wizarding world is highly dependent on CGI, from Harry's broomstick antics to the various transformations of humans, and the sentience of plants and animals. While scholarly discourse has tended to centre on these aspects, as well as issues of class, race, and gender, there has, however, been little discussion of the films' references to 9/11 and their significance for audiences.

Such resonances abound in the *Potter* films, becoming increasingly evident throughout the series, and particularly emerging in *Harry Potter and the Goblet of Fire* (Mike Newell, 2005). This film opens at the Quidditch World Cup, where Harry and the Weasley family plan to camp overnight in the Weasleys' tent. The Dementors, guardians of the wizard prison Azkaban, set the tents alight, burning them to the ground, the smouldering remains echoing those of the 2001 attacks. The scene cuts to the interior of the Hogwarts Express where Hermione reads a newspaper, the 9/11 connection further implicit in the headline. Seen in close-up, it states, 'Terror at the Quidditch World Cup', the combination of words 'terror' and 'World' familiar territory to a post-9/11 audience, whilst Hermione asks the question, 'how can the ministry not know who conjured it? Wasn't there any security?' Subsequently, at Hogwarts, a new Defence of the Dark Arts teacher, Alastor Mad-Eye Moody (Brendan Gleeson), teaches the young apprentices torture and killing curses, the theme of torture becoming increasingly apparent, likely referencing concurrent events at Guantánamo Bay.

The fifth film, *Harry Potter and the Order of the Phoenix* (David Yates, 2007) continues with references to 9/11. The film opens in sunny, suburban Surrey, but the sky soon becomes overcast and the weather suddenly changes. Heavy storm clouds roll in, a common motif of the series, and highly suggestive of the smoke and dust clouds that featured prominently in 9/11 footage. As well as these visual reminders, the language utilised throughout the film is indicative of terrorism. Such comments include for example, 'attack without authorisation', references to 'the war', as well as a theme of recruiting followers to 'Dumbledore's Army', a group led by Harry to practice and perfect Defence

Against the Dark Arts in readiness for Voldemort's attack. When Hermione asks Harry to lead Dumbledore's Army, Harry's response of, 'When you're out there, when you're a second away from being murdered or watching a friend die right before your eyes, you don't know what it's like' also references warfare. In addition, hallucinations increasingly haunt Harry with acute psychic disturbances manifesting as disjointed flashbacks suggestive of post-traumatic stress disorder. References to torture further surface in the 'teaching' techniques of newly appointed Hogwarts teacher Dolores Umbridge (Imelda Staunton) from the Ministry of Magic. Upon discovering that Harry is the leader of 'Dumbledore's Army', she forces him to write lines using a bewitched 'blood quill' as punishment for his role in it. As he writes the words 'I must not tell lies', the same words appear on his hand as bleeding, painful wheals, a form of extreme control that she utilises repeatedly.

The bleaker landscapes of *Harry Potter and the Half Blood Prince* (David Yates, 2009) also see London landmarks under attack. The sombre tone of the film surfaces at the outset, with lightning flashes cutting to a close-up of a still, unfocused eye, establishing a forensic iconography that hints at the darkness to come. A cut to a low-angle shot of distorted reflections of skyscrapers surrounded by black storm clouds onto a glass-fronted building again directly references 9/11. Flashes of lightning then draw attention skyward, where Voldemort's face materialises in the dark clouds, and a swarm of Death Eaters, appearing like missiles, stream down towards London. A cut to a high-angle shot from the perspective of the Death Eaters reveals London rapidly coming into focus, like the military footage of targets televised during the Iraq War. This precedes a dizzying kinetic negotiation of London's streets, and ends in a long shot of a series of explosions that leave bodies scattered on the ground. The Death Eaters' next target is the Millennium Bridge, which subsequently collapses into the Thames, the camera then pulling back sharply to long shot to show them retreating skyward. A radio voiceover reporting on the Millennium Bridge disaster leads into the following scene that cuts to a close up of a newspaper headline stating, 'Bridge collapses – death toll rises'.

Such scenes, distinct from the utopian tendencies of the earlier films, locate the film in the real world of the 21st century, referring to the 9/11 and 7/7 attacks. Indeed, death dominates this film, from the demise of Aragog, Hagrid's (Robbie Coltrane) pet tarantula, to the murder of Dumbledore. A theme of loss also emerges in the film's finer details, for example, Horace Slughorn's (Jim Broadbent) recounting of the day that he arose to find his goldfish bowl empty, and the feeling of loss this engendered. The realist and nihilist tendencies of the film persist in the scenes of Quidditch, which see the pitch surrounded by stark steel towers rather than festooned with their usual brightly coloured team colours. In addition, the *mise-en-scène* is mostly one of darkness and rain. References to terrorism continue throughout the film, for example, security is evident as Filch (David Bradley), the caretaker, asks the students for identification when arriving at Hogwarts, and searches their belongings for weapons. In the closing scenes, as the Death Eaters and Severus Snape cause mayhem, and Harry is lying injured on the ground, an extreme low-angle shot of Hogwarts, with dark clouds billowing behind it, again resembles the destruction of the Twin Towers.

Indeed, throughout the *Half Blood Prince*, homes also become increasingly unsafe in the world outside of Hogwarts with even the welcoming Weasley home destroyed by the Death Eaters. In this scene, an extreme long shot shows the Weasley family dwarfed by a towering inferno as their home blazes. Thus, imagery of the Twin Towers' destruction repeatedly materialises in the *Harry Potter* films. In addition, themes of torture and terrorism emerge, while death and injury are common elements of the entire series, becoming especially prominent in the later films.

The Lord of the Rings

The Lord of the Rings follows a comparable narrative pattern to that of the *Harry Potter* series with its child protagonist seeking to overcome and destroy evil, while it has commonalities with both *Harry Potter* and *Avatar* in its inclusion of magic, eco-consciousness, and spirituality. Like the latter two films, *LOTR* is also dependent on a high degree of technological input, to the extent that Tom Gunning states that 'the directorial voice [of Peter Jackson] takes second place to the technology of film' (2006: 320). In part, this may explain its comparative critical and commercial success in relation to earlier attempts at its adaptation in that the technologies of CGI and motion capture have enabled Jackson to realise fully Tolkien's characters and settings.

In addition to *LOTR*'s combination of magic and technology, several scholarly studies have identified some general resonances with 9/11 and the war on terror. For example, Douglas Kellner notes that:

> the two Hobbits' choice of war, and that of other more obviously militarist characters in the film, is not for a clear cause against a determinate enemy. They go to make war against the abstract Forces of Evil themselves. Indeterminate crusaders against Evil now reflect Bush's war against terrorism.
>
> (Kellner 2006: 31)

Kellner's analysis of *LOTR* continues to highlight the films' analogies with the Bush Administration through their persistent militarist undertones. For, although Tolkien wrote the novel in the 1950s, inflecting it with his wartime experiences, these readily translate to the films' contemporary context. Indeed, Jackson's trilogy often visually exaggerates scenes of conflict, death, and bloodshed, Gary Westfahl noting that, 'While Tolkien primarily describes a quest, Jackson is primarily describing a war' (2005: 1154). Thus, as Ken Gelder suggests, 'This epic fantasy text from the 1950s gains its power because it now accommodates, and speaks on behalf of, a contemporary war scenario' (2006: 107). Inevitably, the title of the second film also resonates with contemporary audiences in its reference to the 'Two Towers'.

In addition, while much scholarly analysis rests on the sublime or picturesque images of the landscape in Jackson's *LOTR*, there is a distinct visual emphasis on decay in the film versions. These images of decay relate closely to certain spaces, and indeed, specific groups. For example, The Dead Marshes, which constitute one of many physical challenges to Frodo's quest, are a site of horror. Corpses appear to litter the marsh-beds, being just visible underneath the water's surface. The film describes them as 'rotting elves and men'. The Mines of Moria provide a further example, literally being littered with corpses, while at Isengard, deep below the earth's surface, we see the creation of the orcs, entities that appear decaying and bloody.

Boundaries as well as spaces are significant in *LOTR* – attention centres on the borders between different geographical regions and topographies, often with direct reference to Tolkien's map of Middle Earth. Boundary consciousness in the trilogy clearly connects to the racial Other, closely aligning particular settings with 'racial' identities. Such boundary consciousness is relevant to contemporary concerns of national security – Cynthia Weber debates both the nature of warfare in the war on terror and the nature of Al-Qaeda itself, commenting that, '[n]ot only is al Qaeda…located everywhere; it is located nowhere' (2006: 23). She also states that:

> [t]he problem for the United States is that its home front…has not just been attacked by al-Qaeda. It has been infiltrated by al-Qaeda, not (only) because al-Qaeda's operators are clever but because the character of neoliberal globalization is that it does not respect international boundaries.
>
> (Weber 2006: 25)

François Debrix too notes the relevance of boundaries to the war on terror, asserting that, 'it is a different war, with no really distinguishable home and away fronts. It is a war in the border regions of the concept of war. It has no beginning and no end; only battles, spurts of violence along the way' (2005: 1159). Clearly, the boundaries discernible in the *LOTR* chime with post-9/11 anxieties in relation to further 'infiltration' and, whilst containing less explicit imagery in relation to 9/11 and the war on terror than other films considered here, the trilogy still captures the zeitgeist of the new millennium. The transient loss of subjectivity signified by Frodo's trancelike state likely relates to Tolkien's experiences of post-traumatic stress – in Jackson's version, perhaps this loss of subjectivity is consistent with the loss of self in relation to the trained terrorist. The notion of the 'Other' is therefore arguably reflected in both Tolkien's tale as an allegory of the First and Second World Wars, and Jackson's rendering of it as a mediation of threats to national identity. As Fowkes notes, 'Tolkien eschewed an allegorical reading of *Rings*, but there is no denying that both the films' military triumphalism and their emphasis on solidarity and friendship speak to and reflect the historical moment of their release' (2010: 144).

Conclusion

Kathy Smith claims that fantasy films such as *LOTR* provided relief to audiences traumatised by 9/11. In fact, an analysis of some of the most commercially successful fantasy films made since 2001 reveals that the genre has been a vehicle through which to reprise images of 9/11 and the war on terror. The dominance of fantasy since 2001 thus not only reflects an 'Easternisation of the West' as posited by Campbell, as well as the emergence of new technologies critical to the credibility of fantasy narratives, but also indicates its centrality to a historically significant watershed. Taking *Avatar, The Dark Knight, Harry Potter,* and the *LOTR* as examples, this chapter contends that the fantasy film, in its oblique mediations of 9/11 and the war on terror, resonates with post 9/11 audiences and offers a further explanation for the genre's post-millennial success.

This chapter therefore suggests that, in general, such films have enabled the spectator to re-experience terrorism, death, and disaster in a 'safe' way. Seemingly reluctant to witness more realistic imagery audiences have instead turned to fantasy. Films including *Avatar,* the *Harry Potter* series, *The Dark Knight,* and *The LOTR* trilogy have explored various dimensions of 9/11 and the war on terror, and mediated these in ways that are fundamentally unrealistic, in many respects, supporting Campbell's claim that fantasy has supplanted 'real' grand historical narratives.

Technology has an undeniable part to play in this, in that the generic attributes of the fantasy film allow it to maximise the spectacular effects of cinema and the spectacular possibilities of terrorism. Arguably, following Klinger's (2006) model, spectacular and arresting imagery serves to mobilise spectator emotion through its intertextual associations. Perhaps the fantasy film does merely offer escapism during difficult times – however, it is difficult to explain why that escapism invariably foregrounds death and nihilism, and why such films should be so commercially successful. It is possible to interpret 9/11 in any scenes of destruction, and indeed, as Baudrillard (2003) points out, cinematic images prior to 9/11 seemed to anticipate the event. However, such images have assumed new significance in fantasy film since 2001. One explanation for fantasy's dominance lies in its capacity to explore traumatic issues in different, 'safe', but still discernibly familiar forms, perhaps allowing some reconciliation with the horrific aspects of 9/11 and the war on terror.

Chapter 7

A *Hostel* Environment: Sanitised Terror and the 'Torture Porn' Cycle

Graham Barnfield

> Torture is the deliberate infliction of pain by a state on captive persons. It is prohibited and so is the use of its product. The UN Convention Against Torture or Other Cruel, Inhuman or Degrading Treatment or Punishment emphasises that there are no exceptional circumstances at all justifying its use, whether state of war or any other public emergency; none of these may be invoked as a justification.
>
> (Peirce 2010: 3-4)

> I don't really give a good fuck what you know or don't know...but I'm gonna torture you anyway.
>
> (Mr Blonde, *Reservoir Dogs*)

Introducing *Hatchet 2* at its world premiere in 2010, director Adam Green was on boisterous form. Initially marketed under the tagline 'Not a Sequel, Not a Remake, Not a Japanese Film', the *Hatchet* franchise wears its genre-awareness on its sleeve. Yet Green ditched his jocular tone to reflect on a piece of fan-mail. A US combat soldier had written to him telling of terrifying Saturday night

Hatchet screenings while serving overseas. Green contrasted the necessity of the professional solider remaining unflinching in combat, while still needing the cathartic 'safe scare' of a horror film. Green seemed genuinely choked up at his correspondent's closing promise, to get his squad back together for a hometown multiplex screening of *Hatchet 2* by smuggling in the ashes of a fallen comrade who 'didn't make it back'. One would need a heart of stone to be unmoved by Green's statement. Yet he also brought to mind a recurring theme used in the marketing of Eli Roth's *Hostel* films. As we shall see below, the notion that combat troops – specifically marines – enjoy being scared by the contemporary horror movie has been circulated in promotional material supporting such films. More broadly, the explicit association of the *Hostel* and *Hatchet* franchises with military audiences at a time of high-profile troop deployments is no accident. It invites reconsideration of long-running scholarly discussions regarding the societal origins of the horror genre. First, the literary tale of terror is treated as capable of mediating social trends (see, for example, Glover 1996). In turn, critical appraisals of the horror film would come to emphasise its connection to the historically specific conditions from which it emerged in all its forms. Typically, such analysis starts with German expressionist film (for example, Prawer, 1980) before demonstrating the intimate linkage between the 1930s horror cycle, centred upon Universal Pictures, and the broadly coterminous Depression (see, for example, Fearnow, 1997: 15-50). It is therefore tempting to elaborate from this emphasis on a social sensibility to assess *Hostel* and the recent torture porn or 'gorno' cycle as performing some mediating function in contemporary society. Before so doing, we should address the problematic character of the 'torture porn' label itself.

One sensible objection is that its implied conflation of sex and violence is 'damaging, unfair, and misguided. It attempts to trivialise certain movies by suggesting that their only purpose is to titillate – short-circuiting the brain to go straight to the pulse or groin' (Hilden 2007). The label has built-in assumptions that serve to delegitimise the films it describes. That said, with the genie out of the bottle and the term in much wider use than its nearest synonym, gorno, it is used throughout this chapter. To date, the most comprehensive account of the 'torture porn' trend in cinema can be found in Kim Newman's *Nightmare Movies*

(2011: 466-504). It would be redundant to repeat his rich description here, but Newman brings out important points. Firstly, he questions whether torture porn as a distinctive genre or subgenre – never mind as a production cycle – actually exists. Secondly, he treats the boundaries between such films and mainstream cinema (not just mainstream horror) as relatively porous. Thirdly, he links the emergence of this filmmaking genre to the 'war on terror' itself. Each point is more than amply demonstrated by countless erudite plot synopses; if nothing else, the reader marvels at Newman's sheer stamina in getting through what seems the entire corpus of such movies.[1]

Newman (2011: 438) notes that in 'horror criticism, the term "torture porn" is contentious: some informed commentators are reasonably happy with the term, others hotly resist.' (Given that he identifies *The Most Dangerous Game* (1932) as the genre's template, there are also strong grounds for not treating the trend as entirely original.) It is generally accepted that the phrase 'torture porn' was launched by David Edelstein in early 2006 in an article for *New York* magazine, entitled 'Now Playing at Your Local Multiplex: Torture Porn' (although, appearing in the headline, the phrase may not have actually been coined by him). The magazine's chief film critic, Edelstein seemed genuinely bemused by a rising tide of movies 'so viciously nihilistic that the only point seems to be to force you to suspend moral judgments altogether.' Edelstein's conclusions were not censorious, but he seemed perplexed at how the loose equivalents of the European splatter film were now on at the US multiplex.

Contemporary society articulates a general moral hostility to torture, making it disconcerting to see its representation in fiction being widely adopted by the entertainment industries. Needless to say, our revulsion in the face of real torture should not rule out its inclusion in drama – stripped of their murders, the moral examples set within Shakespeare plays would of course be diminished. Yet such a straightforward observation has its limits: it cannot account for the particular conditions in which scenes of torture become a commercially viable form of entertainment.

Film critics sent to preview screenings as part of their professional duties are not alone in their negative responses to this so-called subgenre. Their complaints have achieved a relatively wide circulation, when echoed by commentators who note the existence of such films as part of political punditry or moral entrepreneurialism. Disclosing the details from selected gruesome scenes, such writers tend to link the emergence of gorno with the broader decline of values. Thus a general willingness to indulge in such viewing becomes symptomatic of moral turpitude (see, for example, Tookey 2006). While few op-ed columnists replicate exactly the language of the 1980s 'video nasties' panic, they are content to report alleged similarities between movies such as *Hostel*, the 'authentic' content of various 'shock video' websites, and actual cases of violence and murder (for example, Goodwin 2007).

Unease at the frequency with which new 'torture porn' films were being released was also voiced by fans of the horror film itself. Some sought to distance their favourite genre from what they saw as the intrusion of formulaic pap. For instance, a fan-friendly annual of scholarly essays contrasted gorno unfavourably with its socially relevant predecessors: 'An equally pervasive theme [in horror] has been the emergence of the "torture-porn" films ignited by the *Hostel* series and an equally fragmented world which remains a far cry from...post war, not to mention cold war concerns' (Black 2007: 5). High profile UK-based critic Mark Kermode, whose career owes much to his defence of video nasties on behalf of fandom (2010: 166-7), was initially supportive of Eli Roth's *Cabin Fever* (2002), portraying teenage vacationers afflicted with a flesh-eating virus, yet he turned against *Hostel* and its sequel. In short, some writer-fans criticised the new, horrific emphasis on restraint and dismemberment as an affront to their sensibilities.[2]

So far, this chapter has treated torture porn as a specific subgenre of the horror film. Upon looking at the content of the various movies, it becomes apparent that this is problematic for a simple reason: only a small proportion of them feature scenes of prolonged torture. In my initial estimation, *Hostel* (2005), *Hostel 2* (2007), *Captivity* (2007) and – predictably – *The Tortured* (2010) are the Hollywood films indisputably structured around the capture, confinement and mutilation of individuals (although Newman lists several more). In Roth's films, the torturers are privileged thrill-seekers who pay to indulge in such activities. Initially, *Captivity* seems structured around a conventional lone psychopath; the titular *Tortured* could be either the vengeful professional couple coming to terms with the murder of their son, or their victim, abducted from a prison truck. *Hostel*'s moneyed villains stand in *The Most Dangerous Game*'s minor Hollywood tradition. In contrast, Elise (Erika Christensen) and Craig (Jesse Metcalfe) of *The Tortured* are motivated by a rational, yet corrupting, desire for retribution. At the level of plotting and character motivation, this leaves *Captivity*, and *Hostel* and its sequel, as rare examples of productions that can be accurately characterised as 'torture for its own sake', in that the main violence takes place for primarily sadistic reasons. Despite the perception that such scenes have proliferated since 2003, this seems seem questionable in the light of the actual content of such films.

By reputation, some scenes of torture have had a disproportionate impact on perceptions of the contemporary horror film – to the point of defining a subgenre. 'Though the cutting and gouging understandably gets most of the attention, the subgenre is even more obsessed with *restraint*' (Newman 2011: 482, original emphasis). Yet structurally, such scenes tend to make for bad drama and, without the chance of the victim being released, can often lack dramatic tension – hence the need for escape and pursuit. Nevertheless, word-of-mouth reports of the specific scenes of confined, static individuals being mutilated circulate in the school playground and elsewhere, establishing a wider reputation. Thus *The Human Centipede (First Sequence)* (2009), which uses esoteric surgical techniques to combine restraint and mobility and transform escape and pursuit into a source of extreme pain, became better known – indeed more notorious – through its online trailer and spontaneous-seeming Twitter memes than its box office takings would suggest. Posted on YouTube, excerpts and spoofs further reinforced its notoriety.

Other movies located in the so-called subgenre have more tenuous connections to each other, if subjected to some form of content analysis. The seven *Saw* pictures hinge on a series of carefully engineered traps into which abducted individuals are placed. Through a series of flashbacks, viewers are led to believe that most of these victims somehow deserve their predicament. Once in a trap, they are given instructions on how to escape, typically by taking a route which will result in self-mutilation and permanent disfigurement or disability, or in the murder of a stranger or family member. Typically characters procrastinate, resulting in dismemberment by a machine. Those who seek to set a moral example, straying from the set instructions, may inadvertently kill a potential rescuer or otherwise make things worse. To the squeamish this might seems like hair-splitting, but the 'torture' in the *Saw* franchise involves representations of mental anguish prior to injury, rather than the infliction of pain as an end in itself.

More broadly, if we look at the narrative trajectories of the various movies used retrospectively to assemble the torture porn 'genre', their common characteristic is *the ordeal*, in which one or more protagonists face an apparently unending, terrifying scenario which can only end in their death, or that of their antagonist(s). Thus *Wolf Creek* (2005) becomes an ordeal for its three backpackers when they are abducted and hunted by a 'Crocodile Dundee' figure (John Jarrett), depicted in semi-documentary scenes with a then relatively unknown cast. Likewise, the Belgian production *Calvaire* (2004) – half-heartedly renamed *The Ordeal* for its US-UK release – hinges on abduction, humiliation and thwarted escape, rather than torture as such. More than a few critics have noted that such films were also an ordeal for the *audience* (or at least for the critics themselves at preview screenings: 'I didn't want to identify with the victim or the victimizer', groaned Edelstein). In passing, it is notable that a number of non-Hollywood titles appear above, indicating the way that the genre has gained stature through the inclusion of international productions under its banner.

If so-called torture porn is more accurately seen as structured around individual ordeals, its continuity with earlier staples of US independent horror film becomes apparent. For instance, *The Texas Chainsaw Massacre* (1974) featured closing scenes in which Sally (Marilyn Burns) is reduced to a screaming wreck after escaping a bizarre dinner party with a cannibalistic family; *Driller Killer* (1979) shows a failing painter undergoing a mental breakdown accelerated by his horrendous Union Square apartment block. Both movies set a symbolic precedent for the torture porn imbroglio, in that by reputation each became 'the one where that guy kills all those people' using the eponymous power-tool, even though such action takes up at most minutes of screen time. Inferior sequels and copycat marketing have further consolidated the public impression of these two recently rehabilitated classics as unrelenting murder sprees.

The apparent continuity between grungy, 1970s horror films and the more recent gorno cycle was also strengthened by a slew of profitable remakes and 're-imaginings' of earlier movies. Many 'classic' titles were recycled, and up-and-coming 'extreme' directors were given the helm of big-budget productions. Thus Alexandre Aja went from *Haute Tension* (2003) to *The Hills Have Eyes* (2006), while Rob Zombie's 'Firefly Family' films – *House of 1000 Corpses* (2003), *The Devil's Rejects* (2005) – allowed him to produce and direct the high-grossing remake of *Halloween* (2007). Film marketing also boosted this sense of widespread gruesome horror, meaning revenge thriller *Death Sentence* (2007) – loosely adapted from the 1975 paperback successor to *Death Wish* – was publicised as being from 'the director of *Saw*'. Little wonder that to those unfamiliar with the individual films it could appear that the multiplexes were now home to a rising tide of gore.

This perception was further consolidated by the emergence of a 'Splat Pack' of director-producers dedicated to pushing the boundaries of the horror film. From an auteur-theory point of view, gorno can be tracked through the work of Roth, Zombie, *et al.* (and executive producer Quentin Tarantino) as moving from independent production companies to Hollywood studios over the course of the past decade. This process enjoys a more complex relationship with genre directors internationally, with Roth expressing his appreciation of Takashi Miike (*Audition*, 1999) and a broader process of promoting the francophone directors of *Haute Tension/Switchblade Romance* (Alexandre Aja), *Calvaire* (Fabrice Du Welz) and *Martyrs* (Pascal Laugier, 2009) to US audiences. The invitation of directors from outside the United States to 'join' the Splat Pack – through the promotion of their films, cameo appearances, DVD directors' commentaries, etc. – further consolidates the impression of a distinctive movement.

Passing reference to Tarantino is a reminder that, in cinematic terms, we have been here before. Paul Gormley (2005) details the spawning of the 'new-brutality' film by *Reservoir Dogs* (1992), which elevated style over substance to reintroduce visceral shocks ('affect') to audiences (while articulating wider fears of racial conflict). Like the Splat Pack, new-brutalist directors could claim to be posing questions of audience complicity in fictional violence while acknowledging their fanboy debts to a combination of well-known and obscure

1970s texts. If one mentally substitutes 1973's *Mean Streets* for *The Texas Chainsaw Massacre* as seminal texts, the parallels between these cinematic trends become increasingly apparent. As with torture porn, any social comment within the new-brutality film was largely submerged by its co-option to an early 1990s cycle of post-*Goodfellas* (1990) 'Indywood' crime and gangster films. These days, with a handful of exceptions, the early Splat Pack directors seem caught up in an endless stream of remakes of earlier slasher movies. In terms of an identifiable group of genre directors producing similar output at a fixed point in time, the parallels are clear.

Yet this is where the historical similarity ends. Chronologically, the penultimate scene of Tarantino's *Pulp Fiction* (1994) has Marsellus Wallace (Ving Rhames) promising a sado-rapist he will 'get medieval on yo' ass'; *Hostel* takes fulfilling this threat as its basic premise. Moreover, the social context into which each type of film has been released is markedly different. In Britain and some parts of Western Europe, the new-brutality film provoked considerable controversy. *Reservoir Dogs* was the target of a media panic, especially on the eve of its transfer to home video, while the Tarantino-scripted *Natural Born Killers* (1994) was delayed prior to its UK release amid a controversy over 'copycat' crimes. According to those sceptical of moral panics, this was an example of the mass media drawing upon what one wag called 'reservoirs of dogma' (Murdock 2001). In contrast, despite press coverage which features rhetorical similarities to a moral panic, torture porn has yet to provoke a similar *societal* reaction.

Paradoxically, the absence of a significant public scare over gorno has not diminished *perceptions* of its existence as a major genre. At most, such specific concerns are themselves subsumed within ongoing complaints that mainstream film is becoming more violent. Space does not permit substantial discussion of it here, but the same discourse can also involve a chain of observations linking torture porn, reality TV, jihadist video and YouTube content to moral decline. For instance, author Thomas Hibbs grumbles that:

> at nearly every screening of a gruesome horror film I attend (from Massachusetts to Texas), I see parents in the audience with young children. That strikes me as a serious form of child abuse and a more

convincing sign of the impending apocalypse than anything depicted on the screen.

(Hibbs 2006)

In short, the genre tends to attract mainstream criticism primarily through its inclusion in lists of wider symptoms of decadence and social decay.

In terms of filmmaking itself, the two sets of concerns – about the genre existing and about (fictional) bloodshed and body counts increasing – are accurate in one sense at least. Digital post-production techniques boost the formal verisimilitude in scenes of mutilation. Gone are the rubbery prosthetics of old; bodily destruction can now be integrated into the very pixels of a shot. An earlier couplet of audience conversations – 'how did they do that?' / 'that was so unrealistic' – is heard less frequently in the age of digital editing. Whereas such 'nasties' as *Absurd* (1981) and *Tenebrae* (1982) relied heavily on visual effects shots, such as dismembering prosthetic devices in camera, recent releases combine visual effects with digital clean-up: watch, if you dare, the notorious scene in Gaspar Noé's *Irreversible* (2002) where a character's head is pulped using a fire extinguisher. That the new 'nasties' are characterised by high production values allows for promotion in terms of authenticity and verisimilitude too, hence the marketing of *The Human Centipede: First Segment* as '100% medically accurate'.[3] In short, imagining torture porn to be a distinctive subgenre makes sense to the casual observer accumulating information from reviews and promotional copy, but the same exercise fails accurately to capture much about the movies in their own terms – not least why they coincided with the war on terror.

So far this chapter has emphasised the way that the perception of a tidal wave of torture porn has developed almost independently of the films themselves. Yet it would be foolish to deny either their profitability or their incorporation into the mainstream. Leading the way was the *Saw* franchise, of which a new instalment typically arrives on 31 October each year, culminating in *Saw 3D* (its immediate predecessor was treated as evidence of the subgenre's decline because it *failed* to top the box office on release).[4] *Hostel 2* was less successful commercially than its predecessor, after a leaked work-print was downloaded on a huge scale. (It was also the basis for a pirate DVD which, ironically, toned down the gore as it was stolen prior to the insertion of certain digital effects.)

The gorno phenomenon is also unsettling to those with memories of the 1980s video nasties panic (Thompson 1998: 102-10), which resulted in numerous convictions under criminal law and the eventual passage of the Video Recordings Act (1984). Legislators were shown compilations of (out-of-context) dismemberments from a selection of the 70+ videos that made it onto the Director of Public Prosecutions' list. In contrast, today's individual releases often bring high production values to equivalent content and all but the most extreme examples of the genre seem to enjoy a smooth relationship with local government and the British Board of Film Classification. Whereas conflict with the authorities gave the 1980s video nasties an anti-establishment aura, so-called torture porn has settled into a cosy pattern of peaceful coexistence with the multiplex, DVD retailers and, eventually, with terrestrial broadcasters too.

Rather than succumbing to official regulatory pressure, it is likely that the subgenre will exhaust itself. Some locate this bleak future in the self-defeating nature of realistic-looking scenes of prolonged torture, coupled with a willingness to 'push boundaries'. Once audiences have seen 'newborn porn' (*A Serbian Film*, 2010) or a character's mouth being surgically attached to another's alimentary canal (*Human Centipede*), it does suggest there are few other levels of degradation to which to sink. Newman also notes the twin scripting weaknesses of (a) shallow characterisation not allowing audiences to care about who is tied to a chair, and (b) how keeping the victim tied to a chair could increase audience boredom rather than adrenaline levels.

In purely cinematic terms, so-called torture porn cannot accurately be called a film genre in its own right. As argued above, the comparatively small number of films plotted solely around simulated restraint and torture means that the genre tag is mainly being used as an umbrella term for things critics *dislike*. Continuity with the US horror film tradition, coupled with borrowing from European and South East Asian 'extreme' cinema, also undermines claims to distinctiveness, even before we consider the often formulaic content of the films themselves.

Having considered the generic qualities of torture porn, we now turn its relationship with society. If the horror movie is indeed a cinematic home for developing a veiled critique of society, what exactly is a film like *Hostel 2* trying to say? 'Nothing at all' could seem like an adequate answer. Throughout the recent history of British panics about film violence – 1980s video nasties, *Child's Play 3* (1991), 1990s new-brutalism and more recent, Internet-based 'shock video' – the word 'gratuitous' crops up repeatedly. Its rhetorical currency in these moral panics makes me reluctant to use it here, yet it seems an appropriate term when dealing with films that appear to show torture for its own sake – typically with no direct function in the development of the plot. However, in the absence of an actual moral panic about torture porn, critics of moral panics can be relaxed about using the description 'gratuitous'. If there are few cinematic justifications for such films, their disconnection from society appears equally obvious: torture porn is an example of the horror genre having lost its social bite.

With promotion and marketing emphasising (unofficial) military endorsements, is the early 21st Century horror film becoming a mouthpiece of Empire? Mapping the industry-wide changes lets us, at the very least, identify emergent trends in the genre, but to what extent to these tendencies articulate changes in society? Would it be safe to say it is 'no coincidence' that a super-concentrated cycle of terrifying torture movies emerged during a decade characterised by a 'global war on terror'? To this we now turn.

Two related discourses link the perceived emergence of torture porn to the war on terror. In the first of these, the Bush administration's early public explanation for the 9/11 attacks – popularised in the question 'why do they hate us?' – seemed to overlap with the central question of the 'ordeal' movie: 'why are you doing this to me?'. Both questions imply the absence of a rational motive; on screen and on the world stage, those responsible are merely 'evil-doers'. Casting 'terror' as the enemy meant it existed solely to create hurt and outrage, in defiance of common sense, bringing to mind Joseph Conrad's portrayal of the nihilist Professor planning to destroy Greenwich Observatory: without actually 'throwing a bomb into pure mathematics', how else would one destroy utterly 'the fitness of things'? (1993: 36). Although similar to Conrad's semi-politically minded bombers, perceptions of post-9/11 terrorists aligned them to a new type of cinematic torturer, who did evil things without the narrative props of supernatural assistance or a 1960s-style 'psychosis'. The terrorist acting without a discernible motive found symmetry in on-screen tormentors who simply enjoy their illicit and murderous activities.

Yet at the same time, these dehumanising trends shed light on wider concerns. Fictional antagonists such as *Hostel*'s 'Elite Hunting Group' sacrifice human empathy and solidarity while visiting destruction on the bodies of their victims (Murray 2008). Without wanting to labour the point, the plot descriptions derived from torture porn sometimes resonated with the wider reaction to 'extraordinary rendition' and Abu Ghraib. Writing of the treatment of 'enemy non-combatants', the late Daniel Bensaïd described a process where the enemy 'loses his quality of enemy to fall under the category of the monster. There is a short step from the symbolic bestialization of the enemy to his practical animalization' (cited in Callinicos 2003: 41). If the conduct of the global war on terror appeared inhumane and sadistic, it informed a frame of reference for discussing inhumane and sadistic images on screen, and vice versa.

Certain critics of US foreign policy have seized on these overlapping themes to criticise the politics of torture porn (or *Hostel* specifically). For Jason Middleton (2010), the dynamic appears essentially racialised, pitting good-looking Americans against slimy Euro-trash sadists, for example. 'It's not so much new meaning that this film gives to European anti-Americanism...but new mechanisms of implementation', complained another pundit (Hibbs 2006). (Similar criticisms were aired regarding *Paradise Lost/Turistas* (2006), in which a Brazilian organ-harvesting ring menaces young Anglophone tourists.) Objections to their allegedly chauvinistic outlook provide a political flipside to speculation that these films somehow double up as training videos for abusive guards at Abu Ghraib (for example, Sarracino and Scott 2008: 162-4). Even Christopher Tookey, writing in the *Daily Mail* (hardly an anti-imperialist newspaper), claims that the 'politically aware may find discomforting parallels with the Americans' reprisals against "terrorists" in Abu Ghraib and Guantanamo...it could be argued that we are currently witnessing the effects of that culture in the Middle East' (2006).

Crucially, there seems to be a tension emerging between the description of the new form of screen violence – gratuitous and inexplicable – and the assessment of its (harmful) public role. One explanation for this divergence concerns dramatising fiction itself. Just as 90 minutes of restraint and torture offers limited narrative possibilities, it also improves the image of those productions where torture scenes are a fully integrated part of the storyline. The notion that *Hostel* serves as an advertisement for state torture makes little logical sense, when contrasted to the routine use of torture in mainstream fare such as *24* and *Unthinkable* (2010). Alan Dershowitz's so-called 'ticking bomb scenario', where a necessary moral compromise means that information can be extracted under duress in order to save lives (Dershowitz 2002), features in a growing number of film and television storylines. As Slavoj Žižek (2006) has noted, it would seem that 'extraordinary rendition' carried out by the liberal, humane Jack Bauer exposes a greater depravity then that of a self-consciously evil person. Edelstein's seminal feature article makes this explicit:

> Post-9/11, we've engaged in a national debate about the morality of torture, fuelled by horrifying pictures of manifestly decent men and women (some of them, anyway) enacting brutal scenarios of domination at Abu Ghraib. And a large segment of the population evidently has no problem with this. Our righteousness is buoyed by propaganda like the TV series *24*, which devoted an entire season to justifying torture in the name of an imminent threat: a nuclear missile en route to a major city. Who do you want defending America? Kiefer Sutherland or terrorist-employed civil-liberties lawyers?
>
> (Edelstein 2006)

By the same logic, the torture which is integrated into an unfolding storyline dramatising the need for tough choices could be read as a more persuasive piece of torture advocacy than 'torture for its own sake'. In contrast, it is my contention that the seemingly aimless quality of the violence within the gorno genre that actually demonstrates its historically specific origins in the post-9/11 world.

It would be simplistic to say that the war on terror has somehow directly 'determined' the existence of torture porn. Rather, torture porn has taken shape in a social context where various publics – film critics, movie buffs, casual consumers of cinema – could be forgiven for holding the *a priori* assumption that such a thing was routine. Its place in our imaginations draws strength from the way that, as Joel Best argues, 'claims about different problems are connected through the great inventory of cultural resources available for talking about social problems':

> All manner of imagery can be borrowed by advocates trying to give shape to a new problem or policy...the choice of resources is patterned, not random: particular advocates favour particular imagery at particular times and in particular places. Advocates...emerge in specific historical and geographic contexts, and develop characteristic ways of thinking about new social problems.
>
> (Best 1999: 164-5)

Almost independently of the films themselves, the very idea of such materials acts as a metric for gauging our broader unease with society. In other words, it is not so much that the artistic developments taking place in gorno reflect social problems, but more that society can take the opportunity to give some fixity to its unease via such screen representations.

While a comparatively slow film industry was financing the first, low-budget gorno productions, all manner of video content was being uploaded to the Internet. Home broadband and more powerful computers, coupled with the falling price of basic digital video cameras, increased the technical possibilities; changing attitudes towards privacy and on-screen humiliation supplied points of reference for what was to come next. The label 'shock video' was applied to various clips that acquired a combination of thousands of hits and instant notoriety, ranging from fetish pornography ('2 Girls, 1 Cup', which spawned hundreds of 'reaction videos') to 'happy slapping' to combat footage. Hard evidence with which to assess these developments was overshadowed by a palpable sense that voyeurism was out of control. In such conditions, the relationship between shock video and the war on terror is a vexed one. Images acquired by allied soldiers from assorted combat zones have been uploaded onto the Internet, for instance on the website nowthatsfuckedup.com (February 2004-April 2006), which operated a 'bodies for porn' exchange scheme. Trophy-style pictures of humiliated prisoners (echoing Abu Ghraib) and posed corpses (in the style of the discredited 5th Stryker Combat Brigade, 2nd Infantry Division) proliferated, undermining US moral authority. For some pundits, linking images of degradation to a narrative of cultural decadence was hard to square with *a priori* support for their 'own' troops, whereas connecting debased conduct to the entertainment industry was, if nothing else, familiar territory.

Groping around to impose meaning on the post-9/11 world magnified the sense that *Hostel* and other films of its ilk were in some way representative of the times. Yet if they are neither as widespread nor as aggressively militaristic as their reputation suggests, what do they represent? For me, questions of motive are important if not central. When faced with the allegation that torture porn is 'gratuitous', agreement is the best form of defence. While some would point to an underlying anti-violence critique (for example, Hilden 2007), or mount an artistic case for the content of such movies, the fact remains that the genre – as it is understood, as opposed to the content of some of the actual films – hinges on acts of abuse for the gratification of the torturer. A rational motive for the violence is largely absent. Concurrently, this gives shape on-screen to an otherwise nameless, amorphous threat. Thus perceptions of torture porn as a phenomenon take hold because they hook into wider anxieties. In contrast, the deliberate, plot-driven use of fictional torture on a show like *24* is far easier to see as playing a persuasive role in support of these activities in and around the theatre of war and the penal system. Real 'evil-doers' attacked the United States and, before long, their fictional counterparts would inflict pain for kicks on screen.

Of course, the Bush Administration's emphasis on 'evil-doers' incorporated a crude denial that anyone might have a legitimate grievance with US foreign policy. Dislike of Bush could encourage his critics to look for traits in Al-Qaeda resembling those of a national liberation movement. A cursory look at Al-Qaeda's nihilistic ideology and opportunism would soon put paid to such illusions; comparisons with its 'closest precursors...revolutionary anarchists of late nineteenth-century Europe' (Gray 2003: 2) are more instructive, hence also the quotation from Joseph Conrad used above. If the nihilistic torturer cuts a threatening figure in the entertainment industry today, his plausibility is increased by the equally arbitrary moral make-up of the modern terrorist. Both join the constellation of unpredictable threats which Best (1999) shows to be constructed as 'random violence' in the wider imagination.

The vacuous qualities of the torture porn genre correspond to the emptiness of the contemporary terrorist, who combines spectacular acts of violence with nebulous political objectives. Yet both find symmetry in the global war on terror itself. This can be seen in the scandal-ridden US conduct of extraordinary rendition and the drifting, open-ended detention of dozens of 'enemy non-combatants'. As David Chandler argues:

> it would appear that the much publicised abuses of the war on terror stem from the western inability to cohere a clear view of who the enemy is or how they should be treated....It would appear that global war is a product of social dislocation and disconnection rather than the expression of new universalising hegemony fighting a war of annihilation against alternative ways of life.

(Chandler 2009: 181-2)

In a directionless pattern of drift, we see the components being sutured together like the Human Centipede: motiveless, nihilistic terrorists, a state machine that has lost the plot, and unstable, fearful social mores. Joined together, they inform a context in which the motiveless torturer on screen becomes an appropriate antihero for our times.

Notes

[1] In the early drafts of this chapter, I could identify at most two dozen such pictures, a small proportion of those discussed by Newman (2011), who has since stated that the growth of direct-to-DVD torture porn indicates its emerging commercial decline.

[2] In the same period, both the resurgence of (teenage) vampire films and the depiction of fast-moving zombies provoked similar fan-based complaints.

[3] Conversely, some directors present themselves as defiantly old-school, with *Saw 3* managing its transitions through a series of *visual* effects shots.

[4] Further evidence of the mainstreaming of *Saw* can be seen in the *Saw* rollercoaster at Thorpe Park, a major UK theme park (for the uninitiated, this roughly equates to a Six Flags establishment, with the more lucrative Alton Towers in the 'British Disneyland' role).

Chapter 8

Alien Terrorists: Public Discourse on 9/11 and the American Science Fiction Film

Michael C. Frank

I

At the beginning of October 2001, a little less than a month after the terrorist attacks on New York City and Washington, DC, the news broke that 'government intelligence specialists ha[d] been secretly soliciting terrorist scenarios from top Hollywood filmmakers and writers.' In several meetings held at the University of Southern California's Institute for Creative Technologies – a research institute founded in 1999 to develop virtual environment training software for US soldiers – army officials sought the imaginative expertise of a varied group of people, none of whom had any specialised knowledge of either Middle Eastern history or the strategies and ideologies of Islamist terrorism. Among the participants were screenwriter Steven E. de Souza, of *Die Hard* fame, as well as B-movie director Joseph Zito, whose works include the Chuck Norris vehicles *Delta Force One* and *Invasion USA*. According to a brief report published by *Variety*, the official aim of the meetings, which involved teleconferences with the Pentagon, was 'to brainstorm about possible terrorist targets and schemes in America and to offer solutions to those threats' (Brodesser 2001).

On one level, the US government's recourse to the creative powers of Hollywood constitutes a particularly striking example of what social anthropologist Joseba Zulaika (2009: 2) has described as the 'crisis of knowledge' in counterterrorism. For Zulaika, the shortcomings of counterterrorism stem from the self-referentiality of its discourse, which is predicated on a 'faulty epistemology – beginning with the placement of the entire phenomenon [of terrorism] in a context of taboo and the willful ignorance of the political subjectivities of the terrorists' (Zulaika 2009: 2; see also Zulaika and Douglass 1996). From such a perspective, the decision to generate possible threat scenarios with the help of members of the film entertainment industry may be taken to indicate a reluctance to engage with the real circumstances of terrorism – the political, cultural, and ideological factors that constitute the root of the problem. At any rate, the secret meetings at USC illustrate the point made by sociologist Frank Furedi that after 11 September 2001, '[i]magining evil [was] presented as the medium through which understanding of the terrorist threat may be gained' (Furedi 2007: xxvi). Citing the *9/11 Commission Report* as the most salient example, Furedi demonstrates that the limitations of counterterrorist intelligence were frequently described 'as a problem of imagination rather than of information' (2007: xxiv). Consequently, imaginative speculation soon became an official means of complementing – and, if necessary, substituting for – observation and analysis, making the line between fact and fiction increasingly difficult to draw.

Read at another level, the idea of tapping into the creativity of screenwriters and directors seems like a logical consequence of the common notion that the attacks themselves appeared to have sprung from Hollywood films. Statements to the effect that the events in New York seemed 'like a movie' may be found in countless eyewitness accounts, and the cinematic analogy was immediately taken up by journalists, writers, and scholars. Always quick off the mark, Slavoj Žižek and Jean Baudrillard were among the first internationally renowned theorists to bring their particular approaches to bear on the events of 9/11. As different as their essays were, they both addressed the resemblances between the New York disaster and earlier fictional movie scenarios in an attempt to explain the *'jouissance'* (Žižek 2002: 12) afforded by the images of the collapsing Twin Towers.[1] Despite their different emphases and conclusions, these and many other commentaries have at least one thing in common: they are based on the unquestioned assumption that the (real) happenings of 11 September were so similar to (fictional) filmic images that this uncanny correspondence must be considered one of the essential characteristics of the event.

This chapter asks how and for what reasons Hollywood movies have so persistently served as a frame of reference for representations of 9/11. In doing so, it does not seek to provide another confirmation of the common understanding that 9/11 had an inherently – and disturbingly – cinematic quality. On the contrary, it starts from the assumption that the Hollywood analogy is not as self-evident as may be supposed at first sight. Bernd Scheffer reminds us that 'although seeming identities, or at least striking similarities between Hollywood movies and real events in the USA...do exist, a closer look will reveal no real and especially no complete agreement, only some misleading, albeit frequent, superficial likenesses' (Scheffer 2003). While Scheffer mainly thinks of differences in content, formal discrepancies are just as significant. Geoff King persuasively argues that the images shown in the early phases of the 11 September broadcast news coverage contained several 'modality markers' that clearly framed them as a '"breaking" live news event', most importantly, the quality and quantity of the available images (King 2005). The cinematic analogy, then, was not simply 'there'. Rather, it was the result of a particular perception of the event. While spontaneous references to Hollywood movies among witnesses on the scene of the disaster are one thing, the perpetuation of the cinematic analogy in the weeks, months, and years after the event is quite another. As I shall argue, it may best be understood with reference to a larger discourse, which is responsible for a specific conception of the attacks, their perpetrators, and Islamist terrorism in general, a conception to which the consideration of 9/11 through the prism of Western mainstream cinema has contributed its share.

The following discussion is indebted to the field of Critical Terrorism Studies inaugurated by political scientist Richard Jackson (Jackson 2005; Jackson, Breen Smyth and Grunning 2009). In his 2005 study *Writing the War on*

Terrorism, Jackson reads post-9/11 statements by members of the Bush Administration as part of a political narrative created to generate public support for an unprecedented counterterrorist campaign – both at home (the USA Patriot Act and its incursions into civil rights) and abroad (the various battlefields of the war on terrorism). Such measures, Jackson argues, require a large degree of consensus. The war on terrorism, therefore, had to be normalised – something that the discourse installed by the Bush administration achieved to great effect. According to Jackson, the most important features of this discourse are the interpretation of the terrorist attacks as an 'act of war' necessitating a military response, the legitimisation of this response as a battle between good versus evil (and, hence, a just war), as well as the ensuing demonisation and dehumanisation of the enemy. Jackson also emphasises the exaggeration of the threat of terrorism and the idea of an entirely new kind of war, to which old rules no longer apply. This war, one may add, is represented not as a clash of civilisations (in the plural), but as a clash between civilisation (in the singular) and anti-civilisation, a global conflict in which people of all freedom-loving nations stand together against those who have perverted their faith out of sheer hatred for Western democratic values and ways of life. Excluded from this dominant narrative are explanations implicating American foreign policy, an effect reinforced by the positioning of 9/11 as a radical rupture (see Jarvis 2008), which separates the event from its roots in earlier political conflicts and thus entails a de-historicisation.

Against this backdrop, the following discussion will focus on the role of one particular film genre in the representation of 9/11: science fiction. When witnesses on the scene of the attacks in Manhattan stated that the event had seemed 'like a movie', Roland Emmerich's *Independence Day* was among the most frequently mentioned films. The perceived analogy between the incidents of 9/11 and the alien invasion genre not only concerned the affected targets – American landmark buildings – but also the perpetrators, whose 'alienness' was greatly emphasised by the Bush administration. Considering the discourse-historical trajectory of the 'alien terrorist' metaphor, it seems significant that one of the first high-budget Hollywood productions that was explicitly marketed as a post-9/11 film chose the alien invasion genre to reflect the anxieties of present-day America: before the release of *War of the Worlds* (2005), Steven Spielberg and his screenwriters repeatedly underlined that their adaptation of H.G. Wells's novel was a deliberate evocation of the New York City attacks. Taking this kind of allegorisation for granted entails the risk of ignoring the significant political implications involved in such a representation of the event. It is these implications that the present chapter will attempt to demonstrate.

II

'The building began to disintegrate', Wall Street analyst Ron Insana reported one hour after having seen the south tower of the World Trade Center collapse, his clothes still covered in dust: 'And we heard it and looked up and started to see elements of the building coming down and we ran. And honestly, it was like a scene out of *Independence Day*' (quoted in Monahan 2010: 60). CNBC financial expert Insana was only one of numerous witnesses on the scene of the 11 September 2001 attacks who drew on disaster and science fiction movies to describe their impressions. References to such blockbusters were so remarkably frequent that they almost immediately prompted responses from critics, scholars, and members of the film business.

Among the issues addressed by the earliest discussions of the phenomenon was the question of how it was possible that the worst terrorist incident in history had elicited so many references to shallow entertainments, even among people who had followed events in 'unmediated' form (that is, unframed by television screens and unaccompanied by movie poster-like captions such as 'America Under Attack'). *New York Times* writer Michiko Kakutani was one of the first commentators to attempt an explanation. In an article published on 13 September, she argued that the recourse to cinema offered a means of coping with an otherwise incomprehensible occurrence: 'It may seem trivializing – even obscene – to talk about movies in the same breath as this week's tragedy, but the fact that so many people did was a symptom of our inability to get our minds around this disaster, our inability to find real-life precedents, real-life analogies for what happened in the morning hours of Sept. 11' (Kakutani 2001). According to this line of argument, Hollywood's rich repertoire of images provided a readily accessible frame of reference to process and to communicate an experience for which no analogy existed in the historical memory of the American nation. 'Is this method of pop cultural compensation a bad thing?' cultural critic Bernie Heidkamp asked himself on the day of the event; and he replied with another rhetorical question: 'Is there any other way for us to begin to grasp – or describe – the enormity of the attacks? Ours is, after all, a country that has not been damaged, in our lifetime, by war or natural catastrophe on the level we are now witnessing' (Heidkamp 2001).

While this suggests a successful assimilation of the event, a coming to terms *with* it by finding terms *for* it, other commentators emphasised that references to Hollywood films were often accompanied by expressions of disbelief. Among the witnesses who made statements to this effect was an unidentified woman in New York: 'This is very surreal. Well, it's out of a bad sci-fi film, but every morning we wake up and you're like it wasn't a dream. It actually happened' (quoted in Nacos 2002: 35). For Richard Jackson, such statements testify to a 'deep confusion and a genuine sense of epistemic anxiety', caused by 'the blurring of the lines between the virtual and the real world' (2005: 30). This would contradict the more optimistic approach according to which cinematic analogies gave shocked and bewildered witnesses cognitive support (and hence relief), suggesting instead that the perceived correspondences were an essential part of the *horror* of the situation. If this is correct, then the uncanny effects were certainly increased by the fact that, of all cinematic forms, it was the most outrageous science fiction that came closest to the reality of 9/11.

In 1996, gigantic saucer-shaped spacecraft hovering above American landmark buildings signalled the return of the alien invader to the cinema screen. Despite its stereotypical characterisation, questionable plot turns, and undisguised jingoism, Roland Emmerich's heavily marketed *Independence Day* became the highest-grossing film of the year. Strongly derivative in nature, it uses elements of several classic B-movies. From the George Pal-produced *The War of the Worlds* (1953), it borrows the device (originating in Wells's novel) of making the otherwise invincible invaders susceptible to infection – though in this case, it is a computer virus rather than bacteria that vanquishes the aliens. Even more notable is a reference to a lesser-known classic of the alien-invasion genre, Fred F. Sears's *Earth vs. the Flying Saucers* (1956). During that film's climactic battle scene – graced by Ray Harryhausen's pioneering stop-motion animation – the aliens fire their ray guns and crash their saucers into several symbols of democracy in Washington, DC, including the Capitol dome. *Independence Day* transformed this groundbreaking sequence into the simultaneous attack on three American cities, each time beginning with the destruction of one iconic edifice. The explosion of the White House in particular has left a lasting imprint on the cinematic memory, not least because it was featured in the film's famous teaser trailer, first shown – to great effect – during the Superbowl.

Independence Day was the first in a whole series of science fiction films that combined 1950s plot elements with post-*Jurassic Park* digital wonders: *Deep Impact*, *Godzilla*, and *Armageddon*, all of which premiered in 1998, equally borrowed their premises from 1950s models, using updated versions of familiar plots as vehicles for state-of-the-art special effects. The close of the twentieth century thus saw the revival of three seemingly obsolete science fiction subgenres, which had previously been linked by film historians to specific Cold War interests and concerns: the alien invasion film, the monster movie (or creature feature), and the end-of-the-world picture. All three share a strong emphasis on the theme of urban disaster. In what remains one of the most perceptive studies of the topic, Susan Sontag recognised as early as 1961 that 'the science fiction film...is concerned with the aesthetics of destruction, with the peculiar beauties to be found in wreaking havoc, making a mess' (Sontag 1967: 213). The late-1990s representatives of the genre renewed and reinforced that motif, showing a conspicuous preference for downtown New York and its iconic structures. Again and again, the Empire State Building, the Chrysler building, and the towers of the World Trade Center were either severely damaged or completely demolished, burying streets, cars, and people beneath them. In a tacit competition among studios over the most jaw-dropping devastation scene, every film attempted to outdo its predecessors in the sheer magnitude of the destruction displayed – and in the technological sophistication of its visual effects.

If the 2001 attacks on the World Trade Center and the Pentagon put a – temporary – end to this competition, they did so by apparently following a very similar logic of outbidding. As film critic Neal Gabler wrote a few days after 9/11:

> In a sense, this was the terrorists' own real-life disaster movie – bigger than 'Independence Day' or 'Godzilla' or 'Armageddon', and in the bizarre competition among terrorists, bigger even than Timothy J. McVeigh's own real-life horror film in Oklahoma City, heretofore the standard. You have to believe at some level it was their rebuff to Hollywood as well as their triumph over it – they could out-Hollywood Hollywood.
>
> (Gabler 2001)

Three years previously, Gabler had set out to demonstrate in *Life: The Movie* 'how entertainment conquered reality', putting forth the thesis that Americans increasingly perceive and fashion the world according to the familiar patterns of movie entertainment (Gabler 1998). His own statement on the 11 September attacks could be taken as an illustration of this thesis: while viewing the event through the lens of Hollywood 'entertainment', Gabler does not consider the possibility that there may be a more multi-faceted 'reality' beyond his necessarily limited vision. Since they are so obvious to him, he assumes – or rather postulates – that the filmic analogies were meticulously planned by the attackers and their co-conspirators in all their dramatic detail (although the terrible outcome of the plane crashes, the unprecedented collapse of two entire skyscrapers, could hardly have been foreseen and had not apparently been part of the plan). What Gabler disregards is that all inferences in this matter can only be tentative: film critics who can authoritatively discuss cinematic analogies to 9/11 cannot automatically claim insight into the minds of those who devised and executed the attacks.

Interestingly, even authors who are more qualified to make such assertions have come to the conclusion that the filmic dimension of 9/11 was deliberately achieved. In his February 2002 essay 'Roots of Terror', German-Iranian writer and Islamic scholar Navid Kermani argues that the ideological basis of the attacks drew from various heterogeneous sources, Islamic as well as non-Islamic. He describes the terrorists' agenda as 'a mixture incorporating anti-capitalism, the cult of martyrdom, Third World rhetoric, totalitarian ideology and science fiction'. Although he only incidentally touches upon the topic, Kermani too conjectures that the corresponding 'tales of science fiction' were 'probably familiar to the attackers' (Kermani 2002). Following from there, Albrecht Koschorke calls for a 'political analysis of the images of September 11', adding that 'despite all the analyses that have been accomplished in the meantime', such an investigation 'still has to allow itself to be unsettled by the fact that Islamic terror and Hollywood could meet in exactly the same symbolic field' (Koschorke 2005: 96, my translation). One part of this field, according to Koschorke, consists of shared traditions of anti-urbanism (see Koschorke 2005: 99-101). It would be too short-sighted, though, to consider the cinematic destruction of metropolises only in terms of latent hostility to cities and their lifestyles. For such scenes greatly contributed to the symbolic over-determination and fetishisation of American cityscapes by directing viewers' attention again and again to particular landmarks of economic and political power. In this sense at least, there can be little doubt that there is indeed a connection between Hollywood film and the attacks of 11 September 2001. For, as Heidkamp noted on the day of the attacks, 'it is, in part, the pop cultural representations that have made buildings such as the World Trade Center and the Pentagon iconic symbols of America' (2001).

III

Significantly, however, the cinematic analogy was not only applied to the *targets* of the attacks and the *scene* of the disaster, but also to the *hijackers* themselves, even if this latter dimension of the analogy was not always as obvious as the former. As David Simpson remarks at the beginning of his study *9/11: The Culture of Commemoration*, the events of that day 'looked to many of us...like the work of agents so unfamiliar as to seem almost like aliens' (2006: 6). It was precisely in this sense that the attacks and their perpetrators were represented in official discourse. In their early public declarations, President Bush and his administration strongly reinforced the impression of 'alienness' by emphasising the radical alterity of the attackers. Jackson has meticulously reconstructed the various tropes used by government officials to describe the terrorists. As he demonstrates, the opponents in the 'war on terrorism' were conceived as evil and inhuman barbarians, leading a parasitical existence and being driven by an irrational hatred for 'civilisation', that is, Western democratic freedoms as epitomised by American society (Jackson 2005). Most relevant for the present discussion, the cinematic analogy soon extended to the domain of real politics, both in the construction of the enemy and in the political narratives that accompanied the war on terrorism.

There is general agreement among film historians that American science fiction subgenres such as the alien invasion film 'became popular entertainment during crisis moments' (Matthews 2007: 3). It is not difficult to establish such a connection for the first boom of the genre in the 1950s: the anti-Communist hysteria fuelled by Senator Joseph McCarthy's 'witch-hunts' and the omnipresent nuclear threat make it plausible to explain early Cold War scenarios of alien invasion with reference to contemporary fears (see, for example, Biskind 1983: 101-59). In this context, the anthropomorphic alien functioned as an allegorical substitute for real-life foes. But how are we to explain the fact that, after a relative absence of more than twenty years, the figure of the evil space invader came back just in time for the turn of the millennium? In a pre-9/11 study on the topic, Markus Koch considers 1990s alien invasion films as a response to the fundamentally changed geopolitical situation after the end of the Cold War, when political and cultural boundaries had to be newly defined and demarcated (see Koch 2002). *Independence Day*, he argues, resonated with the vision of a 'new world order' – a vision made famous by George H.W. Bush on 11 September 1990, after the Iraqi invasion of Kuwait, when the American president called for all nations of the earth to defend their interest in Persian Gulf oil together (Bush 1990). Emmerich's film takes this vision one step further by making Iraqi fighter pilots part of the force assembled to battle the aliens. The scene in the Iraqi desert in which British, Israeli, and Iraqi troops await American commands presents a *new* new world order – in which all mankind is united against an entirely different type of foe.

Accordingly, Koschorke suggests that films such as *Independence Day* have to be read as reflections of a 'political imaginary', through which America projected enemy figures and adjusted itself to a new, yet undefined threat. Emmerich's film, he argues, indicates that 'long before the [9/11] attacks, this country had been preparing itself for a faceless enemy, and that is to say: for a discourse of total othering' (Koschorke 2004: 104, my translation). In a sense, this 'faceless enemy' materialised on 9/11. The foreignness and alterity of the terrorists and their supporters were immediately underlined in political and legal discourse. On 29 October 2001, three days after he had signed into law the USA Patriot Act, President George W. Bush directed the establishment of a Foreign Terrorist Tracking Task Force, which was to consist of members of various federal agencies and be headed by the Attorney General (see US Department of Homeland Security 2001). Two days later, Attorney General John Ashcroft informed the American public about his Department's preparations in this matter: '[A]s September the 11th vividly illustrates', he declared, 'aliens also come to our country with the intent to do great evil' (US Department of Justice 2001). While reading Ashcroft's speech, one cannot help noticing that, although the phrase used in the title of the task force is 'foreign terrorist', Ashcroft chooses the word 'alien' whenever he speaks of foreigners who threaten domestic security. The word appears no less than 23 times in the short text.

As legal scholar David Cole has demonstrated in his important book on the subject, 'terrorist alien' is the latest variation of the legal category of the 'enemy alien', whose genealogy can be traced to the time of the French Revolution (Cole 2003). At the outset of the undeclared naval war between the USA and France in the years 1798-1800, Federalist-controlled Congress passed a series of four laws designed to prevent 'alien' radicalism from spreading over to the United States and infecting the polity there. The fourth of these laws determined that in cases of war, 'all natives, citizens, denizens, or subjects of the hostile nation or government, being males of the age of fourteen years and upwards, shall be liable to be apprehended, restrained, secured and removed, as alien enemies' – for the sole reason of their nationality. Known as the Alien Enemies Act, this law is still in effect today (as Chapter 3 of Title 50 of the United States Code). It has repeatedly been invoked during wartime, most notoriously during World War Two: after the attack on Pearl Harbor in 1941, the category of the 'enemy alien' was extended to encompass all people of Japanese descent, including those who had already been naturalised, leading to mass internment of Japanese nationals as well as Japanese-Americans on purely ethnic grounds (Cole 2003: 91-100). In a parallel development, the category of the 'enemy alien' was redefined in such a way that it could also be applied in peacetime. This practice began after the anarchist bombings of 1919, during the so-called Palmer Raids, when thousands of suspected 'alien radicals' were arrested and hundreds were deported (Cole 2003: 116-28). Cole mentions this and other controversial episodes in American legal history to make the point that the double standard implied in laws aimed exclusively at non-citizens is inconsistent with – and, indeed, a danger to – America's fundamental constitutional principles.

For Cole, the fact that detention and deportation have repeatedly been used against 'enemy aliens' is related to a long and persistent tradition of American nativism (2003: 90). As Richard Jackson emphasises, however, John Ashcroft's scenario of aliens 'com[ing] to our country with the intent to do great evil' does more than evoke xenophobic responses: it exploits the unavoidable ambiguity of the term 'alien' (Jackson 2005: 71). This ambiguity has also been noticed by self-styled 'video-remixer' TV Sheriff, who used it for comic effect in a short clip released on YouTube (see TV Sheriff Channel 2006) and later included on the artist's first DVD. Leaving Ashcroft's statement unchanged, TV Sheriff modified the caption to 'America's New War: Ashcroft announces new measures against alien spacepeople' and added appropriate illustrations of various extraterrestrials – supposedly showing the different types of 'aliens' mentioned by the Attorney General. This satirical response seems to corroborate Jackson's contention that:

> American officials cannot use the term 'alien' without their listeners recalling – at least at a subconscious level – hundreds of movies, television programmes, comics, novels and radio broadcasts (such as *War of the Worlds*) where space aliens attacked, invaded or subverted society from within. In a society immersed in the movie mythology of *Invasion of the Body Snatchers*, *Alien*, *Predator*, *Independence Day* and *The X-Files*, the meaning of the term 'alien terrorist' oscillates between 'extra-terrestrial parasite' and 'foreign enemy' without any sense of the absurd.
>
> (Jackson 2005: 71)

The most important aspect of the political narrativisation of the 11 September attacks was their interpretation as acts of war rather than crimes that could be prosecuted within the framework of international law. Some film critics have contended that this interpretation was not simply imposed upon the American public by pro-war propaganda (as Jackson seems to suggest), but that there was a general disposition to accept the readings offered by Bush, Ashcroft, and other government officials. In the words of one critic, it was 'American blockbuster movies [that] laid the groundwork for the public's response to the event as the beginning of war' (Bell-Metereau 2003: 143-4). This would imply that the interpretation of 9/11 in terms of conventional warfare followed the logic of an already established cinematic analogy – and that the narrative pattern was thus predefined.

What is certain, in any case, is that the official responses to the attacks reinforced the perceived cinematic analogy (whether deliberately or not) and that the cinematographic subtext remained an essential part of how the war on terrorism was represented. From a discourse analytical perspective, the alien invasion motif seems particularly well suited for post-9/11 counterterrorism discourse, and it is therefore not surprising that it has been incorporated – in various ways – into the different narratives developed to create support for the government's measures. Sontag's reflections on early Cold War science fiction are once more instructive here. 'Again and again', she writes in her 1961 essay, 'one detects [in these films] the hunger for a "good war," which poses no moral problems, admits of no moral qualifications' (Sontag 1967: 219). In Byron Haskin's *The War of the Worlds* (1953), the prototypical alien invasion film, America is attacked on its own soil, without provocation and without forewarning, by a faceless enemy who wreaks havoc on defenceless civilians. Against such an antagonist, all military measures are permissible. The US Army may even drop an 'A-bomb', less than ten years after Hiroshima. Whereas the genre's 'ur-text', Wells's Victorian novel *The War of the Worlds*, compared the Martian incursion with the extermination of the native Tasmanians (see Wells 2005: 9), casting the aliens as a distorted mirror image of European industrial powers in the period of high imperialism, most alien invasion films are unequivocal about the absolute otherness of the antagonist. As director Paul

Verhoeven succinctly phrased it, 'Alien sci-fi films give us a terrifying enemy that's politically correct. They're bad. They're evil. And they're not even human' (quoted in Corliss 1996). Accordingly, there is no doubt in these films about the legitimacy of retaliation.

In *Independence Day*, US President Thomas Whitmore – a former Gulf War pilot – initially refuses to resort to the atomic option. He soon realises, however, that all attempts at diplomacy fall on deaf ears. Connecting itself to the body of a murdered scientist to express itself in human language, a captured alien categorically rejects the President's peace offer. When asked 'What is it you want us to do?', it twice replies 'Die.' At this point, communication continues in telepathic – and hence inaudible – form, as the alien forcefully enters the President's mind. Like the characters in the film, the viewer depends entirely on the reliability of the President, who offers the following summary of his insights:

> I saw his thoughts. I saw what they're planning to do. They're like locusts. They're moving from planet to planet. Their whole civilisation. After they've consumed every natural resource they move on. And we're next.

Following this epiphanic realisation, the President loses his scruples concerning the use of nuclear weapons: 'Nuke 'em. Let's nuke the bastards.' On 11 September 2001, it was similarly the President who first claimed insight into the minds of the attackers. No declaration of responsibility had been issued, but Bush knew exactly what the principal target of the attack had been: the American 'way of life, our very freedom' (Bush 2001a). When enemies neither show their face nor declare their political goals, negotiations are out of the question. In such cases, warfare is the only viable option, as Bush immediately made clear: 'Our military is powerful, and it's prepared' (Bush 2001a). Unlike his fictional counterpart in *Independence Day*, Bush the former F-101 jet pilot never flew a mission against the enemy. But on 1 May 2003 he notoriously landed in the co-pilot seat of an S-3B Viking on the aircraft carrier Abraham Lincoln (CNN 2003). His dramatic tailhook landing, his emergence from the cockpit in flying gear, and his speech under the banner 'Mission Accomplished' were nationally televised.

As Susan Sontag notes, even the most bellicose alien invasion film usually combines the 'hunger for a "good war"' with a 'yearning for peace, or for at least peaceful coexistence'. The theme of interplanetary warfare then goes hand in hand with what she terms a 'UN fantasy, a fantasy of united warfare', in which 'the warring nations of the earth come to their senses and suspend their own conflicts' (Sontag 1967: 219-20). Once again, Sontag's analysis of 1950s B-movies reads like a description of *Independence Day*, albeit with one important exception: in Emmerich's film, there is no need for time-consuming UN diplomacy. All nations of the earth quickly unite under American leadership – even Arabs and Israelis overcome their enmity and fight side by side – prompting the American President to declare a world-wide Independence Day. Is 'Operation Infinite Justice', as it was initially called, not a very similar fantasy?

IV

In his review of Steven Spielberg's *War of the Worlds*, British film critic Kevin Maher remarks that 'there is something fundamentally paradoxical, and frankly odd, about Spielberg employing the very genre that he helped to establish and that supposedly contributed to 9/11 in an attempt to explain the meaning of 9/11 itself' (Maher 2005). I would make the opposite argument: whereas Spielberg's choice of genre is quite consistent with public discourse on 9/11, it in no way endeavours to 'explain the meaning' of the event – if by 'meaning' we understand its causes, contexts, and aims.

The film's release was accompanied by numerous press conferences and interviews in which the director and his screenwriters emphasised their deliberate evocation of post-9/11 fears. On one of these occasions, before the film's premiere in Tokyo, Spielberg stated that his version of Wells's novel intended to reflect America's deep 'unease' following the 11 September attacks (quoted in *Tonight* 2005). This, he continued, was not the first time that Wells's original story had been updated to speak to contemporary issues. In 1938, Orson Welles famously caused panic across the US when radio listeners mistook his dramatisation of *The War of the Worlds* for an authentic news report about an ongoing Martian invasion of central New Jersey and New York City (Cantril 2005). 'The radio show happened just before World War Two', Spielberg commented: 'Everybody in America was nervous about Hitler and what was happening in Eastern Europe.' Similarly, he added that when George Pal turned

The War of the Worlds into a movie, his film reflected anxieties over the Cold War. Accordingly, both Welles's radio play and Pal's film are 'relevant because they've occurred at a time of history when there was great unease in the world' (quoted in *Tonight* 2005). As Spielberg implies, the same also holds for his own 2005 film.

The film's references to the events of 11 September 2001 take two forms, occurring either at the level of plot or at the level of imagery. The visual references are both more numerous and more striking. As several critics have noted, images that have engrained themselves in the minds of television viewers all over the world recur in the film, sometimes as 'almost literal visual quotes' (Wolff 2008: 189; see also Gordon 2007: 260-2; Thompson 2007: 146-8.). If it was not for the presence of actor Tom Cruise in the frame, the shot of a wall plastered with home-made missing person posters could hardly be distinguished from authentic New York footage from the days after the attacks. Other references are more indirect. At the beginning of the alien attack, a panicked crowd runs away from the tripod's heat-ray, bringing to mind images of New Yorkers fleeing from the rubble of the collapsing towers. When Spielberg's protagonist comes home, he is covered in the ashes of the victims who were incinerated around him – a somewhat macabre reminder of the dust-covered people who emerged from the debris cloud in lower Manhattan. In a similar fashion, the shot of clothes floating from the sky recalls the moment after the World Trade Center had been hit, when office paper filled the air and people trapped in the upper floors fell or jumped to their deaths. In an earlier scene, a Boeing 747 crashes into the neighbourhood in which the protagonist and his two children have found refuge. The site of the disaster – a roofless and shattered plane amidst the rubble of destroyed houses – restages the smouldering ruins at Ground Zero with their twisted metal beams and broken slabs of concrete.

At the story level, the film makes some important modifications to Wells's original invasion scenario. In the 1898 novel, the Martians are shot to Earth in huge cylinders and it is in the pits caused by the impact that they begin to assemble their tripods. Although the Martian fighting-machines eventually emerge from below the ground, the incursion is conceived as an attack from 'above'. The science fiction films of the 1950s further accentuated this theme, which resonated with both a growing belief in UFOs and the very real threat of enemy missiles. One of the earliest representatives of the genre, 1951's *The Thing from Another World*, famously ended with a warning to 'the world' (both inside and outside of the film): 'Tell this to everybody wherever they are: Watch the skies. Everywhere. Keep looking. Keep watching the skies' (quoted in Matthews 2007: 14).

Spielberg's film shows signs of a different kind of paranoia. In this post-9/11 version of Wells's tale, the alien machines are already on Earth, '"sleeper" tripods' waiting to be activated when the time is ripe (Thompson 2007: 147). When the aliens finally 'come down' during a lightning storm, they merely continue an invasion that might have been planned 'for a million years', the machines having been buried 'before the first people were here' (Friedman and Koepp 2005: sc. 58A and sc. 188). Accordingly, one of the taglines used to advertise the film was 'They're already here'. Designed to evoke post-9/11 fears of terrorist sleeper cells, this teaser signalled the advent of a new type of enemy: one who comes from outside, but who, in a sense, is already among us. The introduction of this new type of antagonist is clearly related to the fact that prior to the September 2001 attacks, all four pilots had lived, and received flight training, in the US. Where the 1953 film linked the alien invasion to apprehensions of a Soviet 'sneak attack', Spielberg's 2005 *War of the Worlds* is set in an America whose citizens live in fearful expectation of the next terrorist bombing. After a tripod has risen up from beneath the streets of Bayonne, New Jersey, and begun to wreak havoc on the town, the protagonist's eleven-year-old daughter inquires: 'Is it the terrorists?!' (Friedman and Koepp 2005: sc. 43), the definite article indicating a real-life referent. The following exchange between the protagonist, Ray, and his son Robbie situates the film's action in a new global geopolitical environment:

Robbie: [...] *Is* it terrorists?

Ray: No. This came from some place else.

Robbie: What do you mean, like, Europe?

(Friedman and Koepp 2005: sc. 46)

As outrageous as the notion of giant war machines from outer space may be, the children's responses suggest that the destruction of American cityscapes no longer belongs to the realm of filmic extravaganza: similar things have really happened. On 11 September 2001, television viewers all over the world had seen what authentic footage from a site of disaster looked like; and it is this footage that the film deliberately calls to mind. To enhance this effect, Spielberg's cinematographer repeatedly uses hand-held cameras, emulating the shaky camcorder footage from the scene of the 9/11 bombings. One shot shows the incineration of a victim on the LCD screen of an abandoned camcorder.

It has been suggested that Spielberg's film places American citizens in the position of the Iraqi population during the 2003 'shock and awe' bombings of Baghdad (Friedman 2006: 159). Even if such readings are explicitly supported by screenwriter David Koepp (see Feld 2005: 142), the film's primary purpose is clearly to re-enact a specifically American experience: the historically unprecedented attack against US civilians on US territory on 11 September 2001. The figure of the alien invader is by definition over-determined (partly due to the 'memory' of the genre, which necessarily evokes earlier uses of that figure). To cast the aliens as both terrorists and American invaders, however, illustrates the dilemmas of what David Holloway characterises as 'Hollywood allegory lite': 'a commercial aesthetic so packed with different hooks pitched at different audience groups that a degree of aesthetic and narrative fragmentation has become intrinsic to the way Hollywood tells its stories today, particularly the blockbuster.' He continues:

> In Hollywood allegory lite, controversial issues can be safely addressed because they must be 'read off' other stories by the viewer; while the 'allegory' is sufficiently loose or 'lite', and the other attractions on offer are sufficiently compelling or diverse, that viewers can enjoy the film without needing to engage at all with the risky 'other story' it tells.
>
> (Holloway 2008: 83)

Summoning the image of New Yorkers 'fleeing across the George Washington Bridge in the shadow of 9/11', Spielberg himself explained that his film was 'about Americans fleeing for their lives, being attacked for no reason, having no idea why they are being attacked and who is attacking them' (quoted in Chau

2005). It is notable that this explanation fails to mention either the perpetrators or their possible motives, echoing – and, implicitly, affirming – a particular kind of discourse on the attacks of 9/11: because America is literally attacked out of the blue (and 'for no reason'), there is no need to reconsider the country's military and political entanglements in the Middle East. And the same is true for *War of the Worlds*, in which the causes of the invasion remain completely obscure.

In the wake of 9/11, the question arose as to whether the perceived similarities between the scenes of that day and Hollywood imagery were perhaps not accidental. Five weeks after the incident, veteran director Robert Altman exhorted his fellow filmmakers to reconsider their routine indulgence in violence and mass destruction. Drawing a direct connection between the attacks and American blockbusters, Altman asserted that the latter had clearly served as a template and inspiration for the former: 'Nobody would have thought to commit an atrocity like that unless they'd seen it in a movie....The movies set the pattern, and these people have copied the movies' (quoted in BBC 2001c). Film critic Richard von Busack even went so far as to speculate about a possible paradigm shift in Hollywood: 'Maybe the attack will knock an entire moviemaking style out of existence. It would be no loss: action movies are decadent and baroque now, in need of some clever new approach' (Busack 2001).

As we now know, the expectation that Hollywood film would undergo a radical change was to be short-lived. Like several other prognostications made in the immediate aftermath of the terrorist attacks, it over-estimated the cultural impact of the event. There was a brief period in which releases were postponed on thematic grounds – Arnold Schwarzenegger's skirmish with Colombian terrorists in *Collateral Damage* providing the most famous example – and in which re-shoots and re-edits were made for New York-set films showing the Twin Towers, such as *Men in Black II* (Hoberman 2001), but it took only four years for the alien invader to return to the cinema screen. And, what is more, it was a film of this very genre that was marketed and received as 'the first genuine post-9/11 blockbuster' (Maher 2005). In some ways, Spielberg's film marked a return to business as usual. Far from renouncing the representation of disaster, as some critics had prophesied, Hollywood did what it had always done: it adapted popular genres to the needs of the moment. Thus, *War of the Worlds* showed computer-generated scenes of urban devastation, even if it purposely avoided the 'destruction of famous landmarks'. According to co-writer David Koepp, this was one of the things he and director Steven Spielberg felt they 'shouldn't have in the movie'; it was also agreed that the film would not feature any 'shots of Manhattan getting the crap kicked out of it'.[2]

Although it relocates the disaster to suburban New Jersey, however, Spielberg's film still makes ample use of 9/11 imagery; as Holloway observes, 'the extent to which it force[s] audiences to re-experience 9/11 empathetically through encounters with that imagery, ma[kes] it much harder to concentrate on other aspects of the film' (Holloway 2008: 92). At the same time – and more problematically – *War of the Worlds* echoes the political construction of America's new enemy within the generic code of alien invasion. In doing so, it does not bluntly equate aliens and terrorists; yet it nevertheless presupposes that the experience of 9/11 can be evoked by means of the space invader metaphor. While the film may be said to critique certain aspects of post-9/11 counterterrorism policies by emphasising the futility of military intervention, its critical stance is undercut by the fact that it reproduces one basic premise of official counterterrorism discourse: the radical othering of the enemy. This othering is based on a refusal to look beyond the 'alienness' of terrorists at the complicated connections that tie 'us' to 'them' and that make the post-9/11 present part of a longer history – a history, it should be noted, that happens outside of movie theatres.

Notes

[1] In the online version of his essay, which appeared only four days after the attacks, Žižek read pre-9/11 disaster films in terms of an imaginary anticipation – and libidinal investment – of America's forced awakening to the 'desert of the Real'. His main argument (which was much elaborated for the now better-known printed version of the essay) was that the movie-like images of 9/11 had penetrated and shattered a First-World conception of reality based on the system of 'VIRTUAL capitalism' (epitomised by the Twin Towers), a system which had thought itself insulated from the Third-World 'sphere of material production' (Žižek 2001). Baudrillard, for his part, considered disaster movies as an indication that the catastrophe had been secretly wished for, 'because no one can avoid dreaming of the destruction of any power that has become hegemonic to this degree' (Baudrillard 2003: 5).

[2] See 'Production Notes: *War of the Worlds*', 2005,
www.waroftheworlds.com/productionnotes/index.html.

Chapter 9

The War on Terrorism as Comedy

Philip Hammond

There is a common approach to the analysis of Vietnam war films which assesses them largely according to how far they offer a critical view of the conflict. Even though celebratory Vietnam films (such as *The Green Berets*, 1968) are the exception (even *Rambo, First Blood Part II* (1985) incorporates a critique of sorts), and more-or-less critical films the norm, scholarly discussion tends to focus on the ways in which films' critical perspective is limited (see, for example, Dittmar and Michaud 1990; Anderegg 1991). One could plausibly take a similar approach to analysing films about the 'war on terror', pointing up their faulty or absent explanation of causes, their narrow focus on the victimhood of the US/Western soldier, their one-dimensional or dehumanised portrayal of the enemy, their lack of engagement with anti-war perspectives, and so on. Indeed, some critics have taken this route, often to good effect.

This chapter, however, considers the ways in which it can be limiting to assess war-on-terror films in this fashion. The limitations arise from the fact that, after the end of the Cold War, we inhabit a vastly different political universe. While many films which (to a greater or lesser extent) take a critical view of the war on terror rarely acknowledge this, it is brought to the fore in comic treatments of terrorism and war. Some of these comedies (such as *Four Lions*, 2010) clearly invite a serious response; others (such as *Team America: World Police*, 2004) perhaps not. We should nevertheless take comic treatments seriously, it is argued here, since in some respects they offer greater insight into the contemporary politics of war and terrorism than many straight films, including those that take a 'critical' view of the war on terror.[1] In what follows, we first consider the comedic portrayal of terrorist suicide-bombing in *Four Lions,* and then the portrayal of war in *Team America, In the Loop* (2009), and *The Men Who Stare at Goats* (2009), before returning, in conclusion, to the question of how far such treatments offer insights not available in more serious film dramas.

Comedy of Terror

Four Lions concerns a group of 'home-grown' British terrorists, depicting them as inept, amateurish freelancers who are not particularly religious and whose political motivations are extremely vague and confused. In so doing, it clearly sets out to satirise official misunderstanding of Al-Qaeda style terrorism – in the film, the authorities target not Omar, the leader of the bombers, but his ultra-religious brother. Omar's brother fits the profile, being a devout, orthodox, observant Muslim, so it is his house that gets raided even as Omar and his co-conspirators are hatching their plot; and it is the brother who is picked up by the intelligence services and subjected to a form of 'rendition' at the end of the film. In rejecting the conventional view of 'fundamentalist' Islamist terrorism, *Four Lions* recognises that would-be suicide bombers are much closer to the mainstream of British society. The cultural reference points shared by Omar and his friends are for the most part entirely conventional – they refer to XBox games or gangsta rap stars when fantasising about jihad, for example; and Omar uses *The Lion King* (casting himself in the role of Simba) to tell his son heroic bedtime stories about his (actually catastrophic) trip to a training camp in Pakistan. Perhaps most poignantly, when Omar gives another of the terrorists, Waj, a pep talk to convince him to carry through their deadly mission, he explains that: '[life is] like being stuck in the queue at Alton Towers. Do you want to be in the queues or do you want to be on the rides?' Waj enthusiastically agrees that he would rather be on the rides, especially 'Rubber Dinghy Rapids', a phrase he later repeats at various points in the film in an attempt to steel his resolve. This accurately depicts the way that actual bombers and would-be bombers have been, as Mayor Boris Johnson said of those who attacked the

London transport system in 2005, 'as British as Tizer, and queues, and Y-fronts and the Changing of the Guard' (Johnson 2005).[2] It is worth noting that this is true not only of 'home-grown terrorists' but applies more broadly to would-be Al-Qaeda bombers: as Marc Sageman's (2004: 74-5) study of Al-Qaeda members indicates, they are generally not drawn from the ranks of the marginal and dispossessed, but are 'global citizens', familiar with Western culture.

The comic vision of terrorism in this film challenges not only the official view but also a common radical view of the war on terror, which tends to look at the present in terms of a bygone era of national liberation struggles. Some war-on-terror films, such as *Traitor* (2008), or *Rendition* (2007), attempt a more empathetic treatment of terrorism, showing it to be a rational, understandable – though not, of course, condonable – response to oppression; a problem caused by imperialist foreign policy. This is certainly not the case for the characters in *Four Lions*, whose encounters with white British society (including the police) are always very friendly. Again this rings true: Faisal Devji (2005: 27-8) and Olivier Roy (2004: 68) both note how, although Al-Qaeda rhetoric often refers to real injustices such as the dispossession of the Palestinians, the jihadis are disconnected from such actual struggles, using them only opportunistically for their symbolic value. In most cases, would-be martyrs have little or no first-hand experience of oppression or discrimination.

While officialdom treats contemporary terrorism as an alien threat, the product of a foreign ideology, and while radical critics tend to see contemporary terrorism as a politicised response to oppression, *Four Lions* suggests that the terrorists are hopelessly muddled and vague in their political motivations, and that such views as they do have fall firmly within the political and cultural mainstream. Their most eloquent spokesman is Omar, who makes a number of attempts to explain their beliefs during the course of the film. In his martyrdom video, he condemns 'superficial materialism' and the 'capitalist church of McDonalds', and proclaims that: 'The Western imperialist culture has left you like materialist junkies mainlining iPods and Humvees and TK Maxx into a spiritual void.' It is important to note that these declarations (like those of Mohammad Sidique Khan, the leader of the 2005 London bombings), are all delivered in the character's broad Yorkshire accent.[3] In his most extended speech – made to his fellow terrorists rather than a presumed posthumous audience – Omar declaims earnestly:

> We have instructions to bring havoc to this bullshit, consumerist, godless, Paki-bashing, Gordon Ramsay 'Taste the Difference' speciality cheddar, torture-endorsing, massacre-sponsoring, 'look-at-me-dancing-pissed-with-my-knob-out', Sky One Uncovered, 'who-gives-a-fuck-about-dead-Afghanis?' Disneyland.[4]

These denunciations of Western hedonism and consumer culture – in which a 'bullshit materialism' is as much, if not more, of a target as war or imperialism – suggest that Omar and his friends are influenced more by contemporary distaste for consumerism within British or Western culture than by any specifically religious motivation. Indeed, Omar has little patience with his pious brother, mocking his 'scholarly opinions' and Koranic quotes. Omar and his family are much more Westernised. Again this accords with studies of actual suicide bombers. Devji (2005: 16), for example, notes that today's global jihadis show scant regard for conventions of 'correct' Islamic practice or for 'inherited forms of Islamic authority'. Rather, Devji (2005: 6) observes, the pronouncements of figures such as Osama bin Laden have often seemed to mirror the sorts of conspiracy theories popularised in television shows such as *The X-Files* and films by Oliver Stone. The characters in this film are also prone to wild conspiracy-theorising, such as when one claims that 'the Jews invented spark plugs to control global traffic.' In *Four Lions*, apart from one character's plan to blow up a mosque (in order to 'radicalise the moderates'), the most frequently mentioned targets are 'slags' and shops. This recalls, no doubt intentionally, the outlook of a real-life Omar – Omar Khyam – and his fellow bomb plotters, who in 2007 discussed blowing up the Bluewater shopping centre in Kent and targeting 'slags' at the Ministry of Sound nightclub in London.[5] As some commentators have noted, such 'radical' thinking in fact dovetails neatly with official UK government concerns about binge-drinking, anti-social behaviour, and teen pregnancy, as well as with mainstream liberal aversion to consumerism (O'Neill 2007).

It might seem dangerously unwise not to take suicide bombers seriously, but the ridiculous characters in *Four Lions* capture the essential truth that Al-

Qaeda style martyrs, for all their violence and destruction, are absurd figures, narcissistically playing out a fantasy of global jihad in which media spectacle is of paramount importance. As Devji has remarked, the videotaped statements by British 7/7 bombers Shehzad Tanweer and Mohammad Sidique Khan are not only full of media-derived references to images of jihad, copying the dress, body language and sound-bites of bin Laden and other figures, but are also designed to secure their immortality, not in a religious sense, but via the media (in O'Neill 2006). The characters in *Four Lions* exhibit a similar narcissism, continually making videos and taking photos of themselves. During his visit to an Al-Qaeda training camp in Pakistan, for example, Waj describes himself as 'getting [my] pictures, Mujahid style'. Similarly, a fifth terrorist, whom the group recruits during the course of the film, says he is waging a 'jihad of the mind' and seeking to make dramatic 'gestures'. These are 'mediahideen', obsessively re-doing their martyrdom videos despite having nothing much to say.[6]

Whether among British-born radicals or the leaders of Al-Qaeda, the outlook appears to be closer to the sort of disillusioned self-critique found in Western culture than a coherent foreign ideology confronting the West from without (the official view) or a violent political response to imperialism and oppression (the radical view). *Four Lions* understands this in a way that other films about contemporary terrorism do not, since they stay within a now outdated view; a view from a political universe that no longer exists. Something similar can be said about the comic vision of war.

Comedy of War

Films that take a (more-or-less) critical view of the war on terror, such as *Green Zone* (2010), or *Lions for Lambs* (2007), tend to suggest that war is basically caused by a conspiracy on the part of misguided and/or malicious politicians. The conduct of the war is then often seen to be characterised by extreme brutality, sadism and atrocities, as for example in *Redacted* (2007).[7] In this respect, such films might be said to reflect the radical critique of the war on terror, particularly in Iraq, which understands it as a war of hidden motivations (a 'war for oil'), fought for neo-liberal interests, which people were duped in to supporting by a neo-conservative conspiracy. The comic vision of war is rather different, and –

although no doubt something is lost in making light of something so serious – comic treatments again manage to capture some essential truths better than serious films.

In the comic vision, while there might still be a behind-the-scenes conspiracy in the drive to war, politically it is an empty and absurd one. Malcolm Tucker, for example, the devious UK government spin-doctor from *In the Loop*, provides the essential 'intelligence' about weapons of mass destruction to sway the UN vote in favour of war, by cutting and pasting from a document which had actually made the case against war, and by changing the name of the intelligence source to make it appear like a new one. Like virtually all the actions of politicians, aides and civil servants in this film, however, Tucker's action has no wider political meaning or significance. The characters in the film act from narrow self-interest, completely lacking any principle or conviction. Like *The Thick Of It*, the TV series on which it is based, *In the Loop* satirises today's image-obsessed political culture, in which politicians offer no meaningful vision and it is the opinions of newspapers, polls and focus groups, rather than political conviction or principle, that dictate policy. The characters often act in a dishonest, manipulative or underhand fashion, but almost always only in the interests of maximising their own, or their masters', media profile.

In the Loop tells the story of a new British Minister for International Development, Simon Foster (aptly nicknamed 'Simon Fluster' by his staff), who inadvertently puts himself at the centre of the debate about going to war in the Middle East by his unthinking remark that 'war is unforeseeable'. This is seized upon by the anti-war camp, including the US assistant Secretary of State Karen Clarke, who sees an opportunity to 'internationalise the dissent'. Foster then clumsily tries to 'freestyle' a rationalisation of his comment, explaining that 'to walk the road of peace sometimes we need to be ready to climb…the mountain of conflict.' In saying this, his only intention is to repair the damage done by his earlier remark by manufacturing a good sound-bite. But this second comment is then seized upon by another US politician, the hawkish Linton Barwick, who tries to recruit him as a pro-war voice. Caught in the middle, the truth is that he has no strong convictions. When asked publicly to confirm his position that 'war is unforeseeable', Foster says: 'Yes, that's what I said and I stick to what I said.

That doesn't mean that what I said won't change…in the future…it's not immutable, or mutable.' His nonsense response is merely an attempt to sound good; to get the rhetoric right. Similarly, he describes himself as 'on the verge of taking a stand', or, when it seems as if that might be taken seriously, as 'taking a stand, on the verge'. In a parody of the real-life equivocations of Clare Short, Britain's Minister for International Development at the time of the Iraq war, Foster continually debates whether to resign, but the only point of the calculation is figure out what would be best for his public image.

In the Loop offers an accurate depiction of how the contemporary political class is cut off from the electorate – dramatised in a sub-plot about the minister's meetings with his constituents. The gap between the excitement of the international stage and the small, dull world of everyday domestic affairs is demonstrated when Foster travels back to his Northampton constituency, described by his aide as going 'from White House to shite-house'. Ironically, a complaint about the collapsing wall of his constituency office is the seemingly minor and irrelevant problem that ultimately ends his career.

If the war on terror has been light on political vision, though, it has certainly been heavy on rhetoric – even if of a peculiarly incoherent sort. That bombastic, but fundamentally empty and inarticulate rhetoric is also parodied effectively in *Team America*, which mocks the unthinking assertion of 'American values', the emptiness of words like 'freedom' when used with no real meaning – for example in a maudlin country music song, 'Freedom isn't free', or in the film's theme tune, which declaims simply: 'America – fuck yeah!' (see further Froula 2011: 72, 77). Comedies can hardly be expected to capture the reality of war, though they can depict the military's unthinking brutality and destruction. The eponymous Team American habitually destroy cities in the process of 'saving' them: a successful mission in Paris destroys the Eiffel Tower, the Arc de Triomphe and the Louvre; another in Egypt blows up the pyramids, the sphinx and the monuments to the pharaohs in the Valley of the Kings. The team's computer is called 'Intelligence', allowing for predictable jokes when it crashes: 'We've lost intelligence. Repeat, we have no intelligence.' Similarly, there is a telling moment in *The Men Who Stare at Goats*, when, as the central characters escape in a jeep from Iraqi kidnappers, they try to pick up an Iraqi who is also fleeing. He refuses to stop running, and they accidentally knock him down, shouting: 'It's OK! We're Americans! We're here to help you!...Oh crap...I think I just ran him over.'

While showing the reality of combat and atrocities might be difficult in the context of a comedy, however, what these films do capture is another aspect of the conduct of recent wars – namely their *unreality*. In *Team America* the plot revolves entirely around actors and acting: the team's leader, Spottswoode, says to the main character, Gary, for example: 'The team went on a mission without you, and without an actor they were like pigs to the slaughter.' The film pokes fun at anti-war celebrities, for example by having puppet versions of Hollywood stars declare that 'What the world needs is an international advisory committee who truly understands global politics, namely, us' (Alec Baldwin), or that 'If we focus our acting on global politics, we can change everything and stuff' (Liv Tyler). This rings true to the often self-regarding character of contemporary celebrity protest, but the film offers even greater insight into the pro-war side. The seemingly absurd importance that the elite Team America unit places on recruiting someone with 'acting skills' echoes the way that real episodes in the war on terror have sometimes been highly theatrical. The US special forces who went into Kandahar in October 2001, for example, were essentially actors, staging a stunt and videotaping their exploits for the world's media. The operation was of dubious military value since, as Seymour Hersh (2001) reported in *The New Yorker*, army pathfinders had already gone in beforehand to make sure the area was secure. Similarly, the 'Saving Private Lynch' episode discussed in the Introduction to this volume was simply one of the more memorable escapades filmed by US soldiers, who were following instructions from the Pentagon that using helmet-mounted cameras on combat sorties was 'approved and encouraged to the greatest extent possible'.[8]

The Men Who Stare at Goats portrays the 'unreality' of contemporary war in a different sense. The film's depiction of the self-styled 'Jedi warriors' of the New Earth Army is true to life not only in the narrow sense that it is based on a real unit (the First Earth Battalion, the subject of the book on which the film is based), but also because it captures some distinctive features of the contemporary US military. In the film, the New Earth Army is a (now-disbanded) military unit that sought to practice psychic warfare, employing esoteric methods, such as 'remote viewing', informed by New Age techniques and philosophies. One of the key characters, Lyn Cassady, explains the ethos: 'We're Jedi...we don't fight with guns, we fight with our minds....We're going to use visual aesthetics to instil psychically in the enemy the disincentive to attack.' In Iraq, the coalition did something rather similar, using what the British military calls 'effects-based warfare', or what the Pentagon called 'shock and awe' tactics, designed to disarm the enemy mentally rather than simply to defeat them through force (though since the outcome in terms of military force was never in doubt, perhaps it was more the TV audience back home who was supposed to be awed). This approach was partly derived from the ancient Chinese strategist Sun Tzu, whose book *The Art of War* was reportedly distributed to US commanders. The military strategist who conceived the term 'shock and awe', Harlan Ullman, cites Sun Tzu, while the Pentagon acknowledges that 'Sun was well aware of the crucial importance of achieving "shock and awe"'. As Ben Macintyre noted at the time of the Iraq war:

> The notion of attacking an enemy's psychology without firing a shot was elaborated into modern military theory by the late Colonel John Boyd, an American tactician who argued that an enemy commander might be mentally disarmed even before battle begins. Donald Rumsfeld, the Defence Secretary, has called Boyd 'the most influential military thinker since Sun Tzu.'
>
> (Macintyre 2003)

The allusion is made explicit in *The Men Who Stare at Goats* when one of the 'Jedi' instructors is described as having 'caused quite a stir by advocating his controversial "shock and awe" knife attack method.'

Disingenuous though the official claims may be (after all, 'effects-based' warfare is still deadly when carried out by the world's most powerful military), the fact that political and military leaders felt more affinity with the semi-mystical ancient wisdom of a Sun Tzu than with the more orthodox *Realpolitik* of a Carl von Clausewitz tells us much about the self-doubt of the contemporary US military. In *The Men Who Stare at Goats*, that self-doubt is seen to have emerged from the traumatic experience of defeat in Vietnam. The eventual

founder of the New Earth Army, Bill Django, returns from Vietnam a changed
man, and goes in search of enlightenment in the New Age movements of 1970s
California, experimenting with Naked Hot Tub Encounter Sessions, Primal Arm
Wrestling, Higher Essence Colonic Irrigation Therapy, and so on. In a flashback
scene, we see Django explaining the need for change to a roomful of US
generals:

> We are a hollow army, gentlemen. Vietnam has crushed our soul. We
> have to dream a new America. An America that no longer has an
> exploitative view of natural resources, no longer promotes consumption
> at all cost. But to achieve this dream we must become the first
> superpower to develop super powers....Be all you can be.

The use of the real recruiting slogan, 'Be all you can be', reminds us that New
Age thinking really has made some inroads into the mainstream – explained in
the film as a product of Cold War paranoia (the US has to match the Soviets'
psychic research, which was started because the Russians thought the Americans
were already doing it), with references to Ronald Reagan's admiration for *Star
Wars* and his interest in the paranormal. In fact, however, although the First
Earth Battalion / New Earth Army was disbanded in the 1990s, the trends it
encapsulates really took off after the end of the Cold War.

Writing in the US Army's *Parameters* journal, Charles Moskos (2001) argues
that, 'The concept of "postmodernism", with its core meaning of the absence of
absolute values, [is] increasingly applicable to the contemporary military.' Other
authors have complained that 'Military culture is challenged by a relativistic
civilian ethos' (Williams 2000: 274) and that 'militaries now lack a shared
interpretative framework with their publics' (Snider and Watkins 2000). Moskos
(2001) illustrates the 'absence of absolute values' in the military with a number
of anecdotes of political correctness run amok:

> [In] 1999, the US Army chaplaincy recognized the neo-pagan Wicca as a
> legitimate faith. More than 40 active-duty 'witches', male and female,
> celebrated the Rite of Spring at Fort Hood, Texas.

The American Federation of Government Employees filed a complaint after a squadron commander ordered a male civilian Air Force employee to change his attire. The man had been wearing a dress, bra, and makeup.

[T]he Secretary of the Army hired as a temporary consultant an advocate of replacing a 'masculinist' with an 'ungendered vision' of military culture.

The first example here finds an echo in a scene from *The Men Who Stare at Goats* when a high-ranking officer observes with astonishment a member of the New Earth Army, complete with feathered headdress and teepee, enacting an elaborate Native American ceremony in the middle of a US Army base.

Moskos's last example above refers to Madeline Morris, an American law professor who in 1997, as consultant to the Secretary of the Army, argued for a change in 'military culture from a masculinist vision of unalloyed aggressivity to an ungendered vision' (quoted in Gutmann 2000: 151). As Moskos and his co-authors observe in their book *The Postmodern Military*, Western societies have seen a 'cultural shift in public attitudes and opinions', whereby:

> Old verities are questioned rather than accepted. There are fewer overarching authorities to whom people are willing to defer. There is a shrinking consensus about what values constitute the public good, and little confidence that we know how, by the use of reason, to determine what the public good might be.
>
> (Moskos et al. 2000: 4)

Such doubts about society's values have given rise to some odd worries on the part of the military about appearing offensive. During the 1998 'Desert Fox' bombing of Iraq, for example, not only were operations suspended during the first night of Ramadan, but when one sailor wrote 'Hey Saddam! Here's a Ramadan present from Chad Rickenberg' on a Navy bomb, the Pentagon issued an apology, saying it was 'distressed to learn of thoughtless graffiti mentioning the holy month of Ramadan written on a piece of ordnance' (quoted in Gutmann 2000: 176). Similarly, after a row about airmen scrawling offensive slogans, such as 'High jack this, fags', on bombs dropped in the 2001 Afghan war, the US Navy instructed commanders to 'keep the messages positive' (O'Neill 2003).

In addition to worries about 'offending' the enemies they are attempting to kill, there are also concerns about the corrosive effect of 'relativistic values' on the military's own internal cohesion. One female reservist who was called up in the mobilisation for the 1991 Gulf War, for example, filed for conscientious objector status, complaining that: 'My recruiter told me I would never have to go to war, that I would travel and gain skills and an education….I cannot kill another human being. I cannot even facilitate war' (Gutmann 2001: 135). Her words would not be out of place coming from one of the 'Jedi' in *The Men Who Stare at Goats*. The film's characters also embody the idea that joining the military is about self-fulfilment – being 'all you can be'. As senior British diplomat Robert Cooper acknowledges, though, societies which can offer their citizens no higher goal than 'personal development and personal consumption' find it hard to inspire people to risk their lives:

> Army recruitment becomes difficult – consumerism is the one cause for which it makes no sense to die….Where once recruitment posters proclaimed YOUR COUNTRY NEEDS YOU!, they now carry slogans such as JOIN THE ARMY: BE ALL THAT YOU CAN; self-realization has replaced patriotism as a motive for serving in the armed forces.
>
> (Cooper 2004: 51)

'Self-realization' is what the New Earth Army is all about, but it is a poor substitute for an inspiring cause greater than oneself. After the end of the Cold War – in other words, after the end of the modern political contest between Left and Right – political leaders have found it difficult to articulate any such cause or vision.

Conclusion

Analysts of comedy have often understood it as way of saying the unsayable, broaching difficult or taboo subjects or dealing with uncomfortable topics or situations (for example, Freud 1991). In this case, the uncomfortable truth tackled by these comic films is that the war on terror is politically meaningless. The absurdity of the comic vision of war and terrorism captures this emptiness, this lack of political meaning, in a way that (cinematic) attempts to interpret recent events through the old political framework usually fail to do. What in the past might have been seen as a strength – looking for the real motivations behind war; attempting to understand how the violence of the Other is a response to oppression – now appears as a weakness or limitation. Neither the pro- nor anti-war camps, not the fantasy jihadis nor the leaders of the 'war on terror' have a coherent political vision: the present is not simply a continuation of the ideological clashes of the past. This interpretation implies that we should perhaps evaluate non-comic dramas differently, acknowledging that attempts at conventional political explanation are not necessarily a strength, and that political critique has to take new forms.

Of course, none of this is to suggest that these comic films are perfect vehicles of critical analysis or that they articulate any sort of coherent anti-war politics. If the comic voice allows the broaching of difficult or uncomfortable subjects, it also tends to limit the way in which those subjects are discussed, suggesting that any implied critique is not to be taken too seriously. In the examples discussed above, there are instances where the films retreat into a more conventional outlook: the insights of *In the Loop* are restricted to British politics while the Americans engage in an altogether more serious and more traditional political struggle, for example; and *The Men Who Stare at Goats* appears to find the New Earth Army a genuinely attractive proposition (it concludes with the line: 'Now, more than ever, we need the Jedi').

Nevertheless, whatever their faults, these comic treatments of the war on terror deserve to be taken seriously as critical representations of contemporary realities. Their significance is perhaps best summed up by two, complementary moments from *In the Loop* and *Four Lions*. In the former, an aide discovers Simon Foster standing alone in an anteroom as the crucial UN vote is taking place, and, feeling that she is interrupting a private moment, she withdraws, saying 'I'll leave you alone with your thoughts'. 'I haven't got any thoughts', Foster blurts out, 'I'm just staring vacantly into space.' In *Four Lions*, Waj finds himself in a kebab shop, bomb strapped to his chest, when a police negotiator reaches him on the phone and asks what the group's demands are. 'We haven't got any demands', replies the bewildered Waj: even the possibility of having 'demands' has clearly never occurred to him. Taken together, these scenes are emblematic of the real achievement of these comedies: that they show us the emptiness of contemporary politics and the correspondingly inchoate character of contemporary terrorism.

Notes

[1] I was inspired to take these comedies seriously by Neil Davenport's insightful reviews of two of the films discussed here: *In the Loop* (Davenport 2009) and *Four Lions* (Davenport 2010).

[2] Tizer is a British soft drink – its use here is analogous to saying 'as American as Coca-Cola'. Alton Towers is a British theme park: Omar's reference is similar to invoking Disneyland in a US context.

[3] The character of Barry, a white British convert to Islam, parallels Khan's colleague Martin McDaid, a former Royal Marine who was reportedly a key influence on the '7/7' bombers (*Newsnight*, BBC2, 5 May 2011).

[4] The eclectic cultural references here are related in that they point to what might be thought of as hedonistic, indulgent features of contemporary British consumerism: Gordon Ramsay is a TV chef, 'Taste the Difference' is an 'upmarket' food line, and the mention of 'Sky One Uncovered' refers to documentaries focussing on the antics of British people on holiday, such as *Ibiza Uncovered* (1998) or *Tenerife Uncovered* (2001), broadcast by the Sky satellite channel.

[5] 'Clubbers and Shops Targeted', *The Sun*, 30 April 2007, www.thesun.co.uk/sol/homepage/news/article16964.ece.

[6] International Relations scholar Philip Cunliffe notes the real-life case of *Talai al-Fath* ('Vanguard of Conquest'), a radical group based in London, who were mocked by rivals as *Talai al-Fax*, or the 'Vanguard Faxers', because of their habit of bombarding newspapers with faxes full of grandiloquent rhetoric. See Philip Cunliffe, 'Vanguard Faxers and Mediahedin: The "Double Death of Islamic Fundamentalism" Reconsidered', unpublished discussion paper, August 2004.

[7] An interesting example in this regard is *In the Valley of Elah* (2007), which invites the audience to assume there is a conspiracy on the part of the US military to cover up atrocities committed by coalition troops in Iraq, and to assume that the murdered soldier at the centre of the film's plot was killed to stop him exposing the truth. The film is able to generate much suspense around these assumptions precisely because we are so willing to make them.

[8] 'Public Affairs Guidance on Embedding Media During Possible Future Operations/Deployments in the US Central Commands Area of Responsibility', Department of Defense, February 2003, www.defense.gov/news/Feb2003/d20030228pag.pdf.

Chapter 10

'Evil Arabs'? Muslim Terrorists in Hollywood and Bollywood

Bernd Zywietz

Arabs and Muslims are misrepresented in Hollywood movies and US television. If they are not completely ignored, demeaning depictions prevail. Instead of presenting them as normal citizens, a narrow range of stereotypes reduces Muslims and Arabs to lecherous sheiks with undeserved oil wealth or demonic Middle Eastern terrorists. After the attacks of 11 September 2001, in times of so-called 'Islamophobia' and the 'global war on terror', this is dangerous since it feeds in to real-world policies and political rhetoric, building up images of an enemy which can stir up prejudices against ethnic and religious groups:

> The construction of all Arabs as terrorists and all Muslims as Arab terrorists – through political rhetoric reducing vast populations into a single dark image – has significant consequences not only for the civil rights of individuals living in the United States but also for many other citizens of the world.
>
> (Merskin 2004: 173)

But is this true? Is there really a problem in the Western treatment and imagination of Muslims and Arabs in the face of transnational terrorism and radical Islamist hatred against 'crusaders'? Daniel Pipes (2005), director of the Middle East forum, doubts that American Muslims face significant bias in US society, for they boast among the highest rates of education in any group. Even when their faith is disrespected and cases of discrimination occur, legal satisfaction, public apologies and solidarity statements are quick responses. On the other hand, 'ethnic screening' and governmental misuse of detention are a fact, and suspicion and racial violence remain inexcusable and intolerable. But even if they might not be successful, those reactions remain somehow understandable given the suicide hijackers' background and claim to have done what they did in the name of Allah.[1]

> Cinema as an art form not only reflects the society it is set in, but also acts as a reflector to that society. Some films leave their mark on society; and society, in turn, reacts to these films in a variety of ways.
>
> (Bughara 2006: 1)

At least when it comes to media or entertainment representations the case is much easier – or so it seems. A broad range of publications are concerned with the depiction or stereotyping of Muslims and Arabs (or Arab-Americans). Authors such as Karin Wilkins (2008) have studied their impact and reception using empirical methods; Tim Semmerling (2006) and Jack Shaheen (2001, 2009) have found 'Evil' or 'Reel Bad' Arabs depicted in film and television (see also Dana 2009; Gottschalk and Greenberg 2008; Khatib 2006; Kamalipour 2000). Of course, this subject is not new. The Palestinian-born literary theorist and founding figure of Postcolonial Studies Edward Said (1979) published a seminal study in which he analysed how the West imagines and frames the East – the Middle East and Asia – as inferior, irrational and threatening.

At the same time, after international Palestinian terrorism was introduced to Western audiences, two oil crises (1973 and 1979) unsettled the West, and the Islamic revolution in Iran and the Soviet Union's invasion in Afghanistan instigated a new era of conflict, threat scenarios and Islamic visibility in foreign policy and thus media representation. This is the era when Shaheen began to analyse Muslim and Arab images, first on TV, then in cinema, eventually becoming perhaps the most prominent activist in this field. Based on a survey of over one thousand feature films, Shaheen showed that since its very beginning Hollywood vilified or at least stereotyped Muslims and Arabs, continuing to do so even when similar mistreatment of other groups such as African-Americans or Native Americans ceased. To raise awareness Shaheen and organisations like the Council on American-Islamic Relations (CAIR) and the American-Arab Anti-Discrimination Committee (ADC) offer advice to film producers or criticise and campaign against movies they deem inappropriate or unacceptable. In doing so they speak and act on behalf of approximately 3.5 million Arab-Americans[2] and roughly the same number of American Muslims;[3] groups which account for one or two percent of the United States population.[4]

However, when we look more closely at Hollywood's cinematic depiction of Muslims and Arabs as terrorists, we find certain problems with the most common criticisms of stereotyping. In what follows, I compare popular terrorist movies from Hollywood with those from India. Since (and because of) its founding as a modern nation state, India has faced different kinds of terrorism and communal violence, which has often been utilised politically, fuelling suspicion and hate of Muslims. 'Bollywood' has developed a range of strategies for balancing the Muslim image in movies which – as I will show – Hollywood started to apply after 9/11 too. Considering the advantages and limits of such narrative strategies, I will discuss problems of assessing the appropriateness of Muslims' cinematic representation in the context of contemporary transnational terrorism and how critics often disregard basic conditions like the constitution of the movie industry, genre rules and functions or the audience. To begin, I will firstly discuss two pre-9/11 Hollywood movies – *True Lies* (1994) and *The Siege* (1998) – and the objections against them made by Shaheen and others.

Muslims and Terrorists in Hollywood

James Cameron's post-modernist *True Lies* is an ironic romantic action comedy, a remake of the French film *La Totale!* (1991). This box office success stars the 1980s action movie icon Arnold Schwarzenegger as Tasker, a secret agent fighting Arabian terrorists attempting to smuggle several nuclear warheads into the United States. A second storyline revolves around Tasker's marriage and his bored wife (Jamie Lee Curtis) who toys with the thought of starting an affair with a car salesman who pretends to be a secret agent. As a James Bond with a heavy Austrian accent Tasker handles several spy gadgets, rips off a hand dryer from a wall during a fight in a public washroom, chases terrorist leader Aziz (Art Malik) on a horseback through a hotel, blows the villain away with a Harrier jet's missile, and finally reunites with his wife in front of a kind of romantic atomic sunset when one of the bombs detonates far away on a deserted island. Shaheen addresses the fact that the Arabs are nothing more than one-dimensional cartoon figures: often dressed with a *kufiya*, their sole dramatic purpose is to be threatening, even evil, and to be killed by the hero.

> *True Lies* is a slick film perpetuating sick images of Palestinians as dirty, demonic, and despicable peoples. The reel portraits are so remote from reality as to give normal viewers the willies....After watching Schwarzenegger dispatch upwards of 64 Palestinians, I stopped counting. Did the actor ever pause to consider this film's impact on Arab Americans, their families?
>
> (Shaheen 2009: 536)

Shaheen rates *True Lies* as one of the worst films ever, though it is not clear if he does so despite or because of the movie's tongue-in-check attitude.

The second example is a bit more complicated. *The Siege* foreshadows several details of the 2001 events: the plot concerns a series of terrorist attacks in New York, the terrorists are organised in cells, their attacks are mostly suicide bombings, and the perpetrators entered the US on student visas from Germany. The uncanny resemblance to 9/11 is, however, not entirely accidental because director Edward Zwick and his writers, especially journalist Lawrence Wright who later won a Pulitzer Prize for his book about Al-Qaeda (Wright 2006), used real-life terrorist attacks such as the suicide truck bombing of the Beirut US Marines barracks in 1983, the first World Trade Center attack in 1993 and the 1995 Oklahoma City bombing as templates. When the FBI under Agent Hubbard (Denzel Washington) and his partner, a shady female CIA agent (Annette Bening), are unable to stop or contain the violence the US government declares a state of siege and the army takes over. The general in charge (played by action star Bruce Willis) shuts down the city, rounds up and interns young male Arabs and even tortures and kills a suspect. The terrorists in *The Siege* are clearly Muslims. Nevertheless their demands and motivation – as in *True Lies* – are not (or not only) based on religion but on opposition to particular US policies. While in *True Lies* (two years before Osama bin Laden's *fatwa*) terrorists declare war over America's presence in the Gulf region and its support for undemocratic governments, the terrorists in *The Siege* are even more specific: they are a group from Iraq, once trained and supported to oppose Saddam Hussein but then betrayed by the CIA. With their bombing campaign they want now to free their bin-Laden-like leader who was captured in a covert US military operation of which the general public and parts of the government are unaware.

A remarkable debate evolved around *The Siege*, centred mostly on the representation of Arabs and Muslims. Alice Hall analysed the critics' discourse and published her findings in *Communication Quarterly* in 2001. The debate was mainly about the film's relationship with real-world events (like the US embassy bombings in Tanzania and Kenya just a few months prior to the film's release), the intentions of the film's creators, and the constraints of the genre when it comes to dealing with such a complicated subject. Even before the movie's release there were objections to the use of Arab-Muslims as terrorists, especially by Shaheen and representatives of CAIR who were involved in discussions with the producers and the director. They complained that yet again Islamic terrorists were the baddies. Edward Zwick and his producer Linda Obst countered that one of the good guys, played by Tony Shalhoub, is an FBI agent from Lebanon. As a father whose son becomes a victim of the military internment, his character makes an argument against racial profiling and a clear statement that not every Muslim and Arab-American is evil. Shaheen and others dismissed this, however, arguing that Shalhoub's character served merely as a kind of narrative fig leaf who could 'never offset all those scenes that show Arab Muslims murdering men, women, and children' (Shaheen 2009: 462). Shaheen and representatives from CAIR demanded:

- not linking Islamic practices (e.g. reciting prayers from the Koran, ritual washing before prayer, supplication) with terrorism;
- not projecting Arab immigrants as terrorists;
- not selectively framing nor referring to Palestinians and Muslim religious leaders as perpetrators of terror in the US, Israel, Saudi Arabia, or Lebanon.

Shaheen additionally suggested changing the villains into multicultural terrorists, radical militia men or military extremists. The filmmakers declined.[5] Zwick simply commented: 'I didn't make the world. This is the reality of what radical Islamic groups do' (quoted in Pener 1998).

'Reel Bad Arabs', *Angemessenheit* and the Benefits of Stereotyping

Angemessenheit is German for 'adequateness', 'fittingness' or 'appropriateness'. The word includes 'messen' which means 'measuring' or 'scaling', so the adjective 'angemessen' literally means 'being measured at' but leaves open *how* and according to *what* something is measured This is not a new idea in the analysis of representation in art and fiction, where there are concepts like verisimilitude (truth to life) or Edward Schiappa's (2008) 'representational correctness'. *Angemessenheit* combines both ideas but is more open and far-ranging for meta-critical approaches. Shaheen and other critics of stereotyping evaluate movies by checking if they are *angemessen* – how they are (or are not) appropriate to certain norms or ideas – and during the evaluation process they switch this underlying norm or measure on several steps. Various objections can be made against this kind of criticism. Several are elaborated by Schiappa (2008) who describes 'representational correctness' as an umbrella term under which a variety of specific criteria are summarised: *accuracy*, the demand that representations should be authentic and true to the social group depicted to avoid distortion; *purity*, the demand that representation should avoid ambivalence or ideological contradiction; and *innocence*, the demand that representation should be devoid of offense or insult.

Let us combine this with the 'Evil Arab' problematic and retrace the argumentational steps. First, Shaheen argues that a movie like *True Lies* with its stereotypes offers a distortion of reality, or, it is not *angemessen* to reality ('reel portraits are so remote from reality'). The appropriateness in this case (as in other movies or TV shows) can be measured differently: by simple statistical comparison ('*most* Arabs and Muslims are not terrorists'), complexity ('terrorism is not just between good and bad; there are more aspects to be considered') or fairness ('there ought to be a balanced representation of standpoints'). But at what point – especially concerning terrorism – is a representation balanced enough and what is a neutral approach or point of view? Closely connected with these questions is a problem that has haunted art criticism since its beginning:

that of *correct* interpretation or *meaning*. Peter Gottschalk and Gabriel Greenberg, for example, in their study mainly dealing with Arab and Muslims caricatures, accuse *The Siege* of an inappropriate 'implicit message':

> The Islamic terrorist demonstrates a total absence of regret, remorse, or restraint. Ultimately, religious beliefs and acts not only distinguish the terrorists, they motivate the terrorists' irrational violence....The *implicit* message, then, is that Muslims who do not act religiously can be good, normal Americans, while Muslims who perform Islamic rituals and espouse Islamic beliefs also commit terrorists acts.
>
> (Gottschalk and Greenberg 2008: 62, emphasis added)

However, while this meaning might be very clear (even though 'implicit') to the authors, it is based on their subjective judgements and reading. This seems trivial but it has important implications. We might ask why one movie – or the totality of movies – ought anyway to reflect reality in terms of statistics, fairness or complexity. Why not accept that *True Lies* or *The Siege* show us just *some* but not *all* Muslims and Arabs; that movies are a multitude of single stories without claims to be representative, not even as a totality? When it comes to this argument scholars like Shaheen, Gottschalk and Greenberg switch to another kind (and level) of *Angemessenheit*: that of morality or that of impact and influence. They argue that movies must not stereotype because it might hurt feelings and could cause or at least reinforce prejudices and racism, thus leading perhaps to violence or the acceptance of violence.

This is, of course, a strong argument. The whole history of censorship is built on such threats deriving from the simplistic notion of powerful, manipulating media and passive, defenceless audiences – which could be described as a general case of the Third-Person Effect.[6] And of course, producers and directors are eager to avoid this battlefield since they are in very weak position: they would have to prove that their movies *are* no (or at least a negligible) threat to society – which is hardly possible – while their critics need only state that there *might be* a negative effect. But what if there is no such effective meaning in the first place? Or if audiences are active in using, choosing and even making sense of media content, as audience research has suggested?[7]

Rather than delving deeper into the circular 'chicken or egg' debate about possible media influence, let us turn to a major obstacle on the way to properly conceptualising and handling 'Evil Arab' stereotypes: the disregard of the benefits and functionality that stereotypes have for filmmakers and audiences.[8] Most people associate stereotypes with prejudices or more specifically with racism or sexism, and they are right: stereotypes are closely related to these phenomena. But they are not the same. In fact, stereotyping is not even a distortion of reality (or symptom of a distorted perception). Rather, stereotyping is categorising or (over-)generalising. This idea is most often traced back to Walter Lippmann's book *Public Opinion*, first published in 1922. Lippmann realised that human beings need to apply schemes to the world, to give it an order and reduce reality's complexity so we can handle it. Moreover, stereotyping serves to construct a cultural, political and social identity. It sorts people into an in-group and an out-group and serves to construct a cultural, social, political and personal identity. Hence, it enhances self-esteem and legitimises actions against others. Stereotypes are functional and psychologically rational – not just in our social and political life, but also in movies.[9]

Stereotypes are very useful in Hollywood storytelling because they are ready-made, and therefore very effective and economical: they save time and cognitive investment. On the other hand, movies shape social stereotypes as well as creating their own stereotypical images. This is how 'genres' develop. A genre characterises a mode of stereotypical narration and 'is best thought of as a rough category intuitively shared by audience and filmmaker' (Bordwell and Thompson 1997: 52). Such agreement is based on shared conventions concerning characters, actions and situations – but also moods, values and worldviews. It is about meaning. Genre is a kind of language, and you have to learn it like a language to understand it. Every genre has its own ways of talking about the real world, its own codes and verisimilitude (Neale 2007 [1990]).

When we evaluate movies not according to real-world-*Angemessenheit* but as functional products of art or entertainment we get quite a different picture, for most often we find Hollywood's Evil Arab terrorists in action-adventures or thrillers. And the ways they used are absolutely appropriate in terms of the fictional world, of genres and, moreover, the pay-offs and the economics of storytelling. Of course, we can criticise the worldview or the impact of such genres (see, for instance, Hess Wright 2007 [1974]; Klinger 2007 [1984]). But we should acknowledge that action movies have a different representational status from political or social dramas, and therefore a different power or ideological value. Nevertheless, Lina Khatib (2006) compares Hollywood's popular terrorism popcorn entertainment (like the hijacking-thriller *Executive Decision*, 1996) with realistic character and social (and non-terrorist) dramas from Algeria or Egypt, such as *Bab El-Oued City* (1994), which offer very different kinds of stories reaching (and touching) different audiences in different ways. In her study examining how students with different ethnic backgrounds perceive terrorism in action-adventure films, Wilkins (2008: 6) suggests that the argument about genre limitations is just an excuse to justify problematic portrayals. Yet in the end, she (slightly reluctantly) concedes that the action-adventure genre might not be the right kind of entertainment from which to expect balanced and unproblematic perspectives (2008: 82).

Another popular movie industry aiming for mass entertainment seems to offer a suitable comparison with Hollywood concerning questions of Muslim (though not Arab) stereotyping as a reflection of real-world conflicts in times of terrorism and political violence: Hindu mainstream cinema, better known as 'Bollywood'. Yet it uses stock characters and narratives in a different way.

Muslims and Terrorists in Bollywood

According to the *New York Times* Hollywood movies reach around 2.6 billion people in the world while Indian films find an audience of 3.6 billion worldwide (Mishra 2004). Bollywood contributes only around 200 of the annual 800-1,000 Indian movies, but the mainstream Hindi films produced in Mumbai (formerly Bombay) offer 'the model for popular regular cinema and is in this respect closer to being an all-India cinema' (Mishra 2002: 3). Bollywood movies are best known for their song-and-dance scenes, simple and escapist colourfulness, and romantic and melodramatic emotionality. Despite its growing worldwide appeal – advanced by Non-Resident-Indian (NRI) communities and a new-found Western audience – Bollywood is nevertheless regarded and analysed as a specifically national cinema dealing with cultural and political problems:

[O]ne of the key questions for a 'national' cinema is how to incorporate individual identities into group identities, and this is always a matter of particular inflections and narrative strategies for particular historical and social contexts.

(Chakravarty 2005: 237)

Bollywood's high political and cultural relevance to India's society and collective psyche has been discussed at length elsewhere (for example, Virdi 2003; Kazmi 1999; Chakravarty 1993; Ahmed 1992). I will concentrate here on one of the major challenges to Indian integration and cohesion: the role of Muslims in India and the political as well as racial, religious or communal violence connected with this issue.

While in the USA only around one percent of the population is Muslim, in India this religious and cultural group accounts for 14 percent – around 165 million people out of a total population of almost 1.2 billion.[10] Three closely related conflict situations shape modern Muslims' public image as hostile or at least suspicious. First, the enmity with the Islamic Republic of Pakistan as hostile 'brother state', a nation which arose, like India, from Independence but also from partition as 'the bloodiest and most traumatic event in the history of this part of the world', leaving an 'infected wound that has proved difficult to heal' (Cossio 2007: 220). Both countries fought several wars, and in India Pakistan is known to harbour, finance, train and support anti-Indian terrorist and rebel groups. In times of crisis Indian Muslims are suspected by Hindus of being 'undecidables' (Chakravaty 2005 [2000]: 238) or Pakistan's fifth column. The second main point of conflict is Kashmir with its Muslim majority and separatist movement which led to uprisings and harsh counter-actions by national security forces. International Islamist *mujahidin* from outside (mostly Afghanistan) have used this conflict to import their idea of Holy War.[11] The third and central point for Indian Muslims is the communal discrimination, hatred and violence stirred up by radical Hindu-supremacist nationalism: gaining power from the 1980s onwards, a broad network of political parties and organisations such as Bharatiya Janata Party (BJP), Vishwa Hindu Parishad (VHP) and the paramilitary Rashtriya Swayamsevak Sangh (RSS) have agitated for Hindu ideological and political dominance and against special rights for Muslims. In the 1992 riots in Mumbai (still Bombay at this time) after Hindu radicals tore down the Babri mosque in Ayodhya, and the 2002 riots in Gujarat, incredible atrocities happened and thousands were killed while police often remained passive or uninvolved.

> It is within this culture of suspicion, which is at once ordinary and capable of erupting into extreme forms of violence, that the idea of *strangeness* is born. The Bombay riots saw the slaughter of thousands of Muslims by crowds that included their neighbors and former friends. The events of 1992-93 were a watershed in the imaginative rendering of a city, so crucial to Bombay cinema.
>
> (Mazumdar 2007: 30, original emphasis)

This violence was met with counter-violence: in 1993, for instance, Muslim gangsters retaliated by setting off thirteen bombs in Bombay (Varshnev 2002, Narula 2002, Bhatt 2001, Sen 1993).

Bollywood has not shied away from these issues and events so crucial to India's (co-)existence and internal and external security: they crop up in action adventures and thrillers, dramas and romantic comedies.[12] Bollywood cinema appears highly patriotic and extremely nationalistic: promoting India and its ideal of Hindustan is 'Hindi cinema's own agenda – imagining a unified nation' (Virdi 2003: 1). In action thrillers the jingoistic stance becomes very clear, for example in the title sequence of terrorist-movie blockbuster *Zameen* (2003), when singers hail their Motherland. In Hindi they sing: 'The desire of every Indian / As sacred as the Bible, the Gita and the Koran / It's our motherland….To protect our Motherland, we will lay down our lives' – and, in English: 'My nation is my pride'. As nationalistic as this sounds, already here the idea of unity across religious boundaries under the idealised state concept of *Hindustan* is promoted. Such tolerance, however, does not prevent Bollywood filmmakers relying on stereotypical Muslim terrorists as demonic villains. Often collaborating with Pakistan, driven by religious fanaticism or simple hate, black-bearded, grim and fever-eyed radicals seek to attack the Indian state with bombs and hijackings similar to those unfortunately well known to India's peoples. In the movie *Hijack* (2008) they meet secretly to plan their evil deeds before finally screaming out loud, praising Allah so every spectator is aware of their religious affiliation.

Of course, these grotesque and one-dimensional figures function as ready-made images just as other characters in the movies do. Most of the exaggerated stereotyping is due to generally over-the-top and simplistic representational conventions. 'Evil Indian Muslims' are even more explicit and gruesome than Hollywood's 'Evil Arabs' in mainstream Indian cinema – and both countries' standard enemies are ideologically structured in the same way. These bogeyman terrorists come from *outside* as an indistinct group and represent a collective *Other* threatening the in-group, thereby strengthening identification and identity, legitimising state force and affirming dominant ideological boundaries. These 'Evil Muslims' are, however, just *one* kind of established and prevailing stereotypical terrorist in popular Hindi cinema. The other type represents India's troubled peripheries like Kashmir or the North Eastern States. He or she is a Muslim radicalised – one can even say *produced* – by Hindu-led repression and an ongoing cycle of violence. This tragic-individual terrorist has a personal history of grievance which is usually not only recapitulated in the dialogue but even shown on screen and thus made tangible for the audience. If such characters cannot find peace and reconcile with the community they die melodramatically in the end. These and other (religiously or politically identified) victim-hero terrorists are often played by established or upcoming stars like Bobby Deol, Hrithik Roshan, Ajay Devgan or Aamir Khan, who in other films might act as the policemen and soldiers fighting terrorism.[13] It is hard to imagine something similar in Hollywood cinema, and even unthinkable when it comes to A-list stars such as Schwarzenegger or Harrison Ford.

Bollywood's tragic terrorists, though, are based on hero models like the noble outlaw and on a culturally highly valued code of honour and family commitment. So when Bobby Deol in *Badal* (2000), Hrithik Roshan in *Mission Kashmir* (2000), or Ajay Devgan in *Dil Jale* (1996) become members of 'terrorist' groups they are driven by their rage and desire for avenging their families and fathers in the rural regions of Kashmir, Punjab or elsewhere. Religion does not matter much in their resemblance to classical romantic bandits (or the movies' similarities to the Western genre). In other plots religion is an important part of everyday life but as a reason for hostilities it generally takes a back seat in favour of the narrative's clash between the central state's idealised united multitude and the periphery's plurality – in other words, between the peaceful project of Hindustan and the real social grievances, injustices, corruption, despotism and local law enforcement's brutality working against the national ideal. Hence, religious boundaries between Sikhs, Muslims and others, are transgressed not only in the political national utopia but in postcolonial political misery and pain.

Here ideological needs and the requirements of cinematic (and stereotypical) storytelling merge, for even in constructing a tragic terrorist Bollywood needs a *typical* villain. Tragic-terrorists are victims of corrupt politicians who seek only their personal (i.e. unpatriotic) advantage – for instance by playing the various ethnic groups, as in *Fiza* (2000) when both Muslim and Hindu representatives work secretly together in planning riots. One finds reckless businessmen (*Rang De Basanti*, 2006; *Hero – Story of a Spy*, 2003), cruel feudal landlords (*Chamku*, 2008; *Dil Jale*, 1996) or power-hungry or sadistic policemen misusing their office in the name on counterterrorism (*Badal*, 2000, *Dhokha*, 2007). So while these movies also draw a line between good and bad, it is a *horizontal* line: not, as in *True Lies* and many other Hollywood stories, between different nations, religions or ethnic groups, but between levels of social, economical and political power and between an in-group 'down here' and an out-group 'up there'. The movies thereby perpetuate a peculiar grassroots patriotism which is suspicious of certain classes of its nation's functionaries. In this way Bollywood encodes the country's historical colonial experiences and the socialist dreams buried in India's post-Nehru decline in the 1970s.

In addition to the tragic terrorist, another stereotype countering communalist and especially radical Hindu nationalist resentments is the 'Good Muslim'. He (never she) is a kind of enlightened, well-educated man without moral flaws; calm and patient but always ready actively to promote and defend a peaceful and tolerant Islam. In Subash Ghai's *Black & White* (2008) one Professor Gubta, played by Anil Kappor, accommodates a young man, not knowing that his guest is a would-be suicide bomber – one who in the end decides to spare innocent Indians because of the lesson his experience, and of course the kind, father-like Professor, teach him. One movie combining many of Bollywood's characteristic narrative elements in handling problematic intra-national terrorism, discrimination and single group grievance is Pooja Bhatt's *Dhokha*. Muzammil Ibrahim plays a modern Islamic police officer, Zaid, who even donates blood to a Hindu child after a suicide attack, but then finds out that his own wife Sarha (Tulip Joshi) was the suicide bomber. Attacked by his own neighbourhood and treated as a suspect by his own department, Zaid sets off to investigate. He finds out that his wife's father was suspected of being an extremist and was beaten to death by policemen during interrogation. The same men then rounded up Sarha, her brother and grandfather, threatened and humiliated, maybe even raped her to keep her and her family silent. Zaid faces Muslim extremists who threaten to behead him: they explain that Muslims have to look out for themselves, that their bombings are acts of self-defence and revenge, and tell Zaid that his brother-in-law is also going to become a martyr. This, of course, Zaid can prevent by changing the young man's mind in a highly dramatic finale. After the hero has delivered a patriotic but critical speech to his superiors the real villains are arrested: not the radical Islamists but the fiendish policemen who started the – or at least *this* specific, personal – cycle of violence.

As simple and formulaic as *Dhokha* and other movies are in their description and resolution of terrorist problems, and as overtly, almost propagandistically, as they contribute to a certain agenda thereby affirming the myth by acknowledging some particular flaws (Barthes 1964: 140), their stereotypical plots and characters, varying from action-adventures, thrillers to melodramas, nevertheless offer a successful model of mainstream entertainment that promotes ideological education in an ethical and socially positive form. Bollywood apparently seeks to balance and reconcile, even to counter Hindu extremists' ideas and – as with *Zakhm* (1998), *Rang De Basanti* or others movies – even dares to show nationalists as dangerous, fanatical and intolerant. Of course this 'social contribution' is not merely based on insight and goodwill. Bollywood filmmakers face Indian censorship (Bhowmik 2009), and might be confronted with protests by Muslims groups – equivalents of CAIR or the ADC. Suketu Mehta (2008: 507) describes how worries about possible violent reactions or censors' restrictions have influenced scriptwriting so that governmental or socio-economic rationales for Kashmir's unstable situation are excluded. The terrorism action comedy *Jo Bole So Nihal* (2005) was withdrawn from cinemas after Sikhs protested against the degrading main character and the title (a religious chant used in prayers or battles), and after two bombs exploded in a Delhi movie theatre.[14]

After 9/11: What Hollywood Could Learn From Bollywood

Although Bollywood readily adapts stories from Hollywood – often '(H)Indianised' for the domestic audience (Ganti 2002: 290) – when it comes to terrorism India has its own experience. After the 9/11 attacks the nationalist BJP declared: 'What India has been witnessing for over a decade, the United States has experienced the fury of Islamic terrorism only now on its own soil' (Chakravartty 2002: 206). Most of the Indian media contextualised the events historically and politically, drawing parallels with the rise of fundamentalism in Asia and the Middle East (Chakravartty 2002: 207). In the 'war on terror' and the military engagement in Afghanistan America's strategic partnership with Pakistan is criticised given the neighbour state's own fostering of terrorism against India (as the investigations after the Mumbai attacks in 2008 have shown). Therefore 9/11 and the West's new 'global war' had relatively little influence on Bollywood's narrative treatment of terrorism or the problem of Muslim status and stereotyping (although, reflecting real tendencies in the region, transnational 'jihadism' has become more of an issue). Rather, 9/11 and other events in the war on terror, such as prisoner abuse in Abu Ghraib and its photo documentation, were easily incorporated in the existing generic framework: in *Dhokha*, for example, a grinning policeman shoots pictures of the stripped Sarha with his cell phone; while in *New York* (2009) false accusations and mistreatment of Muslim terror suspects by both Indian and US security services turn formerly harmless NRI Omar (Neil Nitin Mukesh) into a revenge-seeking conspirator.

Hollywood can learn from Bollywood – and it seems to have done so already since 9/11. Shaheen (2008: 38), for example, has noted that 'silver screens have displayed, at times, more complex, evenhanded Arab portraits than I have seen in the past'. 'Sympathising' with Muslim and Arab terrorists was hardly possible before this date and of course immediately afterwards, but films like *Rendition* (2007) and *Syriana* (2005) are at least interested in how and under what conditions terrorism arises in Muslim countries, thereby blurring the simplistic distinction between good and evil. Of course these films are exceptions: they seep in from the industry's fringes and independent low- / no-budget realms,[15] and are not typical (action-) genre movies. But even Peter Berg's *The Kingdom* (2007), despite reverting to 1980s-style machismo, US superiority and heroism, pays a visit to a foreign land which stays strange and ambivalent in its own terms. *Body of Lies* (2008) depicts the war against terrorism in the Middle East as a dirty and obscure day-to-day struggle without any morally superior side, in which US technological supremacy with its god-like satellite real-time surveillance allows America to see everything without understanding anything. Even narratives dealing with secretive members of terrorist sleeper cells have started to grant them a more detailed background, a deeper, more comprehensible story of motivational grievance. Mainstream entertainment – such as the TV series *Sleeper Cell* or the movie *Traitor* (2008) – has also introduced as a new (tragic) hero 'good' Muslims as undercover agents who spy on terrorists and thus automatically present a more differentiated view or at least a new arrangement of formulaic story components. So when in *Traitor* Don Cheadle plays African-born Samir Horn, throughout the first half of the movie it is undisclosed that he is a Western infiltrator – and in fact it does not matter much, for Horn is a broken character, more dedicated to Islam than to the USA where he lost his job because of his religion. Cheadle's character is in this sense a more nuanced and tragic figure, and marks a development of characters like Denzel Washington's Hubbard in *The Siege*. As in Bollywood movies Hollywood has coined a new standard narrative situation, sometimes only a single scene: the false accusation or suspicion of Muslim or Arab (or Arab-looking) individuals. US entertainment has also begun to establish the character of the terrorist who is created by US policy (thereby introducing the so-called 'backlash' phenomenon already picked up by *The Siege*), but also by very harsh counterterrorism policies and actions – as, before *Dhokha*, successful movies such as *Maachis* (1996) had done in India.[16]

The new tendencies in Hollywood cinema and US television are of course not an orientation towards Hindi cinema. They are due, rather, to the real-life problems the United States and Europe face today – problems India has struggled with for quite some time. So Bollywood and Hollywood in fact exemplify that when terrorism and political violence comes too close and rocks society's foundations too hard (whether through a single shock or long-term effects) collective cultural reflections cannot solely rely on black-and-white answers, not even in mainstream storytelling as a form of social and psychological coping. Popular culture can counter the terrorists' narrative by acknowledging their outrage and grief, thereby embracing and *neutralising* it, and simultaneously renouncing official state viewpoints.

There are limits and constraints on Hollywood adopting the Bollywood model. Hindus and Muslims share a long common cultural and social history on the Indian subcontinent: ethnic similarities and the Muslim community's substantial size prevent it being framed as too different from other groups. Some of the biggest Bollywood stars are Muslims – most notably Shahrukh Khan, but also two other famous (not related) 'Khans' Aamir and Salman. It is nevertheless doubtful whether the greater presence of Muslim and Arab-American actors in Hollywood that Shaheen calls for, even if they were assigned to non-'Evil Arab' roles, would help erode stereotypes in the US and Europe. Western societies imagine Muslims and Arabs (even if only of Arab descent) as foreign and alien culturally and in their appearance. It is easier to keep a (mental) distance because the main real-life terrorist causes are understood as originating far away and are generally not perceived as *intra*-national issues. Other constraints lie in the conventions of Western cinema and its storytelling. Bollywood is based on acceptance of distinctive formulaic, generic and political entertainment. Comparable over-simplistic, melodramatic and patriotic storytelling is much more problematic in the US and Europe where serious issues like terrorism or ethnic violence demand an *angemessene*, or appropriate aesthetic and dramatic form which seldom reaches a broad audience or is compatible with comical interludes, references to the hero's mother or extra-diegetic song and dance scenes.

In the end, Western critics are suspicious of anything that looks like a clear agenda in movies when they are not realistic and at the same time new, original, of high aesthetic value, thoughtful or balanced. Everyday audiences, allergic to dull morality messages, tend to feel the same way, but even if they are not familiar with certain ways of blurring boundaries between serious topics and alternative ideological stereotyping, nobody says it has to stay that way.

Notes

[1] Miller and Landau (2008) for example explain, based on Terror Management Theory, how catastrophic events are likely to enforce prejudices, stereotyping and hostility against outer-groups. For the phenomenon of scapegoating in this context see Welch (2006).

[2] According to the Arab American Institute (www.aaiusa.org/pages/demographics/); US Census Bureau figures in the year 2000 show only 1.2 million who reported an Arab ancestry (www.census.gov/prod/2003pubs/c2kbr-23.pdf).

[3] Hard total numbers concerning the religious affiliation of the United States population are hard to find and are reliable only to a limited extent. Figures range from 1.3 million (American Religious Identification Survey - http://livinginliminality.files.wordpress.com/2009/03/aris_report_2008.pdf) and 2.45 million (PEW Forum on Religion and Public Life: 'Mapping the Global Muslim Population. A Report on the Size and Distribution of the World's Muslim Population', Oct. 2009 – http://pewforum.org/newassets/images/reports/Muslimpopulation/Muslimpopulation .pdf), up to over 7 million according the Council on American-Islamic Relations (www.cair.com/AboutIslam/IslamBasics.aspx).

[4] According to the US Census Bureau's 'Population Clock' (www.census.gov/main/www/popclock.html).

[5] For an account of this debate see: Shaheen 1998; Shaheen 2009: 461ff; Peretz 1998; Klinghoffer 1998; Pener 1998.

[6] First discovered or at least described by Davison (1983), the Third-Person Effect refers to people's overestimation of media influence (and mostly underestimation of being influenced themselves). The Third-Person Effect can be found in attitudes towards pornography, media violence or advertising and could account for acceptance of censorship or other sorts of media restrictions.

[7] See, for instance, Vidmar and Rokeach's (1974) very interesting classic study.

[8] Criticism often ignores the requirements and conditions of movies' narrativity and production: Shaheen's suggestion to change the perpetrators in *The Siege* into white militia men simply *could not* be accepted for it would have changed the movie altogether (above all it would have made the fundamental civil rights and internment part of the film's story implausible or even impossible to sustain).

[9] On the processes and functions of social stereotypes see Oakes, Haslam and Turner 1994.

[10] According to the Indian Government's Census Data from 2001 India's population totalled 1.02bn with 138m Muslims and 827m Hindus. In 2010 a population of 1,17bn is estimated (see, for example, the US Census Bureau's International Data Base).

[11] On the Kashmir conflict, Pakistan's role and jihadism see: Latimer 2004; Santhanam et al. 2003; Ganguly 1996; Ganguly and Bajpai 1994.

[12] Because of its own dramatic tradition and theory Indian theatre and cinema is more prone to multi-genre storytelling (therefore 'masala movies'). This leads to, for Western audiences, sometimes uncommonly abrupt changes and twists in mood and dramatic composition. Nevertheless, and due to Western (and especially Hollywood's) cinematic influence, one can apply the concept of genres and assign single movies to them. The main general underlying genre in non-comic entertainments is the melodrama.

[13] For example Deol's role as Sepoy Tarun in *Tango Charlie* (2005) which offers a kind of tour through India's terrorist conflicts. For the role of these actors as victim-hero terrorists see for example: Deol in *Badal* (2000) or *Chamku* (2008), Roshan in *Fiza* (2000) or *Mission Kashmir* (2000), Devgan in *Dil Jale* (1996) and Khan in *Rang De Basanti* (2006) or *Fanaa* (2006).

[14] See 'Delhi police hunt cinema bombers', BBC, 23 May 2005, http://news.bbc.co.uk/2/hi/south_asia/4571987.stm.

[15] For example, *The War Within* (2005), *Civic Duty* (2006), *The Torturer* (2008).

[16] *Maachis* deals with Sikh uprisings in the 1980s and '90s and is about a young man and his fiancée joining terrorists to take revenge for his tortured friend / her brother.

Chapter 11

An Ethico-Politics of Subaltern Representations in Post-9/11 Documentary Film

Joe Parker and Rebekah Sinclair[1]

The World War Without End (WWWoE), formerly known as the War on Terror,[2] is one of those rare occasions when a gendered subaltern population comes to the attention of the nation-state. If the subaltern is understood as something akin to illiterate rural women from the global South, then she now has the full attention of the White House and Downing Street, the US State Department, CNN and *Time* magazine.[3] In official state positions and in media coverage, interest in the subaltern is often expressed in humanitarian attention to the rights or freedoms of these subaltern women in order to justify military invasion and ongoing intervention.

Post-9/11 documentaries that appear to oppose the World War Without End rely on similar liberal beliefs in rights and freedom in order to formulate explicit and implicit political criticisms of the war. In this way the documentaries are agreeing with the arguments of those they claim to oppose: such nation-states as the United States and Britain, who have justified their interventions by use of these same humanitarian terms. This agreement is seen when documentaries show the violation of constitutional or international law and human rights in Afghanistan, as in *Taxi to the Dark Side* (2010), or in the US, as in Sree Nallamothu's *Patriot Acts* (2004).

We might liken our own present historical moment to the nineteenth-century British attention to certain women of India whom they felt they must protect from what they saw as the uncivilised tradition of *sati*, or the burning of upper class and caste widows. In both cases, a dominant world power legitimises its intervention into the affairs of a South Asian country by arguing that outsiders must protect the women of the region from the barbarian practices of their countrymen. So here we examine the figure of the gendered subaltern women in post-9/11 antiwar documentaries to reconsider the grounds for critique of the WWWoE. Our central interest is to reject colonising modes of modern meaning and justice based in humanitarian legal and rights thinking, as well as the appropriations of the subaltern to those ends found in film.

Since the WWWoE is being fought not just in Afghanistan and Iraq, but simultaneously in the US, Britain, Spain, Indonesia, Yemen, and other locations, we cannot follow the classic conception of war as something fought in discrete theatres limited to points of invasion and mass conflict. For this reason we have considered documentaries made about a broad range of theatres of conflict not limited to Afghanistan and Iraq.

We bring postcolonial and queer feminist political theory and an ethics of singularity and the Other into conversation with documentary film to centre our analysis on subaltern populations. This allows us to demonstrate how certain forms of violence can often remain unnameable and invisible because they are made possible and justified by fundamental liberal assumptions. Below, we propose to begin identifying the appropriations and subjugations performed in the name of liberal humanitarian justice in order to recognise and challenge the claims of universal democracy and justice made by the US and other collaboration forces in the WWWoE as a problem. This problem is seen in the way that universalist claims naturalise the violences of globalisation through agricultural regulatory schemas proliferated under the guise of national reconstruction or freedom as defined by the economic. For as we will see in our discussion of the films *Taxi to the Dark Side* and *Rendition* (2007), when the valences of democracy, economy, and occupation or war converge in this way, the subaltern's inability or refusal to conform to sanctioned modes of capitalist exchange also make possible her erasure from the political.

As documentary filmmakers work within homogenising universalist beliefs in human rights, freedom, and democratic constitutional governance, they erase the agency and resistance of the subaltern. Subaltern agency is rendered visible only with careful attention to local configurations of difference within historically specific arenas of struggle. If we wish to ever come to recognise rural, unlettered women of the global south as something other than victim, we must find a way to refuse the monolithic homogeneity of categories like 'Muslim women' (obscuring differences of sexual orientation, class, race, and rural/urban divides), 'Afghan women' (erasing class, literacy and educational, and ethnic or regional differences), or even the universalised category of 'women', that is itself the subject of considerable debate among feminists (Butler 1992: 9, 13, 16-17; Mohanty 2003; Spivak 2008: 142-3, 148-9).

Gayatri Spivak and a number of other activist critics have turned to the notion of singularity to counter liberal presumptions to the universal (Spivak 1995: xxiv-xxv; Spivak 2005: 475-8; Morton 2007: 61-3, 95-134; Derrida 1982: 21; Derrida 1991: 100-2; Deleuze 1990: 52-63). They propose instead to recognise the constitution of the Other through these general categories as a key ethico-political moment in a political ontology of resistance.[4] Singularity is the notion of the unrepeatable, irreducible, historically specific, contingent Other whose existence is marked outside of knowledge and language – a 'social' being that nevertheless is constituted in ways that make her 'unintelligible' to us. In our present approach to justice and responsibility, our goal is to explore practical ways to establish other forms of ethical accountability in documentaries that focus on relations with the Others of ongoing imperialism, globalisation, and the WWWoE. We suggest that ethico-political responsibility is possible through refusing to appropriate the Other into modern schemas of intelligibility, even as this refusal displaces the terms of our own collectivities and subjectivities. In the documentaries we explore, we mark how the figure of the subaltern always already contests these universalist terms and logics that would render the Other decipherable, even as the politically disenfranchised populations to which the subaltern refers are strategically excluded from dominant histories and representations.

The Elusive Subaltern in Post-9/11 Documentaries

The gendered subaltern is characterised by the difficulties of understanding her within the political limits of bourgeois modern knowability. The subaltern has been theorised in different ways by activists in Marxist movements first, and now increasingly across a range of disciplines, movements, schools and regions. This obscurity is produced in obvious ways for documentarians, such as limiting the subject matter almost exclusively to the agency of the educated or men, as in *Taxi to the Dark Side*. More frequently, however, the failure to recognise the resistance of the subaltern takes place in more subtle ways.

To explore examples of when the figure of the elusive subaltern appears in post-9/11 documentaries which seem to critique the WWWoE, we begin with Alex Gibney's Academy Award winning documentary, *Taxi to the Dark Side*. The film documents abuses which are widely known but which have never officially been acknowledged as a tactic.[5] Gibney's film explicitly contrasts the views of military interrogators with legal experts who argue in humanitarian terms that the practices documented are violations of national and international law. Their arguments rely on the foundational presumption of equality and the coherent, free individual that undergird modern national and international legal systems. The movie documents the lack of freedom on the part of the taxi driver (and other detainees at other facilities) at the centre of the film to show that the law was not applied equally to free individuals.

While the film is relentlessly masculinised, there is a fleeting moment when one military intelligence interrogator makes a passing remark about a woman corporal interrogator who suggested that the taxi driver's wife visited him in prison. This is the only mention in the film of a woman from the small, peanut-farming village of Yakubi in Khost Province that the taxi driver was from, and may be the only representation of a rural, possibly unlettered farming woman in the film, even though the woman herself is not shown on screen. Yet the US interrogator being interviewed quickly dismisses the possibility that the wife was able to visit, given the conditions at the prison, and the viewing audience is left with a contradictory and uncertain account.

This ghostly, contradictory appearance of a rural Afghan woman in a film that argues for humane treatment and constitutional rights brings into clarity the gendered tilt not only of the prison population at Bagram air base in 2002-3 and in the documentary, but also of the WWWoE and global capitalism and development. For example, the male taxi driver was able to insert himself into the circuits of capitalism as he transitioned from stone-carrier and farmer to taxi driver. Unlike the male driver, the women in this same village are likely cases of those outside the circuits of capitalism who rarely benefit in any concrete way from national wars of liberation or so-called modern development, globalisation, or democracy. Their nearly complete absence from this documentary is one index of how such rural Afghan and Iraqi women are effaced from the stories that documentarians tell us about the WWWoE, and the ways this effacement is tied to their identity constituted as economic remainders in the theatres of globalisation.

We can see the ways these peanut farmers might be remaindered by globalisation – and thus also left out of the narrative of Gibney's documentary – by pointing to the economic shift from pre-war agricultural self-sufficiency, to globalised, neoliberal policies in Afghan seed policy. Shortly after the Afghan theatre opened with the US-led invasion, an initial 2002 agreement was reached between international and national organisations and the UN Food and Agriculture Organization (FAO) to protect local seeds. The agreement stated:

> [Seed practices] should not distort the local seed systems and it should be aimed at building the foundation for a sustainable seed supply system in the future. As much as possible, says the Code, seed should be produced locally to ensure its adaptation to the local environment....

(Food and Agriculture Organization 2002)

But by 2005, the FAO, in complicity with the European Union and the US, had moved to support a commercial seed market – opening the door to foreign seed companies and agribusiness, and endorsing monopoly rights for seed companies. This effectively shut out small farmers, for whom it is difficult or next to impossible to meet the new minimum standards of germination, purity, and labelling for seed sales established in the seed law passed in June 2009 (Grain 2008). From a perspective considering the rural peanut farmers left out of the human rights discourse in Gibney's film, this agricultural shift marks the specific structures of economic-political disenfranchisement that likely made possible and financially viable the transition of the taxi driver from peanut farmer to urban participant, even as the same mechanisms may be destroying the grounds for his wife's farming practices.

Likewise, in Wasit Province of the Iraqi theatre, under new policies adopted by the Iraqi Ministry of Agriculture in 2008, the Provincial Reconstruction Team (PRT) is funding a loan guarantee programme through Iraqi banks in order to move local farmers into the circuits of financial credit systems (Noel 2008; Husar 2010). This work of globalisation on the ground, in a theatre of conflict of the WWWoE, moves the Afghan and Iraqi national agricultural systems towards replacing the small farmer seed production that has served subsistence farming for millennia. These subsistence food production practices are displaced with commercial seed sales and monopoly rights that instead serve transnational agribusiness interests such as Nestlè, Stine Seed Company of Iowa and the German seed company KWS, in cooperation with the Afghan Ministry of Foods and Light Industry (Grain 2009).[6] In this sense civilian USAID workers, the armed forces of the PRT and local elites do more than erase subalterns from the universalist categories of the 'economic' or 'progress': they promote policies, laws, and regulatory systems that work to destroy means of subaltern subsistence.

Documentarians who give attention to the always already present subaltern agency and its resistance to the forces of globalisation would find rich material in what Spivak calls the 'persistent short-term initiatives of local self-management…against the financialisation of the globe' (2008: 156) that the women of the peanut farming villages of Khost Province have been forced to develop while under siege from the WWWoE. Spivak has linked subsistence and small or medium-size farming to Afghan democracy for these reasons (2008: 157), as the terms of democracy shift from those of liberal humanist practices centring on national class elites of the global south, to those which recognise local decision-making practices among subaltern groups. However, even as we suggest documentary film give attention to these matrices of globalisation amid the WWWoE, as well as the movements that resist them, we must also mark the ways documentary film itself imposes limits to the recognisability of these initiatives. This is one way to critically approach the means by which documentarity structures meaning through its claims to facticity and the power at play in its filmic gaze.

Recognisability and the Ethico-Politics of the Documentary Frame

The documentary image is constituted fundamentally by what is left out — maintained, like the taxi driver's wife, outside the frame. Judith Butler's work on frames of recognisability suggests that democracy and legality are deployed to render certain Others legible during times of war, even as, in the same gesture, they exclude Others like the subaltern from the literal document frame, and thus invites a critique of the politics of framing. The frame is active, interpretive, 'both jettisoning and presenting, and doing both at once', delimiting the domain of representability and its Others (Butler 2009: 73-4). As Butler suggests, 'If there is a role for visual culture during times of war it is precisely to thematise the forcible frame', referring as in her other work to Michel Foucault's conception of power (2009: 100).

This suggests that the ethico-political documentary film might come to document the delimiting operations of the frame itself in order to contest the terms of recognition used to construct the film's ethics and politics (Butler 2009: 71, 73). One example of this can be found in Cassian Harrison and Saira Shah's documentary, *Beneath the Veil* (2001), which claims to be documenting the effects of Taliban rule on Afghan citizens generally, and on women specifically. Because of the danger of encountering Taliban officials, and because video and other cameras were outlawed by the Taliban regime, much of the film is shot from under a burqa or inside a sweater. The film shows Shah and her crew being detained, searched, and questioned — vacillating in and out of the frames presented to the viewer. By this movement, the universalised claims of the sovereignty of the Western humanitarian, and her assumptions of unmediated access to the 'real' of covered and violated women in the frame, are disrupted as both Shah and her crew find the camera turned back upon them. This vacillation makes visible the operations of power that are inscribed by the camera and may be deployed as a documentary method to problematise the ethico-political limits of what is representable.

Conversely, in Nick Broomfield's 2007 docudrama *Battle for Haditha*,[7] we find a failure to interrogate the Western schemas of recognisability. The film portrays the perspectives of US Marines, an Iraqi family, and several Iraqi insurgents on a violent conflict that follows the explosion of a roadside bomb. Though the film appears to be critical of the war, Broomfield perpetuates the political and military justifications for the ongoing occupation of Iraq by appropriating identities of disenfranchised women into the schemas of humanitarian intelligibility that substantiate the claims of collaboration forces as a quest for global democracy. A Butlerian analysis would ask us to mark that the lives of the Iraqi women and children who are killed late in the film are rendered visible and valuable only by first being presented throughout the film as 'normal families', through heterosexual sex scenes, and family and religious gatherings, and the like. Indeed, we can recognise the violence and wrongs done to the possibly subaltern women only because they are depicted through an ontology of a generalised, global human subject constituted through an assumed shared narrative of suffering and coercion with the US soldiers and Iraqi insurgents. By doing this, Broomfield does not make it possible to recognise any way in which the subaltern women might reject the ethico-politics of US military personnel. For Ewa Ziarek, working with Jean-François Lyotard's notion of the differend, this inability of the women to signify the violence done to them in terms other than those offered by Broomfield's generalised liberal ontology, is precisely what maintains the putative unity of the Western, humanitarian identity (Ziarek 2001: 17, 84).

Both documentaries and fictional films circumscribe difference within a particular domain of representability, one to which all forms of subjectivity must sooner or later be referred for their validation and legibility. For this reason Spivak has emphasised the ethico-political importance of the imagination in construing the 'reality' of those populations (such as the subaltern) that generally appear only outside the hegemonic narrative frames of capitalism, 'development', globalisation, justice, or the 'real' (2003: 12, 43, 53-4). While

Spivak's work gives primary attention to fiction and history, we may borrow her insights to develop an analysis of such film genres as 'docudrama' or films marketed as 'based on real events', such as *A Mighty Heart* (2007), *Kandahar* (2001), *Redacted* (2007), *Rendition, Battle for Haditha*, or *Extraordinary Rendition* (2007). It is through the mobilisation of the imagination in films on the margins of the documentary genre that the documentarian may carry out what Spivak (1995: 79) calls the 'opening up of…counterfactual possible worlds'. Such counterfactuals can accommodate the agencies of subalterns or the resistances of unlettered women that are often erased in orthodox economic or national history, or the elite, androcentric narratives of progress, or the colonial/postcolonial, or the family through which subalterns are erased. Documentaries of this sort reconstitute the ethico-politics of the past in order to make room for the 'real' of the subaltern present, and allow for the subaltern to come into her own in a 'counterfactual post future' (Spivak 1995: 82), a term useful for constituting a new subgenre at the margins of documentary film that renders legible the histories and experiences and future contributions of the subaltern.

A Calculus of Affirmative Undecidability

As we have suggested, post-9/11 documentaries operate within the limits of what we might call the 'calculations of answerability' or intelligibility (Spivak 2008: 58), calculations ceaselessly marked by their necessary insertion into complicity with troubled binaries. Such binaries might include, for example, the nation-state which kills under the colour of democracy as opposed to the armed terrorist who appears as anti-democratic, or justice via state legal systems as opposed to the injustice of the 'illegal' (such as non-state armed forces). How might documentarians work within the politically compromised space of this acknowledgement of complicity? In Jacques Derrida's (1989) analysis of Martin Heidegger's relation to Nazi fascism, and in Spivak's (2008: 61-78, 88-89) analysis of the academic's relation to capitalist exploitation and violence – in the act of drinking tea or paying taxes or speaking against war – they urge a caution that takes the form of 'knowing which is the least grave of forms of complicity' (Derrida 1989: 39-40, quoted in Spivak 2008: 63, 65). This approach to critique, one haunted by Nazi electoral successes that compromised Heidegger, deconstruction, and democracy in general, centres on a careful mapping of sites where complicity is acknowledged rather than denied. This acknowledgement may work affirmatively to strategically site ways that the unrecognisable, the subaltern, or the differend might pressure intelligibility into new forms of sense making.

This approach could be summarised as what we might term a calculus of 'affirmative undecidability, responsibility' (Spivak 2003: 101-2). Rather than presumptively claiming that we know the universal values of a common humanity, we may strategically work with the undecidable to allow the figure of the collective (audience, we, nation, Marxist, feminist) to remain irreducible, so that it 'remembers its limits' (Spivak 2003: 52) rather than presumes universality. Such a calculus of undecidability refuses the claim to make the radical other appear and speak, as in ethnography or much documentary film, instead operating with the recognition that the best we may do is to work to make visible the specific circumstances and limits to knowledge that render the speech acts of the subaltern indecipherable or unhearable (Morris 2010: 3, 6). By focusing on the moment of effacement in disclosure (Spivak 1999: 310), as we saw in *Taxi to the Dark Side*, we may 'make visible the foreclosure of the subject whose lack of access to the position of narrator is the condition of possibility' (Spivak 1999: 9) of our own colonising modes of meaning and justice. Affirmative undecidability holds its ethico-political value through a focus on the relation of Subject/Other at the moment when the rules of disciplinary training and the determinisms of academic knowledge break down and there emerges the 'dark night of non-rules and non-knowledge' (Spivak 2008: 60, 63) that allows for an ethical decision. This experience of that which is impossible in hegemonic and disciplinary terms is the moment when we may answer the call of the wholly Other in a responsible manner (Spivak 1999: 428).

Such undecidability is found in *Rendition*, where the gendered, possibly subaltern figure of Fatima is only recognisable in her relations to two, highly politicised, class-stratified, male figures in the film: her father, Abasi Fawal, an interrogation officer who is complicit with the US military, and Khalid El-Emim, a member of the Islamic resistance forces. The film's central plot follows the extraordinary rendition of an Egyptian born US citizen to an undisclosed North African country. But it is Fatima's character that makes legible the political, economic and legal conflicts in this North African state. Her figure is undecideable because she serves as what Ziarek might term a differend, who can never call the US to account; throughout the film she not only remains outside the terms of capitalism, education, democracy, and legality, but her erasure in these ways and the absence of her narrative voice is precisely what allows these central conflicts and the other characters to make sense to us.[8]

Spivak suggests that the subaltern allows us to identify the moment of appropriation and ethical accountability. So we may ask what to make of Fatima, whose undecidable figure haunts the frames of recognisability and prevents her appropriation for either democratic aims or other forms of legibility. For example, the viewer remains uncertain about her position with respect to democracy, since we cannot decipher whether she shares her father's affiliation with US imposed 'democracy', or Khalid's affiliation with resistance; nor with freedom, since she is pictured both wearing and not wearing her head-covering, and having rejected an arranged marriage, while also being uncomfortable with her apparently intimate relations with Khalid. Thus her identity might be rendered as a question to the viewer. The indeterminacy of this figure asks that we consider what the possibilities of postcolonial democracy, modernisation, and economic 'freedom' might mean to her. In this indeterminacy there emerges an opening for imagining ourselves differently, not determined by liberal binaries, and open both to new possible configurations of Self/Other and to a reconstitution of ethico-politics that displaces the limits of the benevolent modern humanitarian.

Fatima is a non-rural figure of the possibly subaltern that might also help us think through urban subalterns in documentaries on Arab or Muslim immigrants in Britain or the US. Sree Nallamothu's 2004 documentary of South Asian immigrant neighborhoods in the northern Chicago area, *Patriot Acts*, depicts two of the men who chose to register with the US government rather than fleeing the country or going underground. Like *Rendition*, the film follows the US government's relentless androcentrism in centring on men who are presumed by the state authorities demanding registration to be prepared for anti-capitalist and anti-state violence, rendering immigrant women secondary. Resistance to state violations of its own guarantees of civil liberties are implicitly defined in this film in terms of systems of immigration law and human rights that rely on liberal universalist foundations. For example, even as the documentarians for this film render immigrant women secondary through their focus on men they advance an implicit argument that all immigrants should be treated equally under the law, an argument that is critical of the post-9/11 registration process as it is applied only to men and only to immigrants from certain countries. Through their use of naturalised identity categories (citizen/non-citizen immigrant, male/female), the filmmakers reproduce the very terms under which the US government carried out not only the post-9/11 registrations but also its justifications for the invasion of Iraq and other uses of military force in the WWWoE.

Pia Sawhney and Sanjna N. Singh's short 2004 documentary on US-based Muslims in the years shortly after 9/11, *Out of Status*, opens up some of the resistance strategies that besieged immigrant families draw on as the nation-state begins to detain, interrogate, deport and abuse them. As the families depicted encounter forcible removals, false charges, and secret detentions that violate the very dictates of the legal system itself, they begin to pursue their own versions of justice through fleeing the country and in other ways. In this way Sawhney and Singh's documentary of urban settings shows resistance that relies not only on the terms of the travesty of liberal democratic legality carried out repeatedly by the nation-state, but something Spivak characterises as the 'persistent short-term initiatives of local self-management' (2008: 156) that are everyday practices among subaltern communities.

The key ethico-political point of such a calculus is that it renders fully human and partially if still insufficiently recognisable those who do not benefit from development, globalisation, and the travesties of democracy that have taken centre stage under the WWWoE. Carefully considering which questions to retain as undecidable in our writing and documentary production also allows us to render as legible our own personal complicities with social practices that are far from democratic and just.

Subalterns Always Already Contest the Terms of Terror

Subalterns on the ground in theatres of conflict both in the US or Britain and abroad contest fundamental liberal presumptions in various ways. For example, the Afghan Institute of Learning (AIL) is a growing collective, locally run by Afghan women, who travel to the mostly rural, and culturally and economically secluded villages in Afghanistan to offer health and other education to women and children. In a revealing incident after a 2009 speaking engagement in the US, AIL's founder, Sakena Yacoobi, was asked by a member of the US college audience, 'So what can *we* do?' This question performs the moment of humanitarian benevolence: what can the middle class, educated, humanitarian from the global North contribute to the struggle for freedom and democracy of poor, uneducated, Others victimised by the backwards patriarchal men of the global South? Yacoobi replied that if we felt we needed to do something, we could release veiled women from the position of victim in which we are complicit with their own government in holding them (Yacoobi 2009). This constitutes a moment when local grassroots movements on the ground resist the totalising narrative of liberal humanitarianism complicit with the nation-state perpetrating and legitimating the WWWoE, and also problematises the distribution of so-called development aid under globalisation as a central transnational mode of modern ethical responsibility (Spivak 2008: 85).

Learning is a key theatre of conflict in the WWWoE, where the struggle is not defined by the Taliban and collaboration forces so much as by local grassroots organisations confronting the massive influx of NGO, US government, and US military efforts to build, staff, fund, and populate schools (USAID 2010b; Winthrop and Graft 2010; Burde and Linden 2009; Catholic Relief Services n.d.). These public sphere interventions by the machinery of the nation-states pursuing the WWWoE and their compliant NGO organisations and citizenry are a major problem in Iraq (Zangana 2007: 81-93) and for the AIL, as they attempt to reframe the representations of local Afghan women and the agency of the subaltern that they carry out. The deeply rooted modern belief that the NGO enactment of humanitarian efforts will promote development and equality persists in the face of many decades of evidence to the contrary, shored up by the universalist teleology but disrupted by subaltern resistance when it becomes intelligible.

The women of the Revolutionary Association of the Women of Afghanistan (RAWA) mark another moment of subaltern agency and resistance, as they insist that the Taliban, the Afghan governmental forces, and the US, British, and other international troops not only share a coevolutionary history as oppressors,[9] but share equally in the displacement of the educational, sexual, and political rights of the women of Afghanistan. Their literature and website consistently reject the terms of stories run in newspapers around the world that attempt to misperceive Afghan women as 'needing international aid or occupying forces', or as 'destitute and without hope' (Hairan 2010).

One example of RAWA's subversion of feminist and other Western vocabularies of freedom is their suggestion that the burqa – seemingly a global symbol not only of the oppression of women, but of anti-democratic and 'terrorist' violence generally – can be taken back and redeployed as a tool of resistance.[10] *Beneath the Veil* opens with a view of a woman in a burqa, Zarima, who is subsequently dragged into the centre of a public stadium and shot in the head. The image was captured on film by Salima, who upon reflecting on the images and her experience in the stadium, suggested that RAWA might have to reconsider their stance on burqas, since they could not have carried out this and other tasks (including documentary film-making) without the covert protection of these mandatory garments (Brodsky 2003: 20). Here, the burqa that seems, under modern Orientalism, to appear as a silencing mechanism of anti-freedom that makes it impossible for Muslim women to join with their Western sisters in baring uncovered skin required for modern objectification of women under globalisation, is complicated by its new role as an undercover documentary film-making device.[11]

Indeed, in Meyda Yeğenoğlu's (1998: 43-4, 62-3) analysis, the veiled woman becomes a site for the inversion of the omnipotent, invasive gaze of modern panopticism, since she can see without being seen, displacing the seemingly stable, unidirectional 'truths' of modern objectivist documentary realism and destabilising the putative unified viewing subject position of the documentary camera's gaze. By refusing the urge to 'lift the veil' to see the ethnographic realist 'truth' of the Oriental woman, as in Sharmeen Obaid's 2007 documentary *Lifting the Veil* about wartime Afghan women, Yeğenoğlu suggests a frame that can accommodate the ambivalent economies of desire and unavoidable trace of difference that opens up to the possibility of a subject status of woman as undomesticated Other. RAWA and the AIL are players in transnational networks of resistance to those modes of globalisation supported by the WWWoE, the IMF and the World Bank, and transnational corporations that remain vigilant to contest their appropriation as global subjects in order to retain agency in the terms of their own rendering.

Akin to the moments of subaltern resistance we see in RAWA's subversive use of the burqa, other forms of resistance include those acts of mimicry that Homi Bhabha (1994) has highlighted in his rewriting of history, and the playfulness that Yeğenoğlu (1998) finds useful in Luce Irigaray's work to avoid the liberal mode of resistance through reversal. For those who are forced to subject themselves over and over to the categories and mechanisms of the hegemonic, this playful repetition allows a woman to refuse to be reduced to the place of exploitation by discourse and/or by force. The possibility of exploiting a social role deliberately, in order to thwart a form of subordination by rendering it visible with playful repetition and variation – even when it is supposed to remain invisible – allows the woman to 'also remain elsewhere' (Irigaray 1985: 76, quoted in Yeğenoğlu 1998: 64).

Still another form of resistance can be seen later in Shah's documentary, when a moment of undecidability occurs as three young women, ages 15, 12, and 8, who were targets of Taliban violence, refuse to speak about the events following their mother's death, when they were left alone with local Taliban officials. This refusal momentarily disrupts the unity and authority of Shah's narrative voice, and exposes her to the differend – the failure of signification to capture what is irreducible or untransferable to Western audiences (Ziarek 2001: 95; Lyotard 1988: 13). We must ask ourselves, in view of their agential silence, if there has been no testimony to a legal offense, how can we respond with law? If there has been no clearly documented violation of rights, what can democracy bring? Here it is our identity that might be rendered as a question as we take this moment of undecidability, the moment of the differend's appearance, as an opening for 'institut[ing] idioms which do not yet exist' (Ziarek 2001: 103). Spivak terms this a 'silent interruption' (2008: 19, 56), meaning an interruption in the idiom of the peasant rather than in the language of the film critic, philosopher, or the highly educated filmmaker.

A similar moment occurred in the collective production of the self-portrait photographs documenting post-9/11 Muslim women in Britain from the exhibit *After Cameron*, when several group members decided not to allow their pictures into the public domain (Jennings 2005).[12] In this case the collective process allowed particular immigrant women, many of them more educated than the subaltern in its traditional conception, to exercise their own agency in exposing the nature of authorship and the risky politics of documentary production for public view in a racist time. In participating fully in a project that ultimately questions the work of Julia Margaret Cameron, a photographer from a colonial family in India, the women who refused to enter public space perform the digital media equivalent of what Spivak (2008: 148, 160) characterises as the 'secret writing' of the subaltern. This form of resistance is writing by girls trained to write for their own democratic agency rather than trained to reproduce the docility of the modern democratic citizen under the gaze of the panopticon. This lack of knowledge, this undecidability, puts us in the humble place of learning from below, of asking the subaltern how she might see us, and how she might suggest we respond.

Conclusion: Concrete Practices for Documentary Film

Our ultimate political goal is to confront the limits of liberal notions of democracy and justice in a search for ethically and politically effective strategies for documentary production on the WWWoE (Spivak 2003: 25-71; Mouffe 1992; Derrida 1994; Rancière 2009). The ethico-political moment is precisely when we refuse deterministic, indentitarian appropriations of Others to allow ourselves to be imagined by the subaltern Others of the WWWoE through what we have called an ethico-politics of an affirmative calculus of the undecidable. Practicing an ethico-politics of the subaltern allows us as documentary viewers to find the moment where Eurocentric, colonising universalisms betray their exclusion of those never meant in the modern to have full constitutional rights, to have success in capitalist exchange economies, or to have full participation in representative governance systems.

Showing this 'real' in a documentary is important not because it completes the factographic record, introducing a small but hidden group into the panopticon of modern objectivity. Rather, it brings into visibility those everyday successes at resisting the travesties of democracy and the violence of capitalist progress that characterise the agency in quotidian experiences of the subaltern, while also disrupting the Enlightenment political ontology that depends for its foundations on abstract universalisms that cannot accommodate the historically specific singularity of the subaltern.

Through the encounters with the subaltern, the differend, the ungrievable and the unrecognisable, we hope that documentary films still to come might be able to see framing as one of their most important political statements. For framing is one moment of a gendered, class-selective, rendering of justice as a central moment of exclusion and erasure, and the subsequent intelligibility is a profound ethico-political problem rather than a neutral lens through which we look to find what we know as the 'real'. By marking and troubling the limits of documentary recognisability, by exposing ourselves in our own colonising patterns of recognition rather than seeking to expose the Other, we might rethink what constitutes a political intervention. Such foundational reconceptualisations can create openings for recognising otherwise effaced agency for subalterns, and for filmmakers and audience members, agency which may serve as possibilities for justice that have yet to be imagined in film.

Notes

[1] The authors thank Becca Spence for research assistance for this chapter.

[2] The Obama administration, which no longer uses the Bush era 'war on terror' terminology, now uses terms like 'Global Counterintelligence' (G-COIN) and 'Overseas Contingency Operations', among others.

[3] See *Time*'s 29 July 2010 cover photos. For the US State Department, see its 2001 'Report on the Taliban's War Against Women', and more recently Hillary Rodham Clinton's January 2010 statement on the women of Afghanistan and Pakistan (US State Department 2010). USAID estimates that the illiteracy rates of women in rural areas is about 90%, and about two fifths of the overall population is illiterate (USAID 2010a).

[4] An introduction to the new political ontology in postmodernist theory may be found in White (1991; 2000), Dillon (2006), and Marchart (2007), among many other sources.

[5] A useful analysis of the ways these open secrets shape the public sphere and rewrite the jurisdiction of international law may be found in Bhattacharyya (2008: 54-72, 117-33, 134-44).

[6] For a brief overview of the history of agribusiness expansion under globalisation of the seed industry, see Grain (2010).

[7] *Battle for Haditha* begins by instructing the audience that the story to come is based on real events. It opens with the words: 'On November 19, 2005, an IED planted on the roadside in Haditha Iraq, killed one marine and injured two others. In the following hours, marines killed 24 Iraqi men, women, and children.'

[8] Cynthia Weber builds a similar argument in her book *Imagining America at War* about the feminine providing a site for staging conflicts over the morality and legitimacy of war in films about World War II (2006: 13, 169 n6), Vietnam (2006: 42-6), and the post-9/11 wars (2006: 83-90).

[9] In the historical view of RAWA these forces include the US supported insurgents fighting the Soviets in the 1970s, the 'elected' governmental officials from the Northern Alliance financially and militarily backed by US troops, and the US and international presences, whose occupation continues to signify the oppression of the people.

[10] For a similar argument about the veil during the Islamic revolution in Iran, see Mohanty (2003: 33-4).

[11] This is suggested again in a 4 April 2010 interview with a RAWA activist in Kabul, who suggests that the burqa can be used as a subversive tool, against the violent regimes, to mask identity in a dangerous location where resistance activity gets women killed (Boone 2010).

[12] *After Cameron*, National Museum of Photography, Film, and Television, 2004, www.nmpft.org.uk/aftercameron.

Chapter 12

Screening for Meaning: Terrorism as the product of a Paranoid Style in Politics and Popular Culture

Hugh Ortega Breton

Since the mid 1990s danger, risk and conspiratorial fears have appeared to characterise the safety-conscious world we inhabit. Since President Bill Clinton's declaration of a war on terrorism in 1998, and particularly since the attacks on the US in 2001, the response has been an expansion, or rather an irruption (Baudrillard 2003) in representations of the terrorist threat. A glut of representations in news, current affairs, documentary and drama using the genres of investigation, thriller and melodrama in particular, testify to a fantasy world of conspiratorial fears and terrorist dangers. Such programmes extend the speculation prominent in news and political discourse about the forms and severity of the terrorist threat. In a period of increased emotional expression, decreased political engagement and aversion to taking risks, the representation of subjectivity is driven from the perspective of a fearful, isolated self. It is important to assess and evaluate this shift in popular conceptions of subjectivity because these representations can help us to understand why fear, security, persecution and victimhood dominate political and popular discourse today.

Using a psycho-cultural studies approach I will present analyses of the representation of subjectivity in terrorism-related factual and fictional programmes.[1] I will suggest that 'paranoid'[2] subjectivities and recurring ideas in these television narratives elicit and are determined by a crisis of meaning and identity. In object relations psychoanalysis, 'paranoid' refers to a coping technique for such a crisis which can also be formulated as a mode of representation, as in Richard Hofstadter's (2008 [1964]) *The Paranoid Style in American Politics* (see also Knight 2008). The analysis will show how communicative mechanisms driven by socially repressed fears shape the representation of terrorism, counterterrorism and extremism in a manner which can resonate with fundamental aspects of individuated emotional experience by representing fears of persecution. Examples from the successful espionage-thriller-melodrama *Spooks* (Kudos Productions, 2002-2011 – titled *MI-5* in the US) and from the documentaries *Dispatches: Undercover Mosque* (Hardcash Productions, 2007) and *Dr David Kelly: The Conspiracy Files* (BBC, 2007) will be used. Before doing this it is necessary to outline the politico-cultural context shaping the creative process of these programmes.

Crucial to understanding contemporary political and popular culture today is the significance of the loss of modern political subjectivity and meaning (Laïdi 1998). There has been a chronic need for politicians to re-fashion a meaningful connection with the electorate ever since the collapse of the Cold War, declining rates of political participation and the declining relevance of traditional political ideologies of Left and Right. Whilst the US and the UK alongside them have great military and economic power, clearly evident as part of the propaganda spectacle that is postmodern war (Baudrillard 2004; Hammond 2007), governments' hegemony (moral and cultural leadership) is dependent upon achieving meaningful identifications with the electorate. In Western societies since the mid 1990s such meaningful identifications are based upon the expression of personal, emotional experience in relation to perceived dangers. Personalised emotional engagement and risk perception are the central planks upon which this new form of engagement is based. Terrorism is only one of a number of social problems framed and shaped by what is referred to as 'a discourse of fear' (Altheide 2002); 'risk aversion' (Furedi 2005); 'dangerization'

(Lianos and Douglas 2000); 'traumaculture' (Luckhurst 2003) and 'post-traumatic' culture (Farrell 1998) in American and European societies. These concepts refer to a single cultural script, the predominance of which suggests that this is the single most meaningful way to express how we subjectively *feel* about the world and its others in this post-modern political period. This means that suspicion of others (a belief in malevolence with no evidence to support it) and fear for survival are prevalent characteristics of British and American societies in particular.

The greater 'consciousness' of perceived dangers in the world provides a credible mode of expression for film and television programme makers as well as for the political elite in its efforts to re-engage with the electorate as its protector. Like political leaders, series creators and writers/producers need to connect meaningfully in order to gain an audience, through the dominant cultural script. The drama, excitement, fear and emotional intensity associated with terrorism, extremism and the tragic loss of life is a product of this representational work. While *Spooks/MI-5* is ostensibly about responding to attacks on the nation, identifications are based on the emotional suffering and conflicts of the main characters. While the fictional world of victims and persecutors they inhabit gives symbolic form to a fundamental and universal part of individual emotional experience, this is not to suggest that this cultural phenomenon is not historically specific and socially constructed. I will now turn to my rationale for using a psycho-cultural approach to analyse these representations.

The representation of social life in terms of its fearfulness is considered to have reached such a scale that 'fear has emerged as a framework for *developing identities and for engaging* in social life' (Altheide 2002: 3, my emphasis). Rather than fear being a framework, fear is the conscious, taken-for-granted response to the projection of characteristics which develop identities. My attention to the relationship between meaning, emotion and the re-configuration of subjectivity in popular representations employs the British object relations school of psychoanalysis (Klein 1975 [1946]; Fairbairn 1952, 1954, 1958; Meltzer 1978; Ogden 1991) combined with a contextualised semiotic approach to textual analysis. This form of psychoanalysis provides a socially- and practice-based means for understanding the affective dynamics of the human subject and society. It posits, on the basis of successful and reliable clinical practice, a set of communicative mechanisms which form the basis of human subject formation and interaction. My method focuses on the construction of meaning and subjectivity through these communicative mechanisms using the formal elements of audio-visual representation. This means focusing on how formal elements of texts function as communicative mechanisms to shape subject types in relation to one another.

This relational psychoanalytic approach is based on the premise that taken-for-granted and ostensibly rational signification practices conceal ideological or unconscious dynamics which shape these representations. Experiences and emotions which are extremely painful and unbearable (that cannot be thought about) are repressed. This act of repression makes these particular object relations unconscious and dynamic. 'Object relations' refers to these significant experiences (the 'object' is anything which has meaning, and therefore an emotional connotation), which because of their significance become a fundamental part of perceptive and cognitive structures. In order to manage or cope with these ideas and experiences, objects are often split. Splitting is a fundamental concept of object relations psychoanalysis because it refers to what we do when subjectivity is in crisis. In the absence of a meaningful frame we revert back to simplistic polarisations to construct order. Once ideas are split, that is to say once they have been simplified into binary relationships of good and evil for example, then one part of this binary can be projected onto another group or attached to a specific object or signifier. In other words, it can be got rid of by attributing it to someone else through representations. The chief 'mechanisms' through which unconscious object relations become expressed are projection, introjection, and identification, and these form a process producing distinct but related subject roles or identities. The emotions that are generally associated with the 'war on terror' – fear, persecutory anxiety, helplessness and of course terror – are the fabric of these communicative mechanisms. Their association with terrorist subjects and acts of terrorism appears natural but is in fact socially constructed through these communicative and unconscious mechanisms. For example, the projection or objectification of specific, negative characteristics (evil, maliciousness or malevolence, violence, deception) map out and distinguish different subjectivity types (in this case 'the persecutor') in terrorism-related news stories, reifying the fear and paranoid anxieties that can then be associated with the character (the terrorist or extremist) from the perspective of audiences addressed or positioned as potential victims. In this way emotions with unconscious determinants (historical experiences which have been forcefully ignored) are systematically rationalised through their objectification as risks in news and political discourse.

The paranoid technique consists in the projection of disavowed, unbearable emotions of all types that are subsequently conjoined in unconscious fantasy. This partly accounts for the contradictory repulsion and fascination Anglo-American culture has with Islamic extremism as well as our culture's general fascination with practices, people and characters we consider to be morally wrong, such as serial killers and gangsters, in history and popular television. Our interest in malevolent subjectivity continues to increase with many successful television shows which are based on anti-heroes – fundamentally bad people who audiences nonetheless want to know and experience – for example, Donald Draper in *Mad Men* (AMC, 2007-present), Dexter Morgan in *Dexter* (CBS, 2008-present), and Tony Soprano and others in *The Sopranos* (HBO, 1999-2007).

Terrorism-related programming occurs within an entertainment industry already predisposed to emotional intensity as engaging and meaningful through the widespread use of the genre of melodrama, which has expanded through this post Cold War period (Joyrich 1992). The shift towards the use of melodrama reflects the social atomisation of society which has been in process since the 1980s (Geraghty 2006). The increased use of melodrama as a response to negatively experienced social change (Gledhill 1987) is the aesthetic corollary of the resort to the paranoid perspective as a coping strategy when identity is threatened in psychoanalysis. The use of melodramatic devices in *Spooks* – such as victim and villain caricatures, extreme violence and the chronic threat of it, and the visual representation of emotional states, in particular through close-ups – all contribute to the paranoid style of representation. Melodrama focuses on the individual's emotional experience and portrays the world in a Manichean form. The clear-cut hero and villain structure of narratives organises emotions which express subjectivity as split into simplified and polarised extremes. The following examples demonstrate how melodrama, in these respects at least, has a paranoid structure.

Spooks/MI-5: 'None of the normal rules of identity apply'[3]

In *Spooks/MI-5* British political elite concerns and popular suspicions, such as the falsity of news, and threats posed by other states, are expressed through stories about a team of intelligence officers preventing persecutory threats to the British state. Story topics are normally chosen from topical security concerns and international conflicts. Plot lines developed from news narratives are rendered meaningful through an intimate engagement with the emotional lives of the main characters; a trait of melodrama. Surveillance technologies, especially visual and aural, are foregrounded as an expression of sophistication and power. Risk and excitement are conveyed through the narrative structure of the programme via a narrative device called 'jeopardy', which attempts to maintain engagement by consistently problematising protagonists' attempts at achieving their aims, thus consistently heightening the level of tension (Van Loon 2003) by deferring the resolution of the protagonists' objectives. Re-titled *MI-5* for the French and American markets, it has generic elements of action, police and melodrama genres, in particular: the clear divide between good and evil (splitting in melodrama); the foregrounding of identity changed through routine deceptions (the action series: see Miller 2001); and of what can be seen and so known and how conclusions are drawn (the police series: see Bignell 2009). The heroes are portrayed as normal, typical human beings through their personal problems and flaws, characteristic of the *verité* style (Cooke 2001). *Spooks* is an example of the 'play between the internalization of political crisis and the projection of repressed fears' (Donald 1985: 133). Through seeing the hidden lives of MI-5 agents we are witness to the multitude of threats to the national 'way of life'. The very *raison d'être* of the 'spooks' is to manage or eliminate these persecutory threats. The audience know that MI-5 will prevail but not without loss, trauma and personal suffering, elements characterising victimhood. Double agents, undercover agents, the manipulation of informants, lying to sexual partners: all these activities add to the levels of suspicion and tension that signify a paranoid map of suspicious and potentially malevolent relations. The deceptions carried out on a regular basis by the main characters convey suspicion and uncertainty about characters' true identities.

Spooks/MI-5 is not the only example of successful terrorism-related drama exploring uncertainties about subjectivity in the twenty first century. The American spy dramas *Alias* (ABC, 2001-06) and *24* (Fox, 2001-present) feature spies transgressing the boundaries of acceptable behaviour in the name of the security of others. What is significant is that these dramas, amongst others from the same period, also have subjectivity and suspicion as key themes. In addition, a number of films, drama-documentaries and mini-series have also dealt with these issues, for example *Dirty War* (BBC Films/HBO, 2004) and *The Grid* (BBC/TNT/Fox, 2004).

Such narratives inevitably involve victimisation or persecution and attempts to prevent and protect. In one episode of *Spooks/MI-5*, for example, an alleged terrorist falsely imprisoned is characterised as a victim not only of the police but also of a group forcing him to commit a terrorist act on pain of the death of his family. In keeping with the consistent theme of identity in the series, this man is also the victim of a case of mistaken identity. In the same episode (Episode 4.6), a civil liberties organisation (a 'protector') is associated with terrorists plotting a strike, suggesting that the organisation may in fact be in league with the terrorists. The potential or actual victim can be a loved one of one of the officers, a sympathetic collaborator such as the helpful Algerian intelligence officer fleeing from foreign persecution (Episode 2.2.), or one of the officers themselves (Episodes 4.7, 7.1). These are just a few examples of where persecution-victimhood is used as a meaningful structure of identification.

Perhaps the key paranoid motif which can be exploited by audio-visual representation is the distrust of appearances (Bersani 1989). This concerns the problematised ability to know and identify others, evoking suspicion. *Spooks* contains familiar, stereotypical representations of otherness in the form of enemy Iranians and Muslims to clearly express, visually and culturally, the difference in paranoid subjectivities. However, it represents some characters ambivalently as security officers or collaborators with MI-5 who also perform as the terrorist other. The following example (Episode 4.4) illustrates the rejection of any ambivalence in the paranoid style, which is based on its opposite, polarisation (splitting). This foregrounds the centrality of the visual dimension as a source of knowledge and misperception. The presence of Adam (the main protagonist) as an undercover white Arab (an ethnic minority from Syria) makes the white English truck driver (trafficking illegal immigrants) anxious, arousing suspicion. Lighting, mise-en-scène and close-ups create a focus on skin colour reduced to tonal differences. Lighting and the similarity in background colours draws attention to the similarity in skin colour between the British and Arabic men. Shots of Adam and the traffickers alternate and are followed by a close-up on the bundle of money that Adam offers them for his passage on the illegal truck. The downward-looking gazes of Adam and the other passengers contrast with the direct and commanding gaze of the traffickers. Adam is hit by the driver because the driver does not trust him as his ambivalent appearance makes him anxious. In this example aggression is the product of the ambivalence of familiarity and unfamiliarity (a white Arab) provoking anxiety. Acting out this anxiety by attacking the other displays a paranoid mindset of victims and persecutors, where the subject is unable to cope with the ambivalence because it does not offer clear distinctions between the self and the other. Although in this example the distrust of appearance is overcome, the decision to accept Adam on the truck proves fateful for the truck driver. The driver's suspicion is later confirmed when he is beaten and taken by Adam's accomplices, proving to the driver and to the audience that his anxiety about a white Arab was warranted. This effectively underwrites anxiety around ambiguity and identities which do not conform to stereotypes.

Melodramatic devices such as the use of light and shadow, slow motion and music are used to distinguish terrorists, giving them a sinister but stylish aura. A characteristic motif of paranoid representation is evident in *Spooks/MI-5* where a sinister, threatening characterisation is created by capturing the subject in darkness, watching. For example in Episode 4.4 low lighting and the use of curtains to create shadows and conceal the gazing eye connote partial knowledge of the subject, making him more threatening. These differing audio-visual characterisations distinguish the two identities of protector and persecutor, which is important because in terms of action both protagonists and antagonists are killers following orders.

Episode 4.4 is a good example of a paranoid style narrative because in it a suspicious mind-set is validated. The viewer is encouraged to believe in the character Yazdi through the security officers' partial trust in him. The narrative twist in this episode's storyline is that the intelligence authorities wrongly believe Yazdi to be intending to commit a terrorist attack on British civilians and consequently make the mistake of trusting Yazdi to question a senior Arab dignitary who they wrongly believe to be working with him. When Section D's concerns about this are ignored by senior officials, the foreign dignitary is murdered. Yazdi achieves his real mission by manipulating MI-5's attempt to use him. The MI-5 team have effectively failed to be suspicious enough. The message is that we should trust neither terrorists nor political masters, only our emotional selves, our intuitions. Deception and the ability to know and trust others are prominent themes of this and many other episodes involving officers going undercover.

As with many political and news discourse narratives, a central concern of *Spooks/MI-5* is identification/definition of the perceived threat. In Episode 5.3 the paranoid anxiety associated with unknown others, the problematisation of identity, is apparent from the beginning. We are shown a close-up of a trembling/quivering piece of hessian, anchored by a deep, monotone male voice (Ibrahim – the antagonist) conveying indifference, detachment and rationality as he says 'This man is an MI-5 spy'. The cut to a wider distanced shot shows us that the hessian conceals the face of a person, who is on his knees and lit from above in the centre of a circle of men standing in a large, dark warehouse. This organisation of people gives the scene a ritualistic quality as the men are evenly spaced forming a perfect circle around the lit area and on the edge of the darkness that dominates the visual field, the aura of light seeming to emanate from the man's head. This focuses attention on to the prisoner whilst associating those standing silently around him with darkness. This use of light visually depicts the polarised splitting characteristic of the paranoid style, of innocent victimhood (light) and persecution (darkness). The focus is on the experience of persecution of a wholly innocent victim in a world of persecuting villains. The fourth shot reveals to us that one of the men is an MI-5 officer, punctuated by the use of a foreboding low bass tone and the mention of the word 'spy' in the dialogue.

Once the possibility of victimisation has been established the shot naturalistically peels to the right to reveal another layer of this world, and this is complemented by the sound of the antagonist's voice changing from a clear, naturalistic quality to a lower quality associated with radio reception or standard audio recording equipment. We are shown three members of the MI-5 team, two sitting at large screens with headphones, and the main protagonist, Adam, running into the office and putting on his headphones/microphone headset. Through dialogue it becomes apparent that there is another team of MI-5 officers near to the location of the main scene who do not know where the man is being held. A lack of knowledge means that MI-5 are powerless to intervene. The MI-5 teams are positioned as radio audiences: they can do nothing but witness the action via their headsets; they do not have 'a visual on the warehouse'. This lack of view, combined with dialogue and their positioning as witnesses to the action conveys a sense of powerlessness which is characteristic of the paranoid style. Zaf, the undercover officer in the group at the warehouse, makes an argument for not killing the prisoner, claiming to have recognised him as a council employee and pointing out that the prisoner has not seen them. The significance of visual knowledge is thus emphasised again as determining whether someone is considered a danger or not.

The antagonist, Ibrahim, removes the bag covering the prisoner's head. There is a close-up shot of the prisoner's fearful expression followed by a low angled view of Zaf from the point of view of the prisoner, who is on his knees, looking up at him. From this perspective the officer appears ominous and threatening, as he is surrounded by darkness with the shadow thrown by the light concealing his eyes. The next shot is a slow zoom close-up into the prisoner's eyes before a wide angle is used to show the shooting of the prisoner. This is followed by a rapid zoom which bends in its trajectory as it moves towards a semi-profile shot of Zaf. The movement of the camera is used to signify the emotional effect of the shooting on the officer who tried to save him in a situation where showing any kind of sympathy may endanger him.

The use of the sack and of lights as masking devices which prevent sight and the exchange of shots between the innocent victim and Zaf highlights the issue of identity, mistaken and concealed. In a paranoid mode of representation the only identities which are meaningful are the ones on display here, victims, persecutors and protectors. The terrorist cell's suspicions lead them to capture the prisoner and to disbelieve his claim that he is an environmental health officer or 'rat-catcher'. This suspicion is objectified through the arrangement of lighting in the scene. The lights that are shown are pearl bulbs in open lampshades, reminiscent of the lights that feature in interrogations. The men are unknown to one another but their fates are inextricably linked together by other officers' interpretation of the situation, who believe the drawn out event is designed to 'flush out' any undercover officers present. The metaphor of 'rats' and 'rat-catchers' also signals a confusion of the identities of self and other from the victim's perspective. Zaf is metaphorically speaking the real 'rat-catcher' in this situation. Sight, as a source of knowledge, is a prominent motif of this scene and many others in *Spooks*, generating moments of suspense and fear. In the moments before his death the prisoner is seen looking in fear at the MI-5 officer who he falsely believes to be his persecutor. In addition, futility, an emotion characteristic of paranoia (Fairbairn 1952) is evoked by the failed attempt that Zaf makes to save the prisoner's life.

These examples evidence a number of characteristic features of *Spooks*. Through visual style, mise-en-scène, dialogue and narrative, ambivalence is rejected, malevolence is projected, suspicion is validated and a clear distinction between persecutor and victim subject positions is produced. As I will illustrate below, publicised cases of real victimhood give rise to another meaningful aspect of terrorism narratives: conspiracy theories.

Dr David Kelly: The Conspiracy Files

Conspiracy theories have been identified as present within many genres in popular culture (Knight 2000, 2002). Conspiracy theorising became increasingly popular firstly in the USA and then Britain after the Cold War. With increasing cynicism about the 'war on terror', from 2004 conspiracy theorising began to extend beyond the confines of popular entertainment culture (for example *The*

233

X-Files) and contribute to the meaningful mainstream engagement with international terrorism, evidenced for example in the column inches devoted to it in the *New York Times* and the British national newspaper the *Guardian* (Birchall 2006). Most well known are the 9/11 conspiracy theory films *Fahrenheit 9/11* (2004) and *Loose Change* (2005). The secrecy which surrounds intelligence claims, and the general cynicism directed towards both American and British governments, contribute to the increased resonance that 'war on terror' conspiracy theories have. Conspiracy theories attempt to explain losses in meaningful ways, providing alternatives to official explanations which lack this point of identification.

In conspiracy theories, accusations of malevolence are asserted through a process of claims-making that combines the presentation of proofs with the emotional orientation (grief, suspicion) that prompts and drives this process. Without this, such claims would appear ludicrous. *Dr David Kelly: The Conspiracy Files* (hereafter referred to as *Kelly*) investigates the suspicions of conspiracy theorists who question the Hutton Inquiry verdict on Dr David Kelly's death. Kelly was a weapons inspector employed by both the United Nations and the UK Ministry of Defence to find evidence of weapons of mass destruction (WMD) in Iraq. Kelly was found dead in a forest near his home after it became public knowledge that he had expressed his opinion to a BBC journalist that a government report on Iraqi WMD had been 'sexed-up'. *Kelly* was part of a series first broadcast in 2007 which included programmes on the death of Princess Diana, the 1995 Oklahoma City bombing, the terrorist attacks in the USA in 2001 and, in 2008, new programmes on the 1988 Lockerbie bombing and on World Trade Center Building Three which also collapsed on 11 September 2001. In 2009 a further programme was broadcast, on the London bombings of July 2005.

The programme includes reconstructions based on evidence given to the Hutton Inquiry alongside alternative explanations. Such theories are of analytical interest here because they both conceal and attribute agency to others constructed as malevolent. They directly problematise agency in respect of tragic deaths, which in and of themselves are meaningless. Expert opinion and an emotional rhetoric of suspicion and sadness are blended together to make conspiracy claims about well known cases of victimhood, aiming to attribute responsibility by constructing a case which positions political power as persecutory and malevolent.

As in other recent conspiracy theories, there is an explanation produced by an officially sanctioned body, in this case the Hutton Inquiry, with which both the conspiracy theorists and this programme engage. During the presentation of the official explanation, slow, sustained, low chords, familiar from horror films, evoke suspense (anxiety and uncertainty) and danger, establishing and maintaining a sinister mood, anchoring the discrepancies in a fearful frame. *Kelly* is introduced in its voice-over as an exploration of something sinister, immediately suggesting persecution. We thus have two emotionally framed competing positions or explanations. The official explanation is tragic and sad, the other sinister; however it is the sinister tone which is foregrounded through music.

Kelly's own recorded persecutory perception of his situation is enlisted as proof of a conspiracy:

> Narrator: There was one sinister message...it doesn't appear to show that Dr Kelly was a threat to himself but that he felt threatened by others. He told his friend...that there were 'many dark actors playing games'.

This is a quintessential conspiratorial statement. Its significance is increased by the slow iteration of the narrator as she reads the quotation and the very close shot of the quotation on a PC monitor from directly in front and behind the screen. This lends substantial weight to conspiracy claims by using Kelly's own perception that something sinister was occurring around him, combined with concealed and surveillant camera positions connoting a voyeuristic pleasure as well as malevolent spying. Hidden, malevolent agency is shown through low lighting combined with a slow tracking shot taken from behind the subject's back, a shot commonly used in horror and thriller films. As the victim, Kelly's own perception has a privileged value in Anglo-American societies at this time. Additionally, as the former purveyor of intelligence secrets, he is attributed with knowing what is really going on and revealing the truth. However, it is the camera which knows what is really happening by occupying the position of the malevolent persecutor, surveying its unaware victim, thereby connoting danger.

The visual absence and aural presence of the narrator lends *ethos* and *pathos* to the claims being made. The tonality of voice is a very significant conveyor of emotional mood in everyday life. Here, there is a mild but consistent mournfulness, doom and foreboding in the pace and tone of the narrator's voice. This is complemented visually by a shot of fast-moving dark cloud over the headquarters of the UK foreign intelligence service and shots of solitary ravens and gargoyles, throughout the narrative. The effect of these seemingly unconnected shots is to frame the narrative in a melodramatic gothic register by use of visual metaphors which connote evil, evoking a sinister, suspicious mood. The narrator's constant aural presence maintains this sense of foreboding throughout the programme, occasionally changing tone and raising her voice when presenting a piece of conflicting evidence, expressing suspicion and lending credibility to the claims.

Discrepancies in accounts and imprecision in diagnosis are presented as traces of *another agency absent* from the official account. This is done by leaving experts' questions without immediate response and this results in an accumulation of suspicion towards the official explanation. The final quarter of the programme is taken up mainly by eminent experts of high authority agreeing with Hutton's verdict or explaining away the conspiracists' claims. The programme thus offers a diminution of the sinister tension generated by the interviewing of conspiracy theorists and music and in doing this, resolves some of the persecutory anxieties that the programme had raised, providing some closure. We could interpret this heightening and diminishing of anxiety as 'modulation', an idea used by Andrew Hoskins and Ben O'Loughlin (2007) in their study of television news discourse, which they argue functions as a container for anxieties, amplifying and assuaging them in the course of their representation. However, in these programmes paranoid anxieties are amplified much more than they are assuaged.

The belief in the malevolence of powerful others is an attempt to provide a meaningful account for a tragic loss. What appears to be meaningful is the idea of powerful malevolent agents working secretly. Identification with the tragedy, futility and powerlessness associated with loss is conveyed, coupled with a desire to identify someone or some group as responsible for this loss. Conspiracy theories and programmes about them provide a focus for the expression of alienation from political agency, formulated as suspicion and fear of formal political power and the characterisation of its political agency as malevolent.

Agency is concealed by its projection onto others through the conspiracy claim. The claim itself is evidence of the subjectivity of the conspiracist, but this draws attention to others who are constructed as not only more powerful but malevolently powerful. This is the form of powerful subjectivity which we find meaningful in Anglo-American societies today, if we consider the marked rise of interest in and popularity of conspiracy theories since the end of the Cold War. Conspiracy claims therefore evidence an alienation from subjectivity, through its projection and characterisation as malevolent. This is balanced by the related subject position of the 'good' innocent victim – such as Kelly. Conspiracy claims validate our culture of suspicion, in the same way that 'in paranoia, the primary function of the enemy is to provide a definition of the real that makes paranoia necessary' (Bersani 1989: 193). We should understand the WMD saga in the same way: the rhetorical and emotional structure of such theories and the truth claims of Anglo-American governments in the 'war on terror' are the same (Knight 2008). As I will illustrate in the example below taken from an investigative documentary, suspicion can also be mobilised through camera work producing an exciting and fearful representation of malevolent subjectivity.

Dispatches Undercover Mosque

Channel 4's *Dispatches Undercover Mosque* features secret filming in a number of UK mosques using a hidden camera on an undercover reporter. This form of investigative journalism is underpinned by an overt 'will to reveal' (Bratich 2006) the truth that lies behind appearances. In *Dispatches*, this private and hidden surveillance structures the documentary's narrative, supported by DVD footage of preachers and academic experts who express fears about extremist Islamist ideas. I will focus on how the use of the hidden camera and editing structure a paranoid relationship between the subjects of the film – members and imams of the mosque – and the programme's audience.

The premise of the programme and its use of a hidden camera is that the public image of the Green Lane Mosque and the organisation that runs it, The United Kingdom Islamic Mission (UKIM), is false. Statements from the mosque's website promoting inter-faith dialogue are presented alongside comments from selected preachers who use derogatory terms to describe non-Muslims. The title of the programme, *Undercover Mosque*, denotes that the mosque, not just the programme makers, are 'undercover', suggesting that their public-facing appearance as a 'multi-faith', tolerant organisation is disingenuous. The programme's claim, voiced by a female narrator, is that despite appearances to the contrary the public face of these organisations conceals 'a message of intolerance and bigotry' presented as threatening through the tone of the narrator's voice which is fearful, suggesting doom and foreboding. The programme confirms that some imams are homophobic and chauvinistic but these attitudes were quite common in British society only fifty years ago and are still held by some, so the distance the programme creates between mainstream British society and Islamic extremism is unjustified. This problematisation of imported culture and immigrants is a long-standing feature of popular culture. Since the end of the Cold War and the development of multiculturalist policies, and particularly since 2001, Islamic and Arabian culture has been consistently problematised in the mainstream press (Poole 2002, Poole and Richardson 2006). Domestically and internationally the perception of threat has become fixated on Islamism and the south Asian region (Brown 2006), with Muslims becoming the object of a paranoid and suspicious gaze.

The hidden camera is of course one of the conventions of investigative journalism regardless of the subject matter, used to get under the false surface of self-promoting or deceptive self-representation. The belief that, if one cannot be seen observing, then the subject will act 'naturally' and authentically, as if they were not being watched, is the premise of the use of hidden cameras. Hidden filming implies that the true character of the group is secret or inaccessible by other means. Through secret filming the investigator replicates the perceived false appearance of the other to get to the truth of the other's character. This technique produces a paranoid object relationship because of the suspicion and distrust of the subject which it implies. Suspicion of the subject as threatening is reified as it is produced through the filming technique. The use of a caption, 'Secret filming', emphasises the perceived risk involved in this kind of filming, generating tension, excitement and apprehension. The camera view is blurred, obscured or unlevel, at a fixed distance with a central subject, and unsteady and shaky in movement. This partial obscurity conveys the meaning that something hidden is being revealed whilst characterising what is being shown as concealed. This is important because the hidden camera is considered to provide indisputable evidence, regardless of how the choice to film in this way frames the subject in a particular relationship to the viewer. This rhetoric of revelation and truthfulness legitimates the paranoid frame of suspicion which determines the use of the hidden camera.

The audience is watching part of a highly differentiated group from within itself, but at a distance because of the hidden engagement of the reporter. This deception creates a non-dialogic, distanced relationship between the audience and the programme's subjects because, by posing as a member of the group, the cameraman's agency and identity is hidden; so he is not addressed as someone different or actively observing. The point here is that the relationship between the watcher and the subject is concealed by the method of filming so that the subject is othered, denying the existence of a shared cultural context in which to understand the subject. At the same time the hidden camera materialises the paranoid phantasy of being *inside* the persecutory other (Klein 1975 [1946]), creating fear and excitement about the surrounding potential danger. The hidden camera produces this perspective and a boundary marked by being inside the other, inside the mosque, but separate from it because of the absence of a dialogue. The choice of this format prohibits dialogue with others already considered dangerous. Contrast this with *The Mosque* (BBC, 2001), made before 9/11. In this documentary, a standard camera follows three different members of the mosque: its secretary, a sharia law advisor and the head of the mosque as they go about their daily routines. They describe their work and answer the cameraman/interviewer's questions, creating a dialogic relationship with the subjects in the programme.

There is doubtlessly a certain pleasurable form of voyeuristic excitement and danger produced by this type of programme. It clearly positions the audience via the camera operator and direction in a position of anonymous surveillance of a subject represented as dangerous. The audience is positioned as the 'citizen-spy' (Bratich 2006: 500), through the camerawork concealing and revealing, thereby representing the Islamist as dangerous. The 'engagement' the programme attempts to make is based on an unconscious projection of malevolence which others the subject whilst at the same time creating excitement for the viewer because of its perceived dangerousness. This exciting but abhorrent contradiction is characteristic of the paranoid coping technique (Fairbairn 1952, Grotstein 1994). The effectiveness of the representation is based on this repellent-exciting contradiction. This is produced through a combination of the secrecy of the camera and the statements made by the imams. In stark contrast to the absence of the camera bearer, the editing and subtitles highlight statements of violent action expressed by different imams, which in combination with the narration represents Islamic culture as homophobic, chauvinist and therefore dangerous, addressing the majority of audiences who are not and so providing an identification with potential victimhood and malevolence. Subjectivity is represented in simplistic, polarised and reductive terms through these statements. Rather than revealing anything real the secret camera surveillance method is used to produce revelry in British tabloid folk devil culture. This reinforces the simplistic association of extremist Islam with fear, validating a paranoid perspective.

Conclusion

The television programmes analysed here exhibit the socially constructed anxieties characteristic of post-Cold War Anglo-American culture. The challenge is in sufficiently elucidating the link between detailed audio-visual analysis of popular television and the critical political context of which they form a part. In conclusion, I would like to return to the idea of a crisis of meaning and subjectivity and how these programmes and others give expression to this.

We can see from these programmes that the paranoid style produces clear and unequivocal subject positions of victim, persecutor and protector, with suspicion and fear as their fabric. Using melodrama, highly emotionalised and intimate engagements with characters through music, tone of voice, camerawork and lighting, and the aesthetics of mise-en-scène, are often employed to construct paranoid narratives which provide fearful/exciting entertainment and the relief of a clear distinction between 'us' and 'them'. Uncertainty about the self and its knowledge of the world takes the form of persecutory anxieties and suspicions directed towards others. In the objectification of the belief in malevolence, subjects are represented in a Manichean fashion with no tolerance for complexity or ambivalence, as was illustrated by *Spooks/MI-5*. The fears and anxieties that are conveyed in these representations – fears of extremism, suspicion of hidden malevolence, fear of being trapped inside the malevolent other and identity anxiety – all involve the projection, audio-visually and verbally, of malevolent subjectivity. In *David Kelly: The Conspiracy Files* attempts are made at providing proofs to support these projections.

These representations and their concerns suggest a popular cultural coping strategy, giving symptomatic expression to the political crisis of meaning and subjectivity through conspiratorial and persecutory narratives. This is because these programmes seem to be responding to a sense of uncertainty and lack of knowledge about who and what people are. In all three programmes featured here, not knowing and seeking to know more, visually represented as concealment-revelation, is central to the plot. This search for knowledge is, however, driven by a suspicious belief in malevolence. Both melodrama and conspiracy theories have grown in use and popularity since the end of the Cold War, suggesting that they are the cultural forms giving expression to this crisis. Both these forms have a paranoid structure and address the problems of knowledge and uncertainty by providing clear positions of identification that validate suspicion and fear. The crisis of meaning and subjectivity is evident, I suggest, in the focus on active agency as malevolent and other whilst the *passive identity* of the victim is the position from which this world is witnessed and experienced.

The problem with paranoid conceptions of subjectivity is that they only portray people as malevolent when they are active and only positively when they are vulnerable, fearful and passive. Where are the positive and active subjectivities? Why are all the cult figures of recent television culture anti-heroes, compromised by addictive and neurotic defence mechanisms – Don Draper,

Dexter and Tony Soprano? Where are the confident and proud promoters of the 'war on terror' and where are their opponents? Over the last decade we have all witnessed the alacrity with which responsibility and blame are apportioned and projected onto others and how responsibility is disavowed and denied in a string of conspiracy theories and inquiries – two forms which have more in common than we would ordinarily think, given that they are often represented as in opposition to one another.

How can a constructive critique of the paranoid style be made that leads to a progressive opposition to the trend of securitisation in politics? I think the key focus needs to be reclaiming political agency as positive whilst revealing the affective dynamics of risk aversion and fear. Risk aversion and subjective emotional experience have only come to political and cultural dominance because they resonate in the absence of meaningful politics. Revealing the dynamic structure of risk aversion and securitisation in political discourse as well as popular culture is the necessary critical task. If engagement and identification are successfully achieved at the level of individuated emotions then critical public debate is entirely bypassed and important arguments about the diminishing of political agency and the positive potential of it will not be heard. Re-routing this bypass into critical, open-minded public debate is the political task.

Notes

[1] Excerpts of this chapter were published in *Free Associations*, No. 62, July 2011.

[2] Whilst providing a critical analysis of popular television culture and seeking to highlight that in this sense the narratives analysed are 'paranoid' I am not using the term to marginalise, de-value or 'other' these narratives. I am using 'paranoid' as an analytical concept to develop a deeper understanding of televisual representation. In psychoanalytical literature the term is not pejorative but refers to a process of relational identity formation and communication.

[3] *Spooks/MI-5* Executive Producer Jane Featherstone, BBC Television Publicity News Release 2002.

Chapter 13

Screening Terror on
The West Wing

Jack Holland

As Laura Shepherd has reflected, *The West Wing* may appear a somewhat 'esoteric choice of analytical vehicle' (2009: 1), but there are very good reasons for taking this groundbreaking television show seriously; not only for its contributions in the realm of popular culture, but also for its contributions in the 'real world' of American politics and public opinion. Messages in fiction matter in real and political ways, and *The West Wing* was particularly well suited to impacting real life politics. Because of this, *The West Wing* has already attracted academic analysis for its contribution to debates on gender (Shepherd 2009) and race (Wodak 2010), as well as foreign policy, terrorism and war (Gans-Boriskin and Tisinger 2005; Holland 2011). This chapter analyses the role *The West Wing* has played in screening terror, before, during and after the events of 11 September 2001.

This role should be taken seriously for a number of reasons (see further Weber 2006; Weldes 2003). High viewing figures and a devoted audience, as well as the show's tendency to confront topical issues head-on, made *The West Wing* an important medium for communicating about terrorism to the American people as they were confronted with the shock of 9/11. This shock contributed to an immediate post-9/11 period characterised by the difficulty of making sense of events that seemingly fell beyond the expectations of normal life and were briefly resistant to attempts at their articulation. Yet, only three weeks later, on 3

October 2001, over 28 million Americans tuned in to view a special one-off episode of *The West Wing* that stood alone, outside of ongoing storylines, in order to address the events of 9/11 directly.

This chapter situates the special stand-alone episode, 'Isaac and Ishmael', within the broader context of the emerging 'war on terror', arguing that the show played an important role in communicating terrorism for the American public and in narrowing the space for debate in the wake of 9/11. It is argued that *The West Wing*'s approach to screening terror responded to the context of the moment before, during and after the events of 11 September. This response equated to a worrying reinforcement of dominant discourses. To demonstrate this reinforcement and its impact, the chapter is organised in three sections. First, the changing context of terror and American politics, in which *The West Wing* aired and evolved, is set out. Second, the chapter pivots around the date of 11 September 2001 to examine the portrayal of terrorism in *The West Wing* before, during and after the tumultuous moment of 9/11. And third, the chapter reflects on the narrowing of debate performed by screenings of terror in *The West Wing* through a consideration of the role of television in the production of political (im)possibility.

The Context of Terror: Before, During and After 9/11

First airing on American television in 1999, following the Monica Lewinski scandal and subsequent impeachment of President Bill Clinton, *The West Wing* offered an alternative and arguably more idealistic portrayal of American politics. However, the show frequently and notably took its cues from real life, including the foreign policy of the Clinton Administration. While Clinton's presidency may not be remembered primarily for foreign policy, his Administration did inevitably engage with foreign policy issues and was forced to respond to several instances of international terrorism that would later be read as early warning signs of the threat posed by Al-Qaeda and Osama bin Laden. The result of these responses, combined with Clinton's focus on domestic issues, was that the Administration's foreign policy appeared *ad hoc* and reactive. As Republican nominee for the presidency, George W. Bush lamented Clinton's perceived lack of strategic vision:

[America's] temptation is drift – for our nation to move from crisis to crisis like a cork in a current. Unless a president sets his own priorities, his priorities will be set by others – by adversaries, or the crisis of the moment, live on CNN. American policy can become random and reactive – untethered to the interests of our country.

(Bush 1999)

Bush's criticism addressed Clinton's foreign policy in Kosovo, as well as his response to the 1998 US embassy bombings in Tanzania and Kenya. Linked to the terrorist group Egyptian Islamic Jihad, the bombings of American embassies in Dar es Salaam and Nairobi killed over two hundred people. Two weeks later, President Clinton launched Operation Infinite Reach, a series of missile strikes against terrorist training camps in Afghanistan, as well as a pharmaceutical factory in Sudan, believed (incorrectly) to be producing nerve gas. In total, due to the camps being almost completely empty, the strikes likely killed between six and thirty-five people, a relatively small number. While opinion was divided, the strikes were generally supported in the Western world as a proportional and legitimate response to the bombing of US embassies, targeted against specific terrorist sites. It was in the context of debates on the acceptability and appropriateness of responses to terror that *The West Wing* made its first foray into foreign policy debates in 1999, reaffirming prevalent understandings of the need for restraint and proportionality in foreign policy.

One year later, following the 2000 bombing of the American Navy Destroyer the USS Cole, the Clinton and Bush Administrations opted not to take military action in response. Despite evidence linking Al-Qaeda to the attack, Bush was adamant that he did not wish to waste American resources on insignificant enemies. He told Condoleezza Rice that he 'was tired of swatting flies' (cited in NCTAUS 2004). The desire not to 'respond to Al-Qaeda one attack at a time' fitted with Bush's broader disdain for reactive foreign policy, uninformed by a broader strategy to combat the terrorist threat. However, less than a year later and only eight months after taking office, the events of 11 September 2001 would shatter the status quo, force a response and accelerate efforts to develop a grand strategy for confronting terrorism.

9/11 was seen by most watching Americans to instantly and unquestionably herald a moment of temporal rupture (Holland 2009). Bush articulated this rupture as 'the day the world changed' and 'night fell on a different world' (Bush 2001b). However, beyond rupture, it was not clear to many viewers why and by whom the United States was attacked, nor how it should respond. To understand this confusion, it is necessary to re-locate the events of 9/11 within the specific American context in which they occurred.

Conditioned by the truths of American security culture, US citizens did not expect or foresee large-scale, illegitimate violence taking place on American soil (Gaddis 2004). Coming as it did at the end of the 1990s further increased the perceived unlikelihood of such an attack: the decade of 'New World Order' that had followed the end of the Cold War was proclaimed to be America's 'unipolar moment', in which the US was now the 'indispensible nation' (Krauthammer 1990/91). The attack was shocking precisely because Americans were unconditioned to viewing 'foreign' violence on home soil and it came at that moment the US was seen to be at the zenith of its power. Correspondingly, spontaneous reactions from ordinary Americans frequently assumed the events were either news from some other country or from some previous time. Such reactions make sense when it is recalled that, for many Americans, 9/11 was seen to contradict triumphalist claims that history had ended with America's ascension to sole superpower status (Fukuyama 1992).

As events appeared to contradict these deeply ingrained beliefs of US security culture, ordinary Americans struggled to make sense of 9/11. This was compounded by a lack of authoritative voices coming forward to explain the situation to a bewildered public. As I have argued elsewhere, the *wrong* (the disproving of perceived security truths) and the *lack* (the failure to narrate) were the twin arms of the void that held Americans in a stunned, silent embrace (Holland 2009; Holland 2011). On 11 September 2001 language failed. Politicians, practitioners and media commentators initially struggled to place frameworks of intelligibility over the events. At first, the events were literally 'unspeakable' as the US lacked an appropriate vocabulary to describe what it was seeing (Kleinfeld 2003; Steinert 2003). Unlike, for example, British, Spanish or

Sri Lankan experiences, Americans lacked a language to describe and regulate the meaning of terrorism at home.

The lack of an appropriate language to make sense of 9/11 meant that cues were frequently taken from unofficial sources and 'lower' levels of cultural life. In contrast to the more commonplace intersubjective understandings that are produced through discursive regularities, religion and films were frequently drawn upon as American attempts to comprehend 9/11 initially took place at the level of the individual, often with recourse to popular culture. The resulting discursive void saw a plethora of competing and fragmentary understandings in place of more commonplace harmonised meaning (Holland 2009; Campbell 2001). In short, the cultural shock of 9/11 was compounded by the emptiness of the space usually occupied by assured 'official' voices. It was in this space that *The West Wing* delivered the one-off 'Isaac and Ishmael' episode, which would help to fill the uneasy void in meaning that plagued America in the days after 9/11.

Filling the void was an important process. The cultural shock was symptomatic of what Jenny Edkins has identified as 'trauma' (2002; 2004). Succinctly, having fallen outside of expected and predictable patterns everyday life, 9/11 was a traumatic event that was seen and felt to *demand* a response. The insistence on an exceptional response, outside of usual politics, reflected the reading and experience of 9/11 as an exceptional event. Given the difficulty politicians faced in communicating what had happened for the public, this demand to be communicated with and to 'reply' generated an acute tension. It was in this tension that Aaron Sorkin wrote, directed and produced 'Isaac and Ishmael', outside of *The West Wing*'s continuity. The episode helped to the fill the void in meaning for Americans, teaching them how to think about 9/11. Unfortunately, it did so by reinforcing the dominant narratives of the Bush Administration, further limiting the scope for different interpretations and alternative responses. This complicity in the framing of terror was continued as *The West Wing* returned to its normal and ongoing plotlines.

The war on terror was marked by a number of assumptions about the nature of the terrorist threat. First, 9/11 was framed as an act of war and a moment of transition from peacetime to wartime. This paradigm shift meant that the rule of law was seen to be replaced by the rules of war. Second, it was framed as heralding fundamentally new and dangerous times, in which the threat to the United States was unprecedented. To combat this unique threat, the Bush Administration advised that the rules of the game had changed and new strategies would be required. Third, 9/11 was framed as being an attack on fundamental American values, such as freedom, a hatred of which motivated the attacks. And fourth, new policies were introduced to combat the terrorist threat. Most notably, the metaphor of harbouring helped the Bush Administration to locate and localise the terror threat, by making no distinction between terrorists and their state sponsors. More broadly, however, sensitivities to local and cultural differences were now seen to be secondary to the need to advance 'freedom' abroad in order to defend it at home. It was in this context that *The West Wing*'s approach to foreign policy evolved to meet and match the perceived demands of the war on terror. Again, in its approach to screening terror, as well as appropriate responses to it, *The West Wing* served to reconfirm dominant discourses, disseminating them for an American public and ultimately helping to silence dissent.

Screening Terror: Before, During and After 9/11

First airing on NBC in September 1999, *The West Wing* went on to run for seven series. The show drew consistently high audiences, although they declined following Sorkin's departure at the end of the fourth series. The finale of series two, for example, attracted over twenty million viewers in the US. And the show was critically acclaimed, winning three Golden Globes and 27 Emmy Awards (Shamsie 2001). Its plotlines boasted numerous real world parallels, despite the show's creators being adamant that they were creating a work of fiction. Referred to as 'The Left Wing' by the American Right, real-world parallels were most evident in respect of the Clinton White House (Rollins and O'Connor 2003: 3). Key characters were easily read as counterparts of Clinton Administration officials: Sam Seaborn as George Stephanopoulis; Josh Lyman as Paul Begala; and C.J. Cregg as Dee Dee Myers (Waxman 2000). The election of George W. Bush did not hinder the show's tendency to find inspiration in events taking place in the real life West Wing.

Mocking it as naively 'Capra-esque' and as 'political pornography for liberals', critics feared the politicised impact of the show. Accusations included that *The West Wing* had a 'tacit mission of the revival of lagging liberal spirits' and that the show was no more than a 'cultural platform for the revival of liberal politics in America' (quoted in Rollins and O'Connor 2003: 4). Before 9/11, as the 'ultimate Hollywood fantasy: the Clinton White House without Clinton', *The West Wing* broadly supported the president's foreign policy, albeit with a cautious bipartisanship.

A Proportional Response: Teaching Restraint Before 9/11

Aired on 6 October 1999, the third episode of *The West Wing*, titled 'A Proportional Response', closely follows debates about the appropriateness of Clinton's response to the 1998 embassy bombings. The principal storyline revolves around President Jed Bartlet's struggle to formulate a proportional response to the shooting down of an American military plane by the Syrian Defence Ministry. The previous episode laid the groundwork for Bartlet's turmoil, as the final scene closes with the fictional president promising to 'blow them off the face of the earth with the fury of God's own thunder'. It is this desire for vengeance through violent retribution that defines President Bartlet's character for the majority of 'A Proportional Response':

Toby: The President was…barking at the Secretary of State, he's scaring the hell out of [Admiral] Fitzwallace, which I didn't think was possible. He's snapping at the First Lady. He's talking about blowing up half of North Africa…

This desire to strike back does not subside as the episode progresses. Rather, President Bartlet's frustration with those around him slowly increases, as they hinder his desire to strike back immediately and overwhelmingly.

Bartlet: It's been 72 hours, Leo. That's more than three days since they blew [it] out of the sky. And I'm tired of waiting dammit! This is candy ass! We are going to draw up a response scenario today, I'm going to give the order today, we're going to strike back today....Americans were on that plane.

The president's desire to strike back as a deterrent to taking the lives of other Americans manifests itself clearly as the episode moves to the Situation Room where the Chairman of the Joint Chiefs of Staff, Admiral Fitzwallace, outlines 'three retaliatory strike options' that 'meet the obligations of proportional response'.

Fitzwallace: All three scenarios are comprehensive, meet the obligations of proportional response and pose minimal threat to US personnel and assets. To turn our attention to scenario one, or Pericles One, to use its code name...

Bartlet: What is the virtue of a proportional response?

Fitzwallace: I'm sorry?

Bartlet: What is the virtue of a proportional response? Why is it good? They hit an airplane, so we hit a transmitter, right? That's a proportional response....They hit a barracks, so we hit two transmitters?

Fitzwallace: That's roughly it, sir.

The West Wing closely aligns itself with debates in the real White House from the previous year, following Operation Infinite Reach, as Bartlet laments that intelligence has already shown the targets to be empty.

Barlet: But they know we're going to do that, they know we're going to do that. Those areas have been abandoned for four days. We know that from the satellites. We have the intelligence....They did that, so we did this, it's the cost of doing business, it's been factored in, right?...Am I right or am I missing something here?

Fitzwallace: No sir, you're right sir.

Bartlet: Then I ask again, what is the virtue of a proportional response?

Fitzwallace: It isn't virtuous, Mr. President. It's all there is, sir.

At this stage, Bartlet's anger and frustration is clearly expressed. When pressed by Admiral Fitzwallace on what other options might exist, the president is clear in outlining the kind of response and indeed retribution he would ideally like to see.

Bartlet: A disproportional response. Let the word ring forth from this time and this place, you kill an American, any American, we don't come back with a proportional response, we come back [*bangs fist on table*] with total disaster!

General: Are you suggesting we carpet-bomb Damascus?

Bartlet: General, I am suggesting that you and Admiral Fitzwallace and Secretary Hutchinson and the rest of the national security team take the next sixty minutes and put together a US response scenario that doesn't make me think we are just docking somebody's damn allowance!

After Operation Infinite Reach a number of criticisms were launched at the Clinton Administration's response to the US embassy bombings. The timing (only twelve days after impeachment), the (lack of) justification, and the targeting (of what turned out to be an innocent pharmaceutical plant and empty training sites) were all problematic. However, the single largest limiting factor in Operation Infinite Reach was the scale of the response. The limited operation failed to deter Al-Qaeda, with so few terrorists killed and so little damage inflicted on terrorist infrastructure. Bin Laden himself joked that Al-Qaeda had lost little other than a few 'camels and chickens' (cited in Temple-Raston 2007: 119). In view of such concerns, *The West Wing* outlines what a disproportionate response might entail:

Fitzwallace: Mr. President we put together a scenario by which we attack Hassan airport....In addition to the civilian causalities, which could register in the thousands, the strike would temporarily cripple the region's ability to receive medical supplies and bottled water. I think Mr. Cashmen and Secretary Hutchinson would each tell you what I'm sure you already know sir. That this strike would be seen at home and abroad as a staggering overreaction…without the support of our allies, without a Western Coalition, without Great Britain and Japan and without Congress, you'll have doled out a five thousand dollar punishment for a fifty-buck crime, sir. Mr. President, the proportional response doesn't empty the options box for the future, the way an all out assault [does].

Signalling him to finish, Bartlet interrupts Fitzwallace before slowly and reluctantly accepting that the proportional response, which minimises the risk of civilian casualties and cripples 'both their intelligence network and their surface to air strike capabilities', is the best course of action. The choice is vindication of Clinton's own decision to strike back 'proportionally'. However, Bartlet is given a final opportunity to reflect on his frustrations and ultimate desire to secure a world Americans can live in free from the fear of harm.

Bartlet: Did you know that two thousand years ago a Roman citizen could walk across the face of the known world free of the fear of molestation? He could walk across the earth unharmed, cloaked only in the words 'Civis Romanis': I am a Roman citizen. So great was the retribution of Rome, universally understood as certain, should any harm befall even one of its citizens. Where was [the] protection [of those] on that plane? Where is the retribution for the families and where is the warning to the rest of the world that Americans shall walk this earth unharmed, lest the clenched fist of the most mighty military force in the history of mankind comes crashing down on your house?!

By linking a policy of disproportionate response to Rome, *The West Wing* effectively makes the point that securing total safety and freedom from harm would require the establishment of an American Empire. On this point, Bartlet's Chief of Staff, Leo McGarry, sets the president straight:

Leo: We are behaving the way a superpower ought to behave.

Bartelet: Well our behaviour has produced some pretty crappy results. In fact, I'm not a hundred percent sure it hasn't induced them....I'm talking about two hundred and eight-six American marines in Beirut, I'm talking about Somalia, I'm talking about Nairobi.

Leo: And you think racking up the body count's gonna act as a deterrent?

Bartlet: You're damn right.

Leo: Then you are just as dumb as these guys who think that capital punishment is going to be a deterrent for drug kingpins. As if drug kingpins didn't live their day-to-day lives under the possibility of execution. And their executions are a lot less dainty than ours and tend to take place without the bother and expense of due process. So my friend, if you want to start using American military strength as the arm of the Lord, you can do that, we're the only superpower left. You can conquer the world, like Charlemagne, but you better be prepared to kill everyone and you better start with me 'cause I will raise up an army against you and I will beat you!

To reinforce the point, the episode closes by admitting that the situation is not ideal, but that it is the best that can be achieved in the circumstances. *The West Wing* teaches its audience that the proportional response, while not virtuous, is correct, appropriate and moreover informed by the lessons of history.

Leo: It's not good, there is no good. It's what there is. It's how you behave if you're the most powerful nation in the world. It's proportional, it's reasonable, it's responsible, it's merciful. It's not nothing; four high rated military targets.

Bartlet: Which they'll rebuild again in six months.

Leo: So we'll blow 'em up again in six months! We're getting really good at it....It's what our fathers taught us.

In its early stages, *The West Wing* set out a strong liberal position that frequently supported the policies of the Clinton Administration. On foreign policy, there was a recognition that a bipartisan dialogue was required, whereby liberal and conservative views on the need for a proportional response could come together. Actor Martin Sheen, who plays the fictional president, was often troubled that his character was:

> ...often a vengeful president when it comes to the Arab world....I'm always fighting for diplomacy rather than military intervention. This is a constant debate we have on the show. But we do have to satisfy the other side sometimes, give a voice to the right.
>
> (in Dunphy 2000)

This desire for a cautious balance to be found at the intersection of liberal and conservative responses to terrorism would be rapidly abandoned after 9/11. Instead, *The West Wing* would teach Americans that proportionality belonged to a past era. First, however, the show had to explain the nature of the new era, characterised by an unprecedented terror threat, to the American public.

The Klan, Gone Medieval and Global: Teaching 9/11
Three weeks after 9/11 *The West Wing* aired the first episode of its third series. Attempting to confront the events of 11 September head on, the episode did not follow ongoing plotlines. This decision ensured that *The West Wing* helped to construct 9/11 as an exceptional event and a temporal rupture, by responding with its own exceptional episode and temporal rupture. '[S]crambling to meet a virtually unprecedented production schedule' and 'formidable logistical challenge', the speed of this televisual 'response' ensured that *The West Wing* 'was

the first TV show to address the events and aftermath of 9/11' (Lowry 2001; Sorkin 2001; Kel 2001).

From the start, the 'Isaac and Ishmael' episode made viewers aware of its exceptional status and location outside of usual storylines. Addressing the audience as himself, not his character, Bradley Whitford informed Americans that the episode was 'a story-telling aberration'. However, it was far more than that. The episode was a lesson in terrorism for an American public that had struggled to make sense of the events of 11 September in the three weeks after the Twin Towers fell. Moreover, the episode was screened only four days before Operation Enduring Freedom would commence and intervention in Afghanistan would begin. In this context 'Isaac and Ishmael' adopted an explicitly pedagogical theme to teach Americans how to think about terrorism and American responses to it. In both tasks, *The West Wing* would aid and abet the Bush Administration.

The format for the episode sees a group of school pupils, selected for the 'Presidential Classroom' scheme, stuck in the White House Mess Hall due to a lockdown caused by an unspecified threat. One by one the show's main characters join the group to contribute to a question-and-answer style 'lesson' on terrorism. Affording the time to ask questions, the episode reflected and attempted to confront the confusion that characterised the post-9/11 void in meaning. Framing the episode around knowledgeable but scared and confused children asking questions reflected the confusion of the post-9/11 void, in which questions such as 'why do they hate us?' were commonplace (Crockatt 2003; Jackson 2005; Silberstein 2002). With the American public symbolised by the pupils, *The West Wing* reproduces the void in meaning, helping to fill it in particular ways. 'Isaac and Ishmael' perpetuates dominant constructions of both 9/11 and the appropriate response to terrorism through the (re)production of a number of tropes that had already begun to define events. The contribution of 'Isaac and Ishmael' to the production of increasingly hegemonic meaning can be understood around the three principal questions the episode asks and answers: Who is attacking us? Why are they attacking us? And how should the United States respond?

(i) Who is Attacking us?

Answering the first question, 'who is attacking us?', *The West Wing* offered a series of related answers. Joshua Lyman, the fictional Deputy Chief of Staff, delivers the most notable answer:

> Josh: You're juniors and seniors. In honour of the SATs you're about to take, answer the following question. Islamic... extremist...is to...Islamic...as...'blank' is...to Christianity.
>
> *Josh writes this on the board for the students, before turning around, writing 'KKK' and circling it.*
>
> Josh: That's what we're talking about. It's the Klan, gone medieval and global.

This contextualisation of the unnamed Al-Qaeda helped to explain the terrorist network to the population in a way that the Bush Administration had been struggling to achieve (see further Holland 2011). It contributed to an over-lexicalisation of the enemy underway in official government narratives and picked up on by *The West Wing*.

> Toby: When you think of Afghanistan, think of Poland. When you think of the Taliban, think of the Nazis. When you think of the citizens of Afghanistan, think of the Jews in concentration camps.

Not only are the terrorists akin to a medieval Ku Klux Klan, but, as Communications Director Toby Ziegler asserts, when imagining their Taliban protectors Americans should also think of Hitler's National Socialists. *The West Wing* teaches Americans that Al-Qaeda are the KKK, the Taliban are the Nazis and both want to exterminate America and American freedoms, as they are already doing to ordinary Afghan citizens. Using these commonly understood reference points, 'Isaac and Ishmael' teaches Americans little that the Bush Administration had not already sanctioned for public consumption.

(ii) Why are they Attacking us?

On this second question, 'Isaac and Ishmael' joins with the Bush Administration in arguing that terrorists target the United States because of American identity and values.

Girl 1:   Why are Islamic Extremists trying to kill us?

Josh: That's a reasonable question if ever I heard one. Why are we targets of war?

Boy 2:   Because we're Americans.

Josh: That's it?

Girl 3:   Because of our freedom?

Josh: No other reasons?

Boy 3:   Freedom and democracy.

Josh: I'll tell you, right or wrong – and I think they're wrong – it's probably a good idea to acknowledge that they do have specific complaints. I hear them every day – the people we support, troops in Saudi Arabia, sanctions against Iraq, support for Egypt. It's not just that they don't like Irving Berlin.

Donna: Yes, it is.

Josh: No, it's not.

Donna: No, not about Irving Berlin, but your ridiculous search for rational reasons why somebody straps a bomb to their chest is ridiculous.

While this remains one of the more critical readings that 'Isaac and Ishmael' offers, allowing space for a counter-discourse, the show ultimately concludes that terrorists are motivated purely by hatred. The strategy is repeated later in the episode to represent two competing discourses that emerged in the post-9/11 void: 'imperial blowback' and 'they hate our freedoms'. The conclusion, again, is that while terrorists may have legitimate political grievances, they attack the US because of American identity, not because of what the US has done. This is an important political move as it renders introspection unnecessary and naturalises a militaristic response. Since American identity and values are portrayed as fundamental, timeless and unchanging, terrorist violence motivated by a pure and unyielding hatred of them will not end without the elimination of the threat itself.

(iii) How Should the United States Respond?

The West Wing answers the third question in terms of both a generalised strategic mission and the specific tactical considerations that are required. Firstly, on the mission, since terrorists are motivated by a hatred of fundamental American values, 'Isaac and Ishmael' correspondingly teaches Americans that fighting terrorists is always about ensuring freedom.

> Toby: Well, what would you say the point of fighting terrorism is?
>
> C.J.:   It's to ensure freedom, Pokey. I don't need the brochure.

This is a significant framing that reduces the space to oppose official policy and limits opportunities for proposing alternatives. Framed as the defence of freedom, fighting terror abroad becomes a dominant and coercive foreign policy. To challenge this framing is to risk being seen to lack patriotism, as evidenced by a lack of willingness to defend values such as freedom that are understood to be fundamental to American national identity (Krebs and Jackson 2007; Krebs and Lobasz 2007, 2009).

Secondly, addressing the more specific issue of tactics, the cast offer three important and increasingly commonplace tropes. First, Josh reassures the pupils and the watching public that killing terrorists is acceptable:

> Pupil: Do you favour the death penalty?
>
> Josh: No.
>
> Pupil: But you think we should kill these people?
>
> Josh: You don't have the choices in a war that you do in a jury room. But I wish we didn't have to. I think death is too simple.

The West Wing's liberal response regrets having to kill America's enemies, but acknowledges that 9/11 has changed the rules of the game, and America must adapt accordingly in order to survive. For Josh, following these acts of war, it is necessary to switch to a 'war paradigm' in order to fight back and protect America. White House Press Secretary C.J. Cregg delivers an impassioned defence of this position in a discussion on the balance between civil liberties and security:

> C.J.:
>
> Look, I talk civil liberties as seriously as anybody, okay? I've been to the dinners and we haven't even talked about free speech yet and somebody getting lynched by the patriotism police for voicing a minority opinion. That said…we're going to have to do some stuff. We're going to have to tap some phones and we're going to have to partner with some people who are the lesser of evils. I'm sorry but terrorists don't have armies and navies. They don't have capitals. Some of these guys we're going to have to walk up to them and shoot them. Yeah, we can root terrorist nests but some of these guys aren't going to be taken by the 105th armoured tank division. Some of these guys are going to be taken by a busboy with a silencer. So it's time to give the intelligence agencies the money and the manpower they need. We don't hear about their successes. Guess what? The Soviets never crossed the Elbe. The North Koreans stayed behind the 38th parallel. During the Millennium? Not one incident. Do you think that's because the terrorists decided that'd be a good day to take off? Not much action that day?

For C.J., faced with an existential terrorist threat, the liberty/security debate is a 'no brainer': it is imperative that the US increases defence spending and provides intelligence officers the widest possible scope to act. Second, C.J. goes on to reassure the pupils that America need not fight alone. In a new era defined by dangerous enemies, the children are reassured that the US still has friends and that coalition-building is quintessentially American:

| C.J.: | There's nothing more American than coalition-building. The first thing John Wayne always did was put together a posse. |

Third, reassured that fighting terrorists to defend freedom will be done shoulder-to-shoulder with America's allies, the pupils are told where the US is going to have to take action. Replacing Bush's harbouring metaphor with that of 'incubator', intervention in Afghanistan is naturalised by contextualising American foreign policy through widely understood pre-existing conflicts:

Boy 1:	Where do terrorists come from?
Josh:	Where do they come from?
Sam:	Everywhere. Mostly they come from exactly where you'd expect: places of abject poverty and despair. Horribly impoverished places are an incubator for the worst kind of crime.

As Charlie explains, it is no different from the gangs of 'South Central LA, Detroit, the South Bronx' and 'Southeast DC'. By linking the present threat to wars – gang wars, and the war on drugs – that Americans were already familiar with, *The West Wing* emphasises the necessity of fighting and killing terrorists, helping to naturalise an assertive, interventionist response to 9/11. This was an analogy that resonated with viewers, with one noting that 'while all the characters gave amazing performances, there were a few standouts. Charlie's comparison of terrorist camps and gangs was really well written' (Kickdoor 2010). This resonance, and the feeling that the show was accurately articulating the political moment, would be continued as the emerging war on terror took shape.

They'll Like Us When We Win: Teaching Interventionism After 9/11
On 29 January 2002, George W. Bush gave his first State of the Union Address since 9/11. At this stage, it appeared that major combat operations in Afghanistan were coming to a close, with the Taliban toppled and the NATO-led International Security Assistance Force about to step into the vacuum to stabilise the country. In the same month, Guantànamo had received its first

detainees, described as 'illegal, enemy combatants' and the 'worst of a very bad bunch' by Secretary of Defense Donald Rumsfeld and arguably the most influential Vice-President in American history, Dick Cheney. Bush's speech seized on the apparent success to open out the logic of the war on terror. He identified the now infamous 'axis of evil' in the modern world, initially comprising Iran, Iraq and North Korea. Over the course of the coming year it would be Iraq on which attention would be refocused. This was the context in which the fifty-seventh episode of *The West Wing* aired. Coming thirteen weeks after 'Isaac and Ishmael', this episode was one of the first to be written around the new context of the war on terror. *The West Wing*'s approach to the screening of terror, as well as American foreign policy responses to it, were adapted accordingly, standing in stark contrast to the calls for proportionality in the show's early days.

Early in the episode, 'Night Five', Toby Ziegler remarks that his latest draft of a speech for the president's address at the United Nations was inspired by being 'tired of reading about the President's scattershot foreign policy'. Donna confirms that 'we're at the UN on Monday giving a new foreign policy speech that's going to stir some things up'. On reading the draft, the speechwriters are quizzed about 'want[ing] to be responsible for starting World War III'. Reading the draft aloud, it becomes clear that *The West Wing* is mirroring the Bush Administration's attempts to place 'freedom' at the centre of a foreign policy doctrine:

Andy: 'Freedom must run deeper than the free flow of capital. Freedom must mean more than the free trade of goods and services. The world will be free when we have freedom of speech for every nation….The world will be free when there is freedom to worship for everyone. The world will be free…when we finally shake off the rusted chains of tyranny…whether in the guise of fascist dictatorships…or economic slavery, or ethnic hostility…or', wait for it, 'the crushing yoke of Islamic fanaticism'. Gentlemen, start your engines.

The speech is significant, coming as it does in such stark contrast to the previous discursive work the show afforded to a foreign policy of proportionality and humility, in keeping with Bush's own election platform. In the post-9/11 era, *The West Wing* confirmed Bush's assertions that freedom and fear are now at war. The discussion of the speech continues, tellingly:

Andy: America doesn't have a monopoly on what's right. And even if we did, I think you're gonna have a tough time convincing the Arab world....The US Constitution defends religious pluralism. It doesn't reduce all of Islam to fanaticism.

Toby: It's fanaticism whether we call it that or not, so we're going to call it that. We respect all religions, all cultures...to a point. Grotesque oppression isn't okay just because it's been institutionalised. If you ask me, I think we should have gotten into the game three, four decades ago, but they're coming after us now, so it's time to saddle up....We do know what's right.

Andy: This is why they hate us.

Toby: There's a lot of reasons why they hate us. You know when they're gonna like us? When we win.

A renewed confidence in American values and a heightened belief in American exceptionalism were important features of the war on terror at the start of 2002, as the US attempted to re-establish its confidence in world affairs. Previous toleration of cultural differences was seen to be inappropriate in an era when they might lead to a hatred that ultimately fuels terrorism. In this context, liberal and conservative views on foreign policy no longer met at their *cautious* intersection, but rather favoured a muscular defence of treasured values through overwhelming military might. This formulation was central to the emerging neoconservative orthodoxy adopted within the Bush Administration. And with soaring, unprecedented approval ratings, President Bush was succeeding in selling this argument to the American public. It was a simple message to sell: in the war on terror, fanaticism was to be rooted out to make way for freedom. It was a message *The West Wing* delivered with aplomb.

Toby: Our goal *is* to proclaim American values…the reality is, the United States of America no longer sucks up to reactionaries, and our staunch allies will know what we mean…

Andy: What's Egypt going to think? Or Pakistan?

Toby: That freedom and democracy are coming soon to a theatre near them, so get dressed.

Andy: Toby…you guys are on a thing right now. And I'm behind you. You know I'm behind you; a lot of House Democrats are…and plenty of Republicans. But this one moment in time, you have to get off your horse and just, simply put - be nice to the Arab world.

Toby: Be nice? Well…How about when we, instead of blowing Iraq back to the seventh century for harbouring terrorists and trying to develop nuclear weapons, we just imposed economic sanctions and were reviled by the Arab world for not giving them a global charge card and a free trade treaty? How about when we pushed Israel to give up land for peace? How about when we sent American soldiers to protect Saudi Arabia, and the Arab world told us we were desecrating their holy land? We'll ignore the fact that we were invited. How about two weeks ago, in the State of the Union when the President praised the Islamic people as faithful and hardworking only to be denounced in the Arab press as knowing nothing about Islam? But none of that is the point.

Andy: What's the point?

Toby: I don't remember having to explain to Italians that our problem wasn't with them, but with Mussolini! Why does the US have to take every Arab country out for an ice cream cone? They'll like us when we win! Thousands of madrassahs teaching children nothing, nothing, nothing but the Koran and to hate America. Who do we see about that? Do I want to preach America? Judeo-Christianity? No. If their religion forbids them from playing the trumpet, so be it. But I want those kids to look at a globe, be exposed to social sciences, history, some literature. They'll like us when we win.

The inclusion of a humanitarian argument, appealing to education and notions of universal human rights, within a particularly muscular liberalism or neoconservatism is also indicative of real world debates. The two principal military interventions of the war on terror, in Afghanistan and Iraq, were both justified partly by recourse to humanitarian concerns. A lack of access to education for women in Afghanistan, as well as young boys in madrassas was a frequent feature of attempts to sell intervention to those most sceptical of the use of military force. However, the primary message that *The West Wing* communicated to viewers was that winning, above all else, was all that really mattered and the ultimate determinant of American safety and future popularity.

Television and (Im)possibility

The evolution of *The West Wing*'s approach to screening terror, as well as foreign policy responses to it, closely followed the context in which episodes were written, produced and aired. From advocating a proportional response to terrorism, the show altered its stance to reflect the new 'realities' of the war on terror from autumn 2001 – new realities that continued to shape *The West Wing*'s political message as the war on terror progressed (see also Gans-Boriskin and Tisinger 2005: 106). It was a message that supported official foreign policy and frequently expressed views even more hawkish than those of the Bush Administration.

Through episodes such as 'Isaac and Ishmael' and 'Night Five', *The West Wing* actively shut down the scope for debate in American politics and society after 9/11. Alternative voices were silenced by the amplification of official narratives. *The West Wing*, of course, did not perform this narrowing in isolation. In the news media, for example, 'Bush administration officials were the most frequently quoted sources, the voices of anti-war groups and opposition Democrats were barely audible, and the overall thrust of coverage favoured a pro-war perspective' (Hayes and Guardino 2010: 59). What makes *The West Wing* noteworthy is that the show is explicitly written from a liberal perspective, which, after 9/11, nonetheless reinforced the position of a Republican presidency and neoconservative foreign policy. Just as in 1999, when 'A Proportional Response' effectively helped to silence criticism of President Clinton's ill-received Operation Infinite Reach, in 2001 *The West Wing* again defended the Administration of the day, promoting a muscular, militaristic and interventionist foreign policy.

Responding before any other entertainment television show of a similar nature, *The West Wing* episode 'Isaac and Ishmael' should be read as an important contribution to the tumultuous 9/11 moment. The episode facilitated the transition from a void in meaning to a full-blown response to terrorism. 'Isaac and Ishmael' aided the process of confirming the meaning of 9/11, which slowly harmonised across American society, and it aided the Bush Administration in establishing a hegemonic foreign policy discourse that would come to underpin the subsequent war on terror. This task was continued as the show progressed and returned to ongoing plotlines. Presenting a hawkish, neoconservative policy in concert with the Bush Administration, *The West Wing* contributed to the conditions of possibility that enabled the war on terror, helping to make it possible and simultaneously narrowing the space to think and argue otherwise. First, as a popular, intelligent and liberal show, *The West Wing* served to foster the appearance that militaristic interventionism in the war on terror was a bipartisan policy; and second, by mimicking the Bush Administration's invocations of 'freedom', *The West Wing* made speaking out particularly challenging as it came with the added risk of being labelled unpatriotic – a cardinal sin in post-9/11 America.

Conclusion

The West Wing continues to influence and provide an analytical lens to examine American politics. For instance, the rhetoric of Martin Luther King has recently been invoked in both Jed Bartlet's and Barack Obama's White Houses in light of the extra-judicial killing of terrorists. Having ordered the covert assassination of a terrorist suspect, President Bartlet quotes Dr King to reflect that the 'ultimate weakness of violence is that it is a descending spiral. Returning violence with violence only multiplies violence adding deeper darkness to a night already devoid of stars…I'm part of that darkness now.' The same quotation was shared virally, online around the world, in the days following the extra-judicial shooting of bin Laden in May 2011. In the fictional *West Wing*, Leo was left to reassure President Bartlet that 'Dr King wasn't wrong, he just didn't have your job', once again reaffirming the policies of the actual President of the United States. And once again *The West Wing* reinforces dominant understandings that extra-judicial killing is required in the battle against terror, despite questions about the legality and morality of such actions.

Finally, this analysis contributes to a body of work, exemplified in this volume, which shows that disciplines such as Political Science, International Relations and Terrorism Studies, frequently resistant to analysing popular culture, should take fictional dramas seriously. Television shows such as *The West Wing* possess considerable power to shape and guide public opinion, to support or challenge official policies, and to open up or close down the space for debate in American politics. Most generally this chapter has shown that popular culture plays an important role in contributing to political (im)possibility. More specifically, the chapter has shown that politics, terrorism and television are intimately linked. And most concretely, the chapter has shown that, in its evolving approach to screening terror, *The West Wing* served to reinforce existing official policies before, during and after 9/11.

Chapter 14

The Image of Evil: Why Screen Narratives of Terrorism and Counterterrorism Matter in Real Life Politics and Policies

Brigitte L. Nacos

The traditional stereotyping of particular groups, such as blacks, women, Arabs or Muslims, in motion pictures and TV drama has been well documented. These biases have not been restricted to the entertainment realm, but continue to be part and parcel of news, particularly in television. One manifestation of the entertainment-news symbiosis was post-9/11 TV news reports about the pros and cons of torturing terrorists or suspected terrorists that were introduced by clips of torture scenes from motion pictures or television shows. The evil-doers and the heroic defenders of a threatened nation in fictional dramas figured in real life debates. This chapter explores the blurred lines between news and entertainment media, the dominant narrative about the 'evil' enemy in the so-called war on terrorism and the 'good' heroes that protect the people of the wronged nation, the impact of the story line on mass-mediated public debate, and possible effects on counterterrorism policies – especially concerning the treatment of terrorists and suspected terrorists.

News and Entertainment

The dividing line that many, if not most researchers draw between news and entertainment media is even sharper than the common division of labour between those who analyse the spoken and written word on the one hand and visuals on the other. Perhaps we came to assume the news/entertainment divide because of some obvious differences in the way the press and electronic media organise themselves. Typically, newspapers had in the past and still have today different sections for hard news and entertainment/art news; some TV programmes offer predominantly serious news, while others provide mostly infotainment. Television and radio networks, too, have news and entertainment divisions. In the past, the three US TV networks ABC, CBS and NBC tried in fact to separate news and entertainment by establishing a firewall of dos and don'ts between the two. News divisions were charged with presenting public affairs news in the public interest and were not expected to be profitable; rather, they were financed by their well-earning entertainment brethren.

Only against this background could Richard Salant, as head of CBS News, enact rules that would be unimaginable today. For example, it was a no-no to use music in a news report to make it more dramatic or more entertaining; nor was it allowed to give in to television's need for visuals by recreating scenes to clarify what had happened if no such real images existed. As Peter Boyer observes:

> All of television's efforts, high and low, tumble into the American living room from the same tube, with no physical dividing line between *The Evening News* and *The Beverly Hillbillies*. Television journalists, therefore, had to make the distinction themselves, in their work. 'This may make us a little less interesting to some,' said Salant, 'but that is the price we pay for dealing with fact and truth.'
>
> (Boyer 1988: 15)

Such efforts to distinguish between news and entertainment and to refrain from presenting infotainment have long fallen by the wayside to make room for the overriding corporate profit imperatives of giant media companies. Thus, we miss out on understanding mass media and their impact on people's perceptions concerning public affairs if we continue to hold on to the entertainment/news separation. As Michael Delli Carpini and Bruce Williams note:

> Despite the seeming naturalness of the distinction between news and entertainment media, it is remarkably difficult to identify the characteristics upon which this distinction is based. In fact, it is difficult – we would argue impossible – to articulate a theoretically useful definition of this distinction. The opposite of *news* is not *entertainment*, as the news is often diversionary or amusing (the definition of entertainment) and what is called 'entertainment' is often neither.

> ...all of the usual characteristics we associate with news or public affairs media can be found in other media, and those we associate with popular or entertainment media can be found in the news.

> (Delli Carpini and Williams 2001: 162-3)

In order to keep their audiences tuned-in and maintain or increase their ratings, television networks present the news in ways that they perceive as the most entertaining, interesting, dramatic, or shocking offerings. At times, this means resorting to scenes from entertainment media to make public affairs news more 'real', as the following examples attest:

- On 8 March 2002 ABC News anchor Ted Koppel showed participants in an electronic town hall meeting on the issues of torture and curbs of civil liberties a scene from the TV series *NYPD Blue* in which detective Andy Sipowicz brutally 'tuned up' a suspect to make him talk.

- On 4 March 2003 *World News Tonight with Peter Jennings* opened with a segment on 'torture or persuasion' by showing a torture scene from the motion picture *The Siege* with Bruce Willis. The clip underlined that, as correspondent Jackie Judd said, 'Hollywood's version of torture knows no limits.'

Whether exposed to combinations of entertainment and news as in the above examples or distinct entertainment and news programmes, audience members do not neatly distinguish between different kinds of media. In researching the depiction of race in American mass media and the formation of the black image in white Americans' minds, Robert Entman and Andrew Rojecki examined news, motion pictures, and advertising in separate case studies and reported their findings in separate chapters. But in the end, based on what they learned in their extensive focus group sessions about white Americans' views of African-Americans, they concluded,

> There is little reason to believe that such distinctions significantly shape people's responses. The *overall patterns* of images and information establish the mental associations, the schemas, used to process the social world. *The most relevant differentiation is not between genres but between different patterns of communicated information and prototypes they construct.*

(Entman and Rojecki 2000: 208)

How we view the world around us, how we think and talk about issues and problems arising in the public and private spheres is not only affected by the information we receive as news but by what the words, narratives, ideas, images, and stereotypes of different types of mass media – and person-to-person communications that are also likely to be influence by media – implant in our memory.

The premise that it is not media types that matter but the patterns in which information is presented and communicated, lies at the heart of cultivation theory and research. The cultivation school, founded by George Gerbner, is not interested in the immediate impact of leading news stories or a particular television show or a particular motion picture on public opinion about public affairs issues or problems, but rather looks at the persistent patterns of media content, whether entertainment, news or art, as influencing audience members' deep-seated perception of reality. The idea here is that over time the mass media's and particularly television's pervasive narratives and images shape our beliefs, values, ideologies, prejudices, stereotypes and thus our *Weltanschauung* – a term not captured fully by the English translation 'worldview'. As Neil Postman noted:

> Whether we are experiencing the world through the lens of speech or the printed word or the television camera, our media-metaphors classify the

world for us, sequence it, frame it, enlarge it, reduce it, color it, argue a case for what the world is like.

(Postman 1985: 10)

Those 'pictures in our heads' come into play when we process new information and are prompted to think about public affairs.

Speculating that strong links exist between film images and movie-goers perception of reality, Walter Lippmann wrote:

> The shadowy idea becomes vivid; your hazy notion, let us say of the Ku Klux Klan, thanks to Mr. Griffiths, takes vivid shape when you see *The Birth of a Nation*. Historically, it may be the wrong shape, morally it may be a pernicious shape, but it is a shape, and I doubt whether anyone who has seen the film and does not know more about the Ku Klux Klan than Mr. Griffiths, will ever hear the name again without seeing those white horsemen.

(Lippmann 1997 [1922]: 61)

To sum up, then, the strict demarcation lines between news and entertainment or between news and popular culture or high art do not make sense if we are searching for the mass-mediated influences on people's perceptions of reality in general and public affairs in particular.

Does this make the examination of one mass media form incomplete and perhaps not even worth labour-intensive research? Of course not: good research that focuses on particular media genres and particular content illuminates our understanding of persistent patterns of representation over time and how those pervasive features come into play in the political discourse of current public affairs. But we get a much more complete, richer picture if we study and compare the whole range of media.

The Depiction of Terrorism in Entertainment and News

There is a great deal of fine research on the depiction of terrorism in motion pictures, television series, and documentaries before and after 9/11. After reviewing Hollywood's terrorism movies of the last decades, Thomas Riegler (2010) concluded that 'terrorism was first of all a thrilling piece of entertainment: the plots are all but spectacular, the villains mostly represent archetypes of "evil", and ultimately the threat is averted by righteous forces.' He also found that the common preoccupation with the good versus evil dichotomy comes at the expense of dealing with the political roots of terrorism. Similarly, Carl Boggs and Tom Pollard note how in Hollywood terrorism is 'reduced to the diabolical work of certain designated groups':

> Visual images, plot lines, musical scores, and sound effects merge to convey an epochal 'clash of civilizations' thematic, as shady personality types (irrational, fanatical, sadistic) hostile to the US occupy center stage.
>
> (Boggs and Pollard 2006: 348)

These scholars, too, were struck by the lack of 'any political backdrop consistent with complex, balanced views of how armed force is used by an array of state and non-state forces around the world' in terrorism movies that pit modern-day action heroes against evil of terrorists like cowboy superstars once fought the evil forces in the American West.

While Hollywood's terror fiction has always embraced the notion that extraordinary actions are needed to fight terrorist foes, the watchdog press is supposed to bark when civil liberties and human rights are violated in the name of greater security. Yet we see the same fixation with terrorist spectaculars, the focus on episodic rather than thematic frames, and the same storylines of good versus evil in the news, particularly in television newscasts. In what follows, after summarising the news media's obsession with terrorism and the tendency to frame terrorism news overwhelmingly episodically, I discuss the melodramatic post-9/11 coverage patterns in television news. Finally, I use a case study to explore the impact of Hollywood's terrortainment, as depicted in *24* and other television drama series and films, on America's post-9/11 public debates about the treatment of terrorists, including the use of torture.

Just as Hollywood exaggerates the terrorist threat for the sake of box office hits and television ratings, the news media, too, over-cover terrorism. Indeed, each major act of terrorism and, in fact, even relatively minor and failed terrorist deeds result in news coverage. Louise Richardson (2006: 94) observes that '[p]ublicity has always been a central objective of terrorism' and that 'terrorists have been extremely successful in gaining publicity.' While this does not mean that the press is sympathetic to terrorists, it is nevertheless true that terrorist strikes provide what the contemporary news media crave most – sensation, drama, shock, and tragedy suited to be packaged as gripping human-interest narratives. As a result, terrorists get precisely what they want: massive publicity and the opportunity to showcase their ability to strike against even the strongest of nation states. Media organisations are rewarded as well, in that they energise their competition for audience size and circulation – and thus for the all-important advertising dollar. As Simon Cottle (2006: 22) puts it, contemporary television 'is embedded within commercial logics and structures of dominance that often implicates it in times of conflict' and struggles with the 'professional raison d'etre of journalism itself.' In the coverage of terrorism, commercial imperatives seem to triumph over journalism ethics (see further, Nacos 2007).

As for the lack of context in the construction of terrorism in Hollywood movies, television news about terrorism is also overwhelmingly episodic, not thematic or contextual. These framing patterns are of great importance because, as Shanto Iyengar's (1987) research found, people exposed to episodic TV coverage of terrorism (or crime and other problems) were likely to attribute the responsibility to the individuals involved, and more likely to favour the punishment of individuals than were those exposed to thematic reporting. The latter group was more likely to attribute responsibility to societal, political conditions and more likely to favour overall policy responses to correct the problems. Since, as discussed above, all types of media affect the perceptions of individuals, one can assume that these similarities in both Hollywood movies and newscasts contribute to audience perceptions of terrorism and counterterrorism.

On the evening of 9/11, in his address to the nation, President George W. Bush characterised the enemy and the attack four times as 'evil', and left no doubt that the United States was the good force in the 'war against terrorism' as it had been in other wars before. 'America has stood down enemies before, and we will do so this time', he said. 'None of us will ever forget this day. Yet, we go forward to defend freedom and all that is good and just in our world' (Bush 2001a). For Americans who had watched television from the time they learned of the attacks, and most of them did, there was nothing new in what the president said and how he said it. For in the hours before the president spoke,

TV's non-stop news reports had told the same story about the eternal clash between good and evil, heroes and villains, freedom-loving victims and ruthless aggressors over and over again. There were also convenient metaphors and references to historic events or fictional versions of such events. Based on a qualitative content analysis of Fox News on the afternoon of 11 September 2001, Elisabeth Anker (2005: 35) concluded that the reporting was best described as a '[m]elodrama [that] defined America as a heroic redeemer with a mandate to act because of an injury committed by a hostile villain.' The narrative was quite similar on the other networks.

In the 14 hours or so following the 9/11 attacks, anchors, reporters, experts and other sources used the terms 'evil' 16 times and 'war' or 'war on terrorism' 93 times in newscasts aired by ABC, CBS, and NBC. The overt or covert message was that just as the nation battled Nazis, Japanese, and Communists in real wars and Hollywood fiction, there was now another evil to be fought – terrorists, an evil force that most Americans knew as much from the movies as from news reports:

- Less than two hours after the attack, ABC News anchor Peter Jennings said, '[w]e are looking at pictures from a war zone this morning. Not a picture of something that looks like a war zone – looks like an old war zone, but it's a picture of a current war zone in this *endless battle between the United States and its enemies*' [emphasis added].

- On CBS News, former Defense Secretary William Cohen commented, 'Well, the most important thing is that this country is going to respond. It will respond in a way that will certainly send a message to those who have committed this act of *monumental and pure evil*' [emphasis added].

- On NBC News, Ken Allard (introduced as terrorism expert,) told anchor Tom Brokaw, 'We have – we have looked at this thing in terms of the criminal justice paradigm [but] I think most Americans, once the shock fades, are less concerned about bringing them to justice than *sending them to hell*' [emphasis added].

- CBS News anchor Dan Rather told his audience, 'Now it's impossible not to compare this coordinated air attack, this undeclared act of war with the attack on Pearl Harbor almost 60 years ago, the Japanese sneak attack on Pearl Harbor, December 7th, 1941. And it's just as clear as can be that December 7th, 1941, will be forever remembered as, in President Franklin Roosevelt's phrase, "a day of infamy", but so, too, will now September 11th, 2001, go down in American history as a day of infamy. At this moment, you may want to recall that Pearl Harbor was a disaster that brought the United States of America together and propelled it to victory. A thought to ponder as we go through this afternoon.'

In the hours after the attack till midnight, 'Pearl Harbor' was mentioned in newscasts of the three networks 58 times. These references drove home the point that a dangerous enemy had struck once again and needed to be fought and defeated like earlier foes. As Murray Edelman wrote well before 9/11:

> The slogans 'Remember the Alamo', 'Remember the Maine', and 'Remember Pearl Harbor' not only broadened support for the wars in which they were early incidents. Taught to children in history courses and cited in patriotic oratory, they continue to reinforce the assumption that military ventures are an effective way to protect the country.
>
> (Edelman 1988: 70)

While images of the destroyed World Trade Center filled the screen, Tom Brokaw characterised the attacks as 'surrealistic' and soon thereafter explained the news of the president's 'Air Force One' being diverted to an Air Force Base far away from the nation's capital by mentioning a well-known movie:

> We're also told that at Offutt Air Force Base, which is the home of the Strategic Air Command, there is the doomsday plane. It was built to be a flying White House for the president in case of nuclear attack. We think that that's where it is located. There – for a long time, you remember, you heard about the famous Looking Glass Mission, B-52s in the air at all hours so that they could launch an attack if this country were ever [attacked]. The *Dr. Strangelove* movie scenario came out of all of that.

In the weeks, months, and even years following 9/11, the virtuous nation and its heroes received a great deal of prominent news coverage. And so did the villain-in chief Osama bin Laden and the actual attackers who killed themselves in order to murder thousands of innocent Americans. This attention to bin Laden fitted the story line about the 'evil-doer', as President Bush called him, and provided a perfect contrast to the protector-in-chief of the nation who dispatched military forces to Afghanistan to hunt down bin Laden and, later, on to Iraq to remove another evil-doer from power.

Considering that 'collective fear' of terrorism has been the premise 'in the fictional world of many of these [terrorism] films' (Semati 2004) and in the real world of post-9/11 America, it is not surprising that there were striking similarities between the dominant film narrative of the terrorism genre and television news. Just as Hollywood does not let go of a construct that works, the melodramatic story-line of 9/11 was repeatedly retold by news media personnel, by the president, and by other opinion-leaders. And just as Hollywood entertainment exploits images of horror, television news and political leaders exploited the visuals of the struck and falling World Trade Center towers. If that was not enough to keep Americans' fear of further terrorist attacks at high levels, the Bush administration's frequently issued and heavily covered 'terror alerts' raised public anxiety, as did the threats issued by Al-Qaeda that were guaranteed generous news coverage.

Whether terrorism threat messages came in the form of official terror alerts by the US Department of Homeland Security or threats by bin Laden and other Al-Qaeda figures, they received a great deal of news coverage and reminded the public of the threat. Thus, it was not surprising that the Bush administration, after initially asking TV networks not to show complete bin Laden video tapes or extensive excerpts, refrained from further such requests: officials seemed to understand that threats by the terrorist 'evil-doer' heightened public anxiety and thus contributed to their own propaganda of fear. As research revealed, the media and particularly TV news facilitated the Bush administration's effort to sell fear of terrorism and enlist public support for the president's domestic and foreign policy agenda (see further, Nacos et al. 2011).

In short, all the elements that were characteristic of terrorism and counterterrorism *à la* Hollywood made for a compelling news narrative.

The Reel Treatment of Terrorists and the Real Torture Debate: A Case Study

Whether dealing with terrorists or criminals, television drama series became far more violent and torture scenes far more numerous after the events of 9/11. In the six years between 1996-2001 there were 102 torture scenes in prime-time network television, but in the four years after 9/11 (2002-05) there were 624 such scenes (Miller 2007). Just as important was that the characters who tortured changed after the 9/11 attacks. According to Human Rights First, 'It used to be that only villains on television tortured. Today, "good guys" and heroic American characters torture – and this torture is depicted as necessary, effective, and even patriotic.'[1] Mark McGuire, a TV/radio writer, concluded in 2003 that 'Today on TV, sanctioned torture and murder are condoned like never before, not only by the individual characters, but also their employers' (McGuire 2003). While ABC's *Alias*, NBCs long-running *Law and Order* and a host of other programmes showcased brutality and even torture, Fox's hit series *24*, featuring the character Jack Bauer as counterterrorism's superhero, went particularly far in its frequent torture scenes. The frequent premise of *24* was a 'ticking time bomb', or other imminent attack, and a captured terrorist who knew details of the planned strike. In those situations, as Jane Mayer (2007) notes, terrorist suspects 'are beaten, suffocated, electrocuted, drugged, assaulted with knives, or more exotically abused: almost without fail, these suspects divulge critical secrets.'

This unlikely 'ticking time bomb' threat became part of America's public debate about the 'war on terrorism' and the treatment of captured terrorists or suspected terrorists. Never mind that what Jack Bauer faced every week never happened in real life. And never mind that interrogation experts, military and civilian, agree that in real life torture does not succeed. If we accept that both entertainment and news affect people's views of the world and understanding of public affairs, it mattered a great deal that in post-9/11 America movie-goers and TV audiences got used to watching evil terrorists being tortured by Americans who were heroic figures in that they risked their own lives to protect fellow citizens. Referring to the dramatic jump in torture scenes, Robert Thompson, an expert on popular television, pointed out that '[t]he federal government could not have come up with a better set of [TV] series to prepare its audience for the new order of the day' (quoted in Mayer 2007).

The prominence in public affairs discourse of *24* and its hero Bauer would not have surprised communication researchers Delli Carpini and Williams who found in the 1990s that participants in focus groups referred slightly more often to fictional TV shows than news programmes in political discourse about the environment. Their conclusion was that 'understanding the full impact of television on political conversations and on the public opinions formed during them requires expanding the definition of politically relevant television to include both fictional and nonfictional programming', because '[w]hen subjects draw on media in their conversations, they make few distinctions between fictional and nonfictional television' (Delli Carpini and Williams 1994: 793).

If the general public does not separate television entertainment and news strictly, why would one expect differently from people interested in or active in politics? Well before 9/11 and well before Jack Bauer appeared on the screen, Edelman suggested that the mass of people and the policy-making elite were affected:

> The models, scenarios, narratives, and images into which audiences for political news translate that news are social capital, not individual inventions. They come from works of art in all genres: novels, paintings, stories, films, dramas, television sitcoms, striking rumors, even memorable jokes. For each type of news report there is likely to be a small set of striking images that are influential with large numbers of people, both spectators of the political scene and policymakers themselves.
>
> (Edelman 1995: 1)

In post-9/11 America Hollywood fiction and especially Jack Bauer and his actions came to permeate bare knuckle politics and public policy discourse when it came to the treatment of captured terrorists. During election campaigns, at events staged by think tanks, and in classrooms, fictional Hollywood productions and especially *24* were brought up in political debates (Bergman 2008). And just as Jack Bauer had fans among conservatives and liberals, Rush Limbaugh and Barbara Streisand among them, his ways of dealing with terrorists were discussed in conservative and liberal circles and by politicians to the right and left of the political spectrum.

Such was the popularity of *24* that candidates for elective offices hoped to win voters' support by claiming that they would be Jack Bauer's choice in real life. Chuck DeVore, a California state legislator and Tea Party-backed candidate for the 2010 Republican nomination for the US Senate, released a video in which a narrator told Californians:

> Ask yourself this question, Jack Bauer fans: Which person would Jack want as *his* US Senator? Barbara Boxer, a Guantánamo-closing, tax-raising, big-government growing ultra-liberal, who reads Miranda rights to foreign terrorists? Or Chuck DeVore, a US Army Reserve intelligence officer, who likes Guantánamo Bay as it is, thinks foreign terrorists should have an interrogator, not a lawyer...?[2]

Embracing Jack Bauer and his tough actions did not prevent De Vore's defeat, but he was not the first candidate who hoped the *24* superman would energise his campaign. In his quest for the Republican nomination for the 2008 presidential race, US Representative Tom Tancredo participated in a primary debate with other presidential hopefuls. When moderator Britt Hume of Fox News asked how aggressively candidates would question an Al-Qaeda operative with information about a bomb about to go off in a US shopping center, Tancredo answered: 'I'm looking for "Jack Bauer" at that time, let me tell you.' This was an indication that Tancredo would torture the information out of the villain.[3] There was applause from the audience, but endorsing Bauer's way of handling terrorists did not help this candidate either.

During one of the Democratic Party's presidential primary debates, moderator Tim Russert of NBC News described the same unreal time bomb case that Britt Hume had posed to Republicans, and then asked Senator Hillary Clinton: 'Don't we have the right and responsibility to beat it out of him [the terrorist]? You could set up a law where the president could make a finding or could guarantee a pardon.'[4] Senator Clinton rejected the idea. '[T]hese hypotheticals are very dangerous because they open a great big hole in what should be an attitude that our country and our president takes toward the appropriate treatment of everyone', she said. 'And I think it's dangerous to go down this path.' After this exchange, Russert revealed that the hypothetical ticking time bomb scenario and the idea of allowing and pardoning the extraordinary treatment of terrorists had been suggested by her husband, ex-president Bill Clinton, during an interview the previous year.

A few days later, during his appearance on the NBC News programme *Meet the Press*, Bill Clinton tried to row back from his earlier position, arguing that:

> The more I think about it, and the more I have seen that, if you have any kind of formal exception, people just drive a truck through it, and they'll say 'Well, I thought it was covered by the exception.' I think, I think it's better not to have one. And if you happen to be the actor in that moment which, as far as I know, has not occurred in my experience or President Bush's experience since we've been really dealing with this terror, but I – you actually had the Jack Bauer moment, we call it, I think you should be prepared to live with the consequences. And yet, ironically, if you look at the show, every time they get the president to approve something, the president gets in trouble, the country gets in trouble. And when Bauer goes out there on his own and is prepared to live with the consequences, it always seems to work better.[5]

A *24* fan, Bill Clinton mentioned Jack Bauer no fewer than seven times in response to questions about his wife's different position on torturing terrorists. Like many others in the general public and in the political class, he bought into the 'ticking time bomb' justification according to which an imminent threat of catastrophic terrorism calls for an otherwise illegal response – torture. As the comprehensive expert report on interrogation methods by the Intelligence Science Board notes:

> Most observers, even those within professional circles, have unfortunately been influenced by the media's colorful (and artificial) view of interrogation as almost always involving hostility and the employment of force – be it physical or psychological – by the interrogator against the hapless, often slow-witted subject. This false assumption is belied by historic trends that show the majority of sources (some estimates range as

high as 90 percent) have provided meaningful answers to pertinent questions in response to direct questioning (i.e., questions posed in an essentially administrative manner rather than in concert with an orchestrated approach designed to weaken the source's resistance).

(Intelligence Science Board 2006: 95)

But whereas most Americans are familiar with Hollywood heroes fighting the war on terrorism effectively, few have read the 372-page report of the Intelligence Science Board and other documents that repudiate Hollywood's torture saga.

The success of Jack Bauer and other fictional heroes in foiling horrible terrorist plots in record time encourages the general public and public officials to expect rapid and successful outcomes in the real world of terrorism prevention and response. The similarities between the failed Times Square bombing on 1 May 2010 and a *24* episode aired earlier that year were striking in that both dealt with terrorists poised to explode bombs and cause great harm in the midst of Manhattan. But whereas Jack Bauer chased a van with a bomb through the streets, aided by spy drones and clear pictures of the suspect and his car all along the way, New York police and FBI agents had only the fuzzy image of a 'person of interest' available in their hunt for the real would-be bomber. As one astute observer noted, the difference between fiction and reality was clear: 'The video surveillance is far better in the show' (Shear 2010). Indeed, 'the person of interest' in the blurred video frames turned out to be the wrong guy.

When New York City Police Commissioner Raymond Kelly announced the arrest of the right guy, Faisal Shahzad, 54 hours after the attempted Times Square bombing, he couldn't resist drawing a comparison with his fast-moving fictional colleague. During a news conference, Kelly said: 'Fifty-three hours and 20 minutes elapsed from the time Faisal Shahzad crossed Broadway in his Pathfinder to the time he was apprehended at Kennedy Airport. Jack Bauer may have caught him in "24". But in the real world, 53 isn't bad.'[6] Nobody blamed Kelly for resorting to pop culture comparisons to celebrate police officers' and FBI agents' success – although there were some voices critical of reports that agents had lost sight of Shahzad's car on the way to the airport and nearly failed to nab the terrorist before he left the country. But the end of the real chase was as dramatic as fiction in that the would-be bomber was arrested aboard the plane as it was ready to take off from Kennedy Airport. The whole episode was another reminder of how terrorism and counterterrorism fiction and reality intertwine in the minds of many Americans – including the law enforcement community, experts in think tanks and other institutions, and newsroom personnel.

After the failed bombing aboard a Detroit-bound airliner on Christmas Day 2009, law enforcement officers questioned the would-be bomber Umar Farouk Abdulmutallab and, eventually, read him the Miranda warning (the right to remain silent and the consequences of waiving this right, and to retain legal counsel). As a result, Abdulmutallab, a Nigerian citizen, chose to remain silent until convinced otherwise by his father who travelled from Nigeria to the United States. Critics argued that terrorists and suspected terrorists should not be granted Miranda rights but should be interrogated in order to win what could be valuable intelligence for the ongoing war against terrorism. Actually, well before this issue arose, the police could, if deemed necessary for public safety, invoke an exception and question an arrested person without reading the Miranda warning. But this leeway was mostly ignored during the post-9/11 debate. Writing less than a week after the failed Christmas Day bombing, Pulitzer Prize winner John McQuaid noted:

> Revenge fantasies are durable, reliable entertainments because they allow us to experience actions that aren't allowed in real life, and that most of us wouldn't truly want to experience even if given the chance. That would be fine if we were just talking about pop culture. But during the 2000s, the revenge fantasy escaped the realm of fiction. It came to dominate our politics and – for a while – overturned centuries of established US policy and tradition toward prisoners....Even with a new president who says he wants to follow tradition and the rule of law, the Jack Bauer Decade won't end....And as long as terrorists are trying to blow up planes with their underpants, the American political debate will skew towards the emotional popcorn of *24*, ticking time bombs...
>
> (McQuaid 2009)

McQuaid was right. Four days after the Times Square incident, when the Miranda-rights-for-terrorists debate heated up again, US Attorney General Eric Holder announced that the Obama administration would work with Congress on a relaxation of Miranda when dealing with the arrest and detention of suspected terrorists. It was telling that even in this context, the fictional 'ticking time bomb' was invoked to push for withholding rights from terrorists or suspected terrorists. The following are excerpts from an exchange between host David Gregory and Eric Holder on *Meet the Press* on 5 May 2010:

Gregory: You issued a Miranda warning to Shahzad, the right to remain silent, at which point a lot of defendants, suspects could get a lawyer. You did that after eight hours and after you had already gotten him talking. There's criticism about injecting the possibility that a suspect will not provide intelligence if you give them that Miranda warning. Take me through that process of what the balancing test is before Miranda is actually issued.

Holder: Well, I wouldn't say that we talked to him for eight hours without giving his Miranda warnings, but aside from that what you do is you use the public safety exception that the Supreme Court has defined to make sure that there are no immediate threats.

Gregory: *The quote/unquote 'ticking time bomb' scenario.*

Holder: *Ticking time bomb.* And then you make the determination whether or not it is appropriate, whether you think that giving Miranda warnings to that person is going to stop the flow of information or whether the flow of information will continue, and you make the determination. In this particular case, is it more important for us to get intelligence from this person, or is it more important for us to build the case? One of the things that we have certainly seen is that the giving of Miranda warnings has not stopped these terror suspects from talking to us. They have continued to talk even though we have given them a Miranda warning.[7]

If, as the attorney general revealed, terrorists continued to talk even when given the Miranda warning, why change the law? Some years earlier, a report by experts on interrogation provided a plausible answer when it stated:

> Prime-time television increasingly offers up plot lines involving the incineration of metropolitan Los Angeles by an atomic weapon or its depopulation by an aerosol nerve toxin. The characters do not have the time to reflect upon, much less to utilize, what real professionals know to be the 'science and art' of 'educing information.' They want results. Now. The public thinks the same way. They want, and rightly expect, precisely the kind of 'protection' that only a skilled intelligence professional can provide. Unfortunately, they have no idea how such a person is supposed to act 'in real life.'
>
> (Intelligence Science Board 2006: ix)

In the last week of July 2010, Representative Adam Schiff, a Democrat from California, introduced a bill titled 'The Enemy Belligerent Interrogation, Detention and Prosecution Act of 2010' that would extend the period of time that law enforcement has to question a terrorist suspect before bringing him/her before a judge. It was assumed the bill had the backing of the Obama White House and the Department of Justice. For critics on the Right, the proposal did not go far enough; for those on the Left it was a further watering down of civil liberties and human rights. But one way or another, fiction had claimed another piece of reality. David McColgin, an assistant federal defender in Philadelphia, commented critically, 'Overall, this legislation reflects the pervasive misconception that coercion works, and that we just need to let Jack Bauer get to work on our terrorism suspects to get the truth.'[8]

Jack Bauer was the darling of the Bush administration all along. In June 2006, the conservative Heritage Foundation organised a panel discussion about '24 and America's Image in Fighting Terrorism: Fact, Fiction or Does It Matter?' Moderated by right-wing talk show host Rush Limbaugh, the event's panel included Homeland Security Secretary Michael Chertoff, two policy experts

(James Jay Carafano of the Heritage Foundation and David Heyman of the Center for Strategic and International Security Studies), the three co-producers of *24* (Howard Gordon, Joel Surnow, and Robert Cochran) and three members of the *24* cast (Gregory Itzin, Mary Lynn Rajskub, and Carlos Bernard). In his opening remarks, Chertoff talked about the difficult choices that Jack Bauer faced, Bauer's need to make risk assessments in the TV show, and how that 'reflects real life'. Nowhere was the enthusiasm for Jack Bauer greater than in the White House and the rest of the administration. *24* co-producer Surnow was well aware that 'people in the administration love the series [for a good reason]': 'It's a patriotic show. They should love it' (quoted in Mayer 2007). After the panel discussion, he and his colleagues lunched at the real White House.

During the debate at the Heritage Foundation nobody expressed concerns about Jack Bauer's frequent violation of American and international law. In general, when the producers of what Sissela Bok (1999) has called 'entertainment violence' are asked about negative consequences of their work, they tend insist that they deal in fiction, not reality. Joel Silver, for example, defended violence in his movies (*Lethal Weapon*, *Die Hard* and *Predator*) by arguing:

> [I]t's a western, it's entertaining, it's good guys versus bad guys. In that scene in 'The Searchers' when John Wayne went after all those Indians, was that genocide? Was that racist? When James Bond dropped the guy in a pond of piranhas, and he says, 'Bon appetite,' we loved that. That's a great moment. Movies are not real.

> (in Weinraub 1992)

Similarly, the lead writer of *24*, Howard Gordon, told an interviewer, 'I think people can differentiate between a television show and reality' (quoted in Mayer 2007). And Richard Walter, the chair of the graduate screenwriting programme at UCLA, rejected the notion that soldiers were getting training from television dramas: 'Viewers are able to draw a distinction between entertainment and reality. It's pretend' (Bergman 2008).

Others insist that Hollywood's counterterrorism fiction influences people's attitudes about the treatment of terrorist enemies – and even their actions. Tony Lagouranis, a US military interrogator in Iraq, including at Abu

Ghraib prison, said during a panel discussion at the University of California at Berkeley's Law School that he 'definitely saw instances where people took specific ideas from TV shows...what we took from television was the idea that torture would work' (Bergman 2008). Diane Beaver, the top military lawyer at Guantánamo, told Philippe Sands that in searching for an interrogation model that worked, Jack Bauer 'gave people lots of ideas' (Mayer 2008: 196). Beaver revealed that while working in the Guantánamo facility, 'We saw [*24*] on cable' and the series was 'hugely popular' (Sands 2008: 62). Furthermore, she told Sands that *24* scenes 'contributed to an environment in which those at Guantánamo were encouraged to see themselves as being on the frontline – and go further than they otherwise might' (Sands 2008: 62). Concerned about rank and file soldiers' enthusiasm for counterterrorism's action-hero Jack Bauer, Brigadier General Patrick Finnegan of the West Point Military Academy met producers of the show in Hollywood. He told them that promoting illegal behaviour in the series was having a damaging effect on young troops (Shakir 2007). The general did not succeed in getting torture scenes toned down, never mind omitted, in subsequent *24* episodes.

Bauer's just-do-it approach to counterterrorism seemed plausible to civilians and members of the military, to the general public, public officials, and opinion-makers in the media. As Mayer (2008: 196) and Sands (2008) conclude, *24* influenced American interrogation doctrine. This was not a case of media hype. In its extensive report on interrogation methods, the Intelligence Science Board that advises the US intelligence community made the following, direct connection between Hollywood fiction and public and elite attitudes about interrogation methods:

> Prime time television is not just entertainment. It is 'adult education.' We should not be surprised when the public (and many otherwise law-abiding lawyers) applaud when an actor threatens the 'hostile *du jour*' with pain or mayhem unless he or she answers a few, pointed questions before the end of the episode. The writers craft the script using 'extreme' measures because they assume, as our own government has, that police-state tactics

studied for defensive purposes can be 'reverse engineered' and morphed into cost-effective, 'offensive' measures.

(Intelligence Science Board 2006: ix)

The Bush administration lawyers who wrote legal opinions in support of 'aggressive interrogation' bought into the fictitious ticking time bomb premise in order to defend their positions. John Yoo, one of the foremost authors of the Justice Department's infamous 'torture memos', for example, wrote in his account of the administration's war on terrorism:

> What if, as the popular Fox television programme *24* recently portrayed, a high-level terrorist leader is caught who knows the location of a nuclear weapon in an American city. Should it be illegal for the President to use harsh interrogation short of torture to elicit this information?

(Yoo 2006: 172)

Instead of answering the question himself, Yoo mentioned senators Charles Schumer (D-NY) and John McCain (R-AZ), both opponents of torture, who had endorsed the violation of anti-torture laws, if a 'ticking time bomb' threat should materialise in reality. Or take the example of conservative US Supreme Court Justice Anthony Scalia. In a 2007 panel discussion on terrorism and the law in Ottawa, a Canadian judge said, 'Thankfully, security agencies in all our countries do not subscribe to the mantra "What would Jack Bauer do?"'. Scalia disagreed and argued: 'Jack Bauer saved Los Angeles....He saved hundreds of thousands of lives....Are you going to convict Jack Bauer?...Say that criminal law is against him?...Is any jury going to convict Jack Bauer?...I don't think so!'[9]

In sum, then, there are many indications that Jack Bauer was – and still is – an important influence on America's post-9/11 interrogation policies and practices. Yoo justified his 'torture memos' with Hollywood's ticking time bomb fantasy; Scalia signalled immunity for Bauer and presumably for equally effective patriots; and interrogators in detention facilities at Abu Ghraib, Guantánamo and elsewhere took their cues from the screens of horror provided by *24* and similar Hollywood productions. All this was well in line with the Bush administration policies. Shortly after the 9/11 attacks, and thus before Bauer became a fixture on America's screens of terror, Vice President Richard Cheney said during a television interview:

We also have to work, though, sort of the dark side, if you will. We've got to spend time in the shadows in the intelligence world. A lot of what needs to be done here will have to be done quietly, without any discussion, using sources and methods that are available to our intelligence agencies, if we're going to be successful. That's the world these folks operate in, and so it's going to be vital for us to use any means at our disposal, basically, to achieve our objective.[10]

The 'dark side' it was in *24* and similar dramas; 'the dark side' it was in right-wing talk radio.

Rush Limbaugh, the most influential talk show host in the country and perhaps the most influential figure in the conservative wing of the Republican Party, was a relentless defender of the 'dark side' and adept at translating *24* into Washington politics. In early 2009, talking about the new season of *24*, he told his audience: 'Folks, my favorite scene of episode one last night is Jack Bauer being grilled by these pompous senators. Here's the guy who has done everything possible to keep his country safe in the midst of genuine terrorist acts, and these people want to throw him in jail forever for torture and so forth.' Later in the programme, he introduced and played the soundtrack of this scene before commenting on real politics:

Limbaugh: Jack Bauer and Agent Kilner are sitting in a car on a stakeout because terrorism has broken out while Bauer is being grilled by a bunch of pompous senators. This is outside the building where there's a sniper trapped inside and Agent Kilner and Bauer have this exchange.

[…]

Kilner: I just wanted to tell you, what they're making you go through at that Senate hearing, it's wrong.

Bauer: No, it's not. It's better that everything comes out in the open. We've done so many secret things over the years in the name of protecting this country, we've created two worlds, ours and the people we promised to protect.

	They deserve to know the truth, and they can decide how far they want to let us go.
Kilner:	Still, you don't deserve to be treated that way. Not after what you've done for our country. And I'm not the only one that thinks so.
Bauer:	Thank you.
Limbaugh:	Now, I wonder how many short years it will be before this conversation is taken with somebody and President Bush, not Jack Bauer. Stop and think of what these guys faced after 9/11. They had no clue whether the next wave of attacks was going to happen that night, the next day, the next week, they had no idea what was coming, because the intel on this was so bad. We don't need to relive history, but just to mention in the nineties the Clinton administration couldn't have cared less about any of this, so there really wasn't much to go on, and the Bush administration took it deadly seriously, and it led to where we are now with the left-wing fringe just totally rewriting history and making it out to be some giant violation of civil liberties and so forth.[11]

I have no idea whether and to what extent the Jack Bauer syndrome and the ticking time bomb scenario prevented the Obama administration and the Democratic majority in Congress from investigating the gross violation of US and international laws against torture during the Bush presidency. But I have documented elsewhere the reluctance of the mainstream media, print and television, to use the term 'torture' once there was evidence of torture in American-run detention facilities abroad. Unless human rights organisations used the T-word or the administration denied that terrorists were tortured, newsrooms chose more benign terms, such as 'alleged abuse', 'mistreatment', and the like.

A case in point was the CBS *Evening News* on 29 April 2004: In introducing a story about the US Army's response 'to documented mistreatment of Iraqi prisoners by American soldiers', Dan Rather spoke of 'mistreatment' and 'abuses'. In the next segment, correspondent David Martin referred to 'Iraqi prisoners mistreated and humiliated by their American jailers', and mentioned the T-word only in the context of 'the Abu Ghraib Prison outside Baghdad, once infamous under Saddam Hussein as a place of torture and death'. Or take the NBC *Nightly News* of 7 May 2004: In introducing the 'Iraqi prisoner abuse scandal', anchor Brian Williams asked, 'What were military superiors told about the abuse and when were they told?' In the report that followed, after speaking of 'abuses' and 'abuse', Lisa Myers mentioned that the International Red Cross had warned the US government of the 'widespread abuse' of detainees 'tantamount to torture'.

News reports about and criticism of real torture and other extreme interrogation methods at Abu Ghraib did not lessen Bauer's tendency to rough up terrorists. On the contrary, in early 2005, a TV critic observed:

> This is not the first time torture has been featured on the show....But on the present season of '24' torture has gone from being an infrequent shock bid to being a main thread of the plot. At least a half-dozen characters have undergone interrogation under conditions that meet conventional definitions of torture. The methods portrayed have varied, and include chemical injection, electric shock and old-fashioned bone-breaking.

(Green 2005)

In the same way that television series such as *Law and Order, The Agency, Alias*, or *24* adapted real crimes and terrorism plots for their dramas, it seems that the producers and writers of *24* in particular were inspired by shocking visuals and reports of extreme interrogation at Abu Ghraib and other US-run detention facilities to incorporate more torture scenes and justify this interrogation method as an effective weapon in the war on terror. The news and entertainment media fed off each other.

Conclusion

The separation between news and entertainment media is an artificial one. The two media types present fact and fiction – news, entertainment and infotainment

– in similar patterns of information, images, and stereotypes. These patterns construct the environment we live in and the issues we are faced with in ways we can make sense of consciously or subconsciously. This proved to be the case in the post-9/11 period when Hollywood fiction, especially *24*, informed public debate on the treatment and mistreatment of terrorists or suspected terrorists at least as much as information provided by the news media. In times of crisis, especially war, negative images and stereotypes of the enemy rally the nation around the war effort – in this particular case, around the 'war on terrorism'. Concerning the treatment of captured terrorists, the prominence of terrorism themes in both news and entertainment, the common narrative of a clash between evil attackers and heroic defenders, and the prevalence of episodic information provided the rationale for believing that 'the world is a just place and that individuals usually get what they deserve' (Gilens 1999: 162-3). In the case of torture, there is ample anecdotal evidence that Hollywood's depiction of torture as a successful counterterrorism measure in the face of 'ticking time bomb' threats affected policy-makers, interrogators, and the general public. In short, the similarities between real and reel terrorism and counterterrorism are greater than the differences.

Notes

[1] Human Rights First, 'Torture on TV Rising and Copied in the Field', www.humanrightsfirst.org/our-work/law-and-security/torture-on-tv/.

[2] Available at www.youtube.com/watch?v=IZvTXHMYwCc.

[3] The exchange occurred on 15 May 2007 in Columbia, South Carolina during the second debate between Republican presidential candidates running for the 2008 bid. The transcript is available at www.cfr.org/publication/13338/republican_debate_transcript_south_carolina.html.

[4] The debate took place at Dartmouth College, New Hampshire, on 26 September 2007. For the full text see www.cfr.org/publication/14313/democratic_debate_transcript_new_hampshire.html.

[5] Excerpts taken from the Lexis/Nexis transcript of NBC News *Meet the Press*, aired on 30 September 2007.

[6] A transcript of Kelly's remarks is available at www.silive.com/news/index.ssf/2010/05/transcript_of_police_commissio.html.

[7] Emphasis added. The transcript is available at www.msnbc.msn.com/id/37024384/ns/meet_the_press// (accessed 30 July 2010).

[8] The quote was taken from a post on the Politico blog, available at
http://dyn.politico.com/members/forums/thread.cfm?catid=1&subcatid=1&threadid=
4325808.

[9] Reported on the *Wall Street Journal*'s Law Blog,
http://blogs.wsj.com/law/2007/06/20/justice-scalia-hearts-jack-bauer/.

[10] Vice-President Cheney made the remark on NBC's *Meet the Press* on 16 September
2001.

[11] The transcript is available at
www.rushlimbaugh.com/home/daily/site_011209/content/01125111.guest.html.

Notes on Contributors

Matthew Alford is the author of *Reel Power: Hollywood Cinema and American Supremacy* (Pluto Press, 2010). He has written features for *The Guardian*, *New Statesman*, and *Filmfax* and has appeared on several international broadcast stations including Press TV, Canal Plus and Al Jazeera. His latest book, *Puppet Masters of Hollywood*, is due for publication in 2012.

Martin Barker is Research Professor at Aberystwyth University. He has worked on a wide range of research issues, including histories of censorship campaigns, methods of film analysis, the history of adaptations of *The Last of the Mohicans*, and audience responses to a range of films – from *The Lord of the Rings*, to films showing sexual violence (a project commissioned by the British Board of Film Classification). He is currently collaborating on a major study of audiences for online pornography. He is the author of *A 'Toxic Genre': The Iraq War Films* (Pluto Press, 2011).

Graham Barnfield is Programme Leader for BA Journalism at the University of East London. He is a domain editor for *Reconstruction: Studies in Contemporary Culture* and a Fellow of the Wolfsonian-Florida International University. With Philip Hammond, he co-edited the 2011 *Journal of War and Culture Studies* special issue on 'The War on Terror in News and Popular Culture'.

Michael C. Frank is lecturer in English Literature at the University of Konstanz. The author of *Kulturelle Einflussangst: Inszenierungen der Grenze in der Reiseliteratur des 19. Jahrhunderts* ('Anxiety of Cultural Influence: The Figure of the Boundary in Nineteenth-Century Travel Literature', Transcript, 2006), he has co-edited three collections of essays, including *Arbeit am Gedächtnis* ('Memory Work', Fink, 2007), and *Literature and Terrorism: Comparative Perspectives* (Rodopi, forthcoming). As a member of the editorial board of *Zeitschrift für Kulturwissenschaften* (Journal for Cultural Studies), he has co-edited several special issues, most recently, *Kultur und Terror* ('Culture and Terror', 2010). His current research topics include the cultural imaginary of terrorism, invasion narratives from H.G. Wells to the present day, and the narratology of space.

Philip Hammond is Professor of Media and Communications at London South Bank University, where he is head of the Centre for Media and Culture Research. He is the author of *Media, War and Postmodernity* (Routledge, 2007), *Framing Post-Cold War Conflicts* (Manchester University Press, 2007) and, with Andrew Calcutt, of *Journalism Studies: A Critical Introduction* (Routledge, 2011). He is the editor of *Cultural Difference, Media Memories* (Cassell, 1997) and, with Edward S. Herman, of *Degraded Capability: The Media and the Kosovo Crisis* (Pluto Press, 2000).

Brigitte L. Nacos is a journalist and an adjunct professor of political science at Columbia University. She is the author of several books, including *Terrorism and the Media* (Columbia University Press, 1996), *Mass-Mediated Terrorism: The Centrality of the Media in Terrorism and Counterterrorism* (Rowman & Littlefield 2007), and (with co-authors Yaeli Bloch-Elkon and Robert Y. Shapiro) *Selling Fear: Counterterrorism, the Media and Public Opinion* (University of Chicago Press, 2011).

Jack Holland is Lecturer in International Relations at the University of Surrey. His research interests lie in American, British and Australian foreign policy, especially during the 'war on terror'. He is currently writing a book on this topic, titled *Framing the War on Terror*, and has recently written articles on Tony Blair and John Howard's use of language during the 'war on terror'. He has also published articles on the construction of '9/11' (in *International Political Sociology*) and the role that *The West Wing* has played in this construction (in *Millennium Journal of International Studies*).

Hugh Ortega Breton lectures at the University of Surrey in Sociology, Media and Cultural Studies. He has just finished his doctorate entitled *The Paranoid Style on British Television 1998-2007: An Object Relations Approach* (a chapter of which is in *Discourses and Practices of Terrorism: Interrogating Terror*, Routledge, 2010). He specialises in representations of risk in British political culture and the emotional dynamics of popular television, developing a psychocultural approach to textual analysis. He is an advisory group member of the AHRC-funded *Media and the Inner World* research network (www.miwnet.org), which investigates the meanings of popular media usage and representation. He is also Assistant Book Reviews Editor for *Free Associations: Psychoanalysis and Culture, Media, Groups, Politics*.

Joe Parker teaches International and Intercultural Studies at Pitzer College in the Claremont Consortium, where he also teaches Gender and Feminist Studies, Cultural Studies, Religious Studies, and Asian Studies. He is a co-editor of *Interdisciplinarity and Social Justice* (State University of New York Press, 2010) and has published articles in Women's Studies and Asian Studies journals and in such edited volumes as *Theorizing Scriptures: New Critical Orientations to a Cultural Phenomenon* (Rutgers University Press, 2008) and *Writing Against the Curriculum: Antidisciplinarity in the Writing and Cultural Studies Classroom* (Lexington Books, 2009).

Fran Pheasant-Kelly is MA Award Leader and Senior Lecturer in Film Studies at the University of Wolverhampton. Her research interests include abjection and space, which form the basis for her forthcoming book, *Abject Spaces in American Cinema: Institutional Settings, Identity, and Psychoanalysis in Film*. Other recent and forthcoming publications include 'Authenticating the Reel: Simulation and Trauma in *United 93*', in *The International Journal of the Arts in Society* (2009); 'Bewitching, Abject, Uncanny: Other Spaces in the Harry Potter Films', in *The Harry Potter Casebook* (Palgrave, forthcoming); 'Cinematic Cyborgs, Abject Bodies: Post-Human Hybridity in *Terminator 2* and *Robocop*', *Film International* (forthcoming); and 'Authenticating the Reel: Realism, Simulation and Trauma in *United 93*', in *Portraying 9/11: Essays on Representations in Comics, Literature, Film and Theatre* (McFarland Press, 2011).

Rebekah Sinclair is a scholar-activist living in Claremont, California. Areas of interest and publication include contemporary continental philosophy, critical animal and eco-theory, poststructuralist philosophy, and political and feminist theory. Her upcoming projects include guest-editing a journal on poststructural metaphysics and critical animal thought.

Mark Straw is a PhD student in the Department of American and Canadian Studies at the University of Birmingham, UK. He has taught courses on film theory, North American cinema and national identity, and has published articles on contemporary American cinema and its relationship to US foreign policy, victimhood, and damaged masculinity.

Liane Tanguay received her BA in English from the University of Toronto and her MA in English and Critical Theory at the University of Manchester, where in 2006 she completed her PhD under the supervision of Professor Terry Eagleton. Her first book, *History 'After History': Representations of the War on Terror in American Popular Culture*, is scheduled for publication with McGill-Queen's University Press in 2012. She has taught English and Literary/Cultural Theory at both Lakehead University and Acadia University in Canada and is currently an affiliate of the York Centre for International and Security Studies in Toronto.

Guy Westwell is Senior Lecturer in Film Studies at Queen Mary, University of London. He is the author of *War Cinema – Hollywood on the Front Line* (Wallflower Press, 2006) and editor of the Mapping Contemporary Cinema web site.

Bernd Zywietz is a PhD candidate in the Department of Film Studies at the Johannes Gutenberg University of Mainz. He is co-editor of *Mythos 007: Die James-Bond-Filme im Fokus der Popkultur* ('Myth 007: James Bond Films in the Focus of Popular Culture', Bender Theo Verlag, 2007), and the author of *Tote Menschen sehen – M. Night Shyamalan und seine Filme* ('Seeing Dead People: M. Night Shyamalan and his Films', Edition Screenshot Band 1, 2008), as well as articles and reviews for several publications, including *Film-Konzepte*, *film-dienst* and the *Frankfurter Allgemeine Zeitung*. He is a member of the Gesellschaft für Medienwissenschaft (Society of Media Studies) and chairman of the interdisciplinary Netzwerk Terrorismusforschung (Terrorism Studies Network).

References

Aaron, M. (2007) *Spectatorship: The Power of Looking On*. London: Wallflower Press.

Ahmed, A.S. (1992) 'Bombay Films: The Cinema as Metaphor for Indian Society and Politics', *Modern Asian Studies*, 26(2): 289-320.

Alford, M. (2008) 'A Propaganda Model for Hollywood? Representations of American foreign policy in contemporary films', PhD Thesis, University of Bath.

— (2010) *Reel Power: Hollywood Cinema and American Supremacy*. London: Pluto Press.

— (forthcoming) *Puppet Masters of Hollywood*.

Alford, M. and R. Graham (2008) 'An Offer They Couldn't Refuse', *The Guardian*, 14 November, www.guardian.co.uk/film/2008/nov/14/thriller-ridley-scott.

Alpert, R. (2010) 'Kathryn Bigelow's *The Hurt Locker*: A Jack-in-the-Box Story', *Jump Cut*, 52.

Altheide, D.L. (2002) *Creating Fear: News and the Construction of Crisis*. New York, NY: Aldine de Gruyter.

Althusser, L. (1971) 'Ideology and Ideological State Apparatuses (Notes towards an Investigation)', in *Lenin and Philosophy and other Essays*, trans. B. Brewster. New York, NY: Monthly Review Press.

— (1984) *Essays on Ideology*. London: Verso.

Anderegg, M., ed. (1991) *Inventing Vietnam: The War in Film and Television*. Philadelphia, PA: Temple University Press.

Anker, E. (2005) 'Villains, Victims, and Heroes: Melodrama, Media, and September 11', *Journal of Communication*, 55.

Anon (2010) 'The Hurt Locker: Post-Oscar Stress Syndrome', *Hyperbaric Oxygen Therapy News*, 8 March, http://hyperbariclink.blogspot.com/2010/03/hurt-locker-post-oscar-stress-syndrome.html.

Aufderheide, P. (2007) 'Your Country, My Country: How Films About the Iraq War Construct Publics', *Framework: The Journal of Cinema and Media*, 48(2): 56-65.

Bacevich, A.J. (2005) *The New American Militarism: How Americans Are Seduced by War*. Oxford: Oxford University Press.

Bagdikian, B.H. (2004) *The New Media Monopoly*. Boston, MA: Beacon Press.

Barker, M. (2011) *A 'Toxic Genre': The Iraq War Films*. London: Pluto Press.

Barthes, R. (1964) *Mythen des Alltags* [*Mythologies*]. Frankfurt am Main: Suhrkamp.

— (1986) *The Rustle of Language*, trans. R. Howard. Oxford: Blackwell.

Basinger, J. (1986) *The World War II Combat Film: Anatomy of a Genre*. New York, NY: Columbia University Press.

Baudrillard, J. (2003) *The Spirit of Terrorism and other essays*, trans. C. Turner (New Edition). London: Verso.

— (2004) *The Gulf War Did Not Take Place*. Sydney: Power Publications.

BBC (2001a) 'War in Afghanistan: Editorial Policy Guidelines', 25 September, available at www.cpbf.org.uk/body.php?id=90&selpanel=1.

— (2001b) 'Infinite Justice, Out – Enduring Freedom, In', 25 September, http://news.bbc.co.uk/1/hi/world/americas/1563722.stm.

— (2001c) 'Hollywood "inspired US attacks"', 17 October, http://news.bbc.co.uk/1/hi/entertainment/film/1604151.stm.

Bell-Metereau, R. (2003) 'The How-to-Manual, the Prequel, and the Sequel in Post-9/11 Cinema', in W. Winston Dixon (ed.) *TV and Film after 9/11*. Carbondale, IL: Southern Illinois University Press.

Benjamin, W. (1968) *Illuminations*, trans. Harry Zohn. New York, NY: Schocken Books.

Bergman, B. (2008) 'Prime-time torture gets a reality check', *The Berkeleyan*, 5 March www.berkeley.edu/news/berkeleyan/2008/03/05_torture.shtml.

Bersani, L. (1989) 'Pynchon, Paranoia and Literature', *Representations*, 25 (Winter): 99-118.

Best, J. (1999) *Random Violence: How We Talk About New Crimes and New Victims.* Berkeley, CA: University of California Press.

Bhabha, H. (1994) *The Location of Culture.* London: Routledge.

Bhatt, C. (2001) *Hindu Nationalism: Origins, Ideologies and Modern Myths.* London: Berg.

Bhattacharyya, G. (2008) *Dangerous Brown Men: Exploiting Sex, Violence and Feminism in the War on Terror.* New York, NY: Zed Books.

Bhowmik, S. (2009) *Cinema and Censorship: The Politics of Control in India.* New Delhi: Orient Black Swan.

Bignell, J. (2009) 'The Police Series', in J. Gibbs and D. Pye (eds.) *Close-Up 03.* London: Wallflower Press.

Birchall, C. (2006) *Knowledge Goes Pop: From Conspiracy Theory to Gossip.* London: Berg.

Biskind, P. (1983) *Seeing Is Believing: How Hollywood Taught Us to Stop Worrying and Love the Fifties.* New York, NY: Pantheon.

— (1999) 'On Movies, Money and Politics', *The Nation*, 5 April, www.thenation.com/article/movies-money-politics.

Black, A. (2007) 'Foreword', in *Necronomicon Book Five: The Journal of Horror and Erotic Cinema.* Hereford: Noir Publishing.

Block, A.B. (2010) 'Why Oscar didn't embrace "Avatar"', *The Hollywood Reporter*, www.hollywoodreporter.com/news/why-oscar-didnt-embrace-avatar-21390.

Boal, M. (2004) 'Death and Dishonour', *Playboy*, May.

Boggs, C. and T. Pollard (2006) 'Hollywood and the Spectacle of Terrorism', *New Political Science*, 28(3).

— (2007) *The Hollywood War Machine: US Militarism and Popular Culture.* Boulder, CO: Paradigm.

Bok, S. (1999) *Mayhem: Violence as Public Entertainment.* New York, NY: Basic Books.

Boone, J. (2010) 'Afghan Feminists Fighting From Under the Burqa', *The Guardian*, 30 April, available at www.rawa.org/rawa/2010/04/30/afghan-feminists-fighting-from-under-the-burqa.html.

Bordwell, D. and K. Thompson (1997) *Film Art: An Introduction* (Fifth Edition). New York, NY: McGraw-Hill.

Bourke, J. (1999) *An Intimate History of Killing: Face-to-Face Killing in Twentieth Century Warfare*. London: Granta.

Boyer, P.J. (1988) *Who Killed CBS? The Undoing of America's Number One News Network*. New York, NY: Random House.

Bradshaw, P. (2007) 'Lions for Lambs', *The Guardian*, 9 November, www.guardian.co.uk/film/2007/nov/09/thriller.tomcruise.

Bratich, J.Z. (2006) 'Public Secrecy and Immanent Security: A Strategic Analysis', *Cultural Studies*, 20(4-5), July/September: 493-511.

Breckenridge, C. (1989) 'The Aesthetics and Politics of Collecting: India at World Fairs', *Comparative Studies in Society and History*, 31(2), April: 195-216.

Breslau, N. and R.C. Kessler (2001) 'The stressor criterion in DSM-IV posttraumatic stress disorder: an empirical investigation', *Biological Psychiatry*, 50(9): 699-704.

Broder, J.M. (2002) 'Threats and Responses: Hollywood; Celebrities Known for Political Outspokenness Have Little to Say About Iraq', *New York Times*, 6 October, Section 1, p.22.

Brodesser, C. (2001) 'Feds seek H'wood's help: Helmers, scribes probe terrorism at US Army's request', *Variety*, 7 October, www.variety.com/article/VR1117853841?refCatId=18.

Brodsky, A.E. (2003) *With All Our Strength*. New York, NY: Routledge.

Brooks, P. (1984) *Reading for the Plot: Design and Intention in Narrative*. Cambridge, MA: Harvard University Press.

Brown, M.D. (2006) 'Comparative Analysis of Mainstream Discourses, Media Narratives and Representations of Islam in Britain and France Prior to 9/11', *Journal of Muslim Minority Affairs*, 26(3): 297-312.

Bughara, D. (2006) *Mad Tales from Bollywood: Portrayal of Mental Illness in Conventional Hindi Cinema*. Hove: Psychology Press.

Burde, D. and L.L. Linden (2009) 'The Effect of Proximity on School Enrollment: Evidence from a Randomized Control Study in Afghanistan', Center for Global Development, May, www.cgdev.org/doc/events/10.21.09/Proximity_and_Enrollment_2009-05-02.pdf.

Burston, J. (2003) 'War and the Entertainment Industries', in D. Thussu and L. Freedman (eds.) *War and the Media*. London: Sage.

Busack, R. von (2001) 'Just like a movie? With any luck, the Sept. 11 attack will blunt the American taste for cinematic scenes of disaster', *MetroActive*, 19 September, www.metroactive.com/papers/cruz/09.19.01/cinematic-0138.html.

Bush, G.H.W. (1990) 'Address Before a Joint Session of Congress', 11 September, http://millercenter.org/scripps/archive/speeches/detail/3425.

Bush, G.W. (1999) 'A Distinctly American Internationalism', 19 November, available at www.mtholyoke.edu/acad/intrel/bush/wspeech.htm.

— (2001a) 'Address to the Nation in Light of the Terrorist Attacks of September 11', 11 September, *The National Center for Public Policy Research*, www.nationalcenter.org/BushGW91101Address.html.

— (2001b) 'Address to Joint Session of Congress and the American People', 20 September, available at www.americanrhetoric.com/speeches/gwbush911jointsessionspeech.htm.

— (2002) 'State of the Union Address', *CNNPolitics*, 29 January, http://articles.cnn.com/2002-01-29/politics/bush.speech.txt_1_firefighter-returns-terrorist-training-camps-interim-leader?_s=PM:ALLPOLITICS.

Butler, J. (1992) 'Contingent Foundations', in J. Butler and J.W. Scott (eds.) *Feminists Theorize the Political*. New York, NY: Routledge.

— (2009) *Frames of War: When is Life Grievable?* New York, NY: Verso.

Callinicos, A. (2003) *The New Mandarins of American Power*. Cambridge: Polity.

Campbell, C. (2010) 'The Easternisation of the West: Or, How the West was Lost', *Asian Journal of Social Science*, 38: 738-57.

Campbell, D. (2001) 'Time Is Broken: The Return of the Past in the Response to September 11', *Theory and Event*, 5(4): 1-11.

Cantril, H. (2005 [1940]) *Invasion from Mars: A Study in the Psychology of Panic*, with a new introduction by Albert H. Cantril. New Brunswick, NJ: Transaction.

Carruthers, S. (2008) 'No One's Looking: The Disappearing Audience for War', *Media, War and Conflict*, 1(1): 70-6.

Catholic Relief Services (n.d.) 'CRS Partners in Afghanistan', www.crs.org/afghanistan/partners.cfm.

Chakravartty, P. (2002) 'Translating Terror in India', *Television & New Media*, 3(2): 205-12.

Chakravarty, S. (1993) *National Identity in Indian Popular Cinema, 1947-1987*. Austin, TX: University of Texas Press.

— (2005) 'Fragmenting the Nation: Images of Terrorism in Indian Popular Cinema', in J.D. Slocum (ed.) *Terrorism, Media, Liberation*. New Brunswick, NJ: Rutgers University Press. (First published in: M. Hjort and S. McKenzie (eds.) *Cinema & Nation*. New York, NY: Routledge, 2000.)

Chandler, D. (2009) *Hollow Hegemony: Rethinking Global Politics, Power and Resistance*. London: Pluto Press.

Chau, T. (2005) 'Interview: Tom Cruise and Steven Spielberg on "War of the Worlds"', *Cinema Confidential*, 28 June, www.cinecon.com/news.php?id=0506281.

Chesterman, S. (1998) 'Ordering the New World: Violence and its Re/Presentation in the Gulf War and Beyond', *Postmodern Culture*, 8(3), May, www.iath.virginia.edu/pmc/text-only/issue.598/8.3chesterman.txt.

Chicago Sun Times (2008) 'Downey steels the show as irrepressible "Iron Man"; Comic fans won't be only satisfied customers', 1 May, p.33.

Chomsky, N. (1967) 'The Responsibility of Intellectuals', *New York Review of Books*, 23 February, available at www.chomsky.info/articles/19670223.htm.

— (1989) *Necessary Illusions: Thought Control in Democratic Societies*. Boston, MA: South End Press.

— (2003) *Understanding Power*. London: Vintage.

Clover, J. (2009) 'Allegory Bomb', *Film Quarterly*, 63(2): 8-9.

CNN (2003) 'Commander in Chief lands on USS Lincoln', *CNN.com* (International Edition), 2 May, http://articles.cnn.com/2003-05-01/politics/bush.carrier.landing_1_bush-speech-observation-deck-flight-deck?_s=PM:ALLPOLITICS.

Cole, D. (2003) *Enemy Aliens: Double Standards and Constitutional Freedoms in the War on Terrorism*. New York, NY: The New Press.

Cole, W. (2005) '10 Questions for Jessica Lynch', *Time*, 7 August, www.time.com/time/magazine/article/0,9171,1090896-1,00.html.

Conrad, J. (1993) *The Secret Agent: A Simple Tale*. London: Wordsworth Classics.

— (2006) *Heart of Darkness*. New York, NY: Norton.

Cook, D.A. (2000) *Lost Illusions: American Cinema in the Shadow of Watergate and Vietnam 1970-1979*. Berkeley, CA: University of California Press.

Cooke, L. (2001) 'The Police Series (*Hill Street Blues*)', in G. Creeber, T. Miller and J. Tulloch (eds.) *The Television Genre Book*. London: British Film Institute.

Cooper, C. (2008) 'Campaigns Quick to Shake Loose Cannons', *Wall Street Journal*, 25 March.

Cooper, M. (1999) 'Postcards From the Left', *The Nation*, 5 April, www.thenation.com/doc/19990405/cooper.

— (2001) 'Lights! Cameras! Attack! Hollywood Enlists', *The Nation*, 21 November, available at http://ics.leeds.ac.uk/papers/vp01.cfm?outfit=pmt&folder=34&paper=121.

Cooper, R. (2004) *The Breaking of Nations: Order and Chaos in the Twenty-first Century* (Revised Edition). London: Atlantic Books.

Cooper, S. (2006) *Selfless Cinema? Ethics and French Documentary*. London: Legenda.

Corliss, R., et al. (1996) 'The invasion has begun!' *Time*, 8 July, www.time.com/time/magazine/article/0,9171,984815,00.html.

Corn, D. (1999) 'Looking For Mr. Right: Who's Running the Conservative Club in Town? David Horowitz's Wednesday Morning Club Battles Liberalism in Hollywood', *The Nation*, 5 April.

Cossio, C. (2007) '*Dharmputra* and the Partition of India', in H.R.M. Pauwels (ed.) *Indian Literature and Popular Cinema*. London: Routledge.

Cottle, S. (2006) 'Mediatizing the Global War on Terror: Television's Public Eye', in A.P. Kavoori and T. Farley (eds.) *Media, Terrorism, and Theory*. Lanham, MD: Rowman & Littlefield.

Crockatt, R. (2003) *America Embattled: September 11, Anti-Americanism, and the Global Order*. London: Routledge.

Croft, S. (2006) *Culture, Crisis and America's War on Terror*. Cambridge: Cambridge University Press.

Dana, M. (2009) *Big-Screen Aftershock: How 9/11 Changed Hollywood's Middle Eastern Characters*. Master thesis (Communication and Media Technologies). The Rochester Institute of Technology Department of Communication College of Liberal Arts, available at https://ritdml.rit.edu/bitstream/handle/1850/10094/MDanaThesis04-02-2009.pdf?sequence=1.

Davenport, N. (2009) 'In the thick of British warmongering', *Spiked*, 22 April, www.spiked-online.com/index.php/site/article/6566/.

— (2010) 'The slapstick side to Islamic terrorism', *Spiked*, 12 May, www.spiked-online.com/index.php/site/article/8865/.

Davison, W.P. (1983) 'The Third-Person Effect in Communication', *Public Opinion Quarterly*, 47(1): 1-15.

Debrix, F. (2005) 'Discourses of War, Geographies of Abjection: Reading Contemporary American Ideologies of Terror', *Third World Quarterly*, 26(7): 1157-72.

Deleuze, G. (1990 [1969]) *Logic of Sense*, ed. Constantin Boundas, trans. M. Lester with C. Stivale. New York, NY: Columbia University Press.

Delli Carpini, M.X. and B.A. Williams (1994) 'Methods, Metaphors, and Media Research: The Uses of Television in Political Conversation', *Communication Research*, 21.

— (2001) 'Let Us Infotain You: Politics in the New Media Environment', in W. Lance Bennett and R. Entman (eds.) *Mediated Politics: Communication in the Future of Democracy*. Cambridge: Cambridge University Press.

Democracy Now! (2010) 'Michael Moore on his life, his films and his activism', available at http://readersupportednews.org/off-site-news-section/53-53/2366-amy-goodman-michael-moore-an-hour-long-interview.

Denby, D. (2009) 'Anxiety Tests: The Hurt Locker and Food, Inc', *The New Yorker*, 29 June, p.84.

Der Derian, J. (2001) *Virtuous War: Mapping the Military-Industrial-Media-Entertainment Network*. Boulder, CO: Westview Press.

Derrida, J. (1982) *Margins of Philosophy*, trans. Alan Bass. Chicago, IL: University of Chicago Press.

— (1989) *Of Spirit: Heidegger and the Question*, trans. G. Bennington and R. Bowlby. Chicago, IL: University of Chicago Press.

— (1991) 'Eating Well', in E. Cadava, P. Connor and J.-L. Nancy (eds.) *Who Comes After the Subject*. New York, NY: Routledge.

— (1994) *The Politics of Friendship*, trans G. Collins. New York, NY: Verso.

Dershowitz, A.M. (2002) 'Want to torture? Get a warrant', *San Francisco Chronicle*, 22 January, www.sfgate.com/cgi-bin/article.cgi?file=/chronicle/archive/2002/01/22/ED5329.DTL.

Devji, F. (2005) *Landscapes of the Jihad: Militancy, Morality, Modernity*. London: Hurst.

Dickenson, B. (2006) *Hollywood's New Radicalism: War, Globalisation and Movies From Reagan to George W. Bush*. London: I.B Tauris.

Dillon, M. (2006) 'Jacques Derrida', in T. Carver and J. Martin (eds.) *Palgrave Advances in Continental Political Thought*. New York, NY: Palgrave.

Dittmar, L. and G. Michaud, eds. (1990) *From Hanoi to Hollywood: The Vietnam War in American Film*. New Brunswick, NJ: Rutgers University Press.

Donald, J. (1985) 'Anxious Moments: *The Sweeney* in 1975', in M. Alvarado and J. Stewart (eds.) *Made for Television: Euston Films Ltd.* London: British Film Institute.

Downing, L. and L. Saxton (2010) *Films and Ethics: Foreclosed Encounters*. Oxford: Routledge.

Dunphy, T. (2000) 'The President Acting', *Irish American*, available at *The West Wing Episode* Guide, www.westwingepguide.com/.

Ebert, R. (2006) 'I Knew I Would Lose Friends Over This Film', *Sunday Telegraph*, News Review and Comment, 1 January.

Edelman, M. (1988) *Constructing the Political Spectacle*. Chicago, IL: University of Chicago Press.

— (1995) *From Art to Politics: How Artistic Creations Shape Political Conceptions*. Chicago, IL: University of Chicago Press.

Edelstein, D. (2006) 'Now Playing at Your Local Multiplex: Torture Porn', *New York* magazine, 28 January, http://nymag.com/movies/features/15622/.

Eder, J. (2008) *Die Figur im Film: Grundlagen der Figurenanalyse*. Marburg: Schüren.

Edkins, J. (2002) 'Forget Trauma? Responses to September 11', *International Relations*, 16(2): 243-56.

— (2004) 'Ground Zero: Reflections on Trauma, In/Distinction and Response', *Cultural Research*, 8(3): 247-70.

Edwards, D. (2001a) 'Interview With Roger Alton, Editor, *The Observer*, January, 20.12.00', *Medialens*, January, www.medialens.org/articles/the_articles/articles_2001/Interview_With_Roger_Alton.htm.

— (2001b) 'Interview with Jon Snow', *Medialens*, January, www.medialens.org/articles/interviews/jon_snow.php.

Elsaesser, T. (2001) 'Postmodernism as Mourning Work', *Screen*, 42(2): 193-201.

Engelhardt, T. (2007) *The End of Victory Culture: Cold War America and the Disillusioning of a Generation* (Revised Edition). Amherst, MA: University of Massachusetts Press.

Entman, R. and A. Rojecki (2000) *The Black Image in the White Mind.* Chicago, IL: University of Chicago Press.

Fairbairn, W.R.D. (1952) *Psychoanalytic Studies of Personality.* London: Tavistock.

— (1954) 'Observations on the nature of hysterical states', *British Journal of Medical Psychology*, 27: 105-25.

— (1958) 'On the nature and aims of psychoanalytic treatment', *International Journal of Psychoanalysis*, 39: 374-85.

Faludi, S. (2007) *The Terror Dream: What 9/11 Revealed About America.* New York, NY: Atlantic Books.

Farrell, K. (1998) *Post-Traumatic Culture: Injury and Interpretation in the Nineties.* Baltimore, MD: Johns Hopkins University Press.

Fearnow, M. (1997) *The American Stage and the Great Depression: A Cultural History of the Grotesque* (Cambridge Studies in American Theatre and Drama). Cambridge: Cambridge University Press.

Feld, R. (2005) 'Q & A with David Koepp', in J. Friedman and D. Koepp, *War of the Worlds: The Shooting Script.* New York, NY: Newmarket Press.

Ferguson, M. (2008) 'Media Release: Martin Ferguson: Minister Welcomes New Tourism Australia Campaign', www.tourism.australia.com/content/Australia/2008/Minister's%20Campaign%20press%20release%208%20October.pdf.

Food and Agriculture Organization (2002) 'Code of Conduct on Seeds for Afghanistan Reached', News Release, 30 May, www.fao.org/english/newsroom/news/2002/5280-en.html.

Forbes, D. (2000) 'Prime-time propaganda: How the White House Secretly Hooked Network TV on its Anti-drug Message', *Salon*, 13 January, www.salon.com/news/feature/2000/01/13/drugs/index.html.

Fowkes, K. (2010) *The Fantasy Film*. Oxford: Wiley-Blackwell.

Freud, S. (1991) *Jokes and their Relation to the Unconscious*. Harmondsworth: Penguin.

Friedman, J. and D. Koepp (2005) *War of the Worlds: The Shooting Script*. New York, NY: Newmarket Press.

Friedman, L.D. (2006) *Citizen Spielberg*. Urbana and Chicago, IL: University of Illinois Press.

Friedman, T. (2008) 'The Politics of Magic: Fantasy Media, Technology, and Nature in the 21st Century', *Scope*, 14, www.scope.nottingham.ac.uk/article.php?issue=14&id=1138.

Froula, A. (2011) '"America, Fuck Yeah!" Patriotic Puppetry in *Team America: World Police*', in C. Fuchs and J. Lockard (eds.) *Iraq War Cultures*. New York, NY: Peter Lang.

Fukuyama, F. (1989) 'The End of History?', *The National Interest*, Summer, available at www.wesjones.com/eoh.htm.

— (1992) *The End of History and The Last Man*. London: Macmillan.

Furedi, F. (2005) *Culture of Fear: Risk Taking and the Morality of Low Expectations* (Revised Edition). London: Continuum.

— (2007) *Invitation to Terror: The Expanding Empire of the Unknown*. London: Continuum.

Gabler, N. (1998) *Life: The Movie: How Entertainment Conquered Reality*. New York, NY: Knopf.

— (2001) 'This Time, The Scene Was Real', *New York Times*, 16 September, www.nytimes.com/2001/09/16/weekinreview/16GABL.html.

Gaddis, J. (2004) *Surprise, Security, and the American Experience* (Joanna Jackson Goldman Memorial Lecture on American Civilization and Government). London: Harvard University Press.

Ganguly, S. (1996) 'Explaining the Kashmir Insurgency: Political Mobilization and Institutional Decay', *International Security*, 21(2): 76-107.

Ganguly, S. and K. Bajpai (1994) 'India and the Crisis in Kashmir', *Asian Survey*, 34(5): 401-16.

Gans-Boriskin, R. and R. Tisinger (2005) 'The Bushlett Administration: Terrorism and War on the West Wing', *Journal of American Culture*, 28(1): 100-13.

Ganti, T. (2002) '"And Yet My Heart Is Still Indian." The Bombay Film Industry and the (H)Indianization of Hollywood', in F.D. Ginsburg, L. Abu-Loghod and B. Larkin (eds.) *Media Worlds: Anthropology on New Terrain*. Berkeley, CA: University of California Press.

Gardiner, N. (2010) 'Hurt Locker vanquishes Avatar: patriotism triumphs over anti-Americanism at the Oscars', *Daily Telegraph*, 8 March, http://blogs.telegraph.co.uk/news/nilegardiner/100028708/.

Gelder, K. (2006) 'Epic Fantasy and Global Terrorism', in E. Mathijs and M. Pomerance (eds.) *From Hobbits to Hollywood: Essays on Peter Jackson's Lord of the Rings*. Amsterdam and New York, NY: Rodopi.

Geraghty, C. (2006) 'Discussing quality: critical vocabularies and popular television drama', in J. Curran and D. Morley (eds.) *Media and Cultural Theory*. Oxford: Routledge.

Gilens, M. (1999) *Why Americans Hate Welfare*. Chicago, IL: University of Chicago Press.

Gledhill C. (1987) 'The Melodramatic Field: An Investigation', in C. Gledhill (ed.) *Home Is Where the Heart Is: Essays on Melodrama and the Woman's Film*. London: British Film Institute.

Glover, D. (1996) *Vampires, Mummies and Liberals: Bram Stoker and the Politics of Popular Fiction*. Durham, NC: Duke University Press.

Goldman, W. (1996) *Adventures in the Screen Trade: A Personal View of Hollywood and Screenwriting* (Second Revised Edition). London: Abacus.

Gompertz, W. (2010) 'Hurt Locker v Avatar: The decider', BBC, 22 February, www.bbc.co.uk/blogs/thereporters/willgompertz/2010/02/hurt_locker_versus_avatar.html.

Goodwin, C. (2007) 'Sitting comfortably? Ultraviolent sadism is now in Hollywood's bloodstream', *Sunday Times*, 15 April, http://entertainment.timesonline.co.uk/tol/arts_and_entertainment/film/articl e1642008.ece.

Gordon, A.M. (2007) *Empire of Dreams: The Science Fiction and Fantasy Films of Steven Spielberg.* Lanham, MD: Rowman & Littlefield.

Gormley, P. (2005) *The New-Brutality Film: Race and Affect in Contemporary American Cinema.* Bristol: Intellect.

Gottschalk, P. and G. Greenberg (2008) *Islamophobia: Making Muslims the Enemy.* Lanham, MD: Rowman & Littlefield.

Grain (2008) 'Afghanistan Seed Law', www.grain.org/brl/?docid=340&lawid=2834.

— (2009) 'The Soils of War: The Real Agenda behind Agricultural Reconstruction in Iraq and Afghanistan', www.grain.org/briefings/?id=217.

— (2010) 'Global Agribusiness: Two Decades of Plunder', www.grain.org/seedling/?id=693.

Gray, J. (2003) *Al Qaeda and what it means to be Modern.* London: Faber and Faber.

Green, A. (2005) 'Normalizing Torture on "24"', *New York Times*, 22 May, www.nytimes.com/2005/05/22/arts/television/22gree.html.

Grotstein, J.S. (1994) 'Projective Identification and Counter-Transference: A Brief Commentary on Their Relationship', *Contemporary Psychoanalysis*, 30: 578-92.

Grugal, J. (2002) *Democratization: A Critical Introduction.* New York, NY: Palgrave.

Gunning, T. (2006) 'Gollum and Golem: Special Effects and the Technology of Artificial Bodies', in E. Mathijs and M. Pomerance (eds.) *From Hobbits to Hollywood: Essays on Peter Jackson's Lord of the Rings.* Amsterdam and New York, NY: Rodopi.

Gutmann, S. (2001) *The Kinder, Gentler Military.* San Francisco, CA: Encounter Books.

Hairan, A. (2010) 'Is *Time*'s Aisha Story Fake?', *RAWA News*, www.rawa.org/temp/runews/2010/08/29/is-time-s-aisha-story-fake.html.

Hall, A. (2001) 'Film Reviews and the Public's Perception of Stereotypes: Movie Critics' Discourse about *The Siege*', *Communication Quarterly*, 49(4): 399-423.

Hall, C. (1991) 'Quiet On the Wartime Set; Actors Slow to Speak Out on Gulf Conflict', *Washington Post*, 26 January, Final Edition, Style Section, p.D2.

Hall, S. (1993) 'Encoding, decoding', in S. During (ed.) *The Cultural Studies Reader*. London: Routledge.

Hammond, P. (2007) *Media, War and Postmodernity*. London: Routledge.

Harries, O. (1997) 'How not to handle China', *National Review*, 5 May.

Hayes, D. and M. Guardino (2010) 'Whose Views Made the News? Media Coverage and the March to War in Iraq', *Political Communication*, 27(1): 59-87.

Hedges, C. (2002) *War Is a Force That Gives Us Meaning*. New York, NY: Public Affairs.

Heidkamp, B. (2001) 'Now rolling: Ours is a country that has not been damaged, in our lifetime, by war or natural catastrophe. But we've all seen *Independence Day*', *PopPolitics.com*, 11 September, www.poppolitics.com/archives/2001/09/Now-Rolling.

Herman, E.S. (2003) 'The Propaganda Model: A Retrospective', *Against All Reason*, 1: 1-14, http://human-nature.com/reason/01/herman.html.

Herman, E.S. and D. Peterson (2010) *The Politics of Genocide*. New York, NY: Monthly Review Press.

Herman, E.S. and N. Chomsky (2002) *Manufacturing Consent: The Political Economy of the Mass Media*. New York, NY: Pantheon Books:

Herring, E. and P. Robinson (2003) 'Too Polemical or Too Critical? Chomsky on the Study of the News Media and US Foreign Policy', *Review of International Studies*, 29(4): 553-68.

Hersh, S. (2001) 'Escape and Evasion', *The New Yorker*, 12 November.

Hershberger, M. (2004) 'Peace Work, War Myths: Jane Fonda and the antiwar movement', *Peace and Change*, 29(3/4), July: 549-79.

Hess Wright, J. (2007) 'Genre Films and the Status Quo', in B.K. Grant (ed.) *Film Genre Reader III*. Austin, TX: University of Texas Press. (First published in: *Jump Cut*, 1(May/June), 1974).

Hibbs, T. (2006) 'Hostel Territory: Tarantino terrorizes', *National Review Online*, 13 January.

Hilden, J. (2007) 'Free Speech and the Concept of "Torture Porn": Why are Critics So Hostile to "Hostel II"?' *Findlaw.com*, 16 July, http://writ.news.findlaw.com/hilden/20070716.html

Hoberman, J. (2001) 'All as it had been: Hollywood revises history, joins the good fight', *Village Voice*, 4 December, www.villagevoice.com/content/printVersion/167459/.

Hofstadter, R. (2008 [1964]) *The Paranoid Style in American Politics and Other Essays*. New York, NY: Random House.

Holland, J. (2009) 'From September 11th 2001 to 9/11: From Void to Crisis', *International Political Sociology*, 3(3): 275-92.

— (2011) 'When you think of Afghanistan, think of Poland: Teaching Americans "9-11" in NBC's *The West Wing*, *Millennium Journal of International Studies*, 40:1.

Holloway, D. (2008) *9/11 and the War on Terror*. Edinburgh: Edinburgh University Press.

Hoskins, A. and B. O'Loughlin (2007) *Television and Terror: Conflicting Times and the Crisis of News Discourse*. Basingstoke: Palgrave Macmillan.

Hoyle, B. (2009) 'War on Terror backdrop to James Cameron's Avatar', *The Australian*, 11 December, www.theaustralian.com.au/news/arts/war-on-terror-backdrop-to-james-camerons-avatar/story-e6frg8pf-1225809286903.

Hunter, S. (2009) 'The First Decent Iraq-War Movie', *Commentary*, 128(2): 78, www.commentarymagazine.com/article/the-first-decent-iraq-war-movie/.

Huntington, S. (1993) 'The Clash of Civilizations?', *Foreign Affairs*, 72(3), Summer: 22-48.

— (1996) *The Clash of Civilizations*. New York, NY: Touchstone.

Husar, D.G. (2010) 'Pleasant Hill Man Lends Assistance to Iraqi Farmers', *Quincy Herald-Whig*, 8 March (updated 2 June), www.whig.com/story/news/dolbeare-update-030810.

Intelligence Science Board (2006) *Educing Information*. Washington, DC: National Defense Intelligence College, available at www.fas.org/irp/dni/educing.pdf.

Irigaray, L. (1985) *This Sex Which is Not One*, trans. C. Porter. Ithaca, NY: Cornell University Press.

Iyengar, S. (1987) *Is Anyone Responsible? How Television Frames Political Issues*. Chicago, IL: University of Chicago Press.

Jackson, R. (2005) *Writing the War on Terrorism: Language, Politics, and Counter-Terrorism*. Manchester: Manchester University Press.

— (2007) 'The Politics of Fear: Writing the Terrorist Threat in the War on Terror', in G. Kassimeris (ed.) *Playing Politics with Terrorism*. London: Hurst.

Jackson, R., M. Breen Smyth and J. Grunning, eds. (2009) *Critical Terrorism Studies: A New Research Agenda*. New York, NY: Routledge.

Jameson, F. (1979) 'Reification and Utopia in Mass Culture', *Social Text*, 1 (Winter): 130-48.

Jarvis, L. (2008) 'Times of Terror: Writing Temporality into the War on Terror', *Critical Studies on Terrorism*, 1(2): 245-62.

Jennings, T. (2005) 'Documentary Representations of British and European Muslim Women', *Variant 24*, September, available at http://libcom.org/library/documentary-representations-british-european-Muslim-women-essay-review.

Jensen, R. (2007) 'The Faculty Filter: Why the Propaganda Model is Marginalised in Journalism Schools', paper presented at the *Twenty Years of the Propaganda Model* conference, Windsor University, 15-17 May.

Johnson, B. (2005) 'This is a turning point: we have to fly the flag for Britishness again', *Daily Telegraph*, 14 July, www.telegraph.co.uk/comment/columnists/borisjohnson/3618356/This-is-a-turning-point-we-have-to-fly-the-flag-for-Britishness-again.html.

Joyrich, L. (1992) 'All That Television Allows: TV Melodrama, Postmodernism and Consumer Culture', in L. Spigel and D. Mann (eds.) *Private Screenings: Television and the Female Consumer*. Minneapolis, MN: University of Minnesota Press.

Kakutani, M. (2001) 'Struggling to Find Words for a Horror Beyond Words', *New York Times*, 13 September, www.nytimes.com/2001/09/13/arts/critic-s-notebook-struggling-to-find-words-for-a-horror-beyond-words.html.

Kamalipour, Y.R. (2000) 'The TV Terrorist: Media Images of Middle Easterners', *Global Dialogue*, 2(4): 88-96.

Kampfner, J. (2003) 'Saving Private Lynch story "flawed"', BBC, 15 May, http://news.bbc.co.uk/1/hi/programmes/correspondent/3028585.stm.

Kaplan, E.A. (1997) *Looking For the Other: Feminism, Film and the Imperial Gaze*. New York, NY: Routledge

Kazmi, F. (1999) *The Politics of India's Conventional Cinema: Imaging a Universe, Subverting a Multiverse*. London: Sage.

Kel (2001) 'Message 9150', Posted at AaronSorkin@yahoogroups.com, 6 October, http://movies.groups.yahoo.com/group/AaronSorkin/message/9150.

Kellner, D. (2006) '*The Lord of the Rings* as Allegory: A Multiperspectivist Reading', in E. Mathijs and M. Pomerance (eds.) *From Hobbits to Hollywood: Essays on Peter Jackson's Lord of the Rings*. Amsterdam and New York, NY: Rodopi.

— (2010) *Cinema Wars: Hollywood Film and Politics in the Bush-Cheney Era*. Oxford: Wiley-Blackwell.

Kermani, N. (2002) 'Roots of Terror: Suicide, Martyrdom, Self-Redemption and Islam', *Open Democracy*, 21 February, www.opendemocracy.net/faith-europe_islam/article_88.jsp.

Kermode, M. (2010) *It's Only a Movie: Reel Life Adventures of a Film Obsessive.* London: Random House.

Khatib, L. (2006) *Filming the Modern Middle East: Politics in the Cinema of Hollywood and the Arab World.* London: I.B. Tauris.

Kickdoor (2010) 'What can't be learned in classrooms', *TV.com*, 14 June, www.tv.com/the-west-wing/isaac-and-ishmael/episode/77672/summary.html.

Killian, K.D. (2007) 'Batman (and World War III) Begins: Hollywood takes on Terror', *Journal of Feminist Family Therapy*, 19(1): 77-82.

King, G. (2000) *Spectacular Narratives, Hollywood in the Age of the Blockbuster.* London: I.B. Tauris.

— (2005) '"Just Like a Movie?" 9/11 and Hollywood Spectacle', in G. King (ed.) *The Spectacle of the Real: From Hollywood to 'Reality' TV and Beyond.* Bristol: Intellect.

Kirk, S. and S. Kutchins (1992) *The Selling of DSM: the Rhetoric of Science in Psychiatry.* New York, NY: Aldine de Gruyter.

Kirkpatrick, D. (2001) 'Frontline Interviews: The Monster That Ate Hollywood', *Public Broadcasting Service*, www.pbs.org/wgbh/pages/frontline/shows/hollywood/interviews/kirkpatrick. html.

Kivijarv, L. (2005) *Product Placement Spending in Media 2005: History, Analysis and Forecast 1975-2009.* Stamford, CT: PQ Media.

Klein, M. (1975 [1946]) *Envy and Gratitude and Other Works 1946-1963.* London: The Hogarth Press.

Kleinfeld, M. (2003) 'Strategic Troping in Sri Lanka: September Eleventh and the Consolidation of Political Position', *Geopolitics*, 8(3): 105-26.

Klinger, B. (2006) 'The Art Film, Affect and the Female Viewer: *The Piano* Revisited', *Screen*, 47(1): 19-41.

— (2007) '"Cinema/Ideology/Criticism" Revised: The Progressive Genre', in B.K. Grant (ed.) *Film Genre Reader III.* Austin, TX: University of Texas Press. (First published in a slightly different form as '"Cinema/Ideology/Criticism" – The Progressive Text', *Screen*, 25(1), Jan./Feb., 1984.)

Klinghoffer, D. (1998) 'Siege mentality. A ridiculous controversy over a silly film', *National Review*, 7 December, p.38.

Knight, P. (2000) *Conspiracy Culture: From Kennedy to the X-Files*. London: Routledge.

— (2008) 'Outrageous Conspiracy Theories: Popular and Official Responses to 9/11 in Germany and the United States', *New German Critique*, 35(1 103): 165-93.

Knight, P., ed. (2002) *Conspiracy Nation: The Politics of Paranoia in Post-war America*. New York, NY: New York University Press.

Koch, M. (2002) *Alien-Invasionsfilme: Die Renaissance eines Science-Fiction-Motivs nach dem Ende des Kalten Krieges*. Munich: Diskurs-Film-Verlag Schaudig und Ledig.

Kolker, R. (2000) *A Cinema of Loneliness: Penn, Stone, Kubrick, Scorsese, Spielberg, Altman* (Third Edition). Oxford: Oxford University Press.

Koschorke, A. (2005) 'Staaten und ihre Feinde: Ein Versuch über das Imaginäre der Politik', in J. Huber (ed.) *Einbildungen* (*Interventionen*, vol. 14). Vienna and New York, NY: Springer.

Krauthammer, C. (1990/91) 'The Unipolar Moment', *Foreign Affairs*, 70(1), Winter: 22-33.

Krebs, R. and J. Lobasz (2007) 'Fixing the Meaning of 9/11: Hegemony, Coercion, and the Road to War in Iraq', *Security Studies*, 16(3): 409-51.

— (2009) 'The Sound of Silence: Rhetorical Coercion, Democratic Acquiescence, and the Iraq War', in A.T. Thrall and J.K. Cramer (eds.) *American Foreign Policy and the Politics of Fear: Threat Inflation and 9/11*. Oxford: Routledge.

Krebs, R. and P. Jackson (2007) 'Twisting Tongues and Twisting Arms: The Power of Political Rhetoric', *European Journal of International Relations*, 13(1): 35-66.

Laïdi, Z. (1998). *A World Without Meaning: The Crisis of Meaning in International Politics*. London: Routledge.

Lamy, S.L. (2001) 'Contemporary mainstream approaches: neo-realism and neo-liberalism', in J. Bayliss and S. Smith (eds.) *The Globalization of World Politics: An Introduction to International Relations* (Second Edition). Oxford: Oxford University Press.

Latimer, W.S. (2004) *What Can the United States Learn from India to Counter Terrorism?* (Master Thesis in National Security Affairs). Monterey, CA: Naval Postgraduate School, www.nps.edu/Academics/Centers/CCC/Research/StudentTheses/Latimer04.pdf.

Lehman, J. and H. Sicherman, eds. (2000) *American the Vulnerable: Our Military Problems and How To Fix Them*. Philadelphia, PA: Foreign Policy Research Institute.

Levinas, E. (1979) *Totality and Infinity*, trans. A. Lingis. Pittsburgh, PA: Duquesne University Press.

Lewis, A. (1987) 'Abroad at Home: Silence By Libel', *New York Times*, 17 April, Section A, p.31.

Lianos, M. and M. Douglas (2000) 'Dangerization and the end of deviance: the institutional environment', in D. Garland. and R. Sparks (eds.) *Criminology and Social Theory*. Oxford: Clarendon Press.

Link, J. (1991) 'Fanatics, Fundamentalists, Lunatics, and Drug Traffickers: The New Southern Enemy Image', *Cultural Critique*, 19: 33-53.

Lippmann, Walter (1997 [1922]) *Public Opinion*. New York, NY: Free Press.

Lloyd-Parry, R. (2003) 'So who really did save Private Jessica?', *The Times* (London), 16 April.

Lovell, A. and G. Sergi (2009) *Cinema Entertainment: Essays on Audiences, Films and Film Makers*. Maidenhead: Open University Press.

Lowry, B. (2001) '"The West Wing" Is in a Rush to Wrap', *Los Angeles Times*, 2 October, http://articles.latimes.com/2001/oct/02/entertainment/ca-52216.

Luckhurst, R. (2003) 'Traumaculture', *New Formations*, 50: 28-47.

Lyotard, J.-F. (1988) *The Differend: Phrases in Dispute*. Minneapolis, MN: University of Minnesota Press.

MacAskill, E. (2007) 'Rambo image was based on lie, says US war hero Jessica Lynch', *The Guardian*, 25 April, www.guardian.co.uk/world/2007/apr/25/iraq.usa1.

Macaulay, S. (2009) 'Interview: Barry Ackroyd and Kathryn Bigelow', *Filmmaker*, 17(3): 32-8.

Macintyre, B. (2003) 'They fought by the book, and it was Sun Tzu wot won it', *The Times* (London), 23 April, www.timesonline.co.uk/tol/comment/columnists/ben_macintyre/article112950 3.ece.

Maher, K. (2005) 'When the Killing Had to Stop: The Remake of War of the Worlds is the First True Post-9/11 Disaster Movie', *The Times* (London), 30 June, http://entertainment.timesonline.co.uk/tol/arts_and_entertainment/film/article538606.ece.

Marchart, O. (2007) *Post-Foundational Political Thought: Political Difference in Nancy, Lefort, Badiou, and Laclau*. Edinburgh: Edinburgh University Press.

Matthews, M.E., Jr. (2007) *Hostile Aliens, Hollywood and Today's News: 1950s Science Fiction and 9/11*. New York, NY: Agra.

Mayer, J. (2007) 'Whatever It Takes', *The New Yorker*, 19 February, www.newyorker.com/reporting/2007/02/19/070219fa_fact_mayer.

— (2008) *The Dark Side*. New York, NY: Doubleday.

Mayes, R. and A.V. Horwitz (2005) 'DSM-III and the revolution in the classification of mental illness', *Journal of the History of the Behavioral Sciences*, 41(3): 249-67.

Mazumdar, R. (2007) *Bombay Cinema: An Archive of the City*. Minneapolis, MN: University of Minnesota Press.

McCarthy, T. (2001) 'Film Review: Buffalo Soldiers', *Variety*, 24-30 September.

McChesney, R.W. (2000) *Rich Media, Poor Democracy*. New York, NY: New Press.

— (2007) *Communication Revolution: Critical Junctures and the Future of Media*. New York, NY: New Press.

McCrisken, T. (2003) *American Exceptionalism and the Legacy of Vietnam: US Foreign Policy since 1974*. Basingstoke: Palgrave Macmillan.

McCrisken, T. and A. Pepper (2005) *American History and Contemporary Hollywood*. Edinburgh: Edinburgh University Press.

McGuire, M. (2003) 'Good guys are doing bad things this season', *The Times Union* (Albany, NY), 14 January, p.D1, http://alb.merlinone.net/mweb/wmsql.wm.request?oneimage&imageid=61927 60.

McQuaid, J. (2009) 'The Jack Bauer Decade', *Huffington Post*, 31 December www.huffingtonpost.com/john-mcquaid/the-jack-bauer-decade_b_408096.html.

Media Education Foundation (1997) *The Myth of the Liberal Media* (documentary film), dir. Sut Jhally, USA, www.mediaed.org/cgi-bin/commerce.cgi?preadd=action&key=114.

Medved, M. (1993) *Hollywood Versus America*. London: Harper.

Mehta, S. (2008) *Bombay: Maximum City*. Frankfurt am Main: Suhrkamp.

Meltzer, D. (1968) 'Terror, Persecution, Dread – A Dissection of Paranoid Anxieties', *International Journal of Psychoanalysis*, 49: 396-401.

— (1978) *The Kleinian Development*. London: Karnac Books.

Merskin, D. (2004) 'The Construction of Arabs as Enemies: Post-September 11 Discourse of George W. Bush', *Mass Communication & Society*, 7(2): 157-75.

Michaels, W.B. (2000) 'Political Science Fictions', *New Literary History*, 31(4): 649-64.

Middleton, J. (2010) 'The Subject of Torture: Regarding the Pain of Americans in *Hostel*', *Cinema Journal*, 49(4), Summer: 1-24.

Miller, C.H. and M.J. Landau (2008) 'Communication and the Causes and Costs of Terrorism. A Terror Management Theory Perspective', in H.D. O'Hair, R.L. Heath, K/J. Ayotte and G.R. Ledlow (eds.) *Terrorism: Communication and Rhetorical Perspectives*. Cresskill, NJ: Hampton Press.

Miller, M. (2007) '"24" gets a lesson in torture from the experts', *Los Angeles Times*, 13 February, http://articles.latimes.com/2007/feb/13/entertainment/et-torture13.

Miller, T. (2001) 'The Action Series (*The Man from UNCLE/The Avengers*)', in G. Creeber, T. Miller and J. Tulloch (eds.) *The Television Genre Book*. London: British Film Institute.

— (2005) 'Hollywood, Cultural Policy Citadel', in M. Wayne (ed.) *Understanding Film: Marxist Perspectives*. London: Pluto Press.

Miller, T., N. Govil, J. McMurria and R. Maxwell (2001) *Global Hollywood*. London: British Film Institute.

Mishra, P. (2004) 'Hurray for Bollywood', *New York Times*, 28 February, www.nytimes.com/2004/02/28/opinion/hurray-for-bollywood.html.

Mishra, V. (2002) *Bollywood Cinema: Temples of Desire*. London: Routledge.

Mohanty, C.T. (2003) *Feminism Without Borders: Decolonizing Theory, Practicing Solidarity*. Durham, NC: Duke University Press.

Monahan, B.A. (2010) *The Shock of the News: Media Coverage and the Making of 9/11*. New York, NY: New York University Press.

Morris, R. (2010) 'Introduction', in R. Morris (ed.) *Can the Subaltern Speak: A History of an Idea*. New York, NY: Columbia University Press.

Morton, S. (2007) *Gayatri Spivak* (Key Contemporary Thinkers). Malden, MA: Polity.

Moskos, C.C. (2001) 'What Ails the All-Volunteer Force: An Institutional Perspective', *Parameters*, Summer, http://carlisle-www.army.mil/usawc/Parameters/ 01summer/moskos.htm.

Moskos, C.C., J.A. Williams and D.R. Segal (2000) 'Armed Forces after the Cold War', in C.C. Moskos, J.A. Williams and D.R. Segal (eds.) *The Postmodern Military*. Oxford: Oxford University Press.

Motion Picture Association of America, Inc. (2007) 'Entertainment Industry Statistics', available at www.immagic.com/eLibrary/ARCHIVES/GENERAL/MPAA_US/M080925 E.pdf.

Mouffe, C. (1992) 'Feminism, Citizenship, and Radical Democratic Politics', in J. Butler and J.W. Scott (eds.) *Feminists Theorize the Political.* New York, NY: Routledge.

Mueller, C. (2010) 'Foreign Language Films in the US market', *Film Festival Today,* 26 March.

Mulvey, L. (1975) 'Visual Pleasure and Narrative Cinema', *Screen,* 16(3): 6-18.

Murdock, G. (2001) 'Reservoirs of Dogma: An archaeology of popular anxieties', in M. Barker and J. Petley (eds.) *Ill Effects: the Media/Violence Debate.* London: Routledge.

Murray, G. (2008) 'Representations of the body in pain and the cinema experience in torture-porn', *Jump Cut,* 50, www.ejumpcut.org/archive/jc50.2008/TortureHostel2/index.html.

— (2010) 'Fact and Fiction: The Iraq War Film in Absence', *Screening the Past,* www.latrobe.edu.au/screeningthepast/29/fact-and-fiction-iraq-war-film-in-absence.html.

Nacos, B.L. (2002) *Mass-Mediated Terrorism: The Centrality of the Media in Terrorism and Counterterrorism.* Lanham, MD: Rowman & Littlefield.

— (2007) *Mass-Mediated Terrorism: The Centrality of the Media in Terrorism and Counterterrorism* (Second Edition). Lanham, MD: Rowman & Littlefield.

Nacos, B.L., Y. Bloch-Elkon and R.Y. Shapiro (2011) *Selling Fear: Counterterrorism, the Media and Public Opinion.* Chicago, IL: University of Chicago Press.

Narula, S. (2002) '"We have no order to save you." State Participation and Complicity in Communal Violence in Gujarat', *Human Rights Watch,* 14(3C), available at www.coalitionagainstgenocide.org/reports/2002/hrw.apr2002.vol14.no3c.pdf.

NCTAUS (2004) National Commission on Terrorist Attacks Against the United States, Ninth Public Hearing, Hart Senate Office Building, Washington, DC.

Neale, S. (2007) 'Questions of Genre', in B.K. Grant (ed.) *Film Genre Reader III*. Austin, TX: University of Texas Press. (First published in *Screen*, 31(1), 1990: 45-66).

Newman, K. (2011) *Nightmare Movies: Horror on Screen Since the 1960s*. London: Bloomsbury.

Noel, K. (2008) 'Wasit Reconstruction Team Aims to Empower Iraqi Farmers', American Forces Press Service, 23 April, www.defense.gov/news/newsarticle.aspx?id=49672.

Nolte, J. (2008) 'Hollywood loses the war in Iraq', 20 July, available at http://pajamasmedia.com/blog/hollywood-loses-the-war-in-iraq/.

Oakes, P.J., A. Haslam and J.C. Turner (1994) *Stereotyping and Social Reality*. Oxford: Blackwell.

Ogden, T.H. (1991) 'Analyzing the Matrix of Transference', *International Journal of Psycho-Analysis*, 72: 593-605.

O'Neill, B. (2003) 'Gulf War Meets Culture War', *Spiked*, 27 February, www.spiked-online.com/articles/00000006DC92.htm.

— (2006) 'An Explosion of Pity', *Spiked*, 21 July, www.spiked-online.com/index.php?/site/article/1284/.

— (2007) 'Crawley plot: an "Anti-Social Behaviour Outrage"?', *Spiked*, 2 May, www.spiked-online.com/index.php/site/article/3318/.

Peirce, G. (2010) *Dispatches from the Dark Side: On Torture and the Death of Justice*. London: Verso.

Pener, D. (1998) 'Siege Mentality. An action flick with a brain angers Islamic groups despite its best efforts', *Entertainment Weekly*, 13 November, pp.36-8, www.ew.com/ew/article/0,,285700,00.html.

Peretz, M. (1998) 'Siege mentality', *The New Republican*, 30 November, p.62.

Phelan, S.E. (2006) 'A Propaganda Model of Business School Behavior', *Quarterly Journal of Ideology*, 29(1-2), available at www.lsus.edu/Documents/Offices%20and%20Services/CommunityOutreach/JournalOfIdeology/Propaganda%20model%20phelan.pdf.

Pipes, D. (1995) 'There Are No Moderates: Dealing With Radical Islam', *National Interest*, Fall, available at www.danielpipes.org/274/there-are-no-moderates-dealing-with-fundamentalist-islam.

— (2005) 'American Muslims Do Not Face Significant Bias', in A. Verbrugge (ed.) *Muslims in America*. Detroit, MI: Greenhaven Press. (Previously published in: D. Pipes (2002) *Militant Islam Reaches America*. New York, NY: Norton.)

Poe, G.T. (2001) 'Hollywood spectatorship around and about Stanley Kramer's *On the Beach*', in M. Stokes and R. Maltby (eds.) *Hollywood Spectatorship: Changing Perceptions of Cinema Audiences*. London: British Film Institute.

Poole, E. (2002) *Reporting Islam: Media Representations of British Muslims*. London: I.B. Tauris.

Poole, E. and J. Richardson, eds. (2006) *Muslims and the News Media*. London: I.B. Tauris.

Postman, N. (1985) *Amusing Ourselves to Death*. New York, NY: Penguin.

Powers, S., D.J. Rothman and S. Rothman (1996) *Hollywood's America*. Boulder, CO: Westview Press.

Prawer, S.S. (1980) *Caligari's Children: Film as Tale of Terror*. Oxford: Oxford University Press.

Rabin, N. (2007) 'Lions for Lambs', *A.V. Club*, 8 November, www.avclub.com/articles/lions-for-lambs,3207.

Rancière, J. (2009) 'Should Democracy Come: Ethics and Politics in Derrida', in P. Cheah and S. Guerlac (eds.) *Derrida and the Time of the Political*. Durham, NC: Duke University Press.

Ray, R.B. (1985) *A Certain Tendency of the Hollywood Cinema, 1930-1980*. Princeton, NJ: Princeton University Press.

Reich, W. (2006) 'Something's Missing in Spielberg's *Munich*', *Washington Post*, 1 January, www.washingtonpost.com/wp-dyn/content/article/2005/12/3C/AR2005123001581.html.

Rich, J. (2005) 'Monster Budgets', *Entertainment Weekly*, 853, 9 December.

Richardson, L. (2006) *What Terrorists Want: Understanding the Enemy, Containing the Threat*. New York, NY: Random House.

Riegler T. (2010) 'Through the Lenses of Hollywood: Depiction of Terrorism in American Movies', *Perspectives on Terrorism*, 4(2), www.terrorismanalysts.com/pt/index.php/pot/article/view/98.

Robb, D.L. (2004) *Operation Hollywood: How the Pentagon Shapes and Censors the Movies*. New York, NY: Prometheus Books.

Roddy, M. (2007) 'Tom Hanks Tells Hollywood Whopper in "Charlie Wilson's War"', *AlterNet*, 21 December, www.alternet.org/story/71286/.

Rodman, P. (1992) 'Islam and Democracy', *National Review*, 11 May, pp.28-9.

Rollins, P.C. and J.E. O'Connor, eds. (2003) *The West Wing: The American Presidency as Television Drama*. Syracuse, NY: Syracuse University Press.

Rosenbaum, J. (2009) 'On the Denied Politics of *The Hurt Locker*', 14 July, www.jonathanrosenbaum.com/?p=16094.

Rowe, J.C. (2004) 'Culture, US Imperialism, and Globalization', *American Literary History* 16(4): 575-95.

Roy, O. (2004) *Globalised Islam: The Search for a New Ummah* (Revised Edition). London: Hurst.

Sageman, M. (2004) *Understanding Terror Networks*. Philadelphia, PA: University of Pennsylvania Press.

Said, E. (1979) *Orientalism*. London: Vintage.

— (1997) *Covering Islam: How the Media and the Experts Determine How We See the Rest of the World*. London: Vintage.

Sands, P. (2008) *Torture Team: Rumsfeld's Memo and the Betrayal of American Values*. New York, NY: Palgrave Macmillan.

Santhanam, K. et al. (2003) *Jihadis in Jammu and Kashmir: A Portrait Gallery*. New Delhi: Sage.

Sarracino, C. and K.M. Scott (2008) *The Porning of America: The Rise of Porn Culture, What It Means, and Where We Go from Here*. Boston, MA: Beacon Press.

Savran, D. (1998) *Taking It Like A Man: White Masculinity, Masochism, and Contemporary American Culture*. Princeton, NJ: Princeton University Press.

Schatz, T. (2002) 'Old War/New War: Band of Brothers and the Revival of the WWII War Film', *Film and History*, 32(1): 74-7.

Scheffer, B. (2003) 'The Interplay of Fiction and Reality: 9/11 and the USA as a Part of Hollywood', *Medienobservationen*, undated but 2003, www.medienobservationen.uni-muenchen.de/artikel/kino/september_engl.html.

Schiappa, E. (2008) *Beyond Representational Correctness: Rethinking Criticism of Popular Media*. Albany, NY: State University of New York Press.

Scott, A.O. (2010) 'Apolitics and the War Film', *New York Times*, 6 February, www.nytimes.com/2010/02/07/weekinreview/07aoscott.html.

Scott, W.J. (1990) 'PTSD in DSM-III: A case study in the politics of diagnosis and disease', *Social Problems*, 37(3): 294-309.

Segrave, K. (2004) *Product Placement in Hollywood Films: A History*. Jefferson, NC: McFarland and Company.

Semati, M. (2004) 'Entertaining Terror: Popular Entertainment and the Politics of Mediated Terrorism', paper presented at the annual meeting of the International Communication Association, New Orleans, LA, 27 May.

Semmerling, T.J. (2006) *'Evil' Arabs in American Popular Film: Orientalist Fear*. Austin, TX: University of Texas Press.

Sen, A. (1993) 'The Threats to Secular India', *Social Scientist*, 21(3/4): 5-23.

Shaheen, J.G. (1998) 'We've Seen This Plot Too Many Times', *Washington Post*, 15 November, p.C03.

— (2001) *Reel Bad Arabs: How Hollywood Vilifies a People*. New York, NY: Olive Branch Press.

— (2008) *Guilty: Hollywood's verdict on Arabs after 9/11*. Northampton, MA: Interlink Books.

— (2009) *Reel Bad Arabs: How Hollywood Vilifies a People* (Second Extended Edition). New York, NY: Olive Branch Press.

Shakir, F. (2007) 'US Military: Television Series "24" Is Promoting Torture In The Ranks', *Think Progress*, 13 February, http://thinkprogress.org/2007/02/13/torture-on-24/.

Shamsie, K. (2001) 'Triumph of the West Wing', *Prospect*, 66, 20 August.

Sharp, R. (2008) 'Collateral damage: the murder of Richard Davis', *Independent on Sunday*, 8 January.

Shaviro, S. (1993) *The Cinematic Body*. Minneapolis, MN: University of Minnesota Press.

Shear, M.D. (2010) 'Speed of arrest in Times Square bomb attempt draws parallels to TV's "24"', *Washington Post*, 4 May, www.washingtonpost.com/wp-dyn/content/article/2010/05/04/AR2010050403593.html.

Shepherd, L. (2009) 'Feminism Incorporated: Gender and Policy in The West Wing', paper presented at the British International Studies Association Annual Conference, Cambridge.

Sherry, M. (1995) *In the Shadow of War: The United States since the 1930s*. New Haven, CT: Yale University Press.

Shohat, E. and R. Stam (1994) *Unthinking Eurocentrism: Multiculturalism and the Media*. London: Routledge.

Silberstein, S. (2002) *War of Words: Language, Politics, and 9/11*. London: Routledge.

Simpson, D. (2006) *9/11: The Culture of Commemoration*. Chicago, IL: University of Chicago Press.

Sklar, R. (2009) 'The Hurt Locker', *Cinéaste*, 35(1): 55-6.

Smith, K. (2005) 'Reframing Fantasy: September 11 and the Global Audience', in G. King (ed.) *The Spectacle of the Real*. Bristol: Intellect.

Snider, D.M. and G.L. Watkins (2000) 'The Future of Army Professionalism: A Need for Renewal and Redefinition', *Parameters*, Autumn, http://carlisle-www.army.mil/usawc/Parameters/00autumn/snider.htm.

Sontag, S. (1967) 'The Imagination of Disaster' [1961], *Against Interpretation and Other Essays* (Third Edition). New York, NY: Farrar, Straus & Giroux.

Sorkin, A. (2001) 'Interview – Post Terror America: Hollywood Reacts', *Occidental Policy Forum*, 22 October.

Spivak, G.C. (1995) 'Translator's Preface', in M. Devi, *Imaginary Maps: Three Stories by Mahasweta Devi*, trans. G.C. Spivak. New York, NY: Routledge.

— (1999) *A Critique of Postcolonial Reason: Toward a History of the Vanishing Present*. Cambridge, MA: Harvard University Press.

— (2003) *Death of a Discipline*. New York, NY: Columbia University Press.

— (2005) 'Scattered Speculations on the Subaltern and the Popular', *Postcolonial Studies*, 8(4): 475-86.

— (2008) *Other Asias*. New York, NY: Routledge.

Stadler, J. (2008) *Pulling Focus: Intersubjective Experience, Narrative Film, and Ethics*. London: Continuum.

Stahl, R. (2009) *Militainment, Inc.* London: Routledge.

Staiger, J. (1992) *Interpreting Films: Studies in the Historical Reception of American Cinema*. Princeton, NJ: Princeton University Press.

Steinert, H. (2003) 'Unspeakable September 11th: Taken-for-Granted Assumptions, Selective Reality Construction and Populist Politics', *International Journal of Urban and Regional Research*, 27(3): 651-65.

Stewart, G. (2009) 'Digital Fatigue: Imaging War in Recent American Film', *Film Quarterly* 62(4): 45-55.

Sturken, M. (1997) *Tangled Memories: The Vietnam War, the Aids Epidemic, and the Politics of Remembering*. Berkeley, CA: University of California Press.

Taubin, A. (2009) 'Hard Wired', *Film Comment*, 45(3): 30-5.

Temple-Raston, D. (2007) *The Jihad Next Door: The Lackawanna Six and Rough Justice in an Age of Terror*. Philadelphia, PA: Perseus Books.

Thompson, A. (2002) 'Films With War Themes Are Victims of Bad Timing', *New York Times*, 17 October, Section E, p.1.

— (2008) 'Big directors turn to foreign investors', *Variety*, 11 September.

Thompson, K. (1998) *Moral Panics*. London: Routledge.

Thompson, K.M. (2007) *Apocalyptic Dread: American Film at the Turn of the Millennium*. Albany, NY: State University of New York Press.

Thomson, P. (2009) 'Risk and Valor', *American Cinematographer*, 90(7): 44-50.

Todorov, T. (2000) 'The Typology of Detective Fiction', in M. McQuillan (ed.) *The Narrative Reader*. New York, NY: Routledge.

Tonight (2005) 'Spielberg says new movie reflects post-9/11 unease', *Tonight*, 13 June, www.tonight.co.za/index.php?fArticleId=2556230.

Tookey, C. (2006) 'Disgusting, degrading, dangerous', *Daily Mail*, 28 March, www.dailymail.co.uk/tvshowbiz/article-381294/Disgusting-degrading-dangerous.html.

TV Sheriff Channel (2006) 'MF-47 Newsblast – Video Remix', uploaded by davyforce, *YouTube*, 3 December, www.youtube.com/watch?v=Yg391FGkMSs.

United Press International (1991) 'Hollywood's Tribute to Gulf War Vets Rejects Peace Group', *United Press International*, 27 April, Section: Domestic News, BC Cycle.

US Department of Homeland Security (2001) 'Homeland Security Presidential Directive 2: Combating Terrorism through Immigration Policies', 29 October, www.dhs.gov/xabout/laws/gc_1214333907791.shtm.

US Department of Justice (2001) 'Attorney General Ashcroft Outlines Foreign Terrorist Tracking Task Force', 31 October, www.justice.gov/archive/ag/speeches/2001/agcrisisremarks10_31.htm.

US State Department (2001) 'Report on the Taliban's War Against Women', 17 November, www.state.gov/g/drl/rls/6185.htm.

— (2010) 'Advancing the Rights of Women and Girls: Keys to a Better Future for Afghanistan', Fact Sheet, 29 January www.state.gov/s/special_rep_afghanistan_pakistan/2010/136250.htm.

USAID Afghanistan (2010a) 'Education: Increasing Access to Quality Education and Suitable Learning Environments: Program Description', http://afghanistan.usaid.gov/en/Program.23a.aspx.

— (2010b) 'Education: Ongoing Projects', http://afghanistan.usaid.gov/en/Program.23b.aspx.

Valantin, J.-M. (2005) *Hollywood, the Pentagon and Washington: The Movies and National Security from World War II to the Present Day.* London: Anthem.

Valenti, J. (1998) 'Hollywood and Washington: Sprung from the same DNA', speech before the Los Angeles World Affairs Council, 1 October, www.lawac.org/speech/pre%20sept%2004%20speeches/valenti.html.

Van Loon, J. (2003) 'Having it out with Robert', *Text*, 7(1), April, www.textjournal.com.au/april03/vanloon.htm.

Varshnev, A. (2002) *Ethnic Conflict and Civic Life: Hindus and Muslims in India* (Second Edition). New Haven, CT: Yale University Press.

Vidmar, N. and M. Rokeach (1974) 'Archie Bunker's Bigotry: A study in selective perception and exposure', *Journal of Communication*, 24(1): 36-47.

Virdi, J. (2003) *The Cinematic ImagiNation: Indian Popular Films as Social History.* New Brunswick, NJ: Rutgers University Press.

Vogel, H.L. (2004) *Entertainment Industry Economics* (Sixth Edition). Cambridge: Cambridge University Press.

Waxman, S. (2000) 'Inside the West Wing's New World', *George Magazine*, re-printed in Rollins, P.C. and J.E. O'Connor, eds. (2003) *The West Wing: The American Presidency as Television Drama.* Syracuse, NY: Syracuse University Press.

Weber, C. (2006) *Imagining America at War: Morality, Politics, and Film.* Abingdon: Routledge.

Weiner, B. (2010) '"The Hurt Locker": When Great Art Meets Lousy Politics', *Countercurrents*, 9 March, www.countercurrents.org/weiner090310.htm.

Weinraub, B. (1992) 'For this Movie Producer, Violence Pays', *New York Times*, 14 June, www.nytimes.com/1992/06/14/movies/film-for-this-movie-producer-violence-pays.html.

Welch, M. (2006) *Scapegoats of September 11th: Hate Crimes & State Crimes in the War on Terror*. New Brunswick, NJ: Rutgers University Press.

Weldes, J. (2003) 'Popular Culture, Science Fiction and World Politics', in J. Weldes (ed.) *To Seek Out New Worlds: Exploring Links Between Science Fiction and World Politics*. Basingstoke: Palgrave.

Wells, H.G. (2005 [1898]) *The War of the Worlds*, ed. Patrick Parrinder. London: Penguin.

Westfahl, G. (2005) 'The Lord of the Rings: Fellowship of the Ring', in G. Westfahl (ed.) *The Greenwood Encyclopaedia of Science Fiction and Fantasy: Themes, Works and Wonders*. London: The Greenwood Press.

Westwell, G. (2006) *War Cinema: Hollywood on the Front Line*. London: Wallflower.

Wheatley, C. (2009) *Michael Haneke's Cinema: The Ethics of the Image*. New York, NY and Oxford: Berghahn.

White, S. (1991) *Political Theory and Postmodernism*. Cambridge: Cambridge University Press.

— (2000) *Sustaining Affirmation: The Strengths of Weak Ontology in Political Theory*. Princeton, NJ: Princeton University Press.

Wiener, J. (2002) 'Quiet in Hollywood', *The Nation*, 26 November, www.thenation.com/article/quiet-hollywood.

Wilkins, K.G. (2008) *Home/Land/Security: What We Learn about Arab Communities from Action-Adventures*. Lanham, MD: Lexington.

Williams, J.A. (2000) 'The Postmodern Military Reconsidered', in C.C. Moskos, J.A. Williams and D.R. Segal (eds.) *The Postmodern Military*. Oxford: Oxford University Press.

Willis, S. (1997) *High Contrast: Race and Gender in Contemporary Hollywood Film*. London: Duke University Press.

Winthrop, R. and C. Graft (2010) 'Beyond Madrasas: Assessing the Links Between Education and Militancy in Pakistan', The Brookings Institution, June, www.brookings.edu/papers/2010/06_pakistan_education_winthrop.aspx.

Wintonick, P. and M. Achbar (1994) *Manufacturing Consent: Noam Chomsky and the Media*. London: Black Rose.

Wodak, R. (2010) 'The Glocalisation of Politics in Television', *European Journal of Cultural Studies*, 13(1): 43-62.

Wolff, M. (2008) 'Intercultural Awareness and Film: Spielberg's *War of the Worlds* as Post-9/11 Film', in P. Bosenius, A. Rohde and M. Wolff (eds.) *Verstehen und Verständigung: Interkulturelles Lehren und Lernen*. Trier: Wissenschaftlicher Verlag Trier.

Wright, L. (2006) *The Looming Tower: Al-Qaeda and the Road to 9/11*. New York, NY: Knopf.

Yacoobi, S. (2009) 'History of the Afghan Institute of Learning', Public Lecture, Henry R. Kravis Prize in Leadership Luncheon, Claremont McKenna College, Marian Miner Cook Athanaeum, 3 November.

Yeğenoğlu, M. (1998) *Colonial Fantasies: Towards a Feminist Reading of Orientalism*. Cambridge: Cambridge University Press.

Yoo, J. (2006) *War by Other Means*. New York, NY: Atlantic Monthly Press.

Young, M.B. (2003) 'In the Combat Zone', *Radical History Review*, 85: 253-64.

Zangana, H. (2007) *City of Widows: An Iraqi Woman's Account of War and Resistance*. New York, NY: Seven Stories Press.

Ziarek, E.P. (2001) *An Ethics of Dissensus: Postmodernity, Feminism, and the Politics of Radical Democracy*. Stanford, CA: Stanford University Press.

Žižek, S. (2001) 'Welcome to the Desert of the Real', *Reconstructions: Reflections on Humanity and Media after Tragedy*, 15 September, http://web.mit.edu/cms/reconstructions/interpretations/desertreal.html.

— (2002) *Welcome to the Desert of the Real: Five Essays on September 11 and Related Dates*. London: Verso.

— (2006) 'The depraved heroes of 24 are the Himmlers of Hollywood', *The Guardian*, 10 January, www.guardian.co.uk/media/2006/jan/10/usnews.comment?intcmp=239.

— (2010) 'Green Berets with a Human Face', *London Review of Books* Blog, 23 March, www.lrb.co.uk/blog/2010/03/23/slavoj-zizek/green-berets-with-a-human-face/.

Zulaika, J. (2009) *Terrorism: The Self-Fulfilling Prophecy.* Chicago, IL: University of Chicago Press.

Zulaika, J. and W. Douglass (1996) *Terror and Taboo: The Follies, Fables, and Faces of Terrorism.* London: Routledge.

Index

Lightning Source UK Ltd.
Milton Keynes UK
UKOW050505160911

178763UK00001BA/1/P